The Dawn of Tibet

The Dawn of Tibet

The Ancient Civilization on the Roof of the World

John Vincent Bellezza

ROWMAN & LITTLEFIELD
Lanham • Boulder • New York • London

Published by Rowman & Littlefield
A wholly owned subsidiary of The Rowman & Littlefield Publishing Group, Inc.
4501 Forbes Boulevard, Suite 200, Lanham, Maryland 20706
www.rowman.com

16 Carlisle Street, London W1D 3BT, United Kingdom

British Library Cataloguing in Publication Information Available

Library of Congress Cataloging-in-Publication Data

Bellezza, John Vincent.
    The dawn of Tibet : the ancient civilization on the roof of the world / John Vincent
Bellezza.
        page cm.
    Includes bibliographical references and index.
    ISBN 978-1-4422-3461-1 (cloth : alk. paper) — ISBN 978-1-4422-3462-8 (electronic)
    1. Ngari Diqu (China)—Civilization. 2. Ngari Diqu (China)—Antiquities. 3. Tibet
Autonomous Region (China)—Description and travel. I. Title.
    DS797.82.N437B448 2014
    931'.5—dc23
                                                                    2014008853

♾️™ The paper used in this publication meets the minimum requirements of
American National Standard for Information Sciences—Permanence of Paper
for Printed Library Materials, ANSI/NISO Z39.48-1992.

Printed in the United States of America

Contents

Acknowledgments

In a book like this based on many years of research and exploration, the contributions of virtually everyone who has aided me in my adult life should be acknowledged. As such a huge roll is not feasible, I will express my appreciation in mostly general terms. I do so with the sincere wish that each and every individual who has made this work possible through their good words, deeds, or wishes is honored accordingly.

The writing of this book was made possible through a grant from the Shelley & Donald Rubin Foundation (New York City), an organization that commands my highest regard. In particular, I wish to thank Messrs. Donald Rubin, Bruce Payne, and Alex Gardner for their time and interest in my work.

I should continue by thanking the great many residents of Tibet and the Himalaya who have fed me with food and information over the years. They have filled my canteen and watered my curiosity a multitude of times. Quite simply, without the help of the indigenous peoples, I wouldn't have gotten anywhere. Traveling for many months at a time without extraneous means of support meant that I had nowhere else to turn, and rarely was I disappointed with the reception I received locally.

My friendships with Tibetan monastics have been particularly sustaining and inspiring. Foremost among these religious figures is His Holiness the Dalai Lama, who early on took an interest in my research and exploration. Over the years, his moral and material support has been instrumental in my success. His Holiness Menri Trizin, the head of the Bon religion, has also offered his help and encouragement to me countless times. So too has Lopön Tenzin Namdak, the senior-most scholar of Bon, a man who has unstintingly shared his vast knowledge with me. I have significantly benefited from the assistance of various younger Tibetan monk scholars as well. Most notable among these are Geshe Chado Rinpoche, Abott Geshe Tenpa Yungdrung, Geshi Choekhortshang, Geshi Gelek Jinpa, Geshi Changru Trituk, Geshe Rinchen Tenzin, and Geshe Monlam Wangyal. Of all my tutors, the most important has been Yungdrung Tenzin, an unassuming man of tremendous literary capacity. I have also learned much about the culture and history of uppermost Tibet from one of its native sons, Tshering Choephel, an enthusiastic and kind teacher. My dealings over many years with Tashi Tsering of the Amnye Machen Institute (Dharamsala) have also been rewarding.

To conduct major expeditions on an annual basis requires regular institutional support. I was able to fund my undertakings thanks to a number of excellent channels. The organizations that have generously helped me include (listed in descending chronological order): the Shelley & Donald Rubin Foundation (New York City), the Asian Cultural Council (New York City), the American Council of Learned Societies/Henry Luce Foundation (New York City), the Lumbini International Buddhist Institute (Lumbini), the Expeditions Council of the National Geographic Society (Washington, DC), the Unicorn Foundation (Atlanta), the Kalpa Group (Oxford), the Trust for Mutual Understanding (New York City), the Philadelphia Theravadin Meditation Center (Philadelphia), the Spalding Trust (Stowmarket), the Tibetan Medical Foundation (Weslaco), and the Shang Shung Institute (Merigar).

In addition to my excellent family, there are friends whose help has been absolutely essential to the conduct of my work. No acknowledgment on my part could be complete without mentioning Mickey Stockwell, C. Ashley McAllen, Mary and Richard Lanier, Joseph Optiker and Joke van de Belt, Stan Armington, Morgonn Bryant, and Karen Harris. I invoke their names with much affection. In the intellectual sphere, I have also gained from innumerable exchanges with academics. Specifically, I extend a hearty thanks to Ernst Steinkellner (Universität Wien), David Germano (University of Virginia), Charles Ramble (Oxford University), Per Sørensen (Universität Leipzig), and Guntram Hazod (Hummelberg). I beg that all other university savants with whom I have had meaningful dialogue be satisfied with my unrecorded yet unremitting appreciation. Another individual who helped me in formative ways was the late Gene Smith (Tibetan Buddhist Resource Center), certainly one of the greatest Tibetologists of recent times.

My colleagues at the Tibetan Academy of Social Sciences have also freely offered their friendship, never ceasing to take an interest in my research and exploration. Among these scholars, I particularly want to thank Dhondrup Lhagyal, Konchok Giatso, Guge Tsering Gyalpo, and Pasang Wangdu. I am also indebted to numerous officials in the provincial, prefectural, county, and township governments of the Tibet Autonomous Region of the People's

Republic of China for their logistical and technical aid. Without their active assistance, my fieldwork in Tibet would have been very much poorer. In need of special mention are Wang Songping and Shung Garmagyaltsen, two individuals with a deep interest in all things Zhang Zhung.

The overall quality of this book was significantly improved by those whom I relied upon for editorial advice. It is with much gratitude that I acknowledge the technical and literary expertise of Sally Walkerman, Carroll Kelly, Thomas K. Shor, and Steve Farmer. These individuals helped me at various stages in the process of writing this book. Finally, I want to register my deep appreciation of Ted Riccardi (Columbia University), who for many years has inspired me through his erudition and the kindness of his family.

Introduction

This is a story of ancient marvels unearthed in one of the most forbidding places on earth. For more than two decades, I have labored to trace the contours of prehistoric uppermost Tibet, an adventure told here for the first time.

Commonly, when people think of Tibet, Buddhism comes to mind. They imagine a faraway land of monasteries, esoteric rituals, and brightly clad lamas. In the West, romantic notions of Tibet have run riot for more than a century, not least of all because until recently, travel there was difficult and

Location of Tibet in Asia

information about the country relatively scarce. Buddhism is indeed a major part of Tibet; it is a religion that has impinged upon virtually every aspect of her land and people. Yet it has not always been that way. Before Buddhism was introduced, a different type of civilization reigned in Tibet, one with monuments, art, and ideas alien to those of more recent times. A dominant force in this ancient order was the uppermost reaches of the Tibetan Plateau, a place that came to be known as Zhang Zhung.

Zhang Zhung, a realm of ruined castles, wizards, and spirits, is held by Tibetans to be a major source of their culture. The inhabitants of the Tibetan upland flourished in the most debilitating high, dry, and cold conditions imaginable. Austere yet colorful, remote yet human, the tale of Zhang Zhung is one of great endurance and ingenuity. I shall tell the epic of Zhang Zhung through my own exploration and research.

Some three thousand years ago, in a country of limpid lakes and radiant blue skies, a civilization was born. In Tibetan literature and popular imagination, its land, language, and culture have assumed the name Zhang Zhung. The birth of Zhang Zhung occurred in a time of great tumult. Deteriorating environmental conditions were forcing people across Eurasia to adopt a more nomadic lifestyle. In this maelstrom came a fusion of ideas and the development of revolutionary technologies, transforming the face of human existence forever. These irrevocable changes in the fabric of human experience impelled the people of highland Tibet to build the backbone of a new civilization. Demarcated through an enormous network of citadels and burial centers spanning one thousand miles from east to west, it would endure for some fifteen hundred years.

Like neighboring civilizations, the inhabitants of Zhang Zhung adopted the riding horse, metal armaments, and novel social systems springing up all around. Among the most momentous developments was the rise of an aggressive political elite. This upper crust organized Zhang Zhung society into tightly run administrative and military divisions, in which loyalty and honor were among the most cherished values.

The ensemble of monuments announcing the existence of ancient civilization in the highest part of Tibet appeared circa 1000 BCE. Emerging from Stone Age hunting-and-gathering tribes, the highlanders founded a web of settlements supported by trade, agriculture, and livestock herding. The Metal Age castles of Zhang Zhung occupied the high ground, temples hidden nooks, and tombs uninhabited tracts. Many of the fortresses and religious edifices were built using heavy stone members for the roofs. These buildings contained warrens of small windowless rooms, displaying a method of construction that contrasts dramatically with the architecture adopted by later Buddhist settlers.

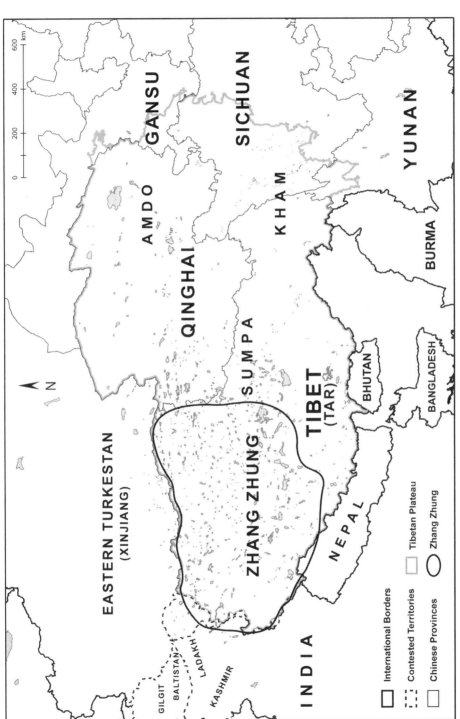

Zhang Zhung and adjoining regions

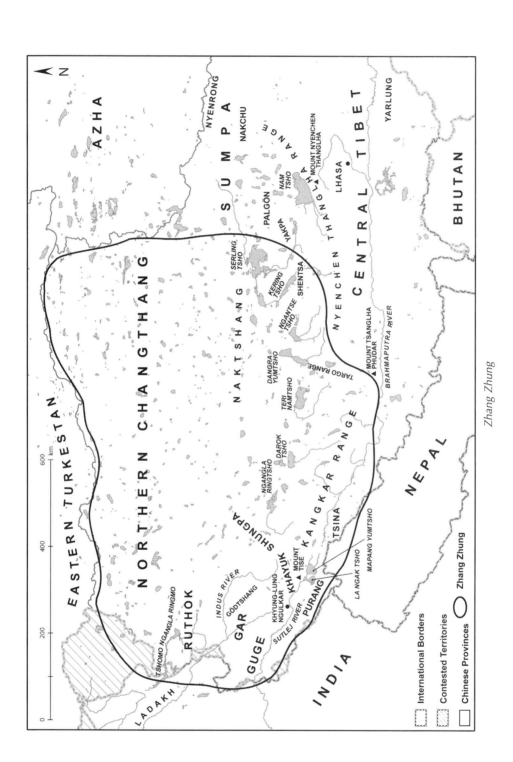

Zhang Zhung

The Metal Age in Upper Tibet was a time of thriving agricultural centers guarded by a chain of mountaintop strongholds and fortified temples. Established at up to 17,000 feet above sea level, these robustly built all-stone structures appear to have housed the chieftains and priests that ruled over Zhang Zhung. At still higher elevations, religious adepts built retreats from which they could monitor the affairs of state below. Nowhere else in the world did humanity construct permanent dwellings in such lofty locations. Raw vitality and religious fervor are implicit in this choice of the most elevated ground possible for the habitations of Zhang Zhung.

The more advanced way of life that dawned with the Metal Age three millennia ago bred new ideas, giving rise to elaborate sets of deities, rituals, and magic. In this period of accelerated cultural development, the building of intricate burial centers marked by arrays of standing stones and stone-lined crypts burgeoned. Lavish artistic tableaux also appeared in upland Tibet dedicated to the profound and everyday realities of life. Throughout this sprawling land, rock carvings and paintings still adorn the walls of cliffs and caves. In graphic detail, they chronicle battles, sporting contests, hunting expeditions, domestic affairs, and religious pursuits. No other archaeological treasure portrays Zhang Zhung in such bold detail as does this rock art. A hardy and eminently practical people are brought into the spotlight, together with their arcane religious practices.

To unravel the mysteries of Zhang Zhung's noble civilization, I have combed Upper Tibet, the region known as the Changthang and Tö to the Tibetans. In tandem with this exploration, I have delved into a literature of immense poetic power to bestow a newfound voice upon its thinkers and builders. Unlike civilizations lost completely in time, the memory of Zhang Zhung is preserved in myths, legends, and histories that began to be written down thirteen centuries ago. The challenges and joys of fashioning a viable high-elevation lifestyle are vividly related in Tibetan manuscripts. They disclose the aspirations and activities of the inhabitants of Upper Tibet, furnishing an animated counterpoint to their majestic but mute ruins. Tibetan literature reveals a people who, while prizing physical prowess, were deeply devoted to the forces of fertility bound up in the maternal aspects of creation.

How ancient civilization in uppermost Tibet actually referred to itself is unknown. In addition to Zhang Zhung, Tibetan scriptures speak of a people, culture, and language in the eastern part of Upper Tibet known as Sumpa. This sister nation shared much in common with the more dominant Zhang Zhung. Tibetan writings illuminate the workings of these two highland cultures and societies and document their castles and temples. Some Tibetan texts name the kings of Zhang Zhung and speak of their exploits in subduing invaders and evil spirits. Still other works describe

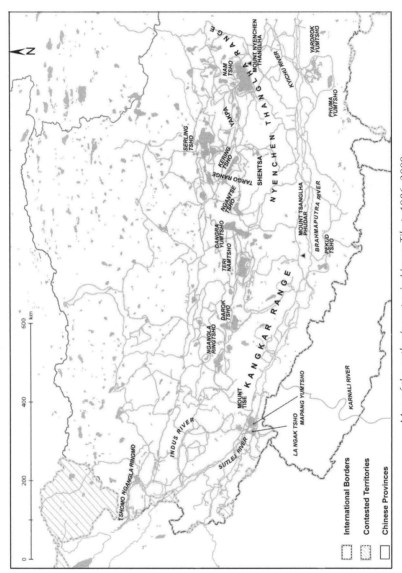

Map of the author's routes in Upper Tibet, 1986–2009

TSHOMO NGANGLA RINGMO

INDUS RIVER

NGANGLA
RINGTSHO

DAROK
TSHO

TERI
NAMTSHO

DANGRA
YUMTSHO

NGANTSE
TSHO

KERING
TSHO

SERLING
TSHO

YARPA

NAM
TSHO

MOUNT NYENCHEN
THANGLHA

SHENTSA

TARGO RANGE

N Y E N C H E N   T H A N G L H A   R A N G E

K A N G K A R   R A N G E

MOUNT
TISE

MAPANG YUMTSHO

LA NGAK TSHO

SUTLEJ RIVER

KARNALI RIVER

MOUNT TSANGLHA
PHUDAR

BRAHMAPUTRA RIVER

PEKUD
TSHO

KYICHU RIVER

PHUMA
YUMTSHO

YARDROK
YUMTSHO

N

0   200   400   600
     km

International Borders

Contested Territories

Chinese Provinces

in rich detail how through supernatural means warrior priests ensured the well-being of royalty and commoners alike.

Most accounts of Zhang Zhung are safeguarded in the texts of Eternal Bon, Tibet's "other" religion. Appealing to those eager to maintain strong links with their ancient heritage, Eternal Bon spread across the Tibetan Plateau and in many Himalayan regions. This Swastika, or "Eternal" Bon, is the thousand-year-old successor to an archaic cultural wellspring. It has achieved this status by overtly propagating traditions whose roots lie deep in Tibet's past. In many other ways, however, Eternal Bon is ethically and philosophically similar to Buddhism. Thus both of these religions can be subsumed under one name: "Lamaism." Unfortunately, this term was used by some Victorian scholars to characterize Tibetan religion in an uncomplimentary manner. Nevertheless, institutionally and doctrinally, the Tibetan faith is indeed dominated by lamas. Shorn of any pejorative undertones, "Lamaism" is used in this work to describe the two prevailing religions of the Tibetans and related peoples—Buddhism and Eternal Bon.

Despite appearing a millennium ago, Eternal Bon affirms that it is many thousands of years old. According to its mythology, it was first spread by divine beings in the legendary western lands of Olmolungring and Takzik, before being brought to Zhang Zhung. Eternal Bon literature tends to portray Zhang Zhung in mythic language, but such accounts are not without merit, for the tales of greatness are reflected in the multitude of ruins that cover the Upper Tibetan landscape. The founder of Eternal Bon is said to be Tönpa Shenrab, a personality in the form of a Buddha who is thought to have lived eons ago. His life story is wrapped up in the parlance of fables and devotion, rendering it difficult to know whether he was an imaginary character or a real-life person. In any case, in the guise of a cultural hero and sacrificial priest, Tönpa Shenrab is cited in Tibet's earliest writings, a literature that predates Eternal Bon.

Although Eternal Bon depicts itself as the guardian of Zhang Zhung wisdom and spirituality, most archaic cultural and religious traditions in Upper Tibet waned over time. With the appearance of Classical Buddhist and Eternal Bon literature circa 1000 CE, what remained of these older traditions also came under the purview of *bon*. The term *bon* is regularly used by Eternal Bon and Buddhism to designate the entire native Tibetan cultural patrimony. This indigenous heritage existed in rudimentary forms long before Tibet's conversion to Buddhism beginning in the seventh century CE. While *bon* and Eternal Bon represent different phases in the cultural history of Tibet, much of what has endured of the former has been incorporated into the latter.

In Old Tibetan literature, written circa 700–1000 CE, *bon* denotes specific mythological and ritual traditions, and *bonpo* are the practitioners of those traditions. In this older historical context, *bon* was not the name of a monolithic religion, nor was it a blanket referent for everyone of early Tibet's myriad cultural traditions. This sense of the word only came about after the archaic religious and cultural traditions were bundled up into one conceptual framework by Lamaism retrospectively. Endowed with a new set of semantics, *bon* and Eternal Bon became mixed up in the minds of Tibetans and were often seen as the same thing. Certain allowances are made when discussing pre-Buddhist *bon* traditions and the Buddhist-like traditions of Eternal Bon, but Tibetans still dicker about which is which.

In order to cope with the rarefied atmosphere and extreme cold of topmost Tibet, a barrage of rituals were developed for the well-being of the people and the natural environment on which they depended. The sky and earth as the source of life were worshipped as kindred souls. Sacred mountains, lakes, and animals were seen as the ancestors and protectors of the Zhang Zhung inhabitants. In the minds of the ancient dwellers, the ontological distinctions between deities, humans, and animals were constantly shifting. Theirs was a world in which ordinary beings assumed the aura of the extraordinary and vice versa. Scriptures composed in the Classical Tibetan language describe secret practices designed to introduce the elect to the true nature of reality. Ultimate truth was conceived of as being as boundless as space and as luminescent as the heavenly bodies. According to Eternal Bon, those who realized this sublime state of knowledge were honored as the superior ones of Zhang Zhung.

Nowadays, the loftiest portion of the Tibetan Plateau is a barren land of alpine deserts and windswept plains, where handfuls of herders and farmers eke out a living. What a contrast to the Metal Age when a proud civilization took hold in Upper Tibet. Most places where the remains of Zhang Zhung monuments can be seen have been utterly abandoned. Coming across these strange structures is like entering a time warp, where trappings of the distant past remain untouched. The hundreds of archaeological sites I have documented point to a land that once hosted larger numbers of more elaborately organized people as compared to more recent times.

In spite of its fine cultural achievements, the soft underbelly of Zhang Zhung would spell its destruction in the end. Upper Tibet grappled with the effects of environmental degradation for centuries as it became progressively colder and drier. By virtue of being on the lee side of the Himalaya and other soaring mountain ranges, it was subject to a powerful rain-shadow effect, causing precipitation to lessen and glaciers to shrink. This chronic desiccation pulled the population centers of Zhang Zhung into a downward spiral. In order to cope with deteriorating conditions in an already marginal environment, ever more ambitious architectural and religious feats were undertaken. However, the various practical and ritual measures relied upon to protect Zhang

Zhung proved inadequate, and its demise was unstoppable. Much weakened, in the seventh century CE, Zhang Zhung was conquered by the expansionist Purgyal kingdom of Central Tibet. The Purgyal rulers controlled a warmer, moister, and lower-elevation land than Upper Tibet. Central Tibet's more generous natural endowment carried the day, and a pan-Tibetan empire under the Purgyal dynasty was formed in the seventh century CE.

By succumbing to Central Tibetan imperial hegemony, the political fortunes of Zhang Zhung quickly waned. The Buddhist religion introduced from India increasingly enjoyed the patronage of the Purgyal emperors, upsetting the old religious balance. As contacts with India intensified, conflicts between proponents of the archaic traditions and the champions of Buddhism grew. Buddhism gained the upper hand through political maneuvering, but also because it appealed to a sophisticated mind-set already enshrined in native customs and traditions. Buddhism's focus on mental projections rather than on physical phenomena resonated with Tibetans in a time of considerable environmental change. Thanks to their impressive cultural and technological base, Tibetans rapidly mastered the intricacies of the Vajrayana, or Thunderbolt Vehicle, of Buddhism. By adopting Buddhism, a cosmopolitan religion with adherents in much of Asia, imperial Tibet grew in prestige.

Tibet's mature civilization and strong monarchy were a fine match for the blossoming of Vajrayana Buddhism, a religion that required a highly vibrant intellectual and economic life. As the preexisting architectural and artisanal traditions of Tibet became receptive to imported Buddhist sensibilities, the way was paved for the re-creation of Tibetan civilization. With Tibetans turning their backs on incompatible elements of their archaic religions, Buddhism marched on victorious. The outcome was nothing less than earth shattering for the holders of the antiquated regime. These practitioners of passé mytho-ritual traditions had no choice but to change with the times and assume Buddhist garb. But Zhang Zhung would not completely disappear, for the new religious establishment borrowed heavily from the old.

Even with the switch to Buddhism, the oldfangled continued to make its presence felt right down to the present day. Zhang Zhung does indeed live on, its ancient traditions reverberating along the path of time to resound in the minds of today's highlanders. These shepherds and farmers are the direct cultural descendants of Zhang Zhung, and timeworn patterns are discernible in the course of their ordinary activities. The herding of livestock, the tilling of soil, the raising of the black tent, the styles of dress, the worship of deities, and many other popular practices stem from antiquity. Moreover, the wisdom of early times, based on a unique understanding of the human mind and its power to shape the universe, still forms the substructure of the Tibetan identity.

Global Timeline

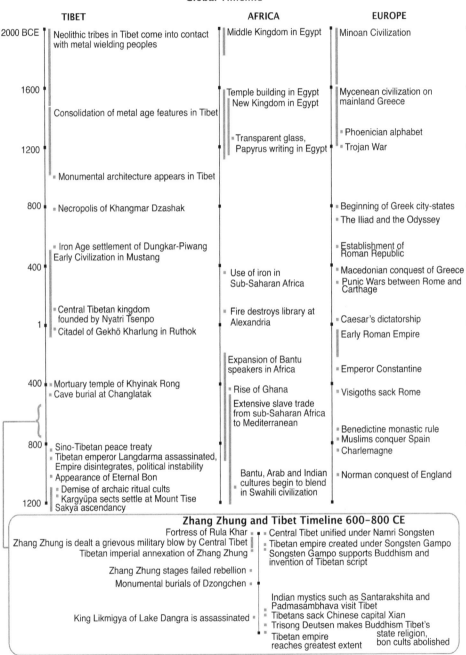

	TIBET	AFRICA	EUROPE
2000 BCE	Neolithic tribes in Tibet come into contact with metal wielding peoples	Middle Kingdom in Egypt	Minoan Civilization
1600	Consolidation of metal age features in Tibet	Temple building in Egypt New Kingdom in Egypt	Mycenean civilization on mainland Greece
1200		Transparent glass, Papyrus writing in Egypt	Phoenician alphabet Trojan War
	Monumental architecture appears in Tibet		
800	Necropolis of Khangmar Dzashak		Beginning of Greek city-states The Iliad and the Odyssey
	Iron Age settlement of Dungkar-Piwang Early Civilization in Mustang		Establishment of Roman Republic
400		Use of iron in Sub-Saharan Africa	Macedonian conquest of Greece Punic Wars between Rome and Carthage
1	Central Tibetan kingdom founded by Nyatri Tsenpo Citadel of Gekhö Kharlung in Ruthok	Fire destroys library at Alexandria	Caesar's dictatorship Early Roman Empire
400	Mortuary temple of Khyinak Rong Cave burial at Changlatak	Expansion of Bantu speakers in Africa Rise of Ghana	Emperor Constantine Visigoths sack Rome
		Extensive slave trade from sub-Saharan Africa to Mediterranean	Benedictine monastic rule
800	Sino-Tibetan peace treaty Tibetan emperor Langdarma assassinated, Empire disintegrates, political instability Appearance of Eternal Bon Demise of archaic ritual cults		Muslims conquer Spain Charlemagne
1200	Kargyüpa sects settle at Mount Tise Sakya ascendancy	Bantu, Arab and Indian cultures begin to blend in Swahili civilization	Norman conquest of England

Zhang Zhung and Tibet Timeline 600–800 CE

Fortress of Rula Khar	Central Tibet unified under Namri Songsten
Zhang Zhung is dealt a grievous military blow by Central Tibet	Tibetan empire created under Songsten Gampo
Tibetan imperial annexation of Zhang Zhung	Songsten Gampo supports Buddhism and invention of Tibetan script
Zhang Zhung stages failed rebellion	
Monumental burials of Dzongchen	
	Indian mystics such as Santarakshita and Padmasambhava visit Tibet
King Likmigya of Lake Dangra is assassinated	Tibetans sack Chinese capital Xian
	Trisong Deutsen makes Buddhism Tibet's state religion, bon cults abolished
	Tibetan empire reaches greatest extent

Timeline of Tibetan and world history

Global Timeline

MIDDLE EAST	ASIA	SOUTH AMERICA
Old Babylon Empire		Potatoes cultivated in Andes
Epic of Gilgamesh		
Code of Hammurabi		
	Shang Dynasty in China	
	Evidence of ideographic script in China	
Hittite Empire in Asia Minor		Olmec civilization in Central America
	Arrival of Aryans, cultivation of Vedic society in India	
Hebrews occupy Canaan	Pre-Scythian tribes raise deer stones in Inner Asia	Cimmerians invade southern Russia
Moses	Zhou Dynasty in China	
Assyrian Empire	Arzhan Scythian tribal confederation in the Altai	
Zoroaster formulates Persian religion	Birth of the Buddha	Confucius
	Pazyryk Scythian culture of Inner Asia	Laozi
Rise and fall of Alexander	Maurya dynasty, India Emperor Ashoka	Mayan civilization in Central America
	Hsiung-nu confederation in Mongolia	
	Unification of China by Qin Dynasty	
Treaty of Samos between Rome and Kush	Han Dynasty Yueh-chih tribes of Gansu	
	Japanese state Corridor pushed westward	
	Kushan rule in northwestern India	
	Buddhism reaches China	
	Barbarian invasions of China	
Life of Muhammad	Huns invade Europe Juan-juan tribal confederation in Mongolia	
	Sui dynasty in China	
Publication of the Qu'ran	Tang Dynasty in China First Turkic khaganate in Central Asia	Tiahuanaco culture in South America
Height of Islamic commerce and industry	Uighurs establish Central Asian empire	
	Song dynasty in China	
First crusade	Muslim invasions of India	Inca civilization in South America
	Ghengis Khan	

Archaic highland civilization collapsed more than thirteen hundred years ago, but for successive generations of Upper Tibetans, its traditions have shown the way forward. Always present but rarely acknowledged, the ancient ethos has been transmuted into a welter of customary responses to everyday affairs. Traces of the world's highest civilization have survived not out of nostalgia, but because they supply the means to successfully live on the margins of the inhabitable world. Changes wrought by time alone could not erase this imperative.

To understand the attainments of Zhang Zhung is to secure a grand sweep of Tibetan history. To delve into the lasting legacies of the archaic is to know today's Tibetans on an intimate level. The foundation of this quest is exploration, so let us see anew.

・ *1* ・

Discovering the First Civilization of Tibet

FROM NOWHERE TO SOMEWHERE

$\mathcal{T}$here are no shortcuts in exploration. One must do the legwork. When my travels in Upper Tibet began in the mid-1980s, I had absolutely no idea what there was to find. Indeed, I didn't even know what to look for. I set out with just one simple objective: to see as much of Tibet as possible. As my acquaintance with the people and land of Upper Tibet deepened, my understanding of their history snowballed. From knowing nothing about the ancient civilization associated with Zhang Zhung to its systematic documentation would prove a journey of over twenty-five years and one hundred thousand miles.

I was well suited to life as an explorer. I felt very comfortable in the wilderness, stemming from my youth spent roving extensively around in the woods. In nature, there was shelter from the cacophony of modern society. Growing up I escaped to the forest as much as possible, to the detriment of schooling and other organized activities. This did not augur well for success in life, at least in any conventional sense. Sometimes I pretended to be wandering around Tibet and the Himalaya in pursuit of archaeological wonders, a foretaste of what was to be.

My efforts to revive Zhang Zhung for all to see were built upon the hard work of the adventurers, scientists, and historians who came before me. An earlier generation of explorers such as the Italian Giuseppe Tucci, the Swede Sven Hedin, and the Englishman H. E. Richardson covered much ground in Tibet.[1] With their outstanding scholarly contributions, they helped to establish Tibetology as a modern field of study. Their fieldwork was only a start, however, for much of Tibet remained unknown to the outside world for most of the twentieth century.

Author and Tibetan friend just before embarking on the winter exploration of an island in Upper Tibet

The father of archaeological exploration in Upper Tibet was George Roerich, the son of Nicholas Roerich, an internationally known Russian painter and spiritualist. The Roerichs' Central Asiatic Expedition of the 1920s quite by accident discovered a number of tombs and standing stones in the northern plains of Tibet.[2] Their finds generated a lot of scholarly and popular interest at the time, but it was not until the last decade that the sites they recorded could be revisited. In addition to the discoveries of George Roerich, there have been several other bright spots in the study of prehistoric Tibet. The history of archaeological exploration in Tibet has been expertly chronicled by the French Tibetologist Ann Chayet and the American archaeologist Mark Aldenderfer.[3]

It was under the Chinese Communists in the 1950s and 1960s that the first highly detailed geographic surveys of the entire Tibetan Plateau were carried out. Except for some high mountain peaks and the lake islands, the Chinese have gone on to explore virtually all of Tibet. They have compiled extremely detailed topographic maps and place-name gazetteers, a hugely important contribution to the study of Tibet.

It was the Chinese who first introduced modern archaeological methodologies in Tibet. In 1976, an expedition launched by the Chinese Academy of Sciences collected Stone Age tools in several regions of Upper Tibet.[4] These discoveries helped push back the origins of man on the Tibetan Plateau to fifteen to thirty thousand years ago. The search for Stone Age implements and other remains has continued to the present day throughout Tibet, greatly adding to our knowledge of its distant past.[5]

One of the most important excavations occurred in the 1980s at the Chogong site in the Lhasa valley.[6] Here Bronze Age technology, intruding upon a Stone Age village, irreversibly changed the way its people lived. The dig at Chogong showed that Tibetans were not immune to the cultural and technological revolution taking place in many parts of Eurasia some three to four thousand years ago.

The discovery of a Neolithic village in eastern Tibet had even more powerful ramifications for our understanding of prehistoric Tibet. Known as Kharo, this site yielded a wealth of buildings and artifacts. Kharo demonstrated that advanced agricultural systems, as well as sophisticated house construction, ceramic making, and the domestication of cattle, were mastered by dwellers on the Tibetan Plateau upwards of five thousand years ago. Traditionally, based on Buddhist historical texts, it was thought that agriculture may have come relatively late to Tibet, in the time of its ninth king, Pude Gungyal. However, Kharo demonstrated that farming on the Plateau predated the time of the legendary Pude Gungyal by some three thousand years.

In the 1980s, the Tibetan archaeologist Sonam Wangdu carried out a succession of major discoveries in various districts of Central Tibet.[7] His team began to excavate gigantic tombs belonging to the ministers of the Tibetan emperors, but their work was halted before it could be completed. The efforts of other Tibetan archaeologists have also been rather short lived and tentative. A lack of trained scientific personnel and a certain resistance from Beijing and its Tibetan government seems to explain the slow progress of archaeology in Tibet.

From the early 1990s to the late 2000s, Professors Huo Wei and Li Yongxian, archaeologists at Sichuan University, carried out far-reaching archaeological projects in western Tibet.[8] On several expeditions, they were joined by Mark Aldenderfer, an archaeologist specializing in ancient highland cultures at the University of California, Santa Barbara.[9] Their excavation of tombs in the Dungkar and Piyang valleys of Guge furnished important insights into the Upper Tibet of twenty-five hundred years ago. Various types of tombs were unearthed, containing a wide array of stone and metal implements, ceramic vessels, ritual objects, and other artifacts. There could be no mistaking the implications: Iron Age western Tibet possessed advanced technological and cultural capabilities. The presence of bamboo in the tombs indicates that Transhimalayan trade routes were already established in that period. A realization was dawning. Rather than a backwater with a rudimentary culture, Upper Tibet was in possession of a full-fledged civilization. This was a fact long before the introduction of Buddhism, which is traditionally seen as the main conveyor of civilization to Tibet.

In 2003, Huo Wei, Li Yongxian, and Mark Aldenderfer were joined by Shargen Wangdu of the Tibetan Provincial Museum in a more thorough survey of a ruined fortress that appears to be the Horned Eagle Valley Silver Castle, a fabled capital of Zhang Zhung.[10] While relatively few artifacts turned up, their work confirmed that this site was a thriving center before the Buddhist era. More recently, stray finds by local monks at what might be the Horned Eagle Valley Silver Castle, and tombs excavated in the vicinity, have revealed an impressive array of artifacts. Dating to the first half of the first millennium CE, these objects, ranging from bronze vessels to stone weights, have added much to our knowledge about the cultural makeup of Upper Tibet before the Buddhist era.[11]

For the most part, Chinese-sponsored surveys of Tibet have not been geared toward systematic cultural and archaeological exploration. To this day, Chinese knowledge of these vital areas of Tibetan life remains incomplete. One major obstacle they face is the lack of a Tibetan-speaking cadre of Han scientists and technocrats. Without deep knowledge of the native languages and dialects of Tibet, Chinese measures to understand the Plateau have been impaired. On the other hand, foreigners have proven willing and able to fill this breach in Tibetan studies.

The years between 1984 and 1988 were a veritable golden age in the exploration of Tibet. During that period, a handful of explorers, mostly from English-speaking nations, visited places never seen before by outsiders. This was a heady time when significant contributions to the cultural and historical geography of Tibet were being made. Names like Bradley Rowe, Victor Chen, Gary McCue, and George Schaller loom large in the annals of Tibetan exploration of that time.[12] In the 1980s, the rivalry between individual explorers was collegial, not least of all because the Tibetan Plateau is so gigantic. There was plenty of territory in which one could claim a first.

In the 1990s, a larger contingent of foreign explorers and researchers appeared in Tibet, eager to go places where others had not been before. Little by little, many corners of Tibet were reached by these intrepid individuals. People with different intellectual perspectives and areas of expertise were involved, bringing the exploration of Tibet to new heights. This unparalleled access to the Plateau allowed the field of Tibetology to burgeon. Tibet, the forbidden land of the past, finally divulged her secrets to those committed to know her. In spirit and in deed, this generation of modern explorers is the worthy successor to its storied predecessors. Their brave efforts notwithstanding, there is still much to discover in Tibet, beckoning the next generation of explorers to see for themselves.

I began my wanderings on the western fringes of the Tibetan Plateau in 1983, a territory under Indian jurisdiction. My first significant encounter with people of Tibetan stock was in the western Himalayan region of Pangi, a week's walk from the nearest road. There in the village of Hoodan, I took refuge from fierce spring snowstorms and avalanches in the labyrinthine mass of houses.

In 1984, China was opening up to the outside world in unprecedented ways, and the trickle of foreign tourists was becoming a steady stream. That year, on the travelers' grapevine came rumors that Tibet was about to be opened up to individuals. Until then only those on expensive organized tours could visit a few select places. Not wanting to be left behind in the quest for new vistas, I made a trip to the region of Amdo in northeastern Tibet. It was not until the summer of 1986 that I could devote myself to the full-time exploration of Tibet. On my first trip to the northern plains, or Changthang, I managed to walk across a swath of open basins without a stove or tent. My only shelter was a woolen robe placed over a ditch or depression at night. For many days I was pummeled by snow and sleet. This jaunt of 175 miles terminated near Namru Dzong, a ramshackle county seat. My entry into the town caused quite a stir, as no other Westerner had come through Namru Dzong since George Roerich's Central Asiatic Expedition in 1928.

For the adventurous, traveling around Tibet without permits was the norm in the 1980s. There was always the risk that one would be nabbed by the police. A battle of wits and wills ensued between travelers and the authorities, fodder for many a future yarn. A few of us had taken writing the accursed confession and apology to a fine art, calling upon our ancestors as witnesses and expressing remorse for our Confucian transgressions. Back in Lhasa, explorers would boast to each other about where they had been and what they had seen. A travelers' co-op, the brainchild of an eccentric but affable English couple, was set up in Lhasa's Banak Shöl hotel, a popular tourist haunt. The co-op provided practical information to travelers and rented out trekking gear at nominal rates. For the more discerning, it also dispensed information about how to get into restricted places, gleaned from conversations with veteran travelers.

A second trip to Upper Tibet in 1986 took me to Mount Kailash, Tibet's foremost holy mountain. During that three-and-a-half-month voyage, I spent much of the time on foot with Tibetan pilgrims learning their ways and language. I was impressed by their ability to cheerfully endure hunger, cold, and other hardships of the journey. A highlight of the pilgrimage was a journey to the source of the Indus River, a remote Transhimalayan location last visited by the Indian savant Swami Pranavananda in the 1930s.[13] I went alone with only meager food reserves and no tent or stove, reasoning that if the Tibetans could travel like that, I could too.

In 1987, a letter written by the eminent Tibetologist H. E. Richardson reached the traveler's co-op in Lhasa. This letter helped focus my wanderings in a more directed manner. Richardson revealed the supposed existence of a gigantic pyramid on the north shore of Nam Tsho, the largest lake in the Changthang. This pyramid was reported in the 1870s by Kishen Singh, a Himalayan native and British subject who spied on behalf of Her Majesty's government. Kishen Singh spoke of a fabulous pyramid with an internal chamber used by an ancient lama to ascend to the heavens.[14] Surely, I fancied, one of the great archaeological discoveries of the decade or maybe even of the twentieth century must be waiting.

With exuberance carrying the day, I set off as quickly as a possible from Lhasa traveling solo. I hiked the rugged north shore of Lake Nam Tsho but could not locate the pyramid. Despite my lack of success in finding this wonder, the spectacular scenery and the intriguing shepherds of the area made the trip a delight. Beautiful vistas greeted me each time I rounded a rocky headland, easing the burden of a ponderous pack. My imagination had been ignited by the local herders, a phlegmatic lot with the air of having lived at Nam Tsho since the beginning of time.

In 1993, 1994, and 1995, I returned to Nam Tsho in search of Kishen Singh's elusive pyramid. I came to hold this lake very dear. Each visit added to my knowledge of its culture and geography, and I made many friends among the shepherds. Yet there was no ancient archaeological miracle over the next horizon. Local elders confirmed that Kishen Singh's pyramid does indeed exist, but it is a natural rock formation, not a man-made structure. Either he or the British agents who filed his report got it wrong.

The large pyramidal mass of limestone stands at a Nam Tsho location called Excellent Orange Horse Headland. Stone steps built in a central cavity lead up to the apex of the pyramid where there are ruins of ancient buildings. Although there was no grand man-made pyramid to be discovered, in those curious ruins and others like them, I detected something else that would prove just as compelling. I had glimpsed for the first time the flicker of another age, the monumental remnants of a buried past. That revelation would lead to more exploration and eventually to cataloging ruins all over Upper Tibet.

In 1992, I managed to visit both the ritual and actual geographic sources of the Karnali, Brahmaputra, and Sutlej Rivers. Along with the Indus, these are the four fabled fountains of Mount Kailash (known to Tibetans as Tise), the lifeblood of millions who live downstream on the Indian Subcontinent. I became the first non-Tibetan to visit all of the ritual and geographic wellsprings of these four rivers. Save for a short article I wrote for *Himal*, a magazine published in Kathmandu, I did not publicize my accomplishment.[15]

Traveling further afield, I got to experience the waterless bleakness of the northern Changthang for the first time in 1992. This austere wonderland required hauling two days' worth of water at all times, as reliable sources of this vital commodity are few and far between. For a lone walker, that payload of seventeen pounds was the margin of error between life and death.

The road to discovery would be long and fraught with many challenges of a physical and personal nature. However, for me, there was no attractive alternative to free-ranging exploration. On a first visit to Lake Dangra, a gorgeous blue lake set in the middle of the Changthang, I was initiated into the lore and hidden places of Zhang Zhung by local luminaries. I called those expeditions to Lake Nam Tsho and Lake Dangra of the mid-1990s "Divine Dyads," a name inspired by the pairing of mother lakes with father mountains in the ancient mythology of the Changthang. This fieldwork at the great lakes led to the publication of my first monograph, *Divine Dyads: Ancient Civilization in Tibet*.

According to a myth circulating around Lake Dangra, this pristine body of water is the source of the universe and living beings. Long and gently curving, Lake Dangra is endowed with a special microclimate that permits tilling of the soil. Some of those who work the land there belong to clans that trace themselves back to the prehistoric times of Zhang Zhung. The natives of Lake Dangra, followers of Eternal Bon, zealously guard their heritage and pride themselves with preserving the last vestiges of the highland's high culture. No mere myth as some in the academic world supposed, I was led to numerous places where signs of a past age of greatness could still be seen. Now only a string of modest villages and monasteries endure where mighty temples and castles once stood.

SOMETHING DEFINITE BEGINS TO EMERGE

How much of Zhang Zhung really existed? Were the ruins of Lake Nam Tsho and Lake Dangra an exception in the wide-open Changthang, or did other locations host similar sites? If I was not to be utterly lost in the vastness of the terrain, firm geographic points of reference were mandatory.

Fortunately, very important allies appeared on my horizon, figures who would help shepherd me to the right places. With findings from the Divine Dyads expeditions, I approached Lopön Tenzin Namdak, the foremost Eternal Bon scholar, at his transplanted monastery in Kathmandu. I also sought out His Holiness Menri Khenpo, the head of the Eternal Bon religion, at his headquarters in Dolanji, India. Right from our first encounters, these gentlemen were supportive and reassuring. They patiently answered a barrage of questions over a number of visits, presenting me with the Eternal Bon texts needed to understand the geographic and cultural scope of Zhang Zhung. Along with junior Eternal Bon scholars deputed to assist me, Lopön Rinpoche and Menri Khenpo personally participated in the laborious task of translating passages from their holy books. This was my crash course in Classical Tibetan.

In those early days of research and exploration, I made another extremely influential friend, His Holiness the Dalai Lama. My first private audience with the Dalai Lama came in September 1997, right after the publication of *Divine Dyads* with the Library of Tibetan Works and Archives. The Dalai Lama remarked that my research would prove valuable to Tibetans but that it might take two or three generations before it was fully appreciated. This paragon among men pledged his support, exhorting me to come and see him any time my work required his assistance. True to his word, His Holiness has been a stalwart backer of my Tibetological undertakings ever since.

Also worthy of special mention is the prominent abbot Chado Rinpoche, and Chögyal Namkhai Norbu, a well-known lama who lived for many years in Italy. These two Tibetan luminaries offered encouragement and information in my search for ancient cultural signposts. Assuredly, I had a pair of strong legs and powerful backers. There could be no going back now!

By readily responding to suggestions offered by experts and by sheer dint of effort, my scholarship gradually improved. During the initial years of exploration there was much to learn about the ways of Western academia. While I had surely done the homework, Occidental scholarship is a tradition with its own modes of framing knowledge. Being versed in the methods of presentation and interpretation is as important as raw knowledge of a subject. Information must be organized in such a way as to lend it maximum relevance and utility; otherwise it is diminished like a pearl in the rough.

Collaboration with Eternal Bon scholars confirmed my suspicion that Zhang Zhung centers are to be found along the shorelines of many big lakes in the Changthang. These great lakes have had a divine aura since time immemorial. To this day, it is believed that they enshrine fertility and wealth-enhancing goddesses. In 1997, I explored a large freshwater lake in the western Changthang known as Darok Tsho. Reaching the northwest corner on foot, a local shepherd family prepared me for what lay ahead. They disclosed that I was venturing into a long-abandoned realm belonging to the archaic Tibetan religious traditions known as *bon*, a place where angry spirits still roam untamed.

It was soon apparent that I had arrived in a world culturally cut off from the rest of Tibet for centuries. The rugged north shore of Darok Tsho hosts a rich mix of prehistoric and early historic temples and hermitages, all of which are in a state of advanced decay. The most tantalizing monuments lay on two offshore islands, Tsho Do and Do Drilbu. I could see the ruins on Tsho Do across a deep strait with my binoculars but did not have means to reach them. The lake would not freeze over for another two months, and I did not have the capability to wait around that long. It would be another nine years before I would be able to visit the islands of Lake Darok Tsho.

In 1998, I hitchhiked on the back of trucks to Tshochen, a county seat in the middle of the illimitable Changthang. I set out to circumambulate Teri Nam Tsho, one of the biggest lakes in Tibet, a journey that would take eighteen days. I had no idea what I would find, if anything. The gamble, however, was handsomely rewarded. On the north shore of Teri Nam Tsho, I spied two headlands near the shiny white limestone mountain of Muro Ri. These twin headlands, former islands known as Pö Do, were connected to the mainland by the most tenuous of routes. In order to reach them, I had to negotiate several kilometers of alkaline flats, pockmarked with pools of quicksand. On Pö Do I confronted traces of ancient edifices, parts of elite cloistered communities, nerve centers of culture that in their time drew in resources from around the region. On the east side of Teri Nam Tsho I walked out on a narrow spit of gravel for four miles to get to Do Drilbu. Like Pö Do, this large rocky headland was an island when water levels in the lake were about twelve feet higher. On Do Drilbu I discovered a series of all-stone houses and a network of shrines belonging to the archaic era civilization. Due to its isolation, some of these structures remain in remarkably good condition. Do Drilbu was once very important real estate, a ritual and cultural center par excellence.

By 1998, I had documented around one hundred residential and ceremonial sites that belonged to Zhang Zhung and the early historic civilization that followed it. Yet the bigger picture was still dim. I had more questions than answers. I needed to know how the stone ruins I discovered tied into Upper Tibet as a whole. How many pieces to the puzzle of ancient civilization were there in this sprawling half of the Tibetan Plateau? To answer the big questions would take another decade and unlimited access to all parts of Upper Tibet. Fortunately, the nature of travel in Tibet was changing. In the late 1990s, the Tibet Tourist Bureau began issuing permits to foreigners wanting to visit restricted areas.

In 1999, I spent nearly half a year in the field. I had put together a wish list of places to visit on what I would call the Changthang Circuit Expedition. I was accompanied on this trip by my friend C. Ashley McAllen, a physician who liked to practice basic medicine in the world's most extreme environments. Our staff of four young Tibetans had no idea what they had signed up for. They were accustomed to going out with tourists, and then only for a week or two. To their credit, they bravely stuck it out, borrowing upon the large reserves of stamina for which Tibetans are famous. There were many challenges that year. Floods, sandstorms, and blizzards took their toll. I lost count of how many times we had to free our vehicles from deep water and mud. At one point, the supply truck plunged off the edge of a ravine, but miraculously it came to rest on a ledge with no major damage to it or the driver. There were still many places in Upper Tibet in 1999 that had not been visited by foreigners, and we were a strange sight to many. Doc, as we called Ashley, ministered to the Tibetan herders and farmers along the way, winning us many friends.

Across Upper Tibet a striking spectrum of ancient castles, temples, villages, menhirs, tombs, cave shelters, and rock art caught my attention. Windowless dry-stone slab walls with tiny entranceways encased pre-Buddhist residential structures. These were strangely constructed edifices very different from Buddhist temples of later times. Some of the archaic structures were built partially underground and contained mazes of dark chambers and narrow passageways. Solitary monoliths or standing stones erected in big groups stood eerily next to tombs of many shapes and sizes. Caves riddled great rock formations, plexuses of long-abandoned habitations. Boulders and cliffs stockpiled ancient artwork incised in stone and painted in rich ochre hues. With the completion of the Changthang Circuit Expedition, the gamut of pre-Buddhist archaeological sites in Upper Tibet had emerged loud and clear as the physical stamp of the Zhang Zhung civilization.

I embarked on the Upper Tibet Circumnavigation Expedition in 2000, a hugely successful undertaking despite the obstacles. Getting to some sites in Upper Tibet was not an easy prospect, the long days of bumpy roads notwithstanding. The trails to many mountaintop citadels had long since collapsed, forcing climbs up and down cliff faces and narrow ledges with only the most minimal of holds for the hands and feet. It was a precarious undertaking using a tape measure on crumbling stone walls along the edges of precipices. There was no room for error or misjudgment. Year after year, the survey work required the Tibetan crews and me to operate within the narrowest of margins. There was no phone to call for help, no one waiting at base camp for support, no travel insurance, no luxury hotel at the end of the long journey. But the exquisite natural beauty of the Tibetan upland, the intellectual challenge, and the satisfaction coming from resisting arbitrary authority were ample compensation.

Remaining an obscure research scholar in a specialized niche came to have unintended benefits. I mostly stayed off the radar screen of the Chinese authorities. There were no big splashes in the media about my explorations that they would feel compelled to contain and neutralize. Lack of media attention acted as confirmation for the Chinese politicos that what was being done under their gaze was not very consequential. With considerable liberty I continued to explore, quietly but relentlessly.

GAINING GROUND TO FURTHER REVELATION

Upper Tibet is an immense region the size of Texas and Oklahoma combined, and I was bent on combing virtually all of it in a bid to assemble a comprehensive inventory of pre-Buddhist archaeological sites. While no one can hope to go everywhere, between 2001 and 2007, I made it to virtually every township in Upper Tibet in search of evidence of the remote past. These annual expeditions relied on motor vehicles and support crews to excellent effect. Thanks to the rugged terrain, however, I still had to hike or go on horseback for long distances. Many sites are located on mountaintops and cliffs or in gorges and caves and are only accessible on foot. A brutal climate and intense physical exertion were constant companions.

In 2001, I launched the four-month-long Upper Tibet Antiquities Expedition (UTAE), which clocked around five thousand miles in vehicles and hundreds more on foot and on horseback. On this crucial journey I documented ninety archaeological sites, providing a wealth of new information for my theories about prehistoric civilization in highland Tibet. Little by little I was closing in on Zhang Zhung, but there remained a great many destinations and questions pending. In 2002, I set off on the High Tibet Circle Expedition, which was also of four months' duration. This trip yielded another hundred archaeological sites over a trajectory of eight thousand miles by motor vehicle, in addition to very considerable distances covered on foot and on horseback.

Each locale in Upper Tibet has its own cultural and physical makeup. A number of tribes with their own dialects call this region home. Some places are higher and colder than others, some with water and some without. The passage of miles was being measured in a steady stream of new discoveries. How lucky to be the first to rend the veil of mystery that had been drawn over the past for a millennium. For the first time in eighteen years of exploration, my work would be officially sanctioned in 2002. Through a bilateral agreement signed between the Tibet Academy of Social Sciences (TASS) and the University of Virginia, it was agreed that there would be an exchange of scholars. Thanks to the efforts of Professor David Germano, I could now organize my expeditions through the auspices of the Tibet Academy of Social Sciences.

On the second expedition of 2002, near ruins that may be the fabled Zhang Zhung capital of Horned Eagle Valley Silver Castle, I recorded the largest burial grounds discovered to date. Called Chunak, or Black Water, it features a network of tombs, mounds, and pillars whose scale was so impressive it led us to consider that it may be the royal cemetery of the Zhang Zhung capital. My partner from TASS on this expedition, Dhondrup Lhagyal, wrote a paper reviewing our findings in the Chinese-language periodical *Tibetan Studies*.[16] His paper elicited much interest in the scholarly community of Tibet and mainland China.

As of 2003, more than half of Upper Tibet still remained unexplored, so that year I mounted another mission with TASS called the High Tibet Antiquities Expedition. The focus of exploration was close to the international border with India, the first access to many of these sectors by an outsider since the time of the British Raj. A People's Liberation Army (PLA) commander interested in culture and history helped my team reach a rock art site called Drak Gyam, the "Rock Formation Cliff Shelter," which boasts a series of adeptly carved stepped shrines known as *chorten*, dating to Tibet's imperium. We also tracked castles connected to an ancient tribe called Mon right to the borders of Ladakh, a fringe region of the Tibetan Plateau under Indian jurisdiction. By canvassing the frontier regions, I was able to fix the western geographic limits for Zhang Zhung–style castles, tombs, and pillars.

In their great physical isolation, the herders of Upper Tibet are not the most communicative lot. It often took years to win their trust. I bided my time, asking their help in finding ancient traces each year we met. Once they were convinced I meant no harm, the shepherds would open up, as cordial a group of people as any. The *drokpas*, as they are called, are highly skilled and trustworthy guides, the pivot point upon which the surveys rested. Without their help, hardly any archaeological work would have been possible. I would have been reduced to searching for the proverbial needle in a haystack.

As many of the ancient monuments chronicled belong to an earlier layer of civilization, they tend to be highly marginal to the doings of contemporary residents. Out of the everyday orbit, pre-Buddhist sites are often greeted with fear and suspicion. On more than one occasion, I was warned about demons infesting a ruin and counseled not to go there. Nevertheless, my perspective on the past was quite different from that of the average Tibetan. I welcomed visiting Zhang Zhung archaeological sites as glorious reminders of a golden era. Holiness is incumbent in the spectacular geographic settings of the early sites.

In 2004, I completed a three-month mission coined the High Tibet Welfare Expedition, in conjunction with the Tibetan Academy of Social Sciences. I was rejoined by my friend Dr. Ashley McAllen, recently back from high adventure in Central Asia and Afghanistan. The 2004 expedition was carried out with the purpose of reconnoitering areas of Upper Tibet not previously visited or where more inquiry was needed. The 2004 expedition proved very difficult. In midstream, Doc had to suddenly return to America. I was left to supervise an unruly crew, hiring and firing a slew of incompetent drivers, cooks, and assistants. I ended up pretty much doing everything, including driving and cooking for myself. Fortunately, a senior commissioner in the provincial government of western Tibet stood in to help. He dispatched a vehicle to keep the expedition afloat. I also had one trusty assistant, a highland shepherd named Ozer, willing to throw in his lot with me. He never said much and did not flinch at climbing yet another mountain in order to reach stone burial chests on a high summit. Once we climbed to nearly twenty thousand feet only to find that we had gone wrong, but Ozer did not even comment on our mistake. We simply looked at each other, shrugged, and headed back down. Being a *drokpa*, Ozer did not mix readily with crews from Lhasa. There was not much common ground between them, as their ways of life are so different. After a couple of weeks, the boys from Lhasa would inevitably miss urban comforts, some managing better than others.

On the forty-five-day-long Tibet Upland Expedition of 2005, I surveyed archaeological sites across the breadth of Upper Tibet not reached on earlier campaigns. Doc returned that year, as he would in 2006 and 2007. He was determined to help the herders with their medical needs and also spend as much time as possible reading through the tall stacks of history and science books he brought along. By 2005, I was able to reach most of the major basins and valleys of Upper Tibet south of the 34th parallel. On a parallel project, I conducted detailed interviews with the shamans of the region, who carry out ancient rites of healing, protection, and prognostication, leading to the publication of my book *Calling Down the Gods* in 2005.

In the winter of 2006, I embarked on the Tibet Ice Lakes Expedition (TILE) so as to reach six islands in four different great lakes of the Changthang. In theory, by traversing the frozen surfaces of the lakes, one could reach the islands, but not without a considerable degree of risk. A warming winter climate did not help matters. Neither Chinese survey teams nor the PLA had made it to the islands of Upper Tibet. With the exception of Swami Pranavananda's pilgrimage to the island of Do Muk, there was no historical evidence to show that any outsider had ever landed on them. This was truly some of the last terra incognita in the mid-latitudes of the planet. The backers of the project, the National Geographic Expeditions Council, decided not to publicize the TILE. I think they were displeased that a staff photographer did not come along, but I was afraid of being burdened with dead weight when moving lightly and quickly was essential.

While outsiders may never have visited the islands and lived to tell about it, they were certainly known to local shepherds. In the wintertime, a few *drokpa* families graze their goats and sheep on these big knobs of rock. An old Tibetan friend of mine, a Buddhist lay practitioner, or *ngakpa*, from Lake Nam Tsho, accompanied me to Semo Do. Semo Do has been closely linked to Buddhist meditators since the eighth century CE. The ice was uncomfortably thin when we arrived at the lakeshore opposite Semo Do. The way across to the island was unnerving. The lake would screech and shudder every time we tried to walk on it. There lay an abyssal black expanse below the frozen surface, and only six to eight inches of ice separated us from it. If it was not for the *ngakpa*, my assistants and I would never have ventured onto Lake Nam Tsho. His confidence carried the day, though. Following his cue, we ambled and slid three miles to Semo Do.

While I had heard that there were old ruins on Semo Do, I had no idea how extensive they were until we arrived. In addition to the derelict shelters of Buddhist hermits, there was a much more extensive monumental infrastructure associated with the pre-Buddhist inhabitants of the region. A series of heavily built but well-worn walls extending toward the lakeshore from the rocky backbone of the island bespoke a once formidable human presence. The island bastion of Semo Do belonged to Sumpa, a sister kingdom of Zhang Zhung that occupied the eastern margin of the Changthang before the seventh century CE. According to Eternal Bon texts, Sumpa and Zhang Zhung shared many religious, cultural, and administrative traits in common.

On the two islands of Darok Tsho, a surprising cache of ancient settlements also awaited my visit. Although Eternal Bon historical documents refer to the island of Tsho Do as the outpost of two eighth-century CE adepts, they fail to note that it was also the object of intense colonization in the time of Zhang Zhung. Rather than merely the refuge of isolated ascetics, a nexus of well-built all-stone houses and fortified structures took root on Tsho Do. In the Zhang Zhung era this nucleus of settlement must have held sway over a wide area. Similarly, the isles of Ngangla Ring Tsho and La Ngak Tsho exhibited robust signs of prehistoric highland civilization. The exploration of the island settlements turned up the key that helped unlock the true character and extent of ancient civilization in Upper Tibet. It was now clear that this string of insular sites formed the geographic and ritual axis of Zhang Zhung. After all those years, the faint outlines of Zhang Zhung were beginning to emerge as bold strokes across the canvas of inquiry.

In the spring of 2006, I completed most of the basic archaeological reconnaissance work in Upper Tibet on the forty-six-day Tibet Highland Expedition. One of the objectives of this expedition was to explore the Changthang north of the 34th parallel. Bereft of people and roads, travel in this colossal region required special logistical preparation. In 2007, I returned once more to the northern Changthang on the Wild Yak Lands Expedition.

It was now evident that far northern Upper Tibet had been left in a pristine state, the haunt of wild animals and hunters. The main arena of ancient highland civilization lay to the south. The builders and inhabitants of Zhang Zhung had gravitated toward the great lakes of the Changthang and the lower-elevation valleys of far western Tibet.

An understanding of the monuments and patterns of settlement that shaped ancient civilization in Upper Tibet was now in my grasp. Thirteen years had passed in pursuit of a single goal. It had taken untold travel, physical effort, and mental exertion, spanning some of the best years of my life, to reach this point. I had not only verified the existence of an ancient civilization in highest Tibet but revealed its basic makeup as well. Announcement to the scholarly community came in a book published by the Austrian Academy of Sciences in 2008 entitled *Zhang Zhung: Foundations of Civilization in Tibet*. Two more volumes followed in 2011, *Antiquities of Zhang Zhung*, published online by the University of Virginia–hosted Tibetan and Himalayan Library (www.thlib.org), and in print form by the Central University of Tibetan Studies in 2014.

My explorations in uppermost Tibet have continued unabated. From 2008 to 2013, I launched a series of expeditions to exhaustively document rock art, better understand archaic funerary traditions, and search for the long lost first temple of the Jain religion.

THE MEANS AND METHODS OF
CHRONICLING ZHANG ZHUNG SITES

My exploration dovetails with that of other archaeologists. While they have focused on a few specific sites, I have analyzed the structural elements and spatial patterns of ancient monuments throughout Upper Tibet, affording a global perspective on highland civilization. This work helps to place specific sites into a broader historical and cultural context. My surveys have been limited to what can be seen aboveground, a prelude to the excavation of tombs and other selected sites. That next step requires highly inclusive studies that draw together experts from various scientific fields.

My aim was to document every visible ancient remain in Upper Tibet. While falling short of this ambitious goal, I was able to document around seven hundred monumental and rock art sites, containing many thousands of individual structures and pictorial compositions. Fortunately, in the highly eroded landscapes of the Changthang, most ruins repose above the surface. The thin soils and incessant winds conspire to keep monuments visible, their crumbling carcasses scoured clean by the elements. How many ancient sites buried by floods, landslides, and earthquakes are out of view I cannot say. Concealed in the bosom of the earth, these markers of the past did not yield to my sweep of the surface.

Over the years, through trial and error, my collection of data became increasingly systematic and detailed. I have not only had to ferret out archaeological sites but to understand how their constituent parts relate to one another. Gaining an understanding of design and construction techniques acted as the basis for determining what types of monuments were created in Zhang Zhung and in the early historic and Lamaist civilizations that succeeded it.[17] In order to fathom holistic features of archaeological settlements, it was essential to work out their patterns of geographic distribution. Seeing how ancient communities spread across the landscape brings into focus the lines of communication and points of schism that helped shape them.

The discovery of Zhang Zhung is an ongoing enterprise. Research and exploration will continue into the foreseeable future, inducting ever more scientists into the process. The holy grail in the search for the ancient past is the excavation of the most promising archaeological sites, those that will spark giant leaps forward in our knowledge of Tibetan prehistory.

Before delving further into the history and archaeology of Zhang Zhung, let us get to better know the land and people of today's Upper Tibet. Learning about a country and its residents is an excellent departure point into the past. This is especially true of upland Tibet where the link between the past and present is so strong.

• *2* •

The Great Sky Realm:
The Land of Upper Tibet

THE PINNACLE ON THE ROOF OF THE WORLD

*T*he uppermost reaches of the Tibetan Plateau are the golden setting in which the jewel of Zhang Zhung once rested. This unique geographic and ecological domain gave birth to a civilization like no other.

The Tibetan Plateau soars above India, China, and Central Asia, occupying the hub of Eurasia. This loftiest elevated landmass on earth covers more than a million square miles, larger in area than Algeria or Greenland. The Tibetan Plateau has an average elevation of fifteen thousand feet above sea level, higher than any mountain in the continental United States.

Undeterred by its great altitude, the Tibetan Plateau grows still higher, uplifted by the inexorable advance of the Indian Subcontinent northward. This colossal highland is one of the most unapproachable territories on the planet, encircled as it is by extremely high mountains. The Great Himalayan Range forms an arc circumscribing the southern and western flanks of the Tibetan Plateau, effectively cutting it off from the Indian Subcontinent. To the north, the Kunlun Range sequesters Tibet from the great deserts and steppes of Central Asia. In the east, a series of high mountain ranges between the mighty Salween and Yangtze Rivers part the cultural and geographic worlds of Tibet and China.

The Tibetan Plateau is crisscrossed by numerous mountains, endowing it with a rich and varied natural environment. There are subtropical jungles in the southeast, lush alpine forests in the east, dry temperate valleys in the center, and an enormous steppe and desert in the north and west. This terrestrial crown of the planet is the source of many of Asia's greatest rivers, including the Brahmaputra, Indus, Yellow, Yangtze, Salween, and

Mekong. As the fountainhead of Asian rivers, the Tibetan Plateau is of critical importance to the well-being of almost two billion people, close to one-third of the world's total population. The sheer height of the Tibetan Plateau endows it with a pivotal role in the global climate system. The shifting of the jet stream south over Tibet helps trigger the summer monsoon on which a multitude of people depend. Heavy winter snow on the Tibetan Plateau contributes to the El Niño phenomenon, which has a profound impact on weather patterns worldwide.

The Tibetan Plateau's central location means that it straddles a number of critical bioecological zones. Southeastern Tibet is closely akin to the flora and fauna of southwestern China, a land of bamboo forests, tigers, and giant pandas. At the great bend in the Brahmaputra River in southern Tibet, there are tropical jungles of the type found on the Indian Subcontinent. In the northeast, the Central Asian steppes and Gobi Desert meld with the Plateau. Central Tibet is intersected by high mountain ranges that shelter forests of rhododendron, juniper, and birch.

North and west of Tibet's foremost city of Lhasa, the Nyenchen Thanglha Mountains separate Central Tibet from the northern hinterlands. This upland region, known as the Changthang, or "Northern Plains," is the largest single physical province of the Tibetan Plateau, occupying one-fourth of its total area. It is dominated by vast grasslands and stony wastelands. From its eastern limits the Changthang extends a thousand miles to the western

Mount Nyenchen Thanglha and Lake Nam Tsho

frontier of Tibet. In the far west, the tablelands of the Changthang give way to a series of lower-elevation valleys and badlands. This is an arid zone of woody scrub and riparian vegetation. Together the Changthang and far western Tibet, or Tö, constitute a seemingly endless highland, a region most aptly called Upper Tibet.

THE ENCHANTING DOMAIN OF UPPER TIBET

Covering almost three hundred thousand square miles, Upper Tibet is the size of France, Austria, and Switzerland combined. It was in this vastness that the ancient civilization most commonly known as Zhang Zhung took shape. Upland Tibet is a paradoxical land where delicate alpine flowers thrive among raging tempests. Formidable and magnificent, absolute silence and the thunderous elements vie for supremacy. This is a land that yields not its secrets easily and is only known after much time and contemplation.[1]

The high-altitude harshness of Upper Tibet is mediated by stunning beauty. The inherent sublimity of the landscape offsets its destructive power, the light overcoming the darkness in nature's perennial mystery play. Glowing with an almost otherworldly resplendence, rock formations and bodies of water assume the richest hues imaginable. At night the sky blazes with a multitude of heavenly bodies far brighter than anywhere else. So pristine is the air that on still, moonless nights, bright stars cast shadows over the landscape.

Upper Tibet is so spacious as to appear limitless. Its rarefied air and intense sunshine accent form and movement in a surreal interplay. The countryside is as vivid with eyes open as it is in dreams. Long vistas are magnified in the sparkling thin air. In this exceptional clarity, it is as if you can reach out and touch faraway places. From certain vantage points it is not unusual to see one hundred or even two hundred miles in all directions.

Remote and self-sustaining, Upper Tibet possesses towering mountains, luminous lakes, unbounded plains, and profoundly deep gorges. It is a land of transcendental qualities, a supernal sphere in which the mystic reigns culturally supreme. To this day, the topographic features of Upper Tibet are imbued with an innate divinity, a projection of the nobility nestled in the hearts of its inhabitants.

The prairies of the Changthang are emblazoned by rock formations of every conceivable color. Bare limestone, shale, and granite mountains in a palette of reds, yellows, and blues dot the sea of plains, breaking up the monotony of untrammeled landscapes. Here and there rolling hills with winding streams and thick carpets of turf rise above the steppes. On higher reaches, the ground is covered in a mantle of tundra that only grows for a few weeks a year. Plates of tundra interlock to form giant jigsaw puzzles that fan out across the landscape.

Some flatlands are nothing more than trackless expanses of sand and gravel devoid of vegetation. These frigid deserts bounded by distant mountains are among the bleakest places on earth. In more congenial locations, the wide plains of Upper Tibet support a thin layer of topsoil on which steppe vegetation grows. During the short summer months, wildflowers and medicinal plants proliferate, enlivening the meadows and rocky slopes in rainbow colors.

The Changthang and far western Tibet form a mosaic of alpine deserts, tundra, grasslands, marshes, sand dunes, woody scrub, and dwarf forests. Zones of geothermal activity create bizarre landscapes of extravagant forms and colors. Around the edges of some lakes and bogs are deadly pockets of quicksand ready to swallow up anything that strays near. Rocky chasms create sheltered microclimates in which miniature willows and junipers specially adapted to the high-elevation environment thrive. Caves abound in limestone formations, providing much-needed refuge from the wind-battered plains. In the extreme west of the Tibetan Plateau there is a massive labyrinth of canyons, some of which are still unexplored. The far northern Changthang is one of the most desolate places on earth. Its uninhabited plains and mountain ranges seem to recede all the way to the ends of the earth.

On all but its northern frontier, the Changthang is circumscribed by two immense chains of mountains, the Nyenchen Thanglha and Kangkar. The peaks of these Transhimalayan ranges rise to twenty-three thousand feet in elevation, making them among the highest mountains in the world. They are the lifeblood of the region, providing much of the water that sustains the rivers and lakes of Upper Tibet. The interconnected Nyenchen Thanglha and Kangkar stretch for a thousand miles, effectively blocking the Changthang from lower regions of the Tibetan Plateau. The highest summit in the Nyenchen Thanglha, or "Great Argali God of the Plain," is its namesake, a snub-nosed peak elevated 23,330 feet above sea level. The pride of place in the Kangkar or "White Mountains" is held by Lopön Kangri, the "Snow Mountain Minister," a rock pyramid that towers to a height of 23,270 feet.

The northern border of Upper Tibet and much of the rest of the Plateau is marked by the Kunlun, one of the world's greatest mountain ranges. The Kunlun acts as a barrier between the boreal biomes of the Changthang and the Taklamakan Desert of East Turkestan, now the Chinese province of Xinjiang. The northeastern border of the Changthang is delineated by the Tangla Range, high glaciated mountains that split the Tibetan Plateau east of Lhasa into southern and northern halves. The lofty plains and basins on the north side of the Tangla Range in what is termed Qinghai Province are similar to those of Upper Tibet, but the cultural histories of these two regions differ considerably. The northwestern corner of the Changthang, a relatively lifeless region known as the Askai Chin, is bounded by the Pamirs, another of the legendary mountain ranges of High Asia.

To the west of the Central Tibetan region known as Tsang, the terrain rises up until it is environmentally and culturally part of the Tibetan upland. This sliver of Upper Tibet along the upper Brahmaputra River is interposed between the Kangkar and Himalaya Mountains. Upper Tibet also extends west of the Kangkar Range, a relatively temperate agricultural and pastoral enclave known as the Gar basin. The Ayila Mountains skirting the west side of Gar demarcate the Tibetan highlands from the badlands of Guge. Smack up against the border of northern India, Guge, with its convoluted topography, is a very distinctive subregion of Upper Tibet.

The Changthang itself is partitioned by north–south-oriented sequences of mountains running perpendicular to the grain of the major fault lines fragmenting Tibet. Called meridian ranges, these are found at fairly regular intervals across the breadth of the region. When the Tibetan Plateau was uplifted by the Subcontinent crashing underneath the Asian plate, colossal tectonic forces were released at right angles, leading to the formation of the meridian ranges. These glaciated chains of mountains are typically 60 to 150 miles in length and twenty thousand feet in height. Their glaciers are of the utmost importance to the maintenance of pastures and lakes, the lifeline of the Changthang's inhabitants. Today, as in ancient times, much of the population of the Changthang is concentrated at the foot of these north–south-running mountain ranges. From east to west, five major meridian ranges partition the southern half of the Changthang: Ama Gyalgang, Targo, Lungkar, Rolpa Kyabdun, and Yalung Selung.

The warm season in the Changthang is only around eight weeks long. Conditions are colder and drier in the north and west, with steppe grasslands dominating the eastern Changthang and alpine deserts the western portion. Most of the northeastern Changthang is overlaid by a thick layer of permafrost, but much of the northwest is too arid for permafrost and the ground remains raw and rocky.

The Changthang has one of the fiercest and most changeable climates on earth, a function of its dizzying height. Gale force winds and blizzards can break out at any time. In the summer, huge squalls flare up unexpectedly, bringing howling winds, hail, and sleet. When summer snow or rain hits, dry dusty plains are transformed into muddy sloughs in a matter of hours, making travel difficult. In this wildly capricious world, it is not unusual for placid sunny weather to replace raging storms repeatedly during the course of a single day. Quite frequently, summertime air currents buffeting the plains are transformed into multiple whirlwinds. The threat of subfreezing weather and blizzards in July and August brands the Changthang with a colder summer climate than most of the Arctic. During the remainder of the year, temperatures are subfreezing, plummeting to an extreme of minus 40 Fahrenheit in the dead of winter. Piercing cold winds blow much of the time, exasperating the already desperate climate. The extreme conditions of Upper Tibet have a devastating impact on the inhabitants of the region. In a particularly bad spell of weather, shepherds can lose 50 to 90 percent of their herds. The lower valleys of the far west have longer summers and milder winters than the Changthang, but the parched terrain makes eking out a living very difficult.

There are nonetheless certain charms to the climate of Upper Tibet that other cold places do not share. Upper Tibet has 270 to 330 days of sunshine a year, ameliorating the worst of the cold, especially in the early afternoons. The sun in the rarefied atmosphere is very intense and has a pronounced warming effect. In the thin air, it is not unusual for diurnal temperatures to vary by forty or even fifty degrees Fahrenheit. Upper Tibet is situated at a relatively low latitude (between thirty and thirty-six degrees above the equator), the same as many subtropical and south temperate areas such as north India, Saudi Arabia, and the southern United States. Being closer to the equator has a moderating effect on the climate, creating warmer winters than there would be otherwise. Most of Upper Tibet has nocturnal winter temperatures of minus 10 to minus 30 degrees Fahrenheit, which is quite mild when compared to the Arctic.

The extreme cold and height of Upper Tibet has traditionally placed stringent constraints on population growth. Most of the region has remained sparsely settled or uninhabited. Even during the height of Zhang Zhung civilization, the northern Changthang was not permanently colonized. By the Iron Age, the climate had deteriorated to the point that this highest and driest tier of Upper Tibet was usable only as a hunting ground. The northern Changthang, exceptionally cold and barren even in the middle of the extremely short summer season, constitutes one of the greatest wildernesses left on earth. The lofty Transhimalayan ranges also remain largely unpopulated, as these mountains are too cold and snowy for human beings to live there year-round. Although Upper Tibet was more intensively occupied in the time of Zhang Zhung than in subsequent periods, the permanent zone of habitation was limited to tracts under 17,700 feet in elevation. In addition to the base of the meridian ranges, the main circles of human settlement in Upper Tibet, now and in ancient times, is the lake belt running across the southern tier of the Changthang, the valleys and basins of far western Tibet, and the upper Brahmaputra valley.

There are worrying signs that arid conditions are intensifying in Upper Tibet. Ironically, flash floods are also becoming more common. This is having a major impact on the environment and is adversely affecting the livelihood of farmers and shepherds. The signs of desertification are plain to see in many areas of Upper Tibet. Marshy pastures used as winter grazing grounds are shrinking throughout the region. Dwindling water supplies are also making farming more difficult. Around the traditional breadbaskets of Lake Dangra and the valleys of far western Tibet, farmers complain that the founts of irrigation water are in steep decline. They say there is now even less water available for cultivation than in the time of their fathers and grandfathers. New irrigation projects are offsetting these losses to some degree, but the situation is critical.

Models used to predict the future climate of Tibet project that upwards of one-third of Himalayan glacial masses could possibly melt away by 2050.[2] The rate of ice loss in the more climatically vulnerable Transhimalayan ranges may be even greater. Glaciers are a source of water for many villages and towns in Tibet, and their loss would have catastrophic consequences for the entire Plateau. As most Tibetans live off the land, any reduction in the animal products and food grains produced would have a grim impact (the effects of climate change are further examined in the last section of chapter 3).

LAKES OF SANCTITY AND BEAUTY

The Changthang is girt by a belt of more than ten thousand lakes. Interposed between India and Central Asia, these bodies of water formed the east–west axis along which ancient highland civilization developed.

Extending across the entire breadth of the region, the lakes of the Changthang are among its most prominent landmarks, breaking up the vast plains into readily distinguishable locales. The great lakes provide travelers with much-needed points of reference in a land so expansive they would otherwise be engulfed. For millennia, these splendid bodies of water have instilled a sense of reverence in the minds of residents and visitors. Daunting yet alluring, the hermit saints of Tibet have habitually sought out their solitudes.

Many of the lake basins are a little lower in elevation than the adjoining plains, and the large bodies of water moderate the temperature, creating a relatively amenable environment for settlement. Around the most important lakes are cliffs and rocky headlands marked with caves and overhangs. These rock shelters are ideal places for human habitation and were intensively exploited in ancient times. Many of the temples and fortresses of Zhang Zhung came up around the lakes, constituting the core of ancient civilization in the Changthang.

A white yak beside one of the many lakes on the Changthang.

The sheer beauty of the Changthang lakes is a crucial factor in their perennial charm. Like a necklace of lapis lazuli and turquoise, they adorn an earthen fabric of bistre and ochre. The lakes contain exceptionally clear and pure water. Each one has special physical characteristics to which a unique personality is attached in local lore. The colors of the Upper Tibetan lakes are accented by the clarity of the water and the rarified air. From deepest blue and green to bronze, black, and gray, their tint varies according to the chemical composition of the water and the weather. During sunrise and sunset, these aqueous expanses sometimes resemble crucibles of molten silver or gold, iridescent and fiery. To see the Changthang lakes in fair weather is a rapturous spectacle. Conversely, in bad weather they are transformed into fearfully dark, brooding seas. In the wintertime the lakes of Upper Tibet freeze over: some have translucent smooth ice, and others have dappled or fissured surfaces, while still other lakes have ice that is opaque and rocklike.

Like moons revolving around planets, the big lakes are ringed by satellite lakes. All of the great lakes are fed by rivers originating in the glaciers and snowmelt of neighboring mountains and in springs that bubble up to the surface. Most of the Changthang lakes are internally draining. The rivers from which they take their sustenance, no matter how large, are entirely consumed. The few existing outlets drain into interconnected lakes from which there is no escape. Only in the extreme east and west of Upper Tibet are a few rivers able to liberate themselves from the clutches of the interior. In the extremely dry and thin air, water simply evaporates from the lakes. As there is no outflow, the concentration of minerals has been increasing over the millennia, leading to amplified levels of alkalinity and sterility.

In these extreme conditions, only specially adapted aquatic life thrives in the Changthang lakes. Among the largest dwellers is the very slow-growing scaleless carp. These primitive-looking fish reach more than three feet in length and prefer deep water near the edges of cliffs and headlands. Upper Tibetans speak of much larger aquatic animals, but these have not been scientifically confirmed. For centuries, it has been said that giant golden fish and dragons lurk in the depths of the biggest lakes. Some local residents as well as visiting pilgrims claim to have seen these fantastic creatures with their own eyes! Perhaps they are confusing savage meteorological phenomena, such as tornados and rare cloud formations, for monsters of the deep, but further inquiry into the matter is warranted. Limnological exploration of the Changthang lakes is still in its infancy. It is also popularly believed that the waters harbor aquatic yaks, horses, and sheep, an unbelievable proposition to the modern mind.

Since ancient times, the Changthang lakes have been considered the abodes of deities and demons. Magnificent goddesses with massive retinues are conceived of as dwelling in lavishly decorated underwater palaces. These regal lake deities are worshipped by shepherds as bringers of well-being, fertility, and fair weather. They are accorded a special role as guardians of livestock, women, and children. Particularly brackish and shallow lakes are believed to be the haunts of demons, a puckish lot better off avoided. These demons are appeased with ritual offerings at specific times of the year or when implicated in troublesome events.

Nam Tsho, the "Celestial Lake," is the largest and deepest body of water in the Changthang. Situated only a hundred miles northwest of Lhasa, its cobalt blue, slightly brackish waters cover seven hundred square miles and have a maximum depth of 350 feet. According to local folklore, Nam Tsho is a gigantic watery mirror that reflects the forms and colors of the sky in perfect fidelity. She is envisioned as a goddess of exquisite beauty and power mounted on a dragon or bird. The mountain Nyenchen Thanglha, which rises above the south shore of Nam Tsho, is thought to be her polygamous mate.[3] Nam Tsho gives as good as she receives and has taken several other mountain god lovers from the region. Archaic cave hermitages and rock paintings, vestiges of Zhang Zhung's sister culture, Sumpa, appear all around Nam Tsho.

One hundred and twenty miles northwest of Nam Tsho is the Changthang's second-largest lake, Zeling Tsho, a shallow and bitter body of water far removed from high mountain ranges. This sterile gray-blue mass is associated with demons. South of Zeling Tsho is the forty-mile-long Kering Tsho, the aquatic stronghold of a serpent goddess known as Kering Bumtsho Chukmo. Seated in the middle of a gigantic basin further west is Ngangtse Tsho, a lake that appears to be the haunt of an old Zhang Zhung goddess named Menchung Yuyi Zamatok, the "Little Woman with the Milk Pail of Turquoise."[4]

In the middle of the Changthang is Lake Dangra Yumtsho, a splendid turquoise sheet encircled by snowy mountain ranges. She is home to the goddess Dangra Lekyi Wangmo, "Ocean Power Lady of Destiny." Dangra Yumtsho, a prime center of Zhang Zhung, boasts the ruins of archaic era fortresses, temples, and settlements all along her shores.[5]

Teri Nam Tsho, located west of Lake Dangra, is another big lake connected to the mythology and settlements of Zhang Zhung. There were once three islands in Teri Nam Tsho, each of which hosted an exclusive community housing the ruling and priestly elites of the region.[6] As Teri Nam Tsho receded over the centuries, these islands became headlands connected to the mainland. Another major lake to the west known as Darok Tsho also had high-status island settlements.[7] Unlike Teri Nam Tsho, the immaculate waters of Darok Tsho are still potable. Emerald green and sapphire blue, Darok Tsho is thought to be inhabited by a comely goddess whose ancestry is also

Island and headlands in Lake Darok Tsho, home to ruined ancient settlements

traced to Zhang Zhung. At 15,385 feet elevation, Ngangla Ring Tsho in the western Changthang is the highest of the big lakes. Long headlands intrude upon its waters on most sides. There is a large island in the center of Ngangla Ring Tsho, accessible during the winter season when shepherds traverse its imperturbable icy mantle.

On the western margin of the Changthang, more than six hundred miles from Lake Nam Tsho, is Tshomo Ngangla Ringmo, a thin ribbon of water that runs to the Indian border. Despite being situated in the northwest, the most arid portion of Tibet, Tshomo Ngangla Ringmo is one of the few large freshwater lakes left in Upper Tibet. It fills an ancient suture zone bound in many places by towering cliffs and rocky outcrops.

Two other lakes of special note are Mapang Yumtsho and La Ngak Tsho, situated in the southwest corner of the Tibetan Plateau. Although not as large as the Changthang lakes, these twin bodies of water are very important pilgrimage destinations. Their waters are perceived as a divine sacrament with healing and restorative properties. Tibetans see sacred Mapang Yumtsho as a mandala containing the palace of a serpent goddess, while for Hindus this lake represents the mind of the creator god Brahma. La Ngak Tsho is shunned by Tibetan Buddhist and Hindu pilgrims because for them it has a demonic persona. However, in Eternal Bon, La Ngak Tsho is the dominion of a goddess of incredible prowess called Drablai Gyalmo who occupies the islands of the lakes.[8] Clad in armor and carrying the weapons of utter devastation, this queen of the warrior deities is thought to have originated in Zhang Zhung. Drablai Gyalmo also dwells on Ngemo Na Nyi, a mountain located just east of La Ngak Tsho. One of the largest massifs in the world, Ngemo Na Nyi is known to the inhabitants of the Indian Subcontinent as Gurlha Mandhata and to Eternal Bon as Takri Trabo. This mountain is offset from the main axis of the Great Himalayan Range, an isolated behemoth recognizable from a great distance away.

COSMIC CENTER MOUNT TISE

Mount Kailash, or Tise in the Zhang Zhung language, is the holiest mountain in Tibet and one of the most famous pilgrimage destinations in all of Asia.[9] Standing above Lakes Mapang Yumtsho and La Ngak Tsho, this mountain pyramid was a major hub of Zhang Zhung. This is demonstrated in a series of ruined temples and strongholds found in the extremely secluded heights.[10] These formidable all-stone edifices were established by archaic religious practitioners as much as three thousand years ago. According to popular folklore, Mount Tise was transferred to the Buddhists in the eleventh

Holy Mount Tise from the middle of frozen Lake La Ngak Tsho

century CE after the famous yogin Milarepa won a magical contest with a *bonpo* magician named Naro Bonchung.[11]

Holy to the Hindus and Jains as well, Mount Tise has drawn pilgrims to its flanks for many centuries. Before the advent of motor vehicles half a century ago, some wayfarers traveled for months to reach the sacred mountain. Those coming from the Subcontinent had to endure a hazardous journey over the Great Himalayan Range, some paying for it with their very lives.

The Sutlej, Karnali, Brahmaputra, and Indus, four mighty rivers watering the Indian Subcontinent, have their sources in southwestern Tibet. In Tibetan sacred geography, these four rivers are envisioned as flowing off the four faces of Mount Tise. While this is not literally true, it is nevertheless remarkable that all four rivers take birth within a hundred miles of the holy mountain. The Sutlej, Karnali, Brahmaputra, and Indus stream out in the four cardinal directions to both breach and flow around the Great Himalayan arc. These rivers course through the Indo-Gangetic plains before emptying into the Arabian Sea and the Bay of Bengal.

The mighty Indus River is spawned in tiny rivulets cascading down the north side of the Kangkar Range. The ritual source of the Indus is the Sengge Khabab, or "Lion Fountain," a spring straddling two streams that form the geographic head of the river. A shrine marks the birth of this north-flowing river from the mouth of a mythic lion, a naturally occurring rock formation. The upper Indus River is lined with pink tamarisk trees and passes through

The vast badlands of Guge with the snowy peaks of the Himalaya in the background

pastures and little agricultural plots. Downstream of Upper Tibet, the Indus ripples through Ladakh, a Tibetan cultural region in Indian territory, before flowing into northern Pakistan.

The wellspring of the west-running Sutlej River, the "Elephant Fountain," is a marsh located a little west of La Ngak Tsho, near the little monastery of Denchu. The upper Sutlej races through a series of gorges gouged out of the Central Himalaya and Western Himalaya on its escape to India. This spectacular badlands region known as Guge, a maze of canyons, mesas, and escarpments, is largely impassable. Unlike the Indus and Brahmaputra, which snake around the western and eastern bastions of the Great Himalayan Range respectively, the Sutlej pushes right through a narrow cleft in the middle of the mountain range.

The ritual source of the south-flowing Karnali River, the "Peacock Fountain," is a high-volume spring nestled on the north side of the Central Himalaya, while its ultimate geographic source is a glacier lying near the crest of lofty peaks. The Karnali winds its way through Purang, an Upper Tibetan farming enclave, before passing to Nepal and blasting through the Himalaya.

The Brahmaputra River's "Horse Fountain" issues from a Transhimalayan glacier seated near the Nepalese border. The roiling headwaters of the Brahmaputra pour out between two rocky peaks known as the "Horse's Ears." As the river gathers strength, it turns east to etch a broad line across much of Tibet.

On the opposite side of Upper Tibet, the Salween, the great lifeline of Burma, originates in lakes west of Nakchu City. The Salween is one of many rivers flowing through the eastern highlands of Tibet. It is not until it turns south in the Kham region of Tibet that it distinguishes itself as a major river.

DIVINE DENIZENS, THE WILDLIFE OF UPPER TIBET

Native wildlife is an inseparable part of the religion, mythology, and economy of Upper Tibet. As much of the region is too high and cold for permanent settlement, it has remained the preserve of wild animals.

In the hyperborean reaches of the Changthang, large herds of wild yaks, antelope, and wild asses still roam freely.[12] Blue sheep are also quite plentiful in many areas of Upper Tibet, but the argali sheep is now rare. The Tibetan brown bear, Eurasian lynx, snow leopard, wolf, and fox are the major predators of Upper Tibet. These carnivores feed on both hoofed animals and smaller burrowing species such as the pica and marmot. Other big meat eaters, namely the tiger and lion, are strongly represented in mythology associated with Zhang Zhung. If indeed tigers and lions did once live in Upper Tibet, they became extinct in ancient times.

The wild yak is by far the largest and most formidable animal of Upper Tibet. It is to the Tibetan highlands what the wild Bactrian camel is to the Gobi Desert of Mongolia. Known as the *drong* in Tibetan, the quintessential wild yak is endemic to the upland. Reputedly, the biggest bulls stand seven feet at the withers and are nearly eleven feet from nose to tail, the size of a sports utility vehicle. Wild yaks are unpredictable and dangerous sorts of animals, best enjoyed from a distance. According to Upper Tibetan tradition, the mountain gods and lake goddesses have manifested in the guise of wild yaks for millennia, underscoring the cultural prominence and great strength of the animal. Numinous wild yaks in many colors also act as magic mounts for a variety of deities. White yaks are preferred by celestial divinities, while terrestrial deities prefer to ride reddish yaks and underworld spirits bluish varieties.

Another intimidating creature of the upland is the Tibetan brown bear, renowned for its variegated pelage ranging from white to tan to bluish in color. These omnivores feed on anything they can get their paws on, but they are generally shy and retiring in nature. Bears seem to invoke a particularly strong sense of fear and curiosity in Upper Tibet. Once one barreled through our camp causing quite a stir among the crew. The protective gods of the region are sometimes depicted attired in the skins of the brown bear. Folklore holds that some of the ancient residents of Upper Tibet were descended from the brown bear. The deep-rooted belief that humans came from beasts is discouraged in Lamaism, as this does not conform to its worldview. Yet such archaic beliefs involving wild animals persist to the present day, albeit in attenuated forms.

Like brown bears, the wolves of Upper Tibet come in a variety of colors, with all-black examples rivaled in rarity only by the all-white albino. The wolf is the most common large predator in Tibet and will hunt both wild and domestic herbivores. Tibetan wolves are leery of humans but less so of a single individual, and it is possible to get almost close enough to touch them. Divine wolves, some of which are multiheaded, appear in the retinues of many local protective deities. They serve as the messengers and attendants of the gods. According to Eternal Bon texts, its ancient religious masters used wolves, bears, and other wild animals as servants.

Lynx and snow leopards live secretive lives in mountainous areas. Eternal Bon writings tell us that the pelts of these great cats were used to make the robes worn by the royalty and high priests of Zhang Zhung. The activities of these shy felines, like those of other wild animals, are believed to be regulated by local territorial deities.

The favorite prey of the lynx and snow leopard are wild sheep. The argali, the largest species of sheep in the world, is called *nyen* in Tibetan. The *nyen* is also the name of a class of ireful terrestrial gods. The much more common blue sheep can be spotted in herds of up to a hundred animals. The horns of the blue sheep and argali are sought after by Tibetan highlanders as offering objects for their deities. These horns grace mountaintop tabernacles and cairns throughout Upper Tibet. The use of blue sheep horns as magical instruments has a long history. In Eternal Bon texts, Gekhö, the most celebrated mountain god of Zhang Zhung, is depicted wielding a blue sheep horn.

In the Nyenchen Thanglha Range near Lake Nam Tsho, the highly endangered musk deer still manages to hold out, despite strong demand on the international market for the sweet-smelling gland found in mature males. Another endangered animal species is the white-lipped deer, which survives in small numbers on the eastern and southern fringes of the Changthang. This proud animal appears to have once roved on many moors and grasslands of Upper Tibet, but overhunting and climate change brought it to the brink of extinction generations ago. The deer is an important motif in the rock art of the region, and shepherds still occasionally unearth the skeletons and antlers of deer in habitats where it is no longer found. Deer as mythological flying creatures appear to have played a vital role in the religious life of Zhang Zhung. It is written in Tibetan texts that its body parts were sought after in the manufacture of ritual objects such a drumheads and tabernacles. It also appears that deer were sacrificed in rites carried out to cure the ill and to ensure the passage of the dead to the afterlife.

Two common wild ungulates of the Upper Tibetan plains are the antelope and wild ass. These fleet-footed creatures are sometimes seen in herds of over two hundred animals. The antelope, known as *tshö* in Tibetan, is relished for its flesh, while the wild ass is only eaten by the most destitute. Traditionally, antelope horns are used as digging tools and as ritual implements for scoring the earth. The wild ass, or *kyang*, has numerous divine aspects. Considered the cousin of the domestic horse in Tibetan literature, the *kyang* is closely aligned to a class of fierce red gods known as *tsen*. Hares notwithstanding, the most common wild herbivore in Upper Tibet is the diminutive gazelle, a species that grazes in small numbers. The gentle gazelle's only defense is its tremendous speed; a healthy adult can easily outrun any predator.

Upper Tibet is home to a rich variety of birdlife including eagles, hawks, vultures, geese, ducks, grouses, choughs, partridges, and cranes, among scores of other species. Avifauna has always figured heavily in the mythology of Upper Tibet. In its unobscured skies, birds have naturally taken on special religious significance. In fact, the mythic horned eagle, or *khyung*, may have been the prime emblem of Zhang Zhung.

Birds such as eagles, falcons, and vultures are thought of as divine progenitors of certain native clans in Upper Tibet. Raptors seem to be frequently portrayed as deities and divine emissaries in the ancient rock art of the highlands. The black-feathered chough is closely linked with a class of semidivine beings known as *dud*. According to Eternal Bon texts, the bellicose *dud* played a dominant role in the prehistoric political and clan history of the northeastern Changthang. Aquatic species like the duck and goose are connected to the *lu*, or water spirits. Birds, like other indigenous animals, are still embodied by the shamans of Upper Tibet when performing curative rites.

Since the takeover of Tibet by the Chinese Communists in the 1950s, pressures on wildlife have grown exponentially. During the Chinese Cultural Revolution (1966–1976), herds of antelope, wild asses, and other animals were relentlessly hunted by the People's Liberation Army to feed its ravenous troops. Armed with motor vehicles and automatic weapons, this plunder by the PLA had a calamitous impact on game in Upper Tibet. The arrival of commercial hunters in the 1980s led to the destruction of many more wild animals, and wild yaks and antelopes were brought to the verge of extinction.

Recently the situation has improved with the creation of the Changthang Nature Reserve in the northernmost tier of Upper Tibet. At nearly one hundred thousand square miles (the size of Colorado), this national park is one of the largest wildlife sanctuaries in the world. It is home to substantial populations of wild ungulates and the large carnivores that prey upon them. Thanks to the measures taken by the Chinese government to preserve native fauna, antelopes are starting to recolonize the plains of the southern

Changthang as well. The tiny population of tawny-colored wild yaks in the Kangkar Range of southwestern Tibet may also be stabilizing.

Despite the measures already taken, there are still grave challenges facing conservation efforts in Upper Tibet. The sheer size of the region makes wildlife protection a daunting prospect. Poachers remain active, capitalizing on lucrative market prospects. Antelope skins are being illegally traded, each of which fetches around $100. The Tibetan antelope produces a soft downy undercoat known as *shahtoosh*, highly coveted for the manufacture of a luxury textile. A single shawl woven with *shahtoosh* brings upwards of $20,000! In the last few years, a market for wild yak heads has appeared in Tibetan towns and cities. With horns spanning as much as seven feet, they are seen as potent household amulets, explaining their growing popularity. Wild yak heads now sell for as much as $1,500 each.

In addition to the wild and domestic animals of Upper Tibet, there are of course the people themselves. Their tenure on the high Tibetan Plateau can be traced back to the Stone Age. Beginning more than ten thousand years ago and extending through Zhang Zhung and historic times, upland Tibet boasts an unbroken legacy of human occupation. From the ancients to their contemporary descendants, the past and present meet as one in the culture of the highlands.

• *3* •

Tillers and Herders, Warriors and Saints: The People of Upper Tibet

A UNION OF FARMERS AND SHEPHERDS

$\mathcal{T}$he sweeping plains and long mountain ranges of Upper Tibet are inhabited by hardy shepherds and farmers. They herd livestock or till the land to extract a meager existence. Heirs to what can be called the Zhang Zhung legacy, Upper Tibetans have been engaged in these subsistence activities for at least three thousand years.[1]

Those residing in the highest realm on earth have had no choice but to muster their courage and stamina in a continuous stream of collective enterprise. They must cope with the ferocity of the natural environment, resolutely pursuing their economic interests despite a constant barrage of difficulties and setbacks. Yet this epic battle for survival has not diminished their spirit, for the Upper Tibetans have cultivated a mind-set in which contentment and comprehension are presiding values.

In significant ways, the techniques used to wrest crops from the land and to rear livestock have changed very little in three millennia. The farmers and shepherds are the inheritors of an economy and culture that have withstood the test of time and its checkered political impositions. They continue to adhere to patterns of thought and behavior derived from early times.

Historically speaking, Upper Tibet is an amalgam of different clans and tribes juxtaposed against one another in shifting alliances. Spacious Upper Tibet has been continuously enriched by peoples of diverse origins, strengthening its social capital. Some agriculturalists and pastoralists belong to the autochthonous clans of the region, while many other lineages came from outside the region. People have immigrated to Upper Tibet from all over the Tibetan Plateau, the Indian Subcontinent, and Central Asia. These assorted groups have been assimilated into the Tibetan ethnos and speak various dialects of Tibetan, the language of Zhang Zhung having died out more than eleven hundred years ago. The Upper Tibetans largely share the same culture and way of life, so they mix and understand one another quite easily. A loose confederation of tribes and clans has thus evolved. The fluid character of this highland society is well suited to optimizing the use of what limited natural resources are available.

THE *DROKPAS*, WANDERERS OF THE TIBETAN UPLAND

The rangelands and mountain meadows of Upper Tibet are inhabited by a people whose mark on the land is as ephemeral as the seasons. These are the *drokpas*, the traditional herders of yaks, sheep, goats, and horses. Through many years in their company, I have come to greatly admire these colonizers of the inhabitable limits of Tibet.[2]

As most of Upper Tibet is not suited to agriculture, it is dominated by the *drokpas*. The name for the shepherds comes from the Tibetan word *drok*, which denotes an isolated or unpopulated place. The *drokpas* are a sturdy lot attired in distinctive sheepskin cloaks, large hats made of fleece and fox fur, and colorful cloth boots. With their ruddy complexions and deeply etched faces, these seminomadic herders are a study in rugged self-reliance.

In possession of proud martial traditions, the *drokpas* were the indisputable masters of their world for many centuries. Carrying swords and knives, the men still cut imposing figures. In the intense sunshine, their skin assumes

A drokpa *shepherdess tending her flock of goats and sheep*

a bronze or ebony cast. The women traditionally accent their rich skin tone with *docha*, a cosmetic prepared by reducing whey to a paste. This dark red unguent is dabbed on the face to beautify and protect the skin. Glistening brilliantly in the sunshine, *docha* has an arresting aesthetic effect.

The *drokpas* walk with a rolling gait but prefer to travel on horseback. Children learn to ride even before they have begun walking. In the time of the Tibetan empire, the equestrian skills of the Upper Tibetan regiments were highly valued by the Purgyal emperors. More recently, *drokpa* horsemen have struck fear into the hearts of interlopers.

Many dozens of clans and several tribes are represented among the *drokpas*, an occupational specialization, not an ethnic designation. Notwithstanding the farmers of the periphery, they are synonymous with the Tibetan highlands. A retiring but cordial group, the *drokpas* traditionally reside in black tents made of woven yak hair. They are people of song and prayer, fiercely devoted to their families, shy but fun loving.

Family members accompany the herds to graze on the plains and mountainsides, often covering long distances before returning home at the end of the day. In the mornings, ewes and female goats are let out of their stone pens, tied together, and relieved of their burden of milk. Female yaks are rounded up and milked as well. Animals are often milked in the evening too. Extracting milk is done by females to the accompaniment of ballads extolling the joys of their religion and homeland in soft, soothing rhythms. When traveling and herding, the *drokpa* men in turn sing about the glories of their way of life and august history. The lilting melodies of the *drokpas* are at once attractive and haunting, exhilarations that temper the character and uplift the spirit.

The *drokpas* are often the object of wistful musings by more settled sections of Tibetan society and foreign observers alike. Their aloof air, free-roaming ways, and closeness to the earth naturally lend themselves to romantic notions. Indeed, their self-composure and fortitude are the basic ingredients from which legends are made. But to overromanticize the *drokpas* and their way of life is to miss much of who they really are. Over the centuries, they have been locked in a titanic struggle for survival that has surely enhanced their character, but it has also taken a big toll. Herding livestock in the Upper Tibetan immenseness is a grueling proposition, one that offers little respite or leeway.

To cope with an unpredictable and frigid climate, the *drokpas* have adopted a lifestyle that is attuned to the maximum conservation of energy. They are not prone to emotional outbursts or incessant chatter. Their quiet bearing is reinforced by a stoicism tinged with deeply held religious beliefs. The *drokpas* are splendidly self-sufficient and will not usually seek out the company of outsiders. When they do encounter foreigners, they tend to be reserved and vigilant. They are in fact kind and hospitable, but in an understated manner. They are not given over to extravagant gestures of generosity and friendship, but rather they comport themselves with calmness and dignity. They make fine companions but treacherous enemies.

The *drokpas* are a high-spirited lot, a quality tied up with their unbounded itinerant lifestyle. They revel in horse races, contests of physical strength, and archery, for they are a people with a warrior heritage. The *drokpas* live by a code of honor underwritten by an eye-for-an-eye philosophy. Before the Chinese Communist takeover of Tibet, the *drokpas* were sometimes mired in feuds that lasted for generations. These internecine conflicts were very costly in human terms, creating a situation in which every provocation had to be redressed before peace could be restored. The arbitration of disputes was carried out by lamas and respected elders, and if their efforts failed, entire communities could be plunged into a state of war. Banditry was also rife, perpetuated by bands of miscreants or the dispossessed. The wide-open spaces of Upper Tibet have always attracted immigrants searching for new opportunities, be they legitimate or illegitimate. Nowadays, the internal conflicts of the *drokpas* have been largely pacified by a strong government presence.

THE *DROKPA* ATTIRE OF GODS AND KINGS

The *drokpas'* colorful dress is modeled on that of their deities and ancient rulers. Their robes, jewelry, coiffure, and other aspects of their apparel are imbued with sacred and regal connotations. Items of clothing are ubiquitous reminders of a *drokpa's* beliefs and of his or her place in the scheme of things. The crown of the hat is a dwelling place of the warrior gods, the leather overcoat is the attire of kings and guardian deities, the designs of the sash pay homage to religious and clan figures, and the soft boots permit one to benignly tread over the realm of the earth spirits.

Virtually every herder carries a braided sling called an *urdo*. It is used to fling rocks at high velocity, a handy tool for controlling livestock and for protection. The *urdo* is also an indispensable object of offering for the warrior and personal gods. The finest *urdo* are braided with "nine eyes," a symbol of the totality of the universe and the primal families of deities.

Drokpa costumes vary geographically and help to pinpoint tribal affiliations. Each region of Upper Tibet has its own headgear, ranging from simple undyed knit caps to elaborate felt and fleece hats with flaps and high crowns. The design of footwear also changes from place to place. The uppers consist of colorful pieces of woolen cloth cut to form a variety of geometric patterns, while the soles are made of leather. Boots are held up by woven cloth ties, which are embellished with flowers, wavy lines, animals, solar discs, and many other motifs. As with other items of clothing, the *drokpas* prepare their own boots, a task that takes several weeks of part-time work.

Much time and effort goes into tanning the sheep and goat hides used to fashion the *drokpa* greatcoats, or *lokpa*. Yogurt is applied to the hides to render them supple and durable. Each hide has to be kneaded with yogurt for many hours at a time. Throughout Upper Tibet, factory-made attire is now replacing homemade clothing. Store-purchased goods are generally inferior in quality, but they do not require time and skill to make and are seen as convenient alternatives. The widespread adoption of mass-produced clothes and tools is blurring the rich regional mosaic that traditionally characterizes *drokpa* communities.

In addition to their everyday clothes, the *drokpas* try to keep a better set of garments for festivals and other special occasions. The luckier among them have also managed to retain precious jewelry and amulets handed down from father to son and from mother to daughter over many generations. *Drokpas* highly prize ancient copper alloy and iron artifacts occasionally found while out grazing the herds. These metallic figurines, arrowheads, and utilitarian objects are perceived as bringers of protection and good luck. Called "primal metal" (*thokchak*) or "sky metal" (*namchak*), they are believed to be of heavenly origins and to reach the earth with lightning strikes.[3]

Ancient patterned agates are also highly coveted by the *drokpas* and can be extremely valuable. These agate beads with their attractive circles and bands are known as *zi*.[4] Those beads with rare "nine eyes" patterning fetch upwards of $100,000 each! Unfortunately, most of the antique patterned agates owned by *drokpas* were sold off to visiting dealers from eastern Tibet in the 1980s, a time when they were relatively inexpensive. *Zi* beads are thought to have been produced by the water spirits and are highly sought after for their reputed therapeutic and apotropaic effects. Actually, the Tibetan *zi* are scored and annealed stones manufactured to high standards of precision. Probably of Zhang Zhung origin, they compare very favorably in form and technical sophistication to the engraved stones produced in ancient India and West Asia.

Herder women, or *drokmos*, are fond of heavy silver and conch bracelets, silver and copper rings, and prominent earrings, as well as reliquary containers fashioned from silver, gold, brass, copper, iron, and white metal. Necklaces of red coral, banded agates, and turquoise are also very popular. These objects are not merely ornamental but have talismanic value as well. They are believed to offer protection against lightning strikes, wild animals, demons, and other hazards of the high plateau.

Drokmos usually wear their uncut hair in pigtails or microplaits that hang freely over their backs. Traditionally, they wore elaborate headdresses, studded with turquoise and red coral, but most of these were lost or sold off in the last fifty years. *Drokmos* tie woolen aprons with stripes or appliqué designs over their bulky sheepskins. Their greatcoats are often decorated with multicolored patchwork. The woman's coat is gathered low on the waist with an intricately designed sash. Woven sashes feature sacred symbols such as the conjoined sun and moon, swastika, endless knot, and ritual thunderbolt. They are also decorated with pairs of deer, antelope, gazelles, and birds. Small knives, sewing kits, spoons, and metal accessory rings from which bells and colorful cords hang are attached to the sash. Ornamental milk-pail hooks and embossed silver plaques are also worn around the waist. With all the things garnishing their waistline, *drokpa* women produce a pleasant jingling sound when they walk. In the western Changthang, *drokmos* sport woolen capes with appliqué designs over their coats. These colorful capes are especially worn on holidays or during wedding celebrations and monastic ceremonies.

Drokpa men also wear their long hair in braids, although cropped hair in modern styles is increasingly gaining wide acceptance. In some areas of the Changthang, men have banged hair across the forehead. In the far eastern Changthang, the braids are wound around the head and tied in place with a bunch of red cord. Males are enrobed in less colorful greatcoats than the women. These are decorated with simple stitch work and patches of black cloth for laymen and red cloth for monks. Men wind their plain or striped woolen sashes higher on the waist than do women. The space created inside the greatcoat above the sash is roomy enough to carry provisions or to even shelter a kid or lamb. A knife and small sword are tucked into the sash. They are used for protection and sundry household tasks. In old Tibet, shepherds would travel with a spear and bow as well. Homemade muskets are still carried by some. While male *drokpas* do not wear much silver jewelry, except for reliquary containers, they are keen on necklaces of turquoise, coral, carnelian, and banded agates.

THE *DROKPA* TENT AS A MICROCOSM OF THE UNIVERSE

The tent of black yak hair is emblematic of the *drokpa* way of life. With its external poles and guys, it resembles a giant spider. Remarkably, the black yak hair tent of the *drokpas* does not appear to have changed much in form or substance since the time of Zhang Zhung. Undoubtedly it is one of the oldest types of residential structures found in Asia, rivaling in antiquity the felt yurt or stone hut.

Woman weaving on a back-strap loom inside a black yak hair tent

The black yak hair tent, or *ba*, is imminently well suited to the pastoral lifestyle and environment. It is highly durable, extremely stable, and relatively light, making it an ideal portable shelter. The tent is made from a coarse yak hair material woven on a back-strap loom. These narrow cloth strips are sewn together with yak hair thread. This material is surprisingly effective at repelling the wind and rain and is very durable. The cloth strips are replaced in rotation as they wear out, precluding the need to make a new tent from scratch.

The square or rectangular yak hair tent is customarily erected with its entrance facing east, the direction of the rising sun and the entry point to the mandalas of various divinities. The doorway is frequently flanked by strips of white yak hair cloth, an auspicious flourish. The *ba* has two ridgepoles constituting its central support. There are also six or more external poles, depending on the size of the tent. Most *ba* measure ten to thirteen feet on each side, but some can be considerably larger. Before the arrival of the Chinese Communists, certain *drokpa* headmen and other dignitaries lived in giant tents, which required many hands to erect. Nowadays, government officials occupy concrete housing blocks in planned towns, a far cry from the domiciles of sixty years ago.

The *ba* can be set up with or without a stone foundation. In more developed campgrounds and for winter use, the ground is excavated to a depth of eighteen inches or more and the hole lined with stones. This foundation is known as a *nangra*, or "home enclosure." Stone steps lead down from the entrance to the main living space of the tent. Niches and small enclosures are built into the stone walls; these serve as secure storage spaces shielded from extremes in temperature.

The *ba* is customarily divided into the male north half and female south half. The gender-based domestic activities of *drokpa* life unfold in these two spheres. Males and females sit and sleep in their respective half of the tent, with children spanning both sides. Milk and other dairy products are prepared and stored in the female half of the tent, while meat and grain is kept in the male half. The two sexes occupy the same amount of space in the tent, underscoring the *drokpas'* notion of gender equality. Men and women fulfill equally essential economic and social roles. Thanks to this ingrained sense of equity, *drokpa* women enjoy a place in society unrivaled in most traditional Asian societies. Whatever property a woman brings into a marriage is always hers to keep. When a man comes to live in his wife's encampment, a not uncommon occurrence, he adopts her household deities, and their children assume the maternal family name. Fraternal polyandry, a traditional Tibetan form of marriage whereby a woman is married to more than one brother, also tends to strengthen a *drokmo's* position in the family.

The *ba* is regarded as the cosmos in miniature.[5] The smoke flap, or *gung-kheb*, is the window to the heavens and portal of the celestial deities. Storage facilities in the foundation are seen as doors to the underworld and the realm of treasure-guarding spirits. The two central poles are referred to as "pillars" by the *drokpas*. They symbolize the mythic world mountain, linking heaven and earth into a harmonious whole. Between the central ridgepoles is the family hearth, consisting of three stones or an iron tripod upon which pots are supported. For the *drokpas*, these three points of the hearth recapitulate the three vertical tiers of the universe, the heavens, earth, and underworld. The hearth is the center of the *drokpa's* existence in both an economic and cosmological sense. It is where a family's food is prepared and the source of fire for daily incense offerings to the gods. Nowadays, sheet metal stoves with long flues are becoming very popular among the *drokpas*. They provide efficient heating and a smoke-free environment, which is welcomed by the herders. However, much of the sacred symbolism of the open hearth is lost with a metal stove.

The family's altar, or *chökhang*, is erected on the west side of the *ba*. This can be either a simple or an elaborate affair depending on a family's wealth and inclination. The altar is typically arrayed with photographs of deities and high lamas, water bowls, incense holders, scriptures, and other religious para-phernalia. Religious paintings known as *thangkas* may hang above it. A shrine for the household protective gods of the male lineage is affixed to the west central pole of the tent. It consists of swords, muskets, and other weapons; bits of ancestral central poles; slings; and strips of white and red cloth. The *drokpas* believe that the god of males (*pholha*), the god of warriors (*dralha*), and the god of the locale (*yulha*) take up residence in this shrine.

On the rear wall of the south side of the tent is a shrine dedicated to the divine protectors of the female lineage. It consists of blue pieces of cloth, blu-ish wool from specially selected sheep, and other items. The god of females (*molha*), female serpent deities (*lumo*), and female archetypal spirits (*menmo*) are said to dwell in this shrine. Similarly, a shrine for male deities consisting of red cloth and sheep astragals is sometimes suspended from the male side of the rear wall of the tent. This type of shrine is set up for the *tsen*, a class of red-colored wrathful gods that empower men.

Outside the tent, behind the altar, prayer flags are attached above the guy lines. They are often arrayed in a gender-specific way, with white prayer flags in the middle as offerings to the *lha* and *lhamo*, or celestial deities; blue prayer flags in the south for the female lineage protectresses; and red prayer flags in the north for male lineage protectors.

The roving *drokpas* must minimize their material possessions. The quantity and quality of personal belongings varies according to a family's wealth, but for the most part it is a Spartan showing. Pots for cooking and tea, buckets for milk storage, basins for food preparation, and a cauldron for roasting barley are essential kitchen items. While these vessels are now being made from plastic and aluminum, they were traditionally crafted by artisans from wood, stone, iron, bronze, and copper. Each family member has his or her own spoon, knife, and bowl, utensils that are carried individually when traveling. Nearly all *drokpa* households own a *lakkor*, a hand-turned mill wheel for grinding dry-roasted barley into the Tibetan staple food known as *tsampa*. Men keep digging implements, tools, whetstones, and weapons in their half of the tent.

Both men and women use drop spindles to spin wool and animal hair. When free from other chores, much of their time is taken up by this activity. With a flick of the hand they spin as they chat, pray, or drink tea. Handspun yarn is used to weave material for tents, clothing, blankets, and rugs. A back-strap loom is employed, a lightweight and portable device nicely adapted to the *drokpa*'s itinerant ways. Their weavings often feature stripes, crosshatches, zigzags, and other geometric designs in earth tones and a mix of rich colors. Sacred symbols and animals are also incorporated into the textile designs. Carpets with and without pile, bags for the storage of meal and incense, worsted blankets, and thick mats are woven by many *drokpa* families, even if they are no longer making their own clothing.

The most valuable items owned by a *drokpa* are either worn on his or her person or stored near the altar. Customarily, *drokpas* had heirloom religious objects and precious jewelry, but these things are fast disappearing as families sell to raise money to meet the demands of the modern cash economy.

The yak hair tent of the *drokpas* is relatively easy to set up, take down, and transport on horseback. The number of times a shepherd family moves during the year is dependent on local topographical conditions and the family's particular set of herding strategies, but on the average a *drokpa* household will move four times a year coinciding with the change of seasons. When it is time to break camp, the entire family swings into action and is packed and ready to move in less than half a day. Three or four people working together can take a tent down quickly, but storing gear in trunks and bags and loading them onto horses and yaks require more time.

Drokpa families band together with those who share the same pastures and migration circuit. Neighbors may or may not be biologically related, but either way they are bound in a pact of mutual cooperation. Having extra hands in times of emergency is essential to an individual family's survival. Traditionally, *drokpas* convene to respond to external threats such as marauding wild animals and enemies, as well as during times of illness and other crises. Contiguous *drokpa* encampments form confederated units known as *ru* and *tsho*, which in olden times were the basic building blocks of the upland military regiments. The *tsho* and *ru* were aggregated to form larger brigades called *de* and *dzong*, akin to the townships and counties of modern times.

The winter camp, or *zhima*, is considered the home base of a *drokpa* family. It is usually located where there are pastures reserved for winter use. Ideally, Upper Tibetan shepherds like to set their *zhima* next to a marshy bottomland where grass is plentiful. Customarily, the deepest and most substantial tent foundation was built at the *zhima*.

Currently, the *drokpa* are in the midst of a house-building frenzy, with support from government agencies. The black tent is being discarded for little mud-brick and stone houses. The *drokpas* appreciate having a house in which to store their food supplies and other belongings. Houses also provide secure shelter from the elements and a more commodious living space than a tent. Government-sponsored housing projects tend to be highly regimented affairs. Identical houses are constructed in long rows in opposition to the organic character of traditional *drokpa* settlements. With its deep historical roots and sacred connotations, nostalgia for the black yak hair tent is growing. In the event of earthquakes, it is a far safer form of housing than more permanent structures. In earthquake- and flood-prone Upper Tibet, the *ba* has proven its worth over the long haul.

Another big economic change affecting the Changthang grasslands is the building of fences. Fences are dividing unrestricted tracts into smaller and smaller parcels. Fencing detracts from the wild and unencumbered feel of the rangelands, blocks customary rights-of-way, and in many instances is of dubious economic value. In a land where there are plenty of hands to tend livestock, the building of fences in all but sensitive winter grazing grounds is a gratuitous expense; however, for some at the government level they are a palpable sign of progress. Fences are used as a tool of administrative consolidation, allowing the state to keep better track of its nomadic citizens.

BESTOWED BY HEAVEN AND EARTH, THE SUSTENANCE OF THE *DROKPAS*

The *drokpas* envision their world as empowered by deities, whose blessings make delicious foods and healing medicines available in abundance. It is the divinities of the sky, earth, and water that determine who will prosper and who will go hungry. They are the allies that every *drokpa* must count among their numbers.

For their part, *drokpas* toil to produce meat and milk for food, hides for clothing, and wool for textiles and cordage. They collect salt from lakeshores, forage for medicinal plants in meadows, and grub for therapeutic minerals. Before the advent of Chinese Communist rule, *drokpas* were self-sufficient in most of their daily needs. In this regard, their lives have not changed very much to the present day. Traditionally, *drokpas* trade their butter, meat, wool, hides, salt, and other produce for artisanal goods and, most importantly, to procure grain. A symbiotic relationship blossomed between the highland shepherds and the farmers residing in adjacent regions. Each group generates what the other needs, leading to the development of thriving trade networks. The traditional system of bartering survives, but in today's cash-dominated economy it is much reduced in scope.

The *drokpas* subsist almost entirely on toasted barley meal, milk, yogurt, butter, and meat. They relish the meat of sheep and yaks but will not eat horses or wild asses except under great duress. *Drokpas* are not accustomed to slaughtering animals in the summer when the females are lactating. In the warm season, they rely on meat left over from the previous winter. The butchering of yaks, sheep, and goats begins in early September. As might be expected, no part of the carcass of an animal is wasted. The intestines are used as sausage casings, while the stomachs are eaten or turned into thin-walled containers that double as butter churns. Some heads and horns are offered to the local deities. Meat is cooked by boiling or, much less commonly, by frying and roasting. Cuts of meat are also partially freeze-dried. Meat processed in this manner is dark and hard on the outside but remains soft and flavorful inside. The extreme cold and sterility of Upper Tibet cures meat without the need for smoking or the application of salts. Partly freeze-dried meat will age for months without deteriorating. Some meats are also fully dried for even longer periods of preservation. A favorite *drokpa* dinner is a stew known as *thukpa*, prepared with fresh or dried meat and hand-pulled noodles.

Drokpas devour huge quantities of yogurt in the summertime when their herds produce the greatest amount of milk. In the summer months they also enjoy buttermilk. Milk is often diluted with hot water and quaffed liberally as well. Butter is mixed with tea and barley meal, but *drokpas* do not often cook with butter. Butter made during the short summer season is stored in dried animal guts for use during the rest of the year. The whey, which remains after the butter is churned, is dried in the sun to create a rocklike fat-free cheese called *chura*. This high-protein food is added to barley meal and stews. A *drokpa* delicacy is dried cream served with a sprinkling of sugar. Other favorite dairy foods are a hard full-fat cheese and cheesecake made from dried whey, butter, and raw sugar.

Dry-roasted barley flour, or *tsampa*, the mainstay of the Tibetan diet, is a very nutritious and substantial food. This coarse parched meal forms the basis of most *drokpa* meals and is mixed with tea, yogurt, or milk to form balls. Once *tsampa* is prepared, it has the advantage of not requiring additional cooking. This is very useful in Upper Tibet where fuel for cooking and heating is in short supply. Local supplies of animal dung and woody brush must be used sparingly if they are to meet a family's needs. Wheat flour and rice are now readily available even in the most remote regions, supplementing barley as basic staples. Rice is mixed with milk or meat to make gruel, and flour is used to prepare breads and noodles.

The *drokpas* are prodigious tea drinkers who, like other Tibetans, prefer low-grade Chinese tea leaves that come compressed in bricks. Tea is served black or is churned with yak butter, salt, and a pinch of soda. Some adults drink twenty or more cups of this salty beverage per day. Tea helps fortify the *drokpas* against the cold and aids in the performance of strenuous tasks.

Drokpas also cast about for wild edible plants, a vital supplement to their diet of grains, meats, and dairy foods. They collect nettles, sorrel, and watercress in the early summer, important sources of vitamins A and C. Several species of edible wild mushrooms appear in the plains in the late summer. The golden mushroom of the Changthang known as *sersha* has a delicate taste reminiscent of almonds and is in demand all over Tibet. Wild chives and garlic also grow in rocky locales during the late summer and are used to flavor stews. Along with salt and imported chili powder, these pungent plants are the only seasonings that *drokpas* regularly add to their cuisine. Small sour red and yellow berries, *ratsha* and *tsarbu*, grow in mountainous tracts and are eaten with relish, particularly by children. Another foraged plant is *droma*, a small tuber that is boiled and served with buttered rice. *Droma* grows wild in much of Tibet and features in a popular sweet dish made for the Tibetan New Year.

HUMAN MINDS AND ANIMAL SPIRITS

Where there are *drokpas*, there is livestock. The two are inseparably linked in a covenant sealed in ancient times. Domestic yaks, horses, sheep, and goats could not survive without human intervention, and humans depend on them for their livelihood. The relationship between the *drokpas* and their livestock, however, is more than a biological symbiosis; it goes to the very heart of the *drokpa* identity and worldview. The presence of livestock in the lives of *drokpas* is strongly reflected in their religion, history, and folklore.

The *drokpas* and their animal charges act almost like a superorganism, a singular living being with many different faces and personas. According to the ancient creation myths, animals and humans appeared from the same divine sources as kith and kin. Holy yaks, horses, goats, and other animals are considered the progenitors of various clans, conferring upon them their powers and protection. *Drokpa* shamans, or *lhapa*, still rely on livestock helper spirits to cure physical and psychological maladies and to rebalance the natural environment.

The yak (*Bos grunniens*) is Tibet's most esteemed and economically crucial animal. This large shaggy bovine, a native of the highlands, has a distinctive grunt and a somewhat unpredictable personality. In the Tibetan language the word *yak* only denotes the male of the species; the female is called a *dri*. There are different names for each year of a yak's sixteen-year or so lifespan, and different terms for each color and fur pattern. Yaks are most commonly black, but they also come in various shades of beige, brown, and gray and in many mixed colors. The all-white yak is considered the most special. White yak tails are traded all the way down to the plains of India for use in Hindu, Jain, and Sikh temples.

The wild yak's habitat is restricted to the Tibetan upland and the Himalayan Mountains. In contrast, domestic yaks are also reared in Mongolia, southern Siberia, and the highlands of eastern Central Asia. Despite its fractious nature, the yak is much loved by Tibetans. It was only through the domestication of this large herbivore that the pastoral way of life could take hold in the Tibetan upland. It has not yet been scientifically established when Tibetans first domesticated the yak, but Chinese historical data suggest that this occurred not less than three thousand years ago, and current scientific opinion holds that this process may have begun around five thousand years ago.[6]

The yak supplies fine-quality meat, lard for cooking, and a high-fat-content milk. Its thick hide is used to make belts, tarpaulins, and boot soles, and its tough hair produces cordage, tent fabric, mats, and bags. The soft, warm undercoat of the yak is much sought after in the manufacture of garments and blankets. The horns of the yak are used as household vessels. Various parts of this animal are also employed to concoct Tibetan medicines. Hornless yaks are used as mounts in some parts of Tibet, but yak riding is not favored by the *drokpas* of Upper Tibet. However, yaks are avidly exploited as a beast of burden. A single yak can carry up to 160 pounds. Unruly yak caravans file across the plains and passes of Upper Tibet transporting *drokpa* household goods and commodities such as wool, hides, and salt for trade.

Given its many functions, it is no wonder that the yak has a divine persona. Specially colored domestic yaks are ornamented and set aside by the *drokpas* as gifts to the local deities. This is done as a means to augment herd size and to bring families good luck. Yak skulls carved with mantras are also offered to the gods. The yak is the symbol par excellence of a shepherd's wealth. In fact, one Tibetan word for yak and wealth are the same: *nor*. The average Changthang family possesses around fifteen or twenty female and castrated yaks and one bull, or *boa*, for breeding. Wealthy families have sixty or more yaks. Given their size and skittish temperament, yaks are usually pastured without human supervision. They tend to graze on high mountain slopes even in the winter, but they regularly come down to the plains and valley bottoms to feed. When it is necessary to drive yaks home, this is accomplished by men on horseback.

Next to the yak, the most significant domestic animal of the Tibetans is the horse. Like their northern counterparts in Mongolia, Upper Tibetans are renowned horsemen. In the far-flung spaces of the highlands, horses are essential for travel. Conventionally, a good horse was an ordinary shepherd's single most valuable possession. Racehorses and trotters form the two main types of horses, and many *drokpa* families like to keep both. In old Tibet the social status of *drokpas* and other members of society was conspicuously displayed in the caparisons of the horse. Noblemen from down country and high lamas possessed elaborately decorated gilt saddles with fancy saddle rugs and stirrups. *Drokpa* chieftains and affluent traders also had fine equestrian accoutrements, while the common herder made do with much simpler but functional gear.

The religious functions of the horse evolved over a long period of time, mirroring the venerable economic and social standing of this animal. So important was the horse in ancient funerary rites that it was entrusted with transporting the souls of the dead to the afterlife. Horses still figure in religious rites carried out by *drokpas* to propitiate deities inhabiting the landscape. Live white horses are proffered to the celestial deities, and bluish horses to the spirits of the underworld. A mythic celestial horse known as the *lungta* is believed to carry a good luck force, which can be transferred to those who invoke it. Tibetan prayer flags frequently depict the *lungta* and its load of spiritual jewels.

After the yak and horse, the sheep is the most valuable animal of the *drokpas*. Live sheep are gifted to local divinities to buy their aid and protection. Mutton is much loved by shepherds, and the creamy white butter of the ewe is a summertime treat. Flocks of sheep are always accompanied by a herder, usually a junior member of a *drokpa* household. The average *drokpa* family has between 100 and 350 sheep and goats, enough to provide a fairly steady supply of meat throughout the year. A particularly affluent household will own upwards of 1,200 sheep and goats, but there are not many families of these means in the Changthang.

Sheep and goats must be constantly guarded against ravening wolves and other predators. Large terriers and mastiff crossbreeds are instrumental in performing this function. Most of the purebred mastiffs were killed off by the Chinese security forces, but an attempt is now under way to resuscitate the breed. Mastiffs are not lapdogs by any stretch of the imagination, but they are easily controlled by even the youngest *drokpa* owner. As regards strangers, a *drokpa*'s dog knows no fear and is a very dangerous adversary. In my early years of solo exploration, I had many run-ins with dogs. When there are two or more large canines in pursuit, a stout wooden staff and rocks must be wielded with great persuasion. Once when visiting a nunnery, I foolishly forgot my trusty staff and came up against a pack of angry dogs. Luckily the nuns dispersed the pack before they could do me grievous harm. I managed to get away with just one serious bite. The scar from that attack wraps halfway around my forearm.

Lambs and kids are corralled separately from the rest of the herd. The young are born in the late spring, and they need special care to withstand the subfreezing nights. Kids and lambs are ensconced in beehive-shaped masonry structures for warmth or are kept inside the family's tent for protection.

Over the last thirty years, the proportion of goats in *drokpa* herds has been increasing. This is because they produce a luxuriant undercoat known as cashmere, or *reku*, a fashion commodity much in demand worldwide. The sale of cashmere has significantly added to the income of herders, but the prices paid are volatile, dictated as they are by middlemen and the international market.

A *drokpa* family's wealth in any given location is determined by sheer physical effort, herding strategies, and lady luck. Some areas are endowed with better grasses than others. The inherent productivity of the land has much to do with whether a family is poor or well off. But there is little an individual family can do to change their natural apportionment, save for defending against overgrazing, a growing problem. The rangeland occupied by the households of an encampment is delineated by historical custom and modern legislation. Upper Tibet is probably near its maximum livestock holding capacity (some experts judge that this has already been exceeded); thus there is little opportunity for *drokpas* to expand the territory under their control. It is therefore necessary to maximize returns from the land available.

To make the best of the situation, good planning and hard work are essential. Knowledge built up over generations of experience is used to determine where flocks will pasture daily and when they will be moved to the next encampment on the annual circuit. Inherited savvy decides the deployment

A lay religious practitioner from Lake Dangra

of satellite camps (*kabrang*), temporary affairs connected to the main *drokpa* household. Satellite camps are used to access grasslands that are too far away to reach in the course of a single day.

The longer animals spend grazing daily and the better they are kept at night, the higher the chances that a herd will grow in number. Nevertheless, even the most adept herder cannot prevent disastrous weather, and flocks may have to be rebuilt repeatedly over the lifetime of a *drokpa*. The fitness of livestock is also traditionally ensured through ritual measures. Lamas, lay practitioners, and shamans are called in to fumigate or lustrate animals to the accompaniment of invocations. Modern veterinary science is now also making a contribution to the health of the *drokpa*'s flocks.

Another traditional source of sustenance for *drokpas* is hunting. The ample herds of large game have been a target of hunters for many centuries. The *drokpa*, however, are not fond of fishing or fowling, as they do not traditionally relish the flesh of fish and birds. Hunters on horseback attempt to control the movements of wild yaks and antelopes by funneling them into strategic bottlenecks where they are finished off by other men lying in wait. Wild sheep are stalked on foot in the mountains, a pursuit that requires much patience and competence.

Traditionally, hunters undergo ritual purifications before embarking on an expedition and hold a thanksgiving ceremony afterward. Hunters have a peculiar pantheon of zoomorphic deities that aid them in the search for game. Even Buddhism and its ethic of nonviolence could not entirely put a halt to hunting, so ingrained is it in *drokpa* culture. In recent years, hunting has been severely curtailed by the Chinese government in an attempt to bolster the dwindling wildlife. As a result, the age-old hunting traditions of Upper Tibet are rapidly disappearing.

Amid much camaraderie, *drokpa* men used to join forces on annual expeditions to collect salt. In the wintertime, gangs of *drokpas* traveled with their yaks and sheep to the northern Changthang. Here salt is easily gathered from the shorelines of some lakes. The salt was carried in panniers tied on the backs of livestock and transported to the agricultural regions of southern Tibet where it was traded for grain. Bags of salt were exchanged for a more or less equal volume of barleycorn. However, this quintessential male activity has been largely discontinued due to changing economic realities. The salt expeditions were viable until circa 1990, when transport by truck finally made the yak caravans a losing proposition. I fondly remember sharing tea with the salt caravanners and discussing local travel and the terrain. Today, the salt and soda of the Changthang is transported in trucks to centralized depots for industrial processing and retail distribution. Without the ebullience of the salters, the Changthang is a little less animated.

A farming village at Lake Dangra

FARMING THE TOP OF THE WORLD

Drokpas reign where no other way of life is possible, but where crops can be coaxed from the land, an alternative lifestyle dominates. The farmers, or *shingpas*, are the occupational counterpoint to the *drokpas*. These two groups form complementary parts of the Upper Tibetan economy and society. Unlike some places in the world where conflicts between nomads and the settled are the norm, the shepherds and herders of highland Tibet cooperate for their mutual betterment.

Although there are fundamental differences in the livelihood and social makeup of the farmers and herders, to survive in the pitiless environment of upland Tibet each group needs what the other has. Together *drokpas* and *shingpas* squeeze out the full productive capacity of the land. To supplement their modest landholdings, many agricultural families keep significant numbers of livestock. They either act as part-time herders, known as *samadrok*, or individual family members are appointed to work full-time as *drokpas*. This shared pastoral focus, as well as clan ties, blurs the divide between *drokpas* and *shingpas*, begetting a common ground of experience.

Clusters of stone and adobe houses have sprung up wherever there are sufficient arable lands to support a stable community. These little villages of winding passages, walled courtyards, and poplar copses present a very different picture of Upper Tibetan life from the *drokpa* encampments. As a rule, farmers possess more material goods than do their shepherd cousins. A fixed abode gives the agriculturalists the luxury to be more acquisitive. The *shingpas* own bulky pieces of furniture and other heavy household goods, agricultural and construction implements, and cumbersome religious objects for which *drokpas* have little need.

The *shingpas* of Upper Tibet are restricted to a few small enclaves in the Changthang and far western Tibet. The largest agriculture enclave in the Changthang is the Lake Dangra basin. Barley is planted above sparkling Dangra in a string of hamlets situated at fifteen thousand feet or more above sea level. This constitutes the highest-elevation cultivation found anywhere in the world. A very limited amount of barley is also raised in the western Changthang regions of Tshakha and Mamik and in a few locales of the extreme eastern Changthang. Along the western margin of Tibet, in the upper Sutlej and Karnali valleys and the basins of Gar and Ruthok, farming is carried out as well.

Armed with plows, hoes, and well-exercised bodies, Upper Tibetans till fields, channel irrigation water, and tend fledgling crops. The beginnings of agriculture in the region are lost in prehistory, but it is likely that crops have been grown for at least three millennia. Over the course of time, invasion and internal strife have created much turmoil for the *shingpas*. In western Tibet, farmers have come under the authority of a long line of kings and chieftains, culminating in the Chinese Communist takeover of 1959. These historical experiences have made them a robustly independent and canny bunch. The *shingpas* carry themselves with a quiet dignity, avoid clashes, and are diffident in their social dealings. A casual observer might see a timid character behind the retiring exterior, but this is not so. The farmers' understated facade veils an indomitable core, a steely determination to succeed in one of the world's most challenging food-growing environments.

Diverse strains of white, black, and red barley are the main crop of Upper Tibet. Turnips, leafy greens, and mustard seeds for oil are also cultivated in some areas. Upper Tibet is too arid for dry farming and is dependent on the maintenance of irrigation systems in each village. Special masters of irrigation known as *chupön* are appointed to oversee the allocation of scarce water resources. Due to reduced infusions of water from the mountains, only a small fraction of extant farmland in upland Tibet is still cultivated.

The growing season in Upper Tibet is no more than three months long, and timing is everything if killing frosts are to be avoided. In addition to relying on their farming skill, agricultural rituals are conducted by monks and laypeople for a community's well-being. Before sowing takes place, the *shingpas* make offerings of incense and dough sculptures to their territorial gods in a ritual known as *lha söl*. At the time of the *lha söl*, the shrines around a village are renewed with a coat of fresh paint and offerings. The *lu*, or serpent spirits inhabiting the fields, must also be placated to ensure the proper growth of crops. After sowing, white stones are piled in the middle of fields to compensate the water spirits for disturbances caused by cutting the earth with the plow. The gods are also feted whenever rain is needed and at harvesttime.

The distinctive costumes and coiffures of some western Tibetan *shingpas* are easily distinguishable from those of the upland *drokpas*. Farmers weave black woolen serge for clothing, eschewing the use of the skin robe. Women don a colorful cape with appliqué designs over their sleeveless woolen tunics. Formerly on festive occasions women of the valleys of Purang and Guge exhibited an elaborate coiffure supported by a wooden rack resembling a pair of horns. This hairstyle contrasts with the freely hanging ornamented plaits of the *drokpas*. Nevertheless, in the Gar, Ruthok, and Dangra Yumtsho regions, the *shingpas* are closely allied to the *drokpas*, and they share the same styles of dress and jewelry.

Like their *drokpa* brethren, the farmers of Upper Tibet are deeply steeped in ancient traditions. They preserve old ballads and circle dances known as *shun*, worship the hoary mountain gods, and erect tabernacles and prayer flags on their rooftops for the household divinities. Using agriculture and trade as an economic foundation, their prehistoric ancestors rose to the heights of civilization. They built an extensive network of temples and citadels that came to be called Zhang Zhung. Subsequently, the Upper Tibetans re-created themselves along Buddhist lines, going on to establish even more

Woman in ceremonial dress for the shun *dance performance in the far western agricultural village of Tang*

ambitious places of worship. Those *shingpas* hailing from Guge and Purang in western Tibet are the proud descendants of a Buddhist kingdom that flourished five hundred to one thousand years ago. Unfortunately, war, disorder, and desertification spelled an end to the golden age in Upper Tibet.

The farming and high culture of Upper Tibet have been in headlong decline for many centuries. The web of desolation has spread far and wide, blotting out one agricultural community after another. For all the hamlets still clinging to an agrarian way of life, many more have turned into ghost towns. A majority of western Tibetan agricultural locales have been partially or fully vacated, the wind blowing forlornly through untilled fields and the carcasses of buildings. Now only scattered *drokpas* survive where there were once flourishing settlements.

Present-day agrarian Upper Tibet is a mere shadow of what it was in ancient times. The rivers and streams that furnished water for irrigation began drying up many hundreds of years ago, locking farmers in a grim race against time, a race still being run today. The severe curtailment of the cereal economy suggests that the indigenous population has been falling. It seems likely that the enhanced production of grains in the past was used to feed a bigger population. The extensive ruins marking the agricultural pockets of Upper Tibet reinforce this perception of a land long past its prime. The adoption of Buddhism, or more recently Communism, could not reverse the inexorable decline in the fortunes of Upper Tibet.

THE CYCLE OF FAITH, FESTIVALS AND PASSAGES

The spinning of prayer wheels, the fingering of prayer beads, and the murmur of mantras fill the lives of the *drokpas* and *shingpas* of Upper Tibet. Despite half a century of atheistic government policies, religion remains an inescapable reality, as natural to the native people as eating and drinking. Like other Tibetans, most highlanders are Buddhists, with less than 10 percent following the Eternal Bon religion. Eternal Bon adherents are concentrated in the eastern Changthang and around Lake Dangra Yumtsho.

The martial history and lingering cultural traditions of Zhang Zhung strongly color the *drokpas*' faith. They mostly pursue practical aspects of religion as a means to achieve peace and well-being in the here and now. Many *drokpas* may not seem like devout Lamaist practitioners, content as they are to enjoy worldly pleasures such as hunting and games of wager. Admittedly, their unbridled ways do not meld well with the strictures of formal religion. The *drokpas* nonetheless have a strong inborn spiritual sense, one engendered from an elementary way of life and the basic rhythms of nature.

As in other parts of the Tibetan world, the highlanders built monasteries, sustaining a cloistered way of life. Monasteries or Lamaseries were and still are centers of intellectual life in Upper Tibet. In ancient times, the temples and citadels of Zhang Zhung performed an analogous role. Over the course of history, it is from these institutions that the region's farmers and herders have obtained much of their strength and inspiration.

Monks cater to the spiritual needs of the Upper Tibetans, providing moral and intellectual guidance. In the sparsely populated Changthang, there are relatively few monasteries, and *drokpas* may travel for several days in order to reach one. Visiting lamas periodically sojourn in the northern tablelands, giving succor to herder camps. Some *drokpa* encampments have lay religious practitioners known as *ngakpa*, who take care of the day-to-day proceedings of religion. *Ngakpa* conduct healing rituals, enact prayer ceremonies, make horoscopes and divinations, and oversee marriages and funerals. The shamans, or *lhapa*, carry out overlapping religious duties.

In western Tibet, there were many monasteries, and the farmers of that region tend to be religious in a more orthodox manner than the *drokpas*. Unfortunately, virtually every monastery and temple in Upper Tibet was damaged or destroyed in the Chinese Cultural Revolution. Formal religion has waned ever since. Only a small fraction of the religious facilities could be rebuilt, as local residents no longer possess the resources to take on such ambitious building projects. Western Tibet is world renowned for a special genre of Buddhist art that took much of its inspiration from neighboring cultures. This highly sophisticated painting and sculpture reflects the flowering of Buddhist ideals and teachings in the time of the Guge-Purang kings. This period of greatness five hundred to one thousand years ago is now just a simmering memory among a broth of ruins.

As in other parts of Tibet, the biggest observance in the highlands is the New Year, or Losar, festival, a time for feasting, merriment, and religious rituals. Losar celebrates spiritual renewal in the beginning of the lunar year. In some locales of Upper Tibet, there is still an older Losar celebration that coincides with the winter solstice. During this holiday, Upper Tibetans tie fresh prayer flags on their tents and houses to win the favor of the household and territorial deities. Livestock anointed with butter and decorated with colorful yarn are set free in the mountains for the same gods. In Lamaseries where there are still sufficient numbers of monks, an elaborate prayer ceremony is held during the first fifteen days of the first lunar month.

In summer months, each Upper Tibetan district holds horse racing and archery contests known as *tagyu*. The *tagyu* is abuzz with excitement and expectation. This is an occasion for people to meet distant friends and relatives and to mix freely with a wide circle of people. At the races, young horsemen with peaked and feathered caps gallop across a long, level expanse. The first horse to pass between the onlookers in the staging area is the winner. In another spectacle, standing archers or ones mounted on horseback must strike targets with arrows from about 150 feet away. Mounted archers swoop low in their saddles to hit a target in an acrobatic show of equestrian prowess.

Saka Dawa, heralding the birth, enlightenment, and ascension into nirvana of the Buddha, is observed on the full moon of the fourth lunar month. This is the chief Buddhist holiday of the year, a solemn time for prayer and contemplation. On the full moon of the first lunar month, Eternal Bon carries out similar religious exercises commemorating their holy founder, Tönpa Shenrab. Dzamling Chisang, or "Universal Purification," is a religious holiday that falls on the full moon of the fifth lunar month. On Dzamling Chisang the *drokpas* and *shingpas* burn generous amounts of incense on behalf of their local deities and the higher gods of Eternal Bon and Buddhism.

For Tibetans, life and death are but signposts along the cycle of existence. These milestones are not seen as an ultimate fate, but as transitions along a well-worn and timeless path. To usher in significant events in their lives, the *drokpas* and *shingpas* bank on an abundant stock of religious customs and traditions. The observances heralding birth, marriage, and death epitomize their aspirations and reflect the depth of their history and culture. In the life cycle rituals, the traditions of Zhang Zhung and Buddhism meet in unique and compelling ways.

Childbirth requires that the newborn and mother be purified with incense, holy water, and prayers, a standard practice throughout Tibet. As a child grows, blessed cords and other talismans are tied around his or her neck or attached to the clothing to repel a host of threats. If a child is thought to have fallen prey to demons, a lama, lay practitioner, or shaman will be called in to divine the precise cause of the illness and prescribe a ritual cure. Should a household experience a string of infant deaths, an ancient-style exorcism called *srico* is performed. The *srico* ordains that senior family members make a pilgrimage, carve prayers on stones, and construct shrines known as *chorten* in order to increase their pool of religious merit.

Marriage customs vary from region to region in Upper Tibet, with those of the shepherds being somewhat more liberal than those of the farmers. Partners are chosen by the parents or by the children themselves. Each stage of espousal has its own cycle of songs and formalized behaviors. Some matrimonial hymns, like the group known as *sridpai tho*, or "registry of existence," are of ancient origins. The singing is stately and joyous, and it is accompanied by a code of etiquette designed to preserve the honor and dignity of the bride and groom's families. A bride-price in livestock, jewelry, or money is paid once negotiations between the two families are concluded. Gifts are also given as a sign of respect to the groom's family. A ceremony is held in the bride's parental home to see her off, and another ceremony is convened to receive her in the groom's home.

For the wedding, the bride, or *nama*, is decked out in the new clothes and jewelry she receives as her trousseau. The summoning of good fortune capabilities, or the *yang*, is paramount in the wedding ceremony. The *yang* rituals are described in Tibet's earliest literature. It is believed that a robust *yang* ensures a couple's happiness and prosperity. The bride's family deities and the groom's family deities must be formally introduced to one another and ritually tied together. There can be no hostility between the two sets of divine protectors if the marriage is to be successful.

Sometimes young people elope and start a family without nuptial formalities. In such circumstances, both sets of relatives make appeasement offerings to each other inducing them to sanction the liaison. Marriage by abduction is occasionally practiced, and if a girl voluntarily agrees to the relationship, she will simply begin living with her abductor as his wife. The boy's family must then go out of its way to win the approval of the girl's relatives. To prevent a feud erupting between the two families, lengthy negotiations and several rounds of gift giving ensue.[7]

The funeral is the most unbending of the *drokpa* life cycle rituals, closely conforming to Lamaist ideals and doctrines. If at all possible, death rituals are performed by Eternal Bon and Buddhist clerics. When monks are not available to conduct a funeral, the local *ngakpa*, or lay practitioner, will suffice. A photograph of the deceased is displayed to attract his or her consciousness to the funeral venue, a modern form of the age-old custom of making effigies of the dead. Dough figures of livestock and humans are fashioned as offerings to placate the demons of death, another ancient tradition. Officiating monks or *ngakpa* perform *phoba*, a Buddhist ritual designed to liberate the consciousness of the deceased or transfer it to a better rebirth. It is averred that an individual after death enters an intermediate state of existence for forty-nine days, a period in which the departed usually experiences much fear and confusion. To alleviate this great suffering, monks attempt to console the deceased and guide him or her to a higher state of existence. As a sign of bereavement, surviving family members do not wash their hair or put on new clothes for forty-nine days. Men also refrain from riding horses, and women from dancing and singing, for upwards of one year.[8]

MANIFOLD CHANGES BUFFET MODERN UPPER TIBET

When speaking of the contemporary cultural scene anywhere in Tibet, it is impossible not to take note of the upheavals of the last sixty years. Through force of arms, ideological persuasion, and economic inducement, the Chinese Communist government is in the process of re-creating Tibet.

Already, the social and economic fabric of the country has been transformed almost beyond recognition. Since 1959, Tibet's traditional cultural and religious institutions have either disappeared or undergone considerable modification. Even the most remote corners of the highlands are not immune to these revolutionary changes.

In Upper Tibet, mining, and the building of roads, railroads, airports, and cities in once barren locations, is radical in scope. The introduction of a market economy, mandatory elementary school education, and an efficient civil administration are extremely potent agents of modernization and Sinicization. Growing numbers of settlers from the Chinese mainland are drastically altering the ethnic makeup of the Tibetan highland. These powerful forces of change, an inescapable juggernaut, pose huge challenges to the cultural integrity of Upper Tibet.

While the benefits of modern life are legion, historical experience worldwide demonstrates that modernity is a proverbial double-edged sword. It empowers materially, but it can also strip away vital layers of human knowledge and well-being. The potential for modernization to hamstring a people is greatly magnified when their government is not directly accountable to them.

The Chinese are involved in settling the *drokpas* of Upper Tibet and other regions of the Plateau in large centrally positioned towns and villages. Government housing represents a secular approach to geography and community at odds with the religion-imbued architecture of the past. These planned settlements sport rows of identical houses with few personalizing features. Gone often are the prayer flags and rooftop shrines for household deities that traditionally embellish Tibetan residences. Reaching outlying pastures from these centralized settlements is more difficult, encouraging some *drokpas* to give up herding altogether and try their hand at something else. Menial work is considered demeaning by most *drokpas*, who cling to the memory of a proud and unhindered way of life. With the loss of their traditional mode of living, boredom, dissatisfaction, alienation, and the social problems associated with these states of mind are on the rise.

In recent years, the Chinese government has begun to restrict traditional grazing practices in the Changthang. Since 2003, it has been official policy to convert actively used pastures into unused grasslands in an effort to preserve their environmental wholeness. This policy is based on three major assumptions: (1) widespread degradation of Changthang grasslands has occurred, (2) irrational and superstitious herding practices contribute to overgrazing, and (3) grazing bans will lead to improved grasslands. However, studies conducted by Melvin Goldstein, Daniel J. Miller, and other rangeland ecologists and pastoral specialists question these basic assumptions.[9] For at least three thousand years, the Changthang grasslands have coevolved with domestic grazing animals, and it appears that livestock play a vital role in maintaining the health and diversity of grass species.

While overgrazing is certainly a problem in some areas, the wholesale curtailment of livestock grazing can have unintended consequences. Preliminary scientific studies suggest that a ban on livestock grazing may impede the ability of grasslands to adapt to climate change.[10] Scientists both inside and outside China readily acknowledge that a better understanding of grasslands ecology and how exactly it is being degraded is vital. However, one thing is already certain: the region is warming at an explosive rate.

The environmental problems associated with modernization in Upper Tibet are being compounded by climate change. *Drokpas* contend that summer rains are more erratic and winter snowstorms more destructive than before. They report that summer grasses are appearing later and later, and what turf there is is shorter and less dense. In addition to climate change, they attribute degradation of the grasslands to outbreaks of rodents and insect pests, as well as overgrazing. These observations have been articulated by a University of Colorado researcher, Yonten Nyima, a native of Nakchu in the Changthang.[11] His interviews with fellow *drokpas* reveal that milk production is beginning later than it did previously, adversely affecting household incomes. The *drokpas* also report that sheep and goats are producing young less frequently than before.

Warming temperatures are expected to further stunt grass growth and reduce rangeland biodiversity. The more traditionally minded *drokpas* relate these environmental problems to the protector deities and their withdrawal of aid and succor. Climate history in Upper Tibet is the object of growing scientific research. The United Nation's Intergovernmental Panel on Climate Change has been sounding the alarm.[12] It is thought that possibly eighty to eighty-five percent of Tibet's forty thousand glaciers are retreating with increasing speed. According to scientific estimates, at least some of the approximately 150,000 Himalayan glaciers are losing six feet to nine feet of thickness on the average annually, probably the most rapid ablation of ice anywhere in the world. In the short term, as the glaciers melt, flooding is expected to become more frequent and lake levels will rise, but in the long term, river volumes will be dramatically reduced, causing Changthang lakes to substantially recede.

Ice cores have been drilled near the summit of western Tibet's Mount Nemo Na Nyi at twenty-three thousand feet above sea level by Lonnie G. Thompson, a leading glaciologist.[13] His study demonstrates that even at this great height there has been a rapid reduction in the amount of ice and snow since around 1950. Yes, climate change is a global problem, but the situation in Tibet appears particularly grave. The China Meteorological Administration calculates that since 1961 the Plateau is warming up by an average of a half degree Fahrenheit per decade, two to three times the global average.

It is not merely the small population of Upper Tibet that will be affected by climate change. The well-being of one and a half billion people in China, Southeast Asia, and the Indian Subcontinent directly hinges upon the great Asian rivers that arise on the Tibetan Plateau. The Yellow, Yangtze, Salween, Mekong, Indus, and Brahmaputra Rivers are all dependent on the glaciers of Tibet for their maintenance. The diminution of these legendary avenues of water threatens catastrophe almost beyond imagination. No longer is Tibet and its cultural and environmental issues merely the concern of a relatively small number of people; they now occupy center stage in the global arena.

How the *shingpas* and *drokpas* fare in the long run remains to be seen, but there is ample room for hope. In the technological push forward, past lessons learned loom large. These call for greater efforts to harmoniously integrate traditional cultural and religious values into the process of modernization. By drawing on their august heritage, the Upper Tibetans can best respond to a deteriorating climate as well as to the demands of the modern world. The promise of a brighter future hangs in the balance for them and for us.

• *4* •

From Sky to Earth:
The History of Zhang Zhung

THE MAGIC AND MYSTERY OF TIBETAN SCRIPTURES

We now turn to the history of Zhang Zhung as it was remembered by Tibetan writers and bards. Zhang Zhung is a name for the prehistoric Upper Tibetan culture and polity marked by advanced technological capabilities that existed until the mid-seventh century CE. Using this traditional label as a designator of ancient civilization in Upper Tibet, its origins are tantamount to the advent of the Metal Age in the region approximately three millennia ago. The rise of Zhang Zhung was signaled by the establishment of citadels, temples, and burial grounds characteristic of the ancient Tibetan upland. Tibetan historical texts inform us that the demise of Zhang Zhung as a political force occurred in the seventh century CE with the assassination of its last king, Liknyikya.

Eternal Bon literature holds that the people of Zhang Zhung were avid users of metal implements, including those made from forged iron, reflecting a fully developed Metal Age culture. In consonance with the available

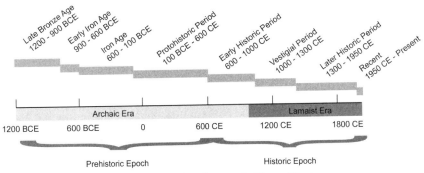

Chronology of civilization in Upper Tibet

archaeological and literary records, a Late Bronze Age or Early Iron Age date for the establishment of highland civilization is best indicated. However, more research and exploration are needed to confirm the precise period in which Zhang Zhung civilization took root in Upper Tibet. This civilization remained a major force in uppermost Tibet for roughly fifteen centuries, twice the length of time of the Roman republic and empire combined.

What the ancient inhabitants of Upper Tibet may have actually called their land in any given period is a moot point. In addition to Zhang Zhung and Sumpa (its lesser neighbor to the east), Old Tibetan (an archaic language) literature refers to all or part of the Changthang as Mrayul Thanggye. Other Old Tibetan documents cite Töd, or "Upper Tibet," as a sizable region. The term "Zhang Zhung" occurs to a lesser degree in Old Tibetan origin myths than do these other two toponyms. It may be that "Zhang Zhung" was the name specifically given to a relatively late kingdom located in the highlands, while "Mrayul Thanggye" and "Töd" were the ancestral geographic designators of Upper Tibet.[1] In any case, "Zhang Zhung" is used in this work as a generic appellation for pre-seventh-century CE Tibetan upland civilization, including its cultural, linguistic, and political aspects. My usage of the term is in conformance with the way it is broadly defined and employed in Eternal Bon literature.

Ever since the invention of their script in the seventh century CE, Tibetans have been keen composers of literature. Theirs is an incredibly rich literary tradition that touches upon virtually all areas of Tibetan knowledge and thought. The most accurate source for the history of Zhang Zhung is texts written in Old Tibetan. Some literature in this obsolete language was composed within two centuries of the kingdom's downfall, when its memory was still relatively fresh in the minds of Tibetans.

An especially fecund source of Zhang Zhung lore is the texts of the Eternal Bon religion, which began to be composed circa 1000 CE. In the style of the bards of yore, a wondrous language, culture, and kingdom are ascribed to Zhang Zhung in this Classical Tibetan literature. Most Eternal Bon accounts of the kings and sages of Zhang Zhung tend to be visionary rather than documentary in nature. By focusing on amazing events in a nebulous past, these texts have a pseudo-historic or mythic slant.

Only with testable evidence can we hope to assess the reliability of Tibetan views concerning their own history. Earlier it was not unusual for historians to accept traditional accounts of the distant past with fewer critical reservations. It was generally thought that received tradition was indeed a reliable indicator of history, that scribes over many generations remained true to the letter of ancient events. In recent decades this basic assumption has been called into question. Today, the trend in historical studies is to view the past more discriminatingly, and with good cause. There are numerous instances of supposedly ancient accounts proving not as old as once imagined. For example, claims that Classical Sanskrit texts are the direct heirs of the Vedas, India's most ancient literature, have been debunked. The same is the case for received Chinese texts; they are proving to be rather distorted records of Bronze Age and Iron Age Sinitic civilization. There are many such examples worldwide of historians who composed fictive or reworked models of the past. Clearly, the same critical concerns that this state of affairs raises are applicable to the Tibetan historical tradition.

Eternal Bon literature enshrines the saga of a noble people, opening the door to a privileged world of magic and mystery. The visionary texts of Eternal Bon idealize the ancient spiritual and political greatness of Zhang Zhung; seldom are they literal records of the past. The fabulous narratives about Zhang Zhung must be read on their own terms. They were primarily authored to inform successive generations of religious practitioners, not as clinical reports of past happenings. That the fantastic is often accented lends these writings much charm. There are tales of magicians controlling the elements and movements of the planets, perfecti knowing everything there is to know in the universe, and saints stopping powerful armies in their tracks with mantras. Poetic, articulate, and colorful, the apologues of Zhang Zhung are riveting reading.

Over time, as archaic civilization faded from the collective consciousness, Zhang Zhung's history became more and more metaphorical in nature. Transformation from the mundane to the extraordinary, from real people and events to reified figures and experiences, marks the long passage of time. Not exclusive to Tibetans, the turning of ancient (and not so ancient) histories into the currency of fables and folklore is a worldwide phenomenon.

Although Eternal Bon, and for that matter many Buddhist texts, are couched in the idiom of the supernatural, they do indeed encapsulate a certain amount of hard data. It is left to the historian to discern temporal reality from the unverifiable truths of the spiritual dimension. Tibetan literature presents us with a spectrum of possibilities regarding the past, leaving it up to the critical reader to determine what may and may not have a spatiotemporal basis.

One of the biggest hitches in using Tibetan literature to sketch the history of Zhang Zhung is the absence of a solid chronology. Hundreds of years may be measured in the thousands, and it is not uncommon to find the happenings of more recent periods endowed with the mantle of antiquity, rendering any attempt at dating problematic. If the Eternal Bon tradition is taken literally, this religion possessed Buddhist-style teachings many thousands of years before the advent of Buddhism. This is a very unlikely prospect and one that bears little resemblance to the true cultural and religious complexion of ancient Upper Tibet.

Myth for history and the mixing and matching of religious traditions: what, then, do Tibetan texts really tell us about Zhang Zhung? The quest for historical reliability and coherence forces the chronicler to pursue various lines of inquiry. Place names that have remained unchanged or the presence of ruins where ancient residences are written to have stood provide benchmarks from which to test the historicity of documents. By corroborating the existence of locations and monuments, the Upper Tibetan archaeological record helps to elucidate broad themes in the historical record. The limitation of this approach is that it does not prove the existence of specific personalities and events. As more empirical data related to Zhang Zhung comes to the fore, however, literary references currently viewed as myth might possibly be carried over into the realm of history.

There is considerable cultural and historical evidence indicating that early religious cults began to adopt Buddhist-style practices and doctrines after the seventh century CE, leading eventually to the creation of the Eternal Bon religion. The wholesale requisitioning of archaic traditions by the authors of Buddhist historical and ritual texts clearly shows that such borrowing was a two-way street. This act of mutual cultural dependence proved to have much practical value in preserving native cultural traditions of the Tibetan Plateau. The widespread borrowing of the archaic to enrich Buddhist teachings in the creation of the Lamaist religions, nonetheless, was tempered by a parochial approach to the writing of history. Eternal Bon and Buddhism were intent on carving out their own intellectual and institutional territories. This rugged independence while fostering sectarian integrity beclouded a shared sense of history.

The interplay between myth and history is very much in evidence in the Tibetan literature examined in the remainder of this chapter. Like objects in a swirling mist, occasionally the actual picture of Zhang Zhung emerges tantalizingly clear, but in other instances it disappears into the gloom of the distant past.

THE COMING TOGETHER OF THE TRIBES

The "archaic era" is a catchall term for the periods predating Buddhist domination of Upper Tibet. It spans the Late Bronze Age (1200–900 BCE), the Iron Age (900–100 BCE), the protohistoric period (100 BCE–600 CE), and the early historic period (600–1000 CE). The Metal Age (Late Bronze Age and Iron Age) and protohistoric period coincide with the so-called Zhang Zhung civilization. The early historic period (600–1000 CE) encompasses the Tibetan empire and its troubled aftermath, a time when a successor civilization to Zhang Zhung thrived in highland Tibet. The vestigial period (1000–1300 CE) coincides with the assimilation into the Lamaist religions of the last highlanders still adhering to archaic religious cults.

Eternal Bon and Buddhist texts, as well as the oral tradition, shed some light on the origins of the Upper Tibetan population. A résumé of its constituent tribes and clans, real and mythic, can be compiled from these sources.[2] The written and oral records suggest that Zhang Zhung was a multiethnic civilization, its society crystallized from the peoples of many surrounding regions. Unfortunately, details about how and when the diverse nations of Upper Tibet came together are very sketchy. The epic journeys of far-flung peoples to their Zhang Zhung homeland are conspicuously lacking in the historical record.

Eternal Bon avers that religious masters belonging to a tribe called Mu colonized the Tibetan Plateau many thousands of years ago. The term *mu* appears as part of many Zhang Zhung words that denote the sky and celestial phenomena. The colonization of the Mu was supposedly part of a move to bring the Eternal Bon religion to more primitive bands of people already residing in Tibet. This account is a half-truth, mixing ancient history with the subsequent reimagining of religion. While the Mu was indeed a primary Upper Tibetan ethnos as alluded to in Old Tibetan literature,[3] there was no Eternal Bon religion before the tenth century CE. The very founder of Eternal Bon himself, Tönpa Shenrab, is said to have been a member of the Mu tribe. While this appears to be so, the legend of Shenrab long predates the establishment of Eternal Bon.

According to Eternal Bon, the Mu tribe with its divine connotations is said to have originally come from a land called Olmolungring. Olmolungring, a mythic paradise where godlike beings lived for eons, is described as having a symmetrical layout with a mountain in the center formed of nine superimposed swastikas. The location of this utopia and whether it is based on a real land is the object of much debate among scholars.[4] There is some textual evidence indicating that Olmolungring was an actual land in the Indo-Iranian borderlands west of Tibet. Olmolungring, the ancestral homeland of Eternal Bon, is thought to lie in Takzik, a country that some Tibetan sources equate with northern Pakistan and eastern Afghanistan. Other historical passages, however, suggest that Olmolungring is tantamount to far western Tibet. According to the eminent Tibetan scholar Samten G. Karmay, it is probable that the area around Mount Kailash, the heartland of Zhang Zhung, is the geographic source of Olmolungring. He theorizes that after the tenth century CE, Eternal Bon began to attribute Olmolungring to Takzik in order to confer an extraordinary spiritual mantle upon it.[5] Wherever it is or is not situated, the primary significance of Olmolungring is religious, as a limpid otherworldly land of spiritual doctrines and sages. Its malleable geographic nature and paradisiacal qualities have led the Eternal Bon studies scholar Dan Martin to compare Olmolungring with two famous Tibetan Buddhist paradises, Shambhala and Kalachakra.[6]

In addition to the Mu, Eternal Bon texts such as the historical work entitled *Treasury of Good Sayings* note that ancient western Tibet was settled by members of the Bru lineage or tribe.[7] The Bru are closely allied with Brusha, a region in northern Pakistan encompassing parts of Gilgit and Hunza. The tongue of the Bru, Burushaski, is one of the oldest languages in the greater Himalayan region. A string of conquests by the Bru in Thokar, perhaps the ancient Tocharia of Central Asia, and in Orgyen, probably a northern Pakistan location, is said to have preceded their arrival into western Tibet. According to the *Treasury of Good Sayings*, the Bru were invited into Tibet by a king named Tsöde.[8]

Another group that occupies a vital place in the early history of Upper Tibet is the Hor. Hor, an ethnonym designating various Turco-Mongolian groups of Central Asia, is first cited in Old Tibetan literature. Eternal Bon sources chronicle a number of legendary prehistoric wars between the Tibetans and Hor. In the text *Yungdrung Bon Gyi Gyübum*, an Upper Tibetan priest named Penegu is said to have invoked the war gods so that the Hor could be defeated by Trithob Namtsen, the twenty-fifth king of Central Tibet.[9] For his efforts, Penegu received special insignia and other badges of courage fashioned from gold and turquoise. The Eternal Bon ritual text *Drawa Nakpo* describes the Zhang Zhung deity Midud's bloody struggle against the Hor.[10] In Tibetan literature, the fates of the Tibetans and the Hor were so closely entwined that they share a common divine ancestor named Gyalbu Thinge. His genealogy is found in the famous history *Langkyi Potiseru*.[11]

An Old Tibetan manuscript notes that some of the horses used in the archaic funerary rites came from Drugu, a region located in the Turkic lands of Central Asia.[12] Some of the early priests known as *bonpo* and one of the chief gods of Zhang Zhung, Traphü, are recorded in Eternal Bon texts as being of Drugu origin as well.[13] Another people of Central Asian origin, the Garlok, are mentioned in a devotional account as having invaded the Purang valley of southwestern Tibet in prehistoric times. This tale is enshrined in *Drangdon Munsel*, an apocryphal text attributed to Drenpa Namkha, a *bonpo* saint reputed to have lived in the eighth century CE.[14]

The various textual accounts of the Mu, Bru, Hor, and Garlok tribes suggest that the Zhang Zhung ethnos was enlarged by peoples coming from the mountainous lands north and west of Zhang Zhung. This rugged country is crisscrossed by the lofty Hindu Kush, Pamir, and Karakorum Ranges. A pattern of migration from the north fits well with Upper Tibetan archaeological evidence, which reveals close affinities to the ancient burial monuments of north Inner Asia. The sheer number of rock art compositions in Ladakh exhibiting steppe influences, if not the actual hands of invaders from the Inner Asian steppes, also indicates that prehistoric cultural forces moved south and east over the western brim of the Tibetan Plateau. Taken together, the literary and archaeological evidence convincingly shows that Upper Tibet was penetrated by peoples filtering through the great mountain ranges on her left flank.

The southern border of Zhang Zhung may also have been porous to migrating tribes. The Mon, another prehistoric group that is believed to have formed a big piece of Zhang Zhung's ethnic puzzle, is generally thought of as a diverse collection of Himalayan tribes that settled across the breadth of Tibet. However, their ultimate geographic origins are unclear. According to the oral tradition of Upper Tibet, the Mon tilled the soil, practiced a black or evil form of the *bon* religion, and built many of the ancient monuments in the region.[15] They are supposed to have died out long before the current occupants of Upper Tibet arrived. These stories handed down over the generations relate that the Mon tribe was once very large and powerful but was subsequently wiped out by a terrible epidemic. It is claimed that the emptied land was eventually recolonized by Tibetans adhering to the Buddhist faith. Buddhist-inspired folklore concerning the Mon deliberately divorces the present-day farmers and herders of Upper Tibet from the ancient heritage of the region. The primary motive for this separation appears to be a desire to give the region a clean historical slate, obviating open acknowledgment of the cultural contributions of Zhang Zhung.

The place of the Mon in the ethnic mosaic of ancient Tibet is undeniable. The distinguished thirteenth-century history *Gyabö Kyi Chöchung* relates how three young boys of this tribe with feathers ornamenting their bodies became the ancestors of three ministerial clans of southern Tibet.[16] Moreover, the thirteenth-century CE *Marlungpa Namthar* documents that thirteen divisions of Mon, the people of the north, were driven south by the Hor tribe.[17] Referring to western Tibet, the precise time frame of this pre-tenth-century CE forced migration is unknown.

In addition to historical sources, the field of comparative linguistics provides tools for discerning the varied origins of the Zhang Zhung people. Over the last sixty years, linguists have attempted to chart the roots and development of the Zhang Zhung language, a tongue extinct for more than a thousand years. So far, while comparative linguistic research offers some insights into the history of Zhang Zhung, a lack of written materials in this language obstructs major strides forward. Researchers only have a couple of rather thin bilingual lexicons in the Zhang Zhung and Tibetan languages and a smattering of Zhang Zhung vocabulary used in Eternal Bon texts with which to work. There are also five enigmatic texts in the collection of early manuscripts from the Dunhuang grottos on the edge of the Gobi Desert that may have been written in the Zhang Zhung language, but they remain undeciphered. These five texts are now undergoing intensive analysis by the Japanese scholars Tsuguhito Takeuchi and Ai Nishida.[18] The extant written materials in the Zhang Zhung language are hardly sufficient for fully reconstructing its vocabulary and grammar. It has not even been agreed upon by linguists whether or not the Zhang Zhung and Tibetan languages are genetically related to one another.

For decades, based on comparative linguistic data, it has been theorized that the Sino-Tibetan borderland regions, a hotbed of ethnic formation and amalgamation, played a crucial role in peopling Zhang Zhung. In his book on the Zhang Zhung language, Seigbert Hummel directly relates it to the eastern Tibetic languages of Sihia and Minyak.[19] The prehistoric peoples thought to have spoken Sihia and Minyak are believed to have been largely of Ch'iang stock. One ethnic group still bearing the ethnonym Ch'iang resides on the eastern fringes of the Tibetan Plateau. These observations prompted Hummel to conclude that the population of Zhang Zhung originated in the east.[20] Similarly, it has been suggested that speakers of archaic Tibetan languages originating in the Sino-Tibetan marches may have pushed up the Brahmaputra River valley to reach Zhang Zhung.

Recent research carried out by Dutch and Japanese linguists indicates that the Zhang Zhung tongue was most closely related to a Western Himalayan group of languages that includes Kinnauri, Rangpa, Byangsi, and others.[21] That Zhang Zhung is akin to languages on the south side of the Himalaya was also arrived at by an earlier generation of scholars, including Helmut Hoffman and Erik Haarh.[22]

George van Driem, a well-known Dutch linguist, argues that Zhang Zhung and the Western Himalayan languages of Bunan, Manchad (both spoken in Lahoul), and Kinnauri probably reached western Tibet in the middle of the third millennium BCE.[23] This Neolithic time span predates the rise of the great castles, temples, and necropolises associated with archaic highland civilization. A Neolithic beginning for the Zhang Zhung language, if accurate, indicates that a long-established cultural bedrock underpinned the establishment of Metal Age civilization in Upper Tibet. Like Hummel, van Driem believes that the Zhang Zhung language originated in the northeast corner of the Tibetan Plateau before migrating west.[24] While this linguistic origins theory has considerable merit, it does not account for words derived from ancient Iranian languages that seem to have crept into Zhang Zhung. More recently, the French linguist Guillaume Jacques argues against a parent relationship between the Zhang Zhung and the Ch'iang family of languages.[25] He rather postulates a direct link with the old Western Himalayan languages as part of an in situ linguistic substrate.[26] His view dovetails geographically with prehistoric ethnic origins as expounded in Eternal Bon literature.

The belt of open plains and widely spaced mountain ranges extending uninterrupted between northeastern Tibet and far western Tibet is a natural geographic conduit. This broad area is liable to have funneled various waves of prehistoric peoples westward into Zhang Zhung and perhaps eastward as well. The ethnic picture of Zhang Zhung, therefore, is liable to be more complicated than the eastern genesis theorists have been willing to consider. From the textual and linguistic data now available, it would appear that prehistoric tribes migrated into the Changthang and western Tibet from many directions. Such diverse ethnic and geographic origins befit an illustrious civilization.

The debate on the origins of the Zhang Zhung language rages on. The contending views of historical linguists will have to be resolved before their theories on geographic relationships between ancient peoples of High Asia can be convincingly applied to the builders of the great monuments of Upper Tibet.

For all this discussion of foreign origins and influences, Eternal Bon texts also speak of clans and tribes native to the Zhang Zhung territory. The most famous of these is called Khyung or Khyungpo, named for the mythic horned eagle of Tibet, the *khyung*. According to an ancient text entitled *Appearance of the Little Black-Headed People*, various sodalities of the Khyung and two allied tribes, the Se and Ra, lent their namesake to a number of places in western Tibet.[27]

The group of genealogical texts known as *Khyung Rab* tells us that the Khyung tribe began with four youths who appeared from the eggs of three *khyung* birds.[28] These divine progenitors went on to found resplendent castles and temples. The emergence of the Khyung clan from horned eagles echoes another ancient myth preserved by Eternal Bon, which states that the clans of Tibet originated from a white eagle and a black eagle. Likewise, ancient Mongolian tribes such as the Buryats believed that a celestial eagle was the progenitor of the human race.

The *Khyung Rab* texts note that Khyungpo clansmen were highly revered priests during the time of the Zhang Zhung kings. It is reputed that even the first kings of Tibet held them in high esteem. The genesis of the Khyung clan and their collective soul receptacles in the *Khyung Rab* is related as follows:

> The one known as King of Luminous Phenomenal Awareness decided to act on behalf of sentient beings, so he manifested the three *khyung* of body, speech, and mind. They flew down from up high and landed in the beautiful flower garden of Khayuk, in the country of Zhang Zhung.

Accordingly, with a sense of wonder arising in the people of Zhang Zhung, they declared that these birds were unknown to them. Some old men remarked that they could be male *khyung*, as they had horns. Those three *khyung* having flown away into the sky, the people of Zhang Zhung examined the place they had been. Where their claws had touched the ground, moisture and warmth had formed four eggs: white, black, yellow, and variegated in color.

From inside each of the hatched eggs appeared a youth with highly favorable qualities. Each was bestowed the name Khyungpo. . . . Each of them had a precious soul stone boulder, a precious nonconstructed castle, and a nonimpounded turquoise lake, respectively. They exercised sovereignty over these, and each member founded salutary castles of the Khyungpo.

Another important native tribe of ancient Upper Tibet was the Mra, which is supposed to have comprised either six or nine clans.[29] According to a text describing the first paternal lineages of Tibet, the tribal symbol of the Mra was a conch-white bull elephant.[30] Various personalities of the Mra tribe figure in the origin myths of numerous Old Tibetan and Eternal Bon ritual traditions. For example, in an early historic period manuscript prosaically glossed Pt 1136, a shepherd named Mrabon Zingkye of the headwaters country in southwestern Tibet is credited with capturing divine horses needed to transport the souls of the dead to the heavens.[31] In Eternal Bon stories set in prehistoric times, families belonging to the Mra were victims of man-eating fiends known as *sri*. These harrowing tales graphically depict the murder of Mra tribal members. Such tales were composed to explain the role of sudden accidents in the mortality of humankind.

Chinese annals from the Tang dynasty studied by the French Sinologist Paul Demiéville record yet another native tribe or clan of Zhang Zhung called Dro.[32] The historian Roberto Vitali chronicles the Dro's involvement in Upper Tibetan political affairs spanning many centuries of the historic epoch.[33]

The oral tradition of the *drokpas* notes many other clans thought to be of ancient origins, some of which must have been derived from the early tribes already mentioned.[34] According to the oral tradition, some of these clans are autochthonous, while others were derived from the neighboring countries of Mon and Takzik. At Lake Dangra, extant clans thought to stem from Zhang Zhung include Chuktshang, Owo, Namru, Chakpa, Phacho, and Rawa. In Shungpa, an important region in the western Changthang, there are said to be nine ancient clans, one for each of its traditional nine districts. In the oral tradition, these clans are stated to be evolved from the white gods of the sky and blue goddesses of the water, deities of Zhang Zhung and Takzik. In Sekhor, another western Changthang region with a big concentration of old clans, clan protective deities, or *rulha*, in the form of wild ungulates are still propitiated. These primitive deities are worshiped in conjunction with the sacred mountains of Sekhor.

The Draktsa clan living in the vicinity of Mount Kailash traces its history to the two bigger islands of Lake La Ngak Tsho and the "houses of existence" located there. The Draktsa's stake in this innermost geographic point in southwestern Tibet underlines their ancient historical position. In the central Changthang area of Shentsa, the Belpa clan is associated with frogs, which may be a carryover from ancient matrilineal traditions. One of the most renowned of the early matrilineal traditions of Tibet in old genealogical texts is known as the "Thirteen Grandmothers."[35] However, little more than the name has survived. The Kye clan of Bartha in the eastern Changthang is said to be related to a group of semidivine beings of Zhang Zhung called *dud*.[36] Known for their ferocity, the *dud* appear to be an apotheosized tribe of indigenous origins. The progenitor of the Ge clan of Nyenrong, found on the eastern edge of the Changthang, has preserved a folktale in which their progenitor appeared on a red earthen throne built by a water spirit.

One of the most famous native clans of Upper Tibet is called Gurub or Gurib. These days it is concentrated in two widely separated corners of the Changthang, Shentsa and Ruthor. The Gurib clan, a constituent part of the Mu tribe, came to prominence because several saints of the eighth to the eleventh centuries CE are counted among its members in Eternal Bon literature. It is a stroke of good luck that the lore of the Gurib preserved in an Eternal Bon manuscript has recently come to light. This extremely rare work was discovered by the Eternal Bon monk Nyima Ozer in the Himalayan district of Dolpo, Nepal. Entitled *The Abridged Origins of the Gurib Paternal Lineage*, it contains valuable historical information on the political role of the Gurib in the kingdoms of Zhang Zhung and Central Tibet.[37] The text begins with a ringing eulogy of the Gurib:

> Hail! Listen to me over here!
> Generally, in the southern continent of the world,
> The greatest sound is that of the dragon,
> The swiftest speed is that of lightning,
> The most variegated is the striped tiger,
> The finest body is that of the lion,
> And the most agile is the horned eagle,
> But the king of sentient beings is the human
> And the king of beasts is the horse.
> We, the clan of Gurib, are not like others.
> We are emanated from the god of effulgence,
> Thus we are radically distinguished from others.

In glowing language, Gurib clan lore recounts the descent of a divine scion of the lineage named Mu Yangje. Mu Yangje was given permission by his mother and father to descend to the world of humans and take a bride among them. Along with his wife Yid Ongma, he settled down and built a dynastic territory inside the country of Zhang Zhung. The text describes the exploits of generations of Gurib, the progenitors of various branches of the clan. One of these prehistoric figures, Mu Berkya, is recorded as marrying the daughter of the king of Khotan, a land to the north of Zhang Zhung.

After listing fourteen generations of Gurib ancestors, it is said that a quarrel broke out between the Zhang Zhung king, Likmikya (also spelled Liknyikya), and a figure known as Lheu Lha Nyak. At that time, a Gurib named Martang was slain, and his older brother Chunmardang fled to Central Tibet. In Central Tibet Chunmardang found favor with Namri Löntsen, the thirty-second king of the Purgyal dynasty. King Namri Löntsen awarded Chunmardang a golden insignia and an insignia made from a precious jewel. According to the Gurib clan history, Chunmardang, with the aid of the Central Tibetan army, attacked and defeated Zhang Zhung. Although this specific event is not mentioned, an Old Tibetan historical text notes the defection of a Zhang Zhung minister to Central Tibet in the time of Namri Löntsen.

There are other such clans in Upper Tibet with ancient origins and exotic pedigrees. Unfortunately, very little of their history and lore has survived. Genealogical information on clans was customarily passed down orally from generation to generation. With inroads made by Buddhist ideas and practices over the centuries, indigenous knowledge of Upper Tibetan clan sources steadily waned. Events of the last sixty years have spelled the death knell for this lore. Today even the spellings of many clan names are in dispute.

In the Eternal Bon tradition, it is popularly held that thousands of years elapsed between the appearance of the first divine king of Zhang Zhung and the time of the kingdom's collapse. Zhang Zhung's royal dynasty is described in a little-known but velvety fluent body of literature, though historical details are scant.

DESCENDED FROM PARADISE, THE ROYAL LINE APPEARS

The kings of Zhang Zhung, a royal line extending from deep in prehistory to the dawn of the historic epoch, are the stuff of legends. In Eternal Bon literature these monarchs exist somewhere in historical limbo between real-life personalities and fanciful specters. The royal annals of Zhang Zhung are peppered with extraordinary doings, the meat and bone of real life just another flavor in the textual stew.

One of the most complete histories of the Zhang Zhung royal line was authored by Lopön Tenzin Namdak, Eternal Bon's foremost living scholar. Entitled *Yungdrung Bon Gyi Tenchung*, this text was compiled from a number of older Eternal Bon scriptures. In these parent writings, the mythic often overrides ordinary events.

According to traditional Eternal Bon reckonings quoted by Lopön Tenzin Namdak, about eighteen thousand years ago various regions of Zhang Zhung were controlled by a ruling lineage known as Triwer Namthuk, which was part of the Hö clan of Olmolungring.[38] The rise eighteen thousand years ago of Zhang Zhung and the Eternal Bon religion bandied about by some sources is impossibly early. This would place them in the Old Stone Age. The attribution of hoary antiquity to Eternal Bon raises its stature above all other Tibetan religions, as its followers would see it. In any case, an Old Stone Age origin is contradicted by other Eternal Bon histories, which ascribe the life of the founder of the religion, Tönpa Shenrab, to roughly four thousand years ago, a more realistic time frame for a metal tool wielding figure. This more recent time frame has been settled upon by the prominent Tibetan historian Namkhai Norbu.[39]

Although the chronology of the Zhang Zhung royal line and Tönpa Shenrab are problematic, useful information can be gleaned from the Eternal Bon historical narrative. These sources speak of a long-lived royal dynasty based in castles throughout Upper Tibet. The locations cited have a strong positive correlation with the ruins of archaic citadels in Upper Tibet that I have documented.[40]

Lopön Tenzin Namdak writes that in the time of the Triwer Namduk ruling lineage of Olmolungring, Tönpa Shenrab propagated the Eternal Bon doctrines at Mount Tise, Lake Mapang, and other regions of Zhang Zhung. This is thought to have occurred during the reign of a Zhang Zhung king named Höje Triwer Nordzin.[41] According to the text *Meri Sangwa Khorlo*, sometime after the life of Tönpa Shenrab there arose in Zhang Zhung a native dynasty of eighteen kings.[42] Another account in *Trije Lungten* states that the life of Tönpa Shenrab overlapped with the first king in the line of eighteen Zhang Zhung monarchs, Triwer Larje.[43] Other texts also support this personal association of the first Zhang Zhung king with the founder of Eternal Bon.

According to Eternal Bon sources, the royal emblem of the dynasty of eighteen potentates was a crown of bird horns, each of which was made from a different precious substance. It is not known what these crowns might have looked like, as none seem to have been excavated. One opinion holds that the headdresses quite literally were surmounted by horns or their replicas, as with the leaders and warriors of various traditional cultures in Eurasia who donned helmets with horns. Another view is that "bird horns" is a metaphor for the feathery crest of some birds. Eternal Bon scholars who support this latter opinion cite scriptural references to the feathered headdresses of the ancient *bonpo* priests, forms of which are still worn by shamans in the Himalayan rimland. Horned and feathered headdresses appear to be depicted in archaic era Upper Tibetan rock art, independently verifying in general terms the textual accounts.

Unfortunately, no detailed royal chronicle of the Zhang Zhung kings seems to have survived in the voluminous literature of Tibet. Biographical information about their regal lives and activities is scant indeed. One of the most important Zhang Zhung historical and geographical texts, *Tisei Karchak*, simply records the names of kings and their Zhang Zhung headquarters.[44] Eighteen throne holders are enumerated, undisputed masters over a gigantic territory. Written by a householder lama named Karru Drubwang (born in 1801), *Tisei Karchak* appears to have been compiled from older Eternal Bon texts and the oral tradition of Upper Tibet, but nowhere in the work is this spelled out. The author, although not very high in the Eternal Bon hierarchy, appears to have been a renaissance man of sorts and quite well traveled. His homeland was Nyenrong, a district on the eastern edge of the Changthang. Right up to the present day, Karru Drubwang's progeny have controlled the monastery he established at Sokde in Nyenrong.

The eighteen throne holders of *Tisei Karchak* are documented as having ruled over eighteen *tride*, or territorial divisions, each of which contained ten thousand administrative or residential units. True to its mythic footing, *Tisei Karchak* claims that some of the eighteen kings lived for two thousand years. So holy were these kings that they are not supposed to have left behind mortal remains. Under these monarchs the Eternal Bon religion is asserted to have spread in all directions of the compass. If any of these kings are based on actual personalities, they would have presided over the archaic religion and not its historical successor, Eternal Bon.

According to *Tisei Karchak*, the eighteen kings were headquartered in ten different locations in the western two-thirds of Upper Tibet. This upland nexus is confirmed by ancient Chinese accounts, which refer to Zhang Zhung as Yang-t'ung. According to Chinese sources, there was a greater and a lesser Yang-t'ung, corresponding to an upper (western) and lower (eastern) Zhang Zhung noted in Tibetan literature.[45] As for Zhang Zhung's northern border, the Kunlun Range forms a natural barrier. North of the Kunlun lies the Tarim basin, a Central Asian region with a historical, ethnic, and cultural complexion in stark contrast to Zhang Zhung. The well-known sixteenth-century CE historical text *Khepai Gatön* hints at this Kunlun divide.[46] It states that Zhang Zhung was situated between Central Tibet and Drugu, a country closely associated with the Turks of the Tarim basin.

The enumeration of ten royal seats in *Tisei Karchak* points to a decentralized command structure, whereby control of Zhang Zhung was left to various regional masters. The sheer size of the territory alone, extending from the central Changthang west to Kashmir, with its royal centers distributed in sundry locations, suggests that Zhang Zhung was divided into a number of autonomous principalities or chiefdoms. Eternal Bon texts name several Zhang Zhung dialects, which also hints at a high level of regional differentiation. The diffusion of archaic era castles throughout much of Upper Tibet without one obviously paramount among them in the archaeological record supports the textual characterization of Zhang Zhung as having various political nerve centers.

The renowned Tibetan scholar Namkhai Norbu speculates that when more than one king is mentioned in conjunction with a specific locale, this implies a dynastic succession.[47] Eternal Bon's senior-most scholar, Lopön Tenzin Namdak, believes that in certain instances two or even three kings may have been contemporaries.[48] During one of our conversations, the venerable Lopön shared his view that some of the Zhang Zhung kings in *Tisei Karchak*, however, may have been fathers and sons, and the possibility of dynastic struggles cannot be ruled out.

The first monarch among the eighteen noted in *Tisei Karchak*, Triwer Larje, was the holder of the golden horns of the bird. *Tisei Karchak* tells us that his prerogative to rule was bestowed by the heavens. He supposedly received his divine apportionment from Tönpa Shenrab, who appeared at Mount Tise and Lake Mapang. This soul mountain and soul lake of Zhang Zhung are envisioned as being in the very middle of its territory, likened in form to a thousand-petaled golden flower. In Eternal Bon literature, King Triwer Larje is often known by the epithet "King of Existence," reflecting his formative role in the history of Zhang Zhung.

According to Eternal Bon ritual texts, King Triwer Larje was a devotee of the god Gekhö, a wielder of thunderbolts and a controller of heavenly bodies. This chief sky god of Zhang Zhung, with his ginger-colored beard, battle hammer, and other attributes, may possibly be related to early Indo-European deities, as he displays some of the same uncanny functions and iconographic features. If so, the origins of Gekhö may date to as early as the second millennium BCE, the epoch of Indo-European mass migrations. We will return to the fascinating identity of Gekhö in chapter 8.

Little else is known about the life and times of Zhang Zhung's first king, Triwer Larje, indeed whether he even really lived or not. Stories about him are interspersed in Eternal Bon literature, but they are patently mythical. The scripture *Trije Lungten* describes Triwer Larje's previous life in moralistic language reminiscent of Buddhist parables about reincarnation and the effects of karma.[49]

Trije Lungten has the Eternal Bon founder Tönpa Shenrab regaling a large circle of disciples with a story about King Triwer Larje's past life. In this retelling of the past, a king of Zhang Zhung named Kunla Kyabpai Gön and his queen, Duktsuk Duk Kyukma, gave birth to two sons. The elder son, called Dalchor Kyeshe, wanted all sentient beings to be happy. The younger brother, Draktsub Kye, was diametrically opposed to his elder brother and spent his time making sentient beings miserable. When the two sons grew up, they began to fight over their parents' wealth and possessions. The object most in contention was a peerless jewel owned by their father, King Kunla. The tensions between the two sons only grew when the king announced that the son who should possess this jewel would rule over his kingdom.

Due to his emotional attachment, King Kunla was unable to choose between his two sons, so a seer named Denpar Mrawa was summoned to examine the boys. The seer could clearly tell that the elder son was morally superior, and he disclosed this as diplomatically as possible to avoid the wrath of the younger brother. As a result of Denpar Mrawa's examination, the Zhang Zhung kingdom was given over to the older son, Dalchor. In a fit of rage over his fate, the younger sibling threatened to kill his parents and brother if he was not given the wish-fulfilling jewel. His older brother offered to share it, but Draktsub refused to be appeased and left the kingdom. Queen Duktsuk, who was intimidated by her son Draktsub, accompanied him into exile. The two fled to the Zhang Zhung country of Metrem Nekha and became servants of its evil king, Lokpai Tobchen.

Using sorcery the mother and younger brother tried to murder King Kunla and Dalchor, but they were unsuccessful because of the wish-fulfilling jewel in their possession. Draktsub expressed a desire to his teacher Salwa Göwar that as he had been unsuccessful in harming his father and older brother in their lifetime, he should come back in the next life and finish the job. At the same time, the virtuous Dalchor wished that when he was reborn he could again see his parents.

In the next life the older brother Dalchor was reborn as Tridü Lampa, the son of Triwer Larje and his wife, Trinyen Zazu, the reincarnations of King Kunla and Queen Duktsuk. The evil younger brother, Draktsub, was reborn as the fiend Kalarasa to the demon parents King Zache Meka and Srinmo Trakthung Mewar. When Kalarasa tried to kill his former brother, he was slain by the divine priest Takla Mebar, a reincarnation of Donla Rabtson, Tridü Lampa's spiritual teacher in his previous lifetime. Tönpa Shenrab then announced to the protagonists their true identities. Queen Trinyen Zazu died in grief realizing that her former younger son was an attempted murderer. Thereafter King Triwer Larje, his son Tridü Lampa, their minister Gawa Gye, and the priest Takla Mebar received teachings from Tönpa Shenrab. Sometime later they went to a place called Brakzur Trizur Dungtse and attained enlightenment. By giving himself over to the spiritual in this fable, it appears that Tridü Lampa forsook becoming king of Zhang Zhung.

The many ruined castle and temple sites located around Mount Tise, Tibet's holiest mountain, mirror the prominent position conferred on this central location in Eternal Bon histories. One of these archaic sites may be the fabled Norbu Pungtsik, a Zhang Zhung–era temple positioned around Mount Tise mentioned in *Tisei Karchak*. *Tisei Karchak* also states that during the reign of King Triwer Larje, a sage named Tridei Öpo established a religious community numbering some six thousand members at Atisangwa. Atisangwa is identified with a jumble of cave shelters and a derelict pre-Buddhist temple situated on the east side of the Mount Tise circuit.[50] While it is hyperbole for *Tisei Karchak* to attribute such a large group of practitioners to Atisangwa, the site's ancient roots cannot be denied.

A disciple of Tridei Öpo, Dangwa Yidring, is recorded in *Tisei Karchak* as propagating the Eternal Bon doctrine to thirty-three hundred realized beings at Mule Tsho. In Eternal Bon sacred geography, Mule Tsho refers either to La Ngak Tsho or Mapang Yumtsho, the two sacred lakes lying south of Mount Tise. There are ruined all-stone domiciles on the islands of La Ngak Tsho that belong to the archaic era.[51] Perhaps these island settlements were associated with Dangwa Yidring, insofar as he really existed. Alternatively, there are two ruined castles on the rocky northwest side of Mapang Yumtsho, Chiu Khar and Chiu Singpai Khar, which may possibly be the Mule Tsho center recorded in *Tisei Karchak*.[52] This text also states that one of the preeminent Zhang Zhung castles of the four cardinal directions, Mapang Pömo Khar, was located at Lake Mapang. A contemporary religious adept from the area named Seralung Tulku attributes the highly dissolute ruins known as the "Great Castle" to Mapang Pömo Khar.[53] This site is found on the east side of Lake Mapang, in the Drak Tsangpo gorge. Other ancient ruins are located nearby at Pöri Ngeden, an Eternal Bon holy mountain.

According to *Tisei Karchak*, King Triwer Larje was followed in the dynastic succession by King Labchen, holder of the horns of the *khyung* bird, and King Hrido Gyerpung Gyalpo Kangka, holder of the crystal horns of the bird. *Tisei Karchak* maintains that the first three kings of Zhang Zhung resided at Gyang Ri Yulojon Dzongkhar, the "Walled Mountain Turquoise Leaf Tree Fortress Castle," located in the lap of Mount Tise. Steeped as it is in history and religion, it is no surprise that Tibet's holiest mountain was chosen as the seat of Zhang Zhung's first capital in *Tisei Karchak*.

Tisei Karchak writer Karru Drubwang identifies the ancient site of Gyang Ri Yulojon with Gyangdrak, a Buddhist monastery of the Drigung Kargyü subsect. This identification is supported by Lopön Tenzin Namdak in his guidebook *Böyul Nekyi Lamyik*.[54] Built in 1215 CE, Gyangdrak sits astride a huge rock in the middle of the inner or secret circuit around Mount Tise, a position of immense geomantic power that underlies the exceptional importance of this mountain to Eternal Bon.[55] The only ancient architectural feature that may have survived at Gyangdrak was the extremely high stone revetments upon which the monastery was built. Unfortunately these walls were destroyed in 2006 during the ill-advised reconstruction of Gyangdrak.

Although the establishment of Gyangdrak monastery seems to have erased virtually all signs of what may have been the Gyang Ri Yulojon castle, my survey work shows that carcasses of archaic temples and hermitages are scattered all over the inner circuit of Mount Tise. These collections of all-stone corbelled edifices reinforce the centrality of Mount Tise to Zhang Zhung. During the reconstruction of Gyangdrak monastery overseen by foreign donors, stones were pilfered from a nearby archaic era archaeological site, causing a great scientific and historic loss.

According to *Tisei Karchak*, the three kings of Gyang Ri Yulojon were succeeded by the three kings of Khyunglung Gyalwa Nyes, the "Victorious Joyous Ones Horned Eagle Valley." This locale is set in Guge, in the Sutlej River basin of far western Tibet. The three Zhang Zhung rulers were King of Guge Letra, holder of the resplendent jewel horns of the bird; King Gyungyar Mukhö, holder of the resplendent rainbow horns of the bird; and King Kyile, holder of the precious conch horns of the bird.

Various Eternal Bon historical sources state that in the "city" of the Victorious Joyous Ones Horned Eagle Valley, there once stood a lavish citadel known as Khyunglung Ngulkhar, the "Horned Eagle Valley Silver Castle."[56] This was the castle of the Zhang Zhung Guge kings. The Khyunglung Ngulkhar citadel is also mentioned in manuscripts of the Dunhuang collection written in the early historic period. These manuscripts note that Khyunglung Ngulkhar was situated in the headwaters of the river country, an allusion to the four major rivers arising in southwestern Tibet.

The thirteenth-century CE Eternal Bon text *Kunbum* affirms that Khyunglung Ngulkhar extended its influence over eighteen subsidiary castles and 360 temples.[57] As with the dynasty of eighteen kings and other royal lore regarding Zhang Zhung, the historical veracity of this information in *Kunbum* cannot be confirmed. The numbers eighteen and 360 are conventional quantities in Eternal Bon ritual traditions and should not be taken literally. The names of the eighteen satellite castles in *Kunbum* do not match any of the names given to scores of ruined strongholds in Upper Tibet by the

The remains of a long rampart at Khardong, the probable location of Khyunglung Ngulkhar

present-day population. Over time, many ancient toponyms were changed as their original significance was forgotten and to reflect more modern cultural values. It is therefore nigh impossible to correlate the castles of *Kunbum* to the facts on the ground.

In *Kunbum*, Khyunglung Ngulkhar is said to have been magically constructed. This ritualistic account portrays the castle as an axis mundi penetrating the three planes of existence, a vertical arrangement of the universe known as *srisum* in Tibetan. This awesome ability to straddle the three tiers of existence is also ascribed to the most important holy mountains of Upper Tibet. *Kunbum* articulates the fabulous appearance of Khyunglung Ngulkhar in noteworthy detail:

> Its foundations were made from gold, its four walls from silver, its four doorjambs from iron, its four doors from conch, its four corners from agate, and its four lintels were made from copper. Its roof rose up into the thirteen celestial tiers. Blizzards harboring a sleeping blue dragon constantly blew around it. Horned eagles hovered around its flanks. The castle had 108 rooms. The upper third of the castle belonged to the gods. On the left side there were formations of three flaming mountains and light; rays and thunder spread forth. This was the abode of the wrathful god Gekhö. The middle third belonged to the Bon priests. . . . The lower

third belonged to the water spirits. Here there was a swirling turquoise lake and turquoise mists thickly gathered.

The precise location of Khyunglung Ngulkhar was lost until the Eternal Bon lama Khyungtrul Jikme Namkha Dorje claims to have rediscovered it in the 1930s.[58] Lama Khyungtrul, a highly respected Eternal Bon practitioner who died in 1956, lived in the Sutlej valley of western Tibet for more than thirty years. According the late monk and doctor Tenzin Wangdrak and others among his disciples, Lama Khyungtrul discovered a life-size stone image of the eighth-century CE sage Drenpa Namkha buried atop a mesa known as Khardong, which overlooks the Sutlej River. The discovery of the likeness of Drenpa Namkha persuaded Lama Khyungtrul to believe that it marked the location of Zhang Zhung's legendary capital, Khyunglung Ngulkhar. The ruins of a particularly large walled citadel blanket the wedge-shaped summit of Khardong.

In *Tisei Karchak*, author Karru Drubwang discloses that Khardong is located in what was the Zhang Zhung city Joyous Victorious Ones, a settlement cited in various Eternal Bon works as the location of Khyunglung Ngulkhar. In making his sensational claim, Lama Khyungtrul was doubtlessly influenced by *Tisei Karchak*, which speaks of the sage Yungdrung Tshultrim, who propagated the Eternal Bon doctrine to countless adepts at Khyungchen Pungpa Ri, a location now known as Khardong.

The identification of Khyunglung Ngulkhar with the Khardong mesa is at odds with the location of Khyunglung Ngulkhar settled upon by eminent Tibetologists such as Giuseppe Tucci and Geza Uray.[59] These Western scholars argued that it is to be found in the village of Khyunglung, located ten miles downstream of Khardong. Tucci visited Khyunglung village in the 1930s, documenting a number of ancient castles and Buddhist monasteries in the surrounding region. However, it does not appear that Tucci had the opportunity to meet the Eternal Bon Lama Khyungtrul. Confusingly, there is also a complex called Khyunglung Ngulkhar in Khyunglung village, a troglodytic site of around 250 caves hewn from conglomerate cliffs. Surely the name of this site impelled Tucci to consider that it was the great citadel of Zhang Zhung fame. Yet, on the summit of this Khyunglung Ngulkhar formation, there are only the ruins of a Buddhist monastery and palace called Khartse (Castle Peak). Khartse's historical and architectural makeup indicates that it was probably established around 1000 CE as part of the second diffusion of Buddhism in western Tibet. In the twentieth century, scholars specializing in Tibetan studies were not familiar with the architecture of Zhang Zhung era monuments. This is likely to have contributed to the misidentification of Khyunglung Ngulkhar with Khartse of Khyunglung village.

While Khartse is a Buddhist facility, the caves of the Khyunglung Ngulkhar cliffs quite probably formed a nucleus of prehistoric settlement in

Khyunglung village. According to local lore, the eighth-century CE saint Drenpa Namkha is supposed to have occupied a cave there called Nakchung Phuk. There are indeed two ruined strongholds in Khyunglung village that potentially date to Zhang Zhung times, the Blue Castle and Brakchak Khongkha, neither of which appears large enough to have been its legendary capital. Rather, the Blue Castle and Brakchak Khongkha are of a size consonant with a local political seat. Moreover, Khyunglung village is set in the bottom of a deep gorge and is not on any trade arteries. Until a road was cut through the canyon a few years back, movements through the region bypassed the village in favor of more expeditious high-plateau routes.

Lama Khyungtrul's equation of the Khyunglung Ngulkhar royal citadel with Khardong has considerable archaeological merit. The Khardong mesa rises above Gurgyam, a cave complex said to have been inhabited by the eighth-century CE Eternal Bon saint Drenpa Namkha. The most telling feature of the structural remains at Khardong is their sheer size; they cover more than two hundred thousand square feet. These structures are in very poor condition, hampering identification, but the presence of stone ramparts running for approximately half a mile along the rim of the mesa are indicative of a castle or fortified settlement.

Khardong occupies a strategic geographic juncture at the margin of the Guge badlands and the high-elevation plains and valleys of southwestern Tibet. Important trade routes must have once been controlled from this point. Khardong also enjoys a powerful geomantic position at the confluence of three rivers. The presence of nearby Chunak, the largest ancient cemetery I have surveyed to date in Upper Tibet, also underscores the locale's special significance. Chunak contains hundreds of large funerary enclosures, mounds, and walled-in pillars. Potentially, Chunak was the final resting place of hundreds if not thousands of people connected to the Khardong settlement. First charted on the High Tibet Circle Expedition in 2002, Chinese archaeologists led by Huo Wei reached Chunak in 2005 to conduct a more detailed survey of its surface remains.

The archaeological evidence collected thus far bolsters Lama Khyungtrul's identification of the Zhang Zhung capital Khyunglung Ngulkhar with Khardong. Perhaps further exploration will fully vindicate his view. Until that time, questions about the real location of the capital city citadel will continue to smolder.

THE DOMINION'S EMBRACE IN KINGS AND CASTLES

From what has been written in Eternal Bon sources, the six kings of Mount Tise and Khyunglung were key rulers of the early Zhang Zhung kingdom.

These legendary figures occupied two of its most important capitals, yet these were purportedly counterbalanced by other centers of kingly power. *Tisei Karchak* enumerates twelve more members of the dynasty of bird-horn holders, which occupied eight alternative sovereign sites.

After the first six of the eighteen kings, next in the royal line were King Pung Gyung Gyer, holder of the resplendent coral horns of the bird, and King Nyelo Werya, holder of the resplendent gilt horns of the bird. These two monarchs are thought to have been headquartered in Pumarhring, better known as Purang. The relatively low-lying Purang valley runs along the southwestern frontier of Tibet. Lopön Tenzin Namdak's history of Eternal Bon and Zhang Zhung tells us that the Zhang Zhung fortress of Purang was called Tiger Hill Castle, one of four primary strongholds on the compass points of the kingdom.[60]

Purang elders report that a highly eroded earthen wall fragment on a summit still known as Tiger Hill was part of a pre-Buddhist castle. Nevertheless, with so little physical evidence to go by, this claim is hard to verify. There are also the extensive ruins of two Buddhist monasteries and administrative buildings of the old Lhasa government on Tiger Hill. These facilities demonstrate that Tiger Hill was indeed a seat of power, at least in historic times. This conical eminence dominates the heart of Purang, a grain-growing enclave, and the caves burrowed in its flanks may have been one of the original centers of habitation in this area. This geographical evidence buttresses the identification of the site in the oral tradition, but more archaeological investigation is required before the Tiger Hill Castle of legendary kings such as Pung Gyung Gyer and King Nyelo Werya can be positively identified.

Tisei Karchak tells us that two Zhang Zhung potentates in the dynasty of eighteen kings resided in Tsina, which more or less coincides with the region more recently known as Droshö. Droshö straddles the headwaters of the Brahmaputra River. The two kings of Tsina are given as Takna Zijid, holder of the iron horns of the bird, and Dzomar Thipung, holder of the resplendent fireball horns of the bird. *Tisei Karchak* speaks of a fortress in Tsina called Takna Waldzong, founded by King Takna Zijid.

Tisei Karchak also notes that Tsina is where a Zhang Zhung–era religious center called Takna Ling was established. According to Eternal Bon savants, Takna Ling is closely linked to Taknarong, a narrow rocky gorge studded with hot springs and bizarre geothermal formations sacred to their religion. Caves and the ruins of an all-stone corbelled hermitage I discovered at Taknarong could possibly be the detritus of Takna Ling.[61] While it is difficult to positively identify specific sites noted in *Tisei Karchak*, the wealth of archaeology in Tsina demonstrates that this region played a leading cultural role in early Upper Tibet.

Forty miles west of Taknarong are the remains of an archaic stronghold known as Takzik Nordzong, named for one of the legendary castles in Tibet's King Gesar epic.[62] The site consists of a network of defensive walls crisscrossing the south face of two rocky ridges. Takzik Nordzong is not a large stronghold, not what one might imagine the Zhang Zhung royal hub of Takna Waldzong to have looked like. While there are many archaic ceremonial sites in the region, I have not detected residential ruins of suitable magnitude in Tsina to have been the home base of individuals with the status accorded King Takna Zijid and King Dzomar Thipung. Possibly the geographic compass of Tsina extended more widely than Droshö, to a castle further afield. The search for the ruins of fabled Zhang Zhung kings continues.

Tisei Karchak also mentions the grove of Chema Yungdrung at the source of the Brahmaputra River in Tsina. Reportedly, a religious community of seventeen thousand highly realized beings was established at Chema Yungdrung by the sage Gungrum Tsukphü. The rise of this community is thought to have occurred in the reign of yet another Zhang Zhung king, Guwer Nor, holder of the bright turquoise horns of the bird. An all-stone residential center in the ancient style of construction is indeed found at Chema Yungdrung, validating the archaic cultural associations of the *Tisei Karchak* legend. However, this facility was home to dozens, not thousands, of people. As for the nature of the spiritual realizations attributed to the Chema Yungdrung inmates, this is a case of seeing the ancient past through the retrospective lens of Lamaism.

According to Eternal Bon literature, one of the most renowned of all Zhang Zhung castles was an installation called Gegi Chiba Khar. It is thought to have been situated in the Brahmaputra headwaters region of Droshö. Gegi Chiba Khar is honored by Eternal Bon as one of the citadels of the four quarters of Zhang Zhung. Geographical and archaeological evidence suggests that this might be the site currently known as Wangchuk Gönpo Khar, an imposing ruined citadel.[63] The ruins consist of a dense collection of stone buildings covering the summit and southern flanks of a hill situated 16,500 feet above sea level. The sprawling Wangchuk Gönpo Khar with its sixty buildings spread over fifty-five thousand square feet and the high quality of construction proclaim this the premier ancient stronghold in Droshö, and one of the most important in all of Upper Tibet. If not Gegi Chiba Khar, perhaps Wangchuk Gönpo Khar was the Takna Waldzong fortress of King Takna Zijid.

The buildings of Wangchuk Gönpo Khar were constructed with locally quarried blue limestone cut into flat blocks laid in random-work courses. There are also a few rammed-earth walls at Wangchuk Gönpo Khar. Many of the buildings were two stories tall and feature wall sockets in which stone corbels were inserted to support the second story. Wooden rafters must have once rested directly upon the corbels or on top of a stone band constructed around the corbelling. There are also surviving examples of rooms with all-stone corbelled ceilings at the site.

According to a local *drokpa* legend, Wangchuk Gönpo was the powerful demon ruler of the region. He came under attack by a Tibetan army that laid siege to his castle. For a few months the castle withstood the assault, but its water supply was finally extinguished. Not wanting this vital fact to be known to the attackers, Wangchuk Gönpo ordered his troops to smear butter on their hair to simulate that they had just bathed. This ruse had the intended effect, and the Tibetan king believed that the castle still possessed ample water reserves. Not willing to wait much longer, the Tibetan king was eager to storm the castle, but his army had used up their salt supply. Consequently, their retreat was imminent. One night, the Vajrayana hero Guru Rinpoche manifested in the dream of the Tibetan king as two yellow ducks that led him to a nearby salt mine. The next morning, using the geographic cues provided in the king's dream, his minister was able to find the salt mine. The attack on the castle could now go ahead, and it proved successful, leading to the defeat of the demon king.

King Wangchuk Gönpo, the ancient demonized ruler of Droshö, is likely to represent a distorted Zhang Zhung royal personage. It is commonplace in the Upper Tibetan oral tradition to associate pre-Buddhist archaeological sites with demons and evil doings in order to lend added legitimacy to the prevailing religious order. This fear and loathing of the past has conspired to diminish the history of Zhang Zhung to a nonentity for most Buddhist inhabitants of Upper Tibet.

Tisei Karchak reports that the Changthang region of Lake Darok Tsho was home to two Zhang Zhung kings, Duddul Wal, holder of the resplendent solar crystal horns of the bird, and Liwergyer, holder of the resplendent lunar crystal horns of the bird. The north shore of Lake Darok Tsho is rich in archaic archaeological sites.[64] Perhaps the two islands of this lake, Tsho Do and Do Drilbu, were royal seats regardless of whether their monarchs were called Liwergyer and Duddul Wal. At this point in the search for Zhang Zhung's capital fortresses, there is no way of conclusively knowing. Another potential candidate for the Darok royal hub is the ruins of a hilltop fortress located just twenty miles north of Darok Tsho. Known as Drarong Mondzong, this impeccably built installation consists of three building complexes sitting atop a limestone tor. All the structures are now in an advanced state of decay. As the name implies, *drokpas* of the region believe that Drarong Mondzong was built by the prehistoric Mon tribe.

A central Changthang locale in *Tisei Karchak* credited with two Zhang Zhung kings is Targo, the snowy meridian range that stands immediately south of Lake Dangra. The two legendary personages of Targo are King Shelgyung Hrido, holder of the resplendent red explosive horns of the bird, and King Likmur Namkha, holder of the resplendent beryl horns of the bird. Shelgyung, a lofty peak in the Transhimalaya, appears to have been the divine protector of King Hrido's clan. Even now this mountain is considered one of the most important ancestral protectors of Upper Tibet. Among the Eternal Bon residents of Dangra and Targo, Shelgyung is the paternal god of the Owo and Chakpa, clans that trace their lineages back to Zhang Zhung.

In the Targo Range, traces of a large citadel and agrarian settlement rest at the foot of Mount Kanglung Lhatse. Massive building foundations and defunct farm fields here ascend a series of slopes and benches. This long-abandoned settlement known as Bumnang Dzong could well be the royal cynosure of ancient Targo.[65] In the oral tradition, as reported in a Tibetan article on the history of the Naktshang region written by the local luminary Letö Jamphel, Bumnang Dzong is identified as a Zhang Zhung stronghold.[66]

As promising as Bumnang Dzong is for further archaeological exploration, there are a number of other prospective sites for a capital that could have been occupied by the likes of King Shelgyung Hrido and King Likmur Namkha. On the east shore of Lake Dangra alone, there are no less than a dozen ruined citadels ascribed by local residents to the time of Zhang Zhung.[67] More important than determining which of these castles might have had royal functions is an appreciation that the coalescence of monumental buildings at Lake Dangra reflects a puissant political presence. Conferred the distinction in Eternal Bon ritual literature of being soul repositories of Zhang Zhung, the role of Dangra and Targo in Upper Tibetan prehistory cannot be overstated. Nevertheless, through centuries of collective forgetfulness, the epic tale of the ancient kings who built up this holiest mountain and lake in the middle of the Changthang has nearly vanished.

Tisei Karchak purports that a King Muwernor, holder of the resplendent precious turquoise horns of the bird, lived in the Zhang Zhung country of Kha Kyor. According to Lopön Tenzin Namdak's history, Kha Kyor is probably an area in the general vicinity of Mount Tise and Lake Mapang.[68] A potential candidate for a royal seat commensurate with the legendary greatness of King Muwernor is a large ruined stronghold now known as Nakra Dzong.[69] Nakra Dzong overlooks the Eternal Bon holy lake of Gunggyü Tsho, located thirty miles east of Lake Mapang. A white goddess clad in a silver helmet and crystal armor is thought to reside in Gunggyü Tsho. Nakra Dzong comprises clusters of crumbling foundations sitting astride three

The main building at the "Castle of the Dwarfs"

rugged limestone outcrops. The highest outcrop has the biggest aggregation of ruins and boasts five different building groups, covering some thirteen thousand square feet. Associated in the oral tradition with an ancient people from the west known as Singpa, the historical complexion of Nakra Dzong is still an enigma.

It is also written in *Tisei Karchak* that a king of the bird-horns dynasty reigned in Khayuk, a region somewhere in or around the badlands of Guge. This was King Sehrigyer, holder of the resplendent blue poppy horns of the bird. His fortress, Mudzong Chenpo, is described implausibly as having a molten pig iron foundation. *Tisei Karchak* recounts that the sage Yeshe Tshultrim headed a community of 1,060 adepts at the Khayuk location of Dudtsi Mennak during King Sehrigyer's reign.

Tsarang, the capital of Guge from the fifteenth century until its downfall in 1630 CE, is thought by some Eternal Bon scholars to be where the Zhang Zhung Khayuk royal hub might have been built. Dominated by a great Buddhist citadel, there is very little physical evidence with which to verify this claim. I have found a more likely candidate for the residence of someone of King Sehrigyer's stature seven miles downstream of Tsarang. Here there are the vestiges of an ancient stronghold and palace known as Balu Khar, the "Castle of Dwarfs."[70] Balu Khar is so named because of its diminutive doorways and rooms, which are believed to have been used by a race of tiny beings.

Built in the archaic style of construction with stone corbels and tiny entranceways, Balu Khar was one of the most important archaic era facilities in the geographic heart of Guge. The site is dominated by a multiroomed building with high walls set upon an extremely prominent foundation. This must have been the temple and/or residence of the chief occupant of the site. This central structure is flanked by lesser all-stone buildings nestled into the side of cliffs and fissures. A network of short defensive walls, as found at many archaic strongholds, protects the vulnerable lower flanks of the citadel. Below the Balu Khar complex, the slopes plunge down to the Sutlej River.

The remains of many other ancient castles rise above the deeply cut valleys of Guge, but which of these may have been a Zhang Zhung capital like that ascribed to King Sehrigyer is an open question. In addition to archaic era hilltop fortresses built with mud bricks in Guge, there are buildings with cobble or slab walls that supported all-stone corbelled roofs in the most common manner of early construction. Two of the largest all-stone strongholds in Guge are Jomo Rirang, located near the old trade mart of Gya Nyima, and Arjak Khar in Zarang.[71]

According to *Tisei Karchak*, the penultimate king of the Zhang Zhung dynasty of eighteen was Nyelo Werya, holder of the razor-sharp celestial iron horns of the bird. He is said to have hailed from Ladakh, a region poised on the western rim of the Tibetan Plateau that has been under Indian jurisdiction for more than 150 years. This region appears to have been part of Maryul, the fabled "Land of Gold" affiliated with Zhang Zhung. Ladakh has a different historical and ethnic composition than Upper Tibet, indicating that its Zhang Zhung connections were likely to have been more political than cultural. The western margin of the Plateau is a productive source of placer gold. Fields of highly eroded shallow pits are what remain of gold mines worked in historic times, and some of the oldest pits may date to the time of Zhang Zhung. The oral tradition of Upper Tibet attributes the first mines to the prehistoric Mon tribe.

In the early twentieth century, a number of ruined castles were reconnoitered in Ladakh by the researcher and Moravian missionary A. H. Francke.[72] Francke determined that some of these sites belonged to the Mon tribe of ancient times. Instead of early ruins as are commonly found in Upper Tibet, many of Ladakh's castles were redeveloped over the centuries and bear little resemblance to their original forms. Ladakh was and still is strongly agricultural and relatively well populated, motive forces behind the remolding of its monuments and settlements. There are, however, at least three sites in Ladakh with ancient citadels that seem to have survived with little architectural modification: Stak Mon Khar, Suryamati's Castle, and Nyarma. These ruins were reconnoitered in the early 1990s by a university student named Neil Howard.[73] They are now being carefully surveyed by the young French archaeologist Quentin Devers and his colleagues.[74] The history of these early Ladakh sites is murky, and one can only guess which ones may have belonged to a monarch in the mold of Nyelo Werya. The Nyarma site in particular, with its all-stone corbelled structures, is of similar construction to archaic installations of Upper Tibet. Wild herbivore rock art in the Eurasian "animal style" and Metal Age rock art consisting of masklike faces and chariots are found in Ladakh and Upper Tibet. These shared artistic traditions also indicate that a cultural stream flowed between prehistoric Upper Tibet and its western neighbor.

The final king in *Tisei Karchak*'s royal line of eighteen bird-horn holders is identified with Ruthok in northwestern Tibet, a region that borders Ladakh. Did its King Mumar Thokgö, holder of the resplendent horns of the bird fashioned from sapphire, really live? While there is little biographical evidence to support his existence or that of the other kings in *Tisei Karchak*, we do know that certain words in their names and titles belong to the Zhang Zhung language. A case in point is the word *mumar* in King Mumar Thokgö's appellation, which means "unworked gold" in Zhang Zhung.

The castle of King Mumar Thokgö, Nam Dzong, is popularly identified with Dzong Ri, a giant stronghold that rose above the old agrarian settlement of Ruthok.[75] Residuum of a Zhang Zhung citadel is not detectable on the hilltop, as this site was intensively occupied in later periods. Local residents say that the broad, flat-topped hill of Dzong Ri has the shape of an elephant and is guarded by an elephant god called Langboche. According to one local myth, in order to save Dzong Ri from a marauding Ladakhi army, this elephant god reared up so high the hill touched the sky. While the visible archaeological evidence alone cannot confirm that Dzong Ri was a monarchial cradle of Zhang Zhung, the site enjoys a central geographic position in what was once a core region of archaic civilization in Upper Tibet.

The disintegrated acropolis of Dzong Ri is known by several other names, including "Ruthok's Castle of the Butcher," "Ruthok's Castle of the White Horned Eagle," and "Ruthok's Castle of the Purple Horned Eagle." By another name, "Ruthok's Lion Fortress," Dzong Ri is reckoned in Eternal Bon to be one of the Zhang Zhung citadels of the four cardinal directions. Two other castles of the compass points, Mapang Pömo Khar and Tiger Hill Castle, have already been noted. The fourth was Lashang Yulo Khar, described in *Tisei Karchak* as being situated north of Mount Tise. Lashang appears to be one and the same as Shang, a well-known region 150 miles north of Mount Tise. There are a number of derelict castles in and around Shang that could possibly be Lashang Yulo Khar.

According to a well-articulated legend handed down over the generations, Ruthok's Dzong Ri was the headquarters of Shenpa Merutse, an ancient Central Asian conqueror.[76] Switching allegiances, he became one of the thirty ministers of Tibet's epic hero Ling Gesar. Local elders report that the relics of Shenpa Merutse were kept in a reliquary enshrined on the east side of Dzong Ri. This fortress and the six Buddhist centers of the acropolis were shelled by the Chinese Communists in 1959 and completely destroyed in the Chinese Cultural Revolution. All texts pertaining to the history of Ruthok in the libraries of Dzong Ri were lost in that devastation.

Tisei Karchak also alleges that a Zhang Zhung religious center known as Sangdrak Yungdrung Tampa, the "Filled by Swastika Secret Rock Formation," is where the Ruthok sage Tsukphü Gyalwa disseminated Eternal Bon teachings to several thousand adepts. This projection of Lamaist religion onto a prehistoric past became standard practice, so committed were Eternal Bon followers to revising ancient religious history along the lines of Buddhist doctrine.

In addition to the ten castles of the bird-horn-holder kings, the eighteen subsidiary castles of Zhang Zhung's capital Khyunglung Ngulkhar, and the four castles of the cardinal directions, there are other legendary Zhang Zhung strongholds mentioned in Eternal Bon literature. The names and a few locations of these have been preserved, but virtually no hard information about their age or usage.

Lopön Tenzin Namdak's history alleges that King Tridem, holder of the iron horns of the bird, and another figure, King Muwer Takna, were part of a latter Zhang Zhung dynasty, which existed around the same time as Central Tibet's first legendary king, Nyatri Tsenpo.[77] According to traditional historical reckonings, King Nyatri Tsenpo was born a little over twenty-one hundred years ago. Other fabled kings of Zhang Zhung mentioned in Lopön Tenzin Namdak's work were Mu tribal figures: Muwer Ösel, Mukhung Namje, Muwer Senggetram, Muwer Tsepo, and Mulakhung Sangje. Purportedly there were also many minor kings from the Himalayan regions of Ladakh, Baltistan (now in northern Pakistan), and Mustang (now in western Nepal) affiliated with Zhang Zhung. The names of still other Zhang Zhung kings have come down to us in Eternal Bon literature. However, they too are disembodied from the toils and trials of real lives. The surviving royal annals of Zhang Zhung are but a mere shadow of what its great citadels once held.

Perhaps someday we will learn more about the kings of Zhang Zhung and better pinpoint their royal headquarters. Until that time, we must be content with the embers of history, the full blaze doused by long years and the capricious nature of the collective human memory.

THE GODS WITHDRAW THEIR FAVOR

As with all worldly kingdoms, it was inevitable that Zhang Zhung would one day disappear from the face of the earth. Its physical remains and a few textual references aside, it persists only in popular imagination, the fine latticework of informed discourse long since dismantled. The fall of political Zhang Zhung is a classic tale of internal decline, the rise of a rival power, and the time-tested seed of destruction, treachery. This grand defeat coincided with the introduction of writing in Tibet, giving rise to the first true historical accounts of Zhang Zhung. With the demise of its political power, the Zhang Zhung language and other aspects of its culture waned, spelling the end to a distinctive Upper Tibetan civilization.

From a position of sovereign might to a vassal state, the Zhang Zhung kingdom met its end in the seventh century CE. A historical study made by the American Tibetologist Christopher Beckwith suggests that at the turn of the seventh century CE, a Zhang Zhung confederacy under the native Liknyi dynasty ruled much of the Tibetan Plateau.[78] This coincided with the reign of the thirty-second Central Tibetan king, Namri Löntsen. Helmut Hoffman, a German Tibetologist, characterized Zhang Zhung as the most powerful military power on the Tibetan Plateau at that time.[79] Yet despite its traditional strength, in the early seventh century CE, political Zhang Zhung was on the verge of collapse, taking with it the ancient civilization it safeguarded.

The Eternal Bon historical text *Yungdrung Bon Gyi Gyübum* claims that a cultural unification of sorts between Zhang Zhung and Central Tibet transpired during the reign of Khritsen Nam, the twenty-fifth king of the Purgyal dynasty.[80] This king, as best as he can be historicized, was perhaps active circa 400 CE. As we have seen, the Gurib clan history attributes the fall of Zhang Zhung to the time of Namri Löntsen, the thirty-second and last protohistoric Purgyal king. This account probably refers to a partial defeat of Zhang Zhung suffered at the hands of Khyungpo Pungse Zutse, one of King Namri Löntsen's key ministers, in the 610s or 620s CE. According to the *Old Tibetan Annals*, a register of the royal activities of the Purgyal dynasty probably written in the ninth century CE, this minister defected from Zhang Zhung to join the Central Tibetans.[81] Pungse Zutse remained a prominent figure in Tibetan politics until he committed suicide after his failed attempt to take the life King Songtsen Gampo. This botched assassination plot occurred sometime before 650 CE.[82]

Prior to the 620s CE, the Purgyal rulers of Tibet were based in the southern Tibetan region of Yarlung. As pointed out by the British Tibetologist H. E. Richardson, the *Chinese Sui Annals* record that in the period from 581 to 600 CE, the Tibetan king (probably Namri Löntsen) led an army of one hundred thousand men, and his kingdom extended to the borders of India.[83] The definitive conquest of Zhang Zhung, however, did not occur until the reign of Songtsen Gampo, the son of King Namri Löntsen. King Songtsen Gampo ruled his Tibetan empire from circa 629 to 650 CE.[84]

The early historic period texts known as the *Old Tibetan Chronicle* and the *Old Tibetan Annals* are among the oldest and most exacting records of the disintegration of Zhang Zhung. According to these historical works composed in the Old Tibetan language, the very last monarch of Zhang Zhung was called Liknyashur or Liknyirhya. Unlike the prehistoric kings of Zhang Zhung in Eternal Bon literature, Liknyashur's existence is relatively well documented in Old Tibetan documents. His Eternal Bon counterpart is called Liknyikya or Likmikya, a Zhang Zhung epithet said to mean "All-Conquering King of Existence." An Old Tibetan ritual text found in the Dunhuang collection pertaining to funerary ritual horses affirms that a King Liknyashur resided in the castle of Khyunglung Ngulkhar.[85] Whether the last king of Zhang Zhung or another member of the same royal dynasty is meant here is uncertain. According to the Dunhuang funerary text, the royal seat of King Liknyashur was in the "headwaters of the river country," the source of the four great rivers that arise in southwestern Tibetan. The celebrated mid-sixteenth-century CE historical text *Khepai Gatön*, by Pawo Tsuklak Trengwa, states that King Liknyashur had two chief ministers, Khyungpo Rasangje and Tonglam Mache.[86] Little else is known about his administration.

Four poems in the circa mid-ninth-century CE *Old Tibetan Chronicle* translated into English by the Hungarian scholar Geza Uray record the failed marriage of Zhang Zhung's King Liknyirhya to Princess Semarkar, the sister of King Songtsen Gampo.[87] The double dynastic marriage of Semarkar to Liknyirhya may have seemed a superb idea to the ruling families of Zhang Zhung and Central Tibet. The joining of their dynasties would forge a powerful alliance that controlled much of the Tibetan Plateau. But this was not to be. What the political elites could not calculate were matters of the heart.

The marital strife between King Liknyirhya and Princess Semarkar would have enormous ramifications for the history of the Tibetan Plateau. The Purgyal kings and ministers were the ascendant political and military force on the Plateau in the early seventh century CE, and their hunger for new conquests and territory knew no limits. Perhaps therefore they never intended for the double dynastic marriage to succeed. As the Italian historian Luciano Petech observes, in order for the Central Tibetan kingdom to expand westward, the annexation of Zhang Zhung was essential.[88]

The four poems by Princess Semarkar cry out to her home kingdom and express a disinclination to consummate the royal marriage. Alarmed by this turn of events, Central Tibet dispatched an emissary named Mangchung to encourage Semarkar to produce a royal heir. In response to his visit, Semarkar enclosed her poems in a cloth packet with turquoise and sent them back with him. In her first song, Semarkar laments her servants and the Zhang Zhung diet of fish and barley. From this account we can deduce that the great lakes of Upper Tibet were once exploited as fisheries. In more recent centuries Tibetans have frowned upon eating aquatic life, probably because of its perceived negative effect on the climate. Semarkar depressingly described her new home, Khyunglung Ngulkhar, as "gray and empty." She also scorned her herds of deer and wild asses, calling them "wild," which almost certainly they were. Her second song is an allegory featuring a wild yak hunt in the northern wastelands, a veiled call for war against Zhang Zhung. Semarkar's second song also acknowledges the place of Central Tibet's six main clans in the conquest of Zhang Zhung and the rewards that each of them would receive for their participation. Semarkar's other two songs are also allegories, which incite war and herald the ensuing defeat of Zhang Zhung.

As the Tibetan scholar Namkhai Norbu makes known, upon Minister Mangchung's return from Zhang Zhung, he sang the four songs composed by Princess Semarkar to her brother King Songtsen Gampo.[89] King Songtsen opened the sealed packet his sister had sent and saw that it contained thirty pieces of turquoise. Pondering the significance of the gift, it finally dawned on him that he should be man enough to wear them around his neck, not like a woman in her hair, and bring about the destruction of Zhang Zhung. The *Old Tibetan Chronicle* notes that Semarkar's dissatisfaction with her marriage to Liknyirhya was used as a pretext for the successful invasion of Zhang Zhung.

The *Old Tibetan Chronicle* and *Old Tibetan Annals* studied by Geza Uray, H. E. Richardson, and other historians furnish the oldest and most accurate accounts of the fall of Zhang Zhung. According to these texts, King Songtsen Gampo brought about the subjugation of Zhang Zhung circa 644 CE by assassinating its king, Liknyashur. The first administrative chief or governor sent by King Songtsen Gampo to Zhang Zhung was Pukgyim Tsang Menchung.[90]

The *Old Tibetan Chronicle* tells us that after the conquest of Zhang Zhung, its capital, Khyunglung Ngulkhar, was the residence of the Central Tibetan administrative chiefs.[91] A recently published improved translation of the *Old Tibetan Annals* by the American scholar Brandon Dotson shows that these administrative chiefs began to intervene in the affairs of Zhang Zhung as early as the 630s CE, a decade before its conquest.[92] After their subjugation, Zhang Zhung and the other highland kingdom, Sumpa, were organized into administrative and military units know as *tongde*. Each *tongde* consisted of a thousand households or residential camps. The *Old Tibetan Annals* add that Zhang Zhung was divided into lower and upper halves, each with five *tongde*.[93] In 653 or 654 CE, the Purgyal minister Pukgyim Tsen Machung was appointed governor of Zhang Zhung.[94] Presumably Pukgyim Tsen Ma-chung was one and the same as Pukgyim Tsang Mangchung, the emissary to Zhang Zhung whose mission was to assist Princess Semarkar. The *Old Tibetan Annals* record that circa 662 CE, the administration of Zhang Zhung was headed by the chief minister Gar Tongtsen.[95] According to Brandon Dotson, this was a time when Central Tibet's political grip on the region tightened further. Circa 675, Zhang Zhung was being administered by the minister Gar Sennya.[96]

Royal alliances between Central Tibet and Upper Tibet continued after the subjugation of Zhang Zhung, for in 671 CE, a Tibetan princess married a Zhang Zhung prince.[97] Not many other details concerning the Purgyal kings' annexation of Zhang Zhung have survived in early historic period writings. We do know that in 677 CE, Zhang Zhung staged a failed rebellion,[98] in 719 CE a census was taken of the former kingdom,[99] and circa 724 CE its administration was reorganized.[100]

With the conquest of the Zhang Zhung and Sumpa kingdoms, the Central Tibetan Purgyal dynasty became the undisputed master of uppermost Tibet. Like Zhang Zhung, the kingdom of Sumpa was organized into units known as *tongde* and ruled by an administrative chief. The Buddhist his-torical work *Narrative of Legislation and Organization* records King Songtsen Gampo's selection of Horcha Zhuring as administrative head of Sumpa.[101] A cartographic study of place names in the *Old Tibetan Annals* conducted by the Austrian scholar Guntram Hazod suggests that the old Sumpa capital Namra Zhadon, or Namra Chakgong, is geographically related to the sacred mountain Namra.[102] Namra, nicknamed the "Great Black One," is situated in the eastern Changthang, in Bartha. In addition to very large ancient cem-eteries in the vicinity of Namra, I have surveyed the remains of two ancient strongholds under its shadow. How these ruins might relate to the political organs of Sumpa remains to be determined.

In his history of Eternal Bon and Zhang Zhung, Lopön Tenzin Nam-dak proposes a twofold demise for Zhang Zhung. While he affirms that King Liknyirhya or Likmikya was killed by King Songtsen, the *lopön* is persuaded to believe that he was not the final king of Zhang Zhung. Based on Eternal Bon sources, Lopön Tenzin Namdak confers this distinction on Likmigyal, a king said to have resided at Lake Dangra. In the Eternal Bon version of his-tory, King Likmigyal was assassinated by King Trisong Deutsen, the emperor of Tibet between 755 and 797 CE. Lopön Tenzin Namdak writes,

> In the end, during the time of the Tibetan kings Songtsen and Trisong, King Likmikya of Zhang Zhung and King Likmigyal of Dangra were killed by the Tibetan Lords. As a result, Tibet ruled most of central and eastern Zhang Zhung. The south and west of Zhang Zhung declined as

well, and there was no one left in the royal dynasty capable of securing the future of the kingdom.[103]

As Lopön Tenzin Namdak's account makes clear, Eternal Bon preserves an alternative version of the fall of Zhang Zhung, one not corroborated by other historical sources. Eternal Bon texts contain much partisan lore about the disappearance of their patron kingdom in a bid to ameliorate Zhang Zhung's defeat and soften the blow dealt to native culture by the introduction of Buddhism. It may be that Likmigyal was a renegade vassal of the Tibetan empire put down by King Trisong Deutsen, but we may never know the truth.

The *Zhang Zhung Nyen Gyü* is an important Eternal Bon collection of mind-training and biographical texts. According to the *Zhang Zhung Nyen Gyü*, the last king of Zhang Zhung was indeed from the Liknyi (or Likmi) dynasty, but his name is rendered Likmikya rather than Likmigyal.[104] This king is portrayed as being so powerful that his army numbered 990,000 soldiers or units, an impossibly large number. By comparison, it is reported that King Trisong Deutsen commanded just forty-two thousand soldiers or units. The *Zhang Zhung Nyen Gyü* maintains that as the Tibetans could not prevail against Zhang Zhung in open battle, a plot was hatched to bring it down using the most nefarious of means.

In the time of King Likmikya, the royal seat is said to have been Dangra Khyung Dzong, a fortress located on the east side of Lake Dangra. Dangra Khyung Dzong was one of a chain of well-built strongholds that stood above the shores of this scenic lake.

According to the *Zhang Zhung Nyen Gyü* legend, King Trisong Deutsen sent Namnam Lekdrub as an emissary to King Likmikya's youngest queen, Nangze Dronglek, a woman of just eighteen years. Namnam Lekdrub presented the young woman with a wild yak horn full of gold dust and inveigled that she should not endure being the junior wife of the Zhang Zhung king. The wily Namnam Lekdrub made Nangze Dronglek a spurious offer: if she would help the Tibetans bring down the Zhang Zhung kingdom, King Trisong would take her as his primary wife and present two-thirds of his kingdom to her.

Her heart filled with evil desire, Nangze Dronglek divulged that her husband would be traveling to Sumpa in the next month with just his personal attendants. It was agreed that Nangze Dronglek would place a sign on the Turquoise Dragon pass revealing to the Tibetan army when King Likmikya would come that way. On Turquoise Dragon pass, King Trisong Deutsen and his minister Namnam Lekdrub found a cauldron filled with water inside of which were three objects: a small piece of gold, a small piece of conch, and a poisoned arrowhead. King Trisong Deutsen was able to read these signs. The full cauldron of water meant that the Zhang Zhung king would be traveling on the full moon. The gold and conch signified that the Tibetan army was to lie in wait at Gold Cave and Conch Cave, grottos situated east of Lake Dangra. The poisoned arrowhead designated the manner in which the king was to be murdered. The ambush was executed accordingly, and Trisong Deutsen slew King Likmikya.

Zhang Zhung Nyen Gyü goes on to describe the punitive action taken by Zhang Zhung. The senior wife of the Zhang Zhung king, Khyungza Tshogyal, was eager to avenge her husband's death. She enlisted the help of a highly reputed sage named Nangzher Löpo. He was willing to be of service to Khyungza Tshogyal because the Buddhist king Trisong Deutsen posed a grave threat to the prevailing religious traditions. Eternal Bon of course holds that these early historic traditions are one and the same as those enshrined in their faith, choosing not to recognize that in the late eighth century CE, archaic religion was still a powerful shaper of Tibetan spirituality.

To aid Zhang Zhung, Nangzher Löpo offered to build and deploy a magical golden bomb known as a *dzo*. He repaired to Tsho Do, an island fastness in Lake Darok Tsho, where he performed the *dzo* ritual for a week. Nangzher Löpo directed two parts of the *dzo* against a herd of deer and a sacred lake belonging to the Purgyal dynasty. These were probably considered to be mystic soul repositories of the royal family. Nangzher Löpo hurled the final part of the *dzo* at Chiwa Taktse, the castle of King Trisong Deutsen. As a result of the attack, the castle caught fire and the king became seriously ill. King Trisong Deutsen soon realized that he had been targeted because of his killing of Zhang Zhung's king Likmikya and for his suppression of the native religion. King Trisong Deutsen sent envoys to seek out Nangzher Löpo. The envoys boarded a boat bound for the island of Tsho Do, where they encountered the shining crystal horn of a blue sheep laid out on a brocade mat. As they presumed this sacred object was actually the saint, the horsemen prostrated and offered gold dust while making supplications. Lo and behold, the crystal blue sheep horn was miraculously transformed into Nangzher Löpo.

Nangzher Löpo confidently defended his actions, telling the king's envoys that it was in his right to kill King Trisong Deutsen, but for the sake of Tibet he would not. The saint reminded the Tibetans that they were responsible for the death of the Zhang Zhung king and the decline of Eternal Bon. The envoys beseeched Nangzher Löpo to come to the Tibetan royal center at Yarlung Sokka and become the preceptor of King Trisong Deutsen. The saint retorted that if they wanted his help, three conditions would have to be met: a golden *chorten* containing the mortal remains of the Zhang Zhung king was to be built, his Gurub clansmen must be exempt from taxes when visiting Yarlung Sokka, and the Eternal Bon doctrine was to be restored. The Tibetan envoys readily agreed to Nangzher Löpo's demands.

Zhang Zhung Nyen Gyü further relates that after King Trisong Deutsen and the Tibetan ministers and subjects submitted to Nangzher Löpo's spiritual authority, he performed a secret rite called *thi*. This caused a great deal of gold that looked like horsetail hairs to appear on King Trisong Deutsen's body, blemishes from the magical bomb attack. The health of the king was restored, and thus the Tibetan people were freed from their sufferings.

At the end of the *Zhang Zhung Nyen Gyü* story, the dignity of the slain King Likmikya is reclaimed, and the indigenous religion is reinstated to its paramount position. This supposed restoration of the ancient status quo, if indeed it occurred, was but a minor blip in the advance of Buddhism. In fact, both Buddhist and Eternal Bon histories agree that it was King Trisong who abolished the old religious order in the 780s CE. As Buddhism continued to gain headway on the Tibetan Plateau, Zhang Zhung faded into obscurity. It was replaced by a cultural and political regimen enforced by the dictates of the Tibetan empire. By the time of the appearance of Eternal Bon, some three centuries after the downfall of Zhang Zhung, the memory of this erstwhile kingdom had been diluted almost to the point of oblivion.

Political vicissitudes notwithstanding, the vagaries of nature must have played a significant role in the demise of Zhang Zhung. The research of Ohio State University's Lonnie G. Thompson, a leading paleoclimatologist, indicates that circa 600 CE there was an abrupt change in the climate of Upper Tibet.[105] The analyses of ice cores and lakebed deposits reveal that in the seventh century CE, the region began to dry out in a most pronounced manner, an environmental legacy that has continued to the present day. This deterioration of the climate in an already depleted region may have led to sharp cuts in Zhang Zhung's agricultural production. A steep fall in the grain supply would only have added to the woes of the teetering kingdom. Expanding the historical scenario to take in the natural environment of the time opens up intriguing avenues of inquiry into the collapse of Zhang Zhung. In the years to come, environmental history may prove one of the most effective tools in prizing open more information about the rise and fall of Zhang Zhung.

Although the historical memory of Zhang Zhung has been consigned to isolated Tibetan texts and handed-down stories, there are still other ways to retrieve its past greatness. As we have seen, Tibetan texts enumerate many places and monuments associated with Zhang Zhung. What is left of these sites and structures and what they tell us about the erstwhile magnificence of Zhang Zhung is our next topic of discussion.

Touching the Sky: The Citadels and Temples of Zhang Zhung

STONES OF TIME

$\mathcal{T}$his chapter explores the actual places where the inhabitants of ancient Upper Tibet built their strongholds and places of worship. Today, the farmers and herders of the region go about their lives without much fanfare, but their homeland was not always so quiet. In the time of Zhang Zhung, their forebears were masters of a gigantic territory. As symbols of political resolve and cultural discernment, they filled the highlands with noble monuments of many kinds. These physical manifestations of archaic civilization linger on as vivid reminders of an extraordinary past.

It is to the upland, a world of limitless horizons, that Eternal Bon traces many of the cultural and religious origins of Tibet. At first glance, Upper Tibet is much too high and dry to be anything more than a backwater, a hardscrabble land that prevented human beings from rising above mere subsistence. Yet it is here on the highest reaches of the Tibetan Plateau that Zhang Zhung and her sister culture, Sumpa, made their debut.

The seven hundred archaeological sites I have surveyed in Upper Tibet span roughly two thousand years.[1] They were founded between approximately 1000 BCE and 1000 CE, a period I call the archaic era. These two millennia encompass the Late Bronze Age and Iron Age (1200–100 BCE), the protohistoric period (100 BCE–600 CE), and the early historic period (600–1000 CE).

On reconnaissance missions carried out in the 1990s and 2000s, I had to be content with realizing fairly modest objectives. Confined to what could be seen and qualified on the ground, I undertook to assemble a database of the general architectural traits and environmental conditions that characterize archaeological sites. These surveys of archaic monuments furnish a bird's-eye view of ancient Upper Tibet, a stepping-stone to more specialized studies.[2]

Discerning the identity of monuments is crucial in understanding the cultural complexion of prehistoric Zhang Zhung and Sumpa and that of the historic epoch civilization that succeeded them. In the field, I would measure the overall dispersal of ruins and the respective structural components of each site. Running around with a tape measure for hours at a time in the rarefied air was quite an athletic undertaking. I relied on the photography of physical remains as an important tool of documentation. Images help to pinpoint the status of sites and facilitate follow-up study. I collected folklore, myths, and legends about archaeological sites from local residents and Tibetan luminaries. The translation of Tibetan textual sources pertinent to the functions, affiliations, and chronology of places and monuments was also essential to my overall objectives.

Determining the current cultural and economic uses of archaeological sites was part of the survey regimen as well. Assessing man-made and environmental risks to archaeological monuments formed the proactive component of the work. I am hopeful that my inventory of sites will aid in the introduction of an effective program of archaeological conservation in Upper Tibet. This is the demand of the day before more ancient monuments in the region and the extraordinary tale they tell are lost forever to vandalism and inappropriate development.

The vast Tibetan upland boasts a surprisingly diverse mix of alpine and steppe ecosystems watered by glacier-fed rivers and springs. Accessed through chasms and over mountain passes, early Upper Tibetans established themselves in concealed nooks and crannies. The first inhabitants gravitated to caves harbored in vales and amphitheaters near perennial sources of water. Sheltered from the weather-beaten plains, these more verdant microenvironments provided the protection necessary for human civilization to take root.

For untold millennia the residents of Upper Tibet pursued an unfettered hunting-and-gathering way of life.[3] Our present state of knowledge does not permit an accurate assessment of when Upper Tibetans first began tilling the soil and domesticating yaks, horses, and sheep. A better understanding of the historical processes connected to agriculture and pastoralism is essential in furthering an understanding of the genesis and evolution of highland civilization. This knowledge will only come about through systematic archaeological excavation and scientific analyses of the remains and objects recovered. Unfortunately, the Chinese government is still dragging its feet in this regard.

Although the exact date has yet to be fixed, sometime around 1000 BCE, tools made from copper alloys began replacing those fashioned from stone.[4] Thereafter, implements made from iron also appeared in Upper Tibet. These major technological innovations mark the seminal shift from the New Stone Age, or Neolithic Age, to the Metal Age. Upper Tibet appears to have entered the Metal Age relatively late as compared to other ancient civilizations such as those of China or Persia, blurring the technological distinctions between the Bronze Age and the Iron Age. The introduction of the forging of iron in Upper Tibet may have occurred right on the heels of innovations in copper smelting, but this remains to be proven. The transition to an agrarian-based Metal Age economy in Upper Tibet was probably forestalled by a plentiful supply of big game. Having so much food naturally available blunted the need to develop new technologies. Archaeological work carried out in Kashmir and Swat points to a belated start to the Metal Age in these Himalayan regions situated northwest of Upper Tibet. The Neolithic in Swat and Kashmir persisted until circa 1700–1500 BCE.[5] It would not be surprising, then, that Upper Tibet, a land rich in large game animals, would have entered the Metal Age around the same time or even later.

In the first half of the first millennium BCE, the development of new technologies to produce metals and kiln-fired ceramics and to construct large buildings laid the material groundwork for Upper Tibet's civilization. As these technologies came to the fore, fledgling agricultural and pastoral communities expanded and diversified. Along with these new patterns of settlement came the formation of more complex social and cultural systems. These revolutionary technological and experiential changes ushered in a brilliant stage in the history of Upper Tibet. Other regions of the Tibetan Plateau also developed greatly by the middle of the first millennium BCE. Likewise, in Mauryan India, Achaemenian Iran, and Scythian Central Asia, ambitious civilizations took root in this period, part and parcel of a continent-wide upheaval. These changes occurred in response to a deteriorating climate, the demise of older cultural systems, the use of iron as the most strategic of materials, and intensified patterns of migration.

War, trade, intellectual exchanges, and new technologies sparked a cultural conflagration sweeping across Asia. The development of nomadic pastoralism and the equestrian arts post-1000 BCE was the catalyst for the tumultuous changes besetting Eurasia. It was in the Early Iron Age that steppe dwellers fully embraced a more itinerant herding economy based on horse riding. Between 700 BCE and 300 BCE, the widespread introduction of metal bridles and horse bits permitted the horsemen of the steppes to cover long distances much more rapidly than they could before. This improved form of transportation facilitated robust cultural and economic contacts between various corners of the vast Eurasian hinterland. In one of the greatest migrations of the time, the Scythians of Mongolia and southern Siberia moved more than three thousand miles westward to the Black Sea. It was during these wanderings of the steppe tribes that the riding horse probably reached the northern plains of Tibet from neighboring Mongolia. The arrival of mounted riders in Upper Tibet brought with it the zeitgeist enveloping the continent.

The use of metal tools and changes in the social fabric toward more stringently organized workforces aided in the construction of ambitious structures throughout much of Eurasia. Environmental impacts also played a part in the building boom under way twenty-five hundred years ago. The winds of change blowing across the steppes were felt in Upper Tibet as well. In the maelstrom of Iron Age lifestyles, customs, and languages, her inhabitants rose to the challenge of the times, equipping themselves with a bold new social and economic provision. It was in this epic re-creation of human society that highland Tibetan civilization was born.

There are a number of fundamental questions concerning how and why the transition was made from an economy based on stone tools and hunting to one that relied on metallurgy, agriculture, and pastoralism. Generally speaking, we know that the adoption of metal-making technologies was accompanied by important cultural changes, and in turn these contributed to further changes in the ways in which people lived. The circulation of metal tools and weapons in Upper Tibet appears to have contributed to the development of a more stratified society, which sustained the establishment of large residential and ceremonial installations.

The precise age of most Upper Tibetan archaeological sites of the archaic era is clouded in uncertainty. Which ones belong to Zhang Zhung and Sumpa in the broad sense of these traditional terms (circa 1000 BCE to 600 CE) and which date to the early historic period (circa 600 to 1000 CE) is still being ascertained. It appears that some early styles of architecture continued to characterize Upper Tibet even after its takeover by the Central Tibetan Purgyal emperors. In other cases, transitional forms of architecture mark the early historic period.

The dating of sites on typological grounds, through comparisons drawn with other archaeological monuments and from historical sources, constitutes informed opinion. These inferential methods of estimating age have to be scientifically verified in the laboratory. The two primary tools for this purpose are radiometric and accelerator mass spectrometry (AMS) testing, highly technical methods of analysis that determine age by measuring the ratio of carbon isotopes in organic samples.

The scientific dating of upland archaeological sites has come from the twenty-five assays I have commissioned. These chronometric data have begun to verify my suppositions concerning their age. The hard dates obtained confirm that the study of monument types and Tibetan texts do indeed play an important role in understanding Upper Tibet's ancient past.

The radiocarbon dating of human remains from the Upper Tibetan necropolis of Khangmar Dzashak indicates that it was already operational twenty-eight hundred years ago.[6] A tomb at Khangmar Dzashak dated to this period is situated between the concourses of standing stones that mark important Zhang Zhung burial centers. This suggests that typical monumental trappings associated with Zhang Zhung interments may have been in place by circa 800 BCE. The scientific dating of other Upper Tibetan castles, temples, and tombs paints a picture of upland civilization in which its basic monuments continued to be constructed through the remainder of the first millennium BCE and during much of the first millennium CE. The coherence of the Upper Tibetan assemblage of residential and ceremonial structures reflects the existence of a civilization that enjoyed a remarkable level of architectural stability.

With the advent of Zhang Zhung, there appeared an audacious vision of architectural spaces. A web of citadels, temples, and burial grounds covered the Upper Tibetan landscape in novel ways, inaugurating an age of imposing monuments. On a grand scale people began to construct permanent structures for habitation and for burial in a bid to better their lot and elevate their stature. The erection of permanent constructions for habitation, worship, and defense marked a sharp break with the Stone Age past, when the population of the region depended on rudimentary shelters and caves.

Zhang Zhung and the highland civilization of the early historic period fashioned a great variety of acropolises, palaces, temples, hermitages, and villages. The colder and drier climate with the arrival of the Late Holocene was probably a major factor in the switch from a mobile to a more settled way of life. No longer were the inhabitants of Upper Tibet constrained by portable shelters that offered only limited utility. Substantial buildings provided a much better buffer against the brutal climate, and they could help the population better protect itself against enemies.

Residential installations built as part of an exclusive social sphere fueled the development of a more complex society. These elite habitations relied on military, administrative, and labor contingents for their upkeep and defense. Larger residences allowed the privileged of Zhang Zhung to amass more food and material objects. Worldwide, the acquisition of surplus goods has accompanied the formation of class-differentiated societies.

For centuries, civilization in Upper Tibet advanced as new settlements and facilities shot up. It is not yet known when Zhang Zhung and Sumpa reached the zenith of their development. Nor is it known how their social and political dispensation evolved over time. Such big questions will help frame the next stage of scientific research and exploration.

Today, forsaken tracts holding ruined castles and temples paint a picture of an environment that has undergone radical changes since the time of Zhang Zhung. Increasing cold and aridity over the centuries reduced many once productive areas to wasteland. Ancient settlements appear alongside dry riverbeds and where old pastures have turned to desert. In the extremely marginal environmental conditions of the highlands, it is likely that desertification pushed ancient civilization to the breaking point. The uplanders lived at the physiological limits of high altitude, and little added stress was needed to send them over the edge.

Subject to an intense rain-shadow effect, Upper Tibet is the driest portion of the Plateau. The Himalaya, Karakorum, Kunlun, and Pamir, the highest mountain ranges on earth, block every path of rain to the region. While the exact mix of factors that led to the collapse of prehistoric upland civilization is not well understood, the results are clear to see: its signature monuments were discarded and left in ruin. The thriving monumental infrastructure of early historic Upper Tibet, a carryover of Zhang Zhung architectural traditions, also vanished.

In far western Tibet, valley after valley where agriculture was once practiced was either partially or completely vacated. Likewise, many of the lakeshore and mountainside sites of the Changthang were abandoned. Later, in the era of Lamaist domination, the extent of permanent settlement in Upper Tibet was further reduced. Not even the establishment of the famous Guge-Purang kingdom in western Tibet in the tenth century CE could reverse this downward trend. Although numerous great palaces and temples were founded by the Buddhist kings and hierarchs of Guge-Purang, most locales were ignored or only partly redeveloped. By the time of their dominion, climate change had ravished the highland environment beyond repair.

THE ABODES OF THE ANCIENTS

The residential sites of prehistoric and early historic Upper Tibet are concentrated in a few specific areas. These include the lower valleys of far western Tibet, along the shores of Changthang lakes, and on the flanks of sacred mountains. Most strikingly, many ancient domiciles are situated where people no longer reside. These places live on only in old texts and the folklore of the present-day inhabitants.

In the treeless wastes of Upper Tibet, stone was what the ancient inhabitants had to work with, and that is precisely what they put to work for a wide

The all-stone corbelled roof of an ancient Upper Tibetan edifice. Both corbels and bridging stones are visible in this photograph.

variety of building purposes. The residential architecture of Zhang Zhung is most notably characterized by all-stone corbelled buildings.[7] The craftsmen of Zhang Zhung designed roofs with stone members and slabs, obviating the need for wooden rafters. Construction relied on the use of corbels that helped support the extremely heavy roofs. Corbels were either counterbalanced between upper wall courses or inserted in stone sockets. Lengths of rock known as bridging stones, up to seven feet in length, oversailed the corbels to complete the span between the outer walls of rooms. The corbels and bridging stones, the substructure of the roof, were covered by stone sheathing to finish the basic roof assembly. Roofs thus built were sealed with layers of gravel and clay, but few signs of these more ephemeral materials are still visible.

The thick walls of all-stone corbelled edifices were laid down by layering stones in random courses, a particularly durable style of stonework. The slab or block walls are of both dry-stone and mud-mortar composition. The all-stone buildings are punctuated by doorways only three or four feet in height. The tiny entranceways, the general absence of windows, and the low ceilings made these structures very stable and relatively easy to heat, welcome assets in the icy montane environment. In western Tibet, the tiny entranceways have given rise to a body of folklore that attributes all-stone edifices to a mythic race of dwarfs known as *balu*.

All-stone corbelled buildings spill down formations in staggered masses or stand proudly in ranks atop summits. They are massively built affairs set deep into the ground or against rock faces. With sinuous ground plans and meandering walls, these edifices present a very different appearance from structures constructed with wooden roofs. They contain warrens of tiny rooms connected by short passageways, internal spaces isolated from the glare of the sun and the brunt of the wind.

Individual buildings were restricted in size because only small rooms can be constructed using the corbelling techniques developed in Upper Tibet. Zhang Zhung builders never perfected the corbelled archway to create big edifices; rather they joined together many lesser structures. Each room or cluster of rooms remained structurally self-sufficient like cells in a great beehive. By grafting many rooms onto one another, large, rambling complexes were produced.

Comparative archaeological study suggests that all-stone corbelled edifices were being built by 500 BCE. In 2003, the foundations of four residences were unearthed by archaeologists Huo Wei and Mark Aldenderfer in the western Tibetan village of Dindun.[8] One of these foundations has been dated to circa 500 BCE. This Dindun structure possesses many of the morphological features of all-stone corbelled residences I have charted on the erstwhile island of Do Drilbu and in many other locations.[9] While the Do Drilbu buildings are far more intact, their ground plans echo those of Dindun.

The ostensible antiquity of this form of architecture is reinforced by the radiocarbon dating of a piece of wood I recovered from the Gekhö Kharlung citadel, which indicates that large all-stone corbelled complexes were being constructed at the end of the first millennium BCE.[10] The building of corbelled edifices in highland Tibet may considerably predate Dindun and Gekhö Kharlung, but more archaeological work is needed to know for sure. From the fourth millennium BCE onward, the use of corbelling as an elementary form of construction is met with in the Mediterranean, British Isles, and other places in the world.

For all their idiosyncrasies, the all-stone edifices of Upper Tibet were eminently well suited to the bleak environment of the region. So sound were they that *drokpa* oral histories tell us that some were occupied for many centuries. In fact, the all-stone corbelled temples of Dzong Ser and Ne Kunzang located in the central Changthang were maintained as religious centers until the Chinese Communist takeover of 1959.[11]

The centerpiece of Dzong Ser is a building designed with bowed walls and rounded corners perched above a vast pastureland. It is surrounded by an outer courtyard and a circumambulatory walkway. Known as "Happiness Retreat," this structure contains four diminutive rooms, the innermost of which functioned as a shrine for protector deities. Despite being damaged in the Chinese Cultural Revolution, enough of the stone walls and roof of Happiness Retreat have survived intact that restoration is feasible should official interest in the site ever blossom.

The ancient building of Dzong Ser

The relatively intact structure known as Ne Kunzang

Ne Kunzang, an early-style all-stone residence and/or temple, overlooks Lake Dangchung. Although its top two stories were rebuilt more than once by Buddhist meditators using wooden rafters, its corbelled basement is an original architectural feature. Despite being unknown even to most local authorities, ancient monuments like Dzong Ser and Ne Kunzang deserve wider recognition and adequate protection under the law.

Not all of Upper Tibet is devoid of trees. Tamarisk and scrub juniper trees still grow in some Changthang locales, more so in ancient times. In the lower valleys of far western Tibet, poplar and willow trees are cultivated beside homes and fields. These trees furnished the wood needed to make rafters used in the construction of a wide assortment of buildings. Some early residential structures in Upper Tibet built with wooden roofs are distinguished from later structures by their imitation of design features associated with all-stone corbelled edifices. They exhibit stone walls uninterrupted by windows, low-slung entranceways, and inner and outer walls with many crooks and curves.

Some archaic era buildings constructed with wooden roofs have mud brick walls. A piece of wood bonding an adobe wall to a stone foundation recovered from the castle of Rula Khar has been dated to the sixth or seventh century CE.[12] This calibrated radiocarbon date indicates that mud brick architecture in Guge was known by the late protohistoric period. A German-Nepalese archaeological team working in Transhimalayan Mustang (a region that adjoins Upper Tibet) in the 1990s dated organic matter detected inside mud bricks to circa 100 BCE. Given this scientific finding, there is no reason to assume that mud brick edifices in Guge, a region with a similar physical and cultural environment to Mustang, were not also being raised two thousand years ago.

THE REDOUBTS OF POWER AND PRESTIGE

On a spine of rock as tall as a large skyscraper, the remains of an ancient citadel extend upward at an impossible angle. This is Gekhö Kharlung, or the "Demon Subjugating Valley Castle," a political and ritual nerve center of Zhang Zhung. Deftly constructed on rocky ledges, the buildings of Gekhö Kharlung seem to soar freely in the sky.

The Gekhö Kharlung castle in extreme northwestern Tibet broods over a large valley that was once farmed. This valley was devastated in a huge flood. A thick jumble of rocks brought down by the floodwaters covers most of the ancient fields. As noted, a piece of wood removed from one of the minor buildings of the Gekhö Kharlung complex has been radiocarbon dated to 100 BCE to 100 CE. I discovered this small round of wood in an all-stone

A few of the ruined buildings at Gekhö Kharlung

corbelled room set below ground level in one of the subsidiary structures of Gekhö Kharlung. The core installation could possibly be even older.

Gekhö Kharlung takes its name from the twenty-thousand-foot-high mountain rising to the north, Gekhö Nyenlung. Although the castle's inhabitants are long gone, Eternal Bon harks back to its wondrous past by venerating its resident gods. Mount Gekhö Nyenlung is home to Gekhö, the "Demon Destroyer," one of Eternal Bon's chief tutelary deities and the main territorial god of contemporary Ruthok. Gekhö still rules over his namesake castle, imbuing its fallen stones with a mythic aura that gravity could not cast down. Of archaic cultural origins, this sky god and his large retinue are seen as clad in tempests, ornamented with the stars and planets, and armed with thunder, lightning, and other terrific weapons.

Of all Zhang Zhung's residences, strongholds such as Gekhö Kharlung are among the most awe inspiring. Whether of an all-stone composition or made with wooden roofs, these fortified structures invoke a romantic sense of the past. Their crumbling walls stand vigil over hilltops and mountain spurs, locations where human activity is now absent. Once the well-being of society and the outcome of wars must have been decided from these castles.

The ancient castles of Upper Tibet occupied strategic economic and military positions, enjoying unencumbered views of the outlying terrain. Their unassailable geographic aspect would have made attack by an enemy difficult and costly. Aside from strategic concerns, the placement of these points of control in the heights was suffused with social and political symbolism. In both the archaic and Lamaist contexts, social hierarchies were reflected in the relative elevation of buildings.

Only the most powerful members of society would have had mastery over the mountaintop castles. Occupying the pinnacle of each community, they were the preserve of kings, chieftains, and other prominent members of Zhang Zhung and early historic period society. Individually, these castles were the nuclei of localities. Collectively, they formed extensive networks, the administrative backbone of ancient civilization. It was from these bastions of prowess and prestige that society was welded into coherent working and fighting units.

In addition to accommodating leading personalities and their families, the larger fortified installations are likely to have housed administrators, warriors, servants, and artisans. While we can assume that castles were organized into palaces, offices, workshops, temples, and garrisons, the specific functions of buildings at any given site are still ambiguous. Many of the ancient strongholds have been reduced to dissolving walls and foundations, while others were redeveloped in later periods, irrevocably altering their architectural character. The degraded physical condition makes it difficult to know what the original functions of individual buildings were with any assurance.

The sheer size of certain strongholds indicates that hundreds of people once lived in them. Take Jomo Rirang Khar, a sprawling, bright red limestone facility tucked away on an out-of-the-way summit in the old western Tibetan district of Gya Nyima.[13] Its all-stone corbelled ruins are believed

Ruined structures at Jomo Rirang. Note the all-stone corbelled roofs.

to be the haunt of a very dangerous goddess, probably a vestigial form of Drablai Gyalmo, the warrior queen goddess of Zhang Zhung. Nowadays the site is given a wide berth by local shepherds. Despite the pall hanging over present-day Jomo Rirang Khar, a large number of people must once have lived and toiled in its dozens of buildings. The structures of Jomo Rirang line the crags to form a variety of precincts, each of which appears to have had special residential functions. Those balanced on the highest summit, the most defendable position, were probably reserved for the rulers or commanders of the citadel. The central edifices of Jomo Rirang Khar, some of which were two stories tall, are where the majority of the castle's residents were domiciled. More outlying structures are likely to have been active in the defense of the site.

Wherever castles sprung up in Upper Tibet, a ready workforce was required for construction and maintenance. Water, food, fuel, and other supplies had to be transported up to the citadels, presupposing a class of individuals who labored for the upper crust of society. This type of social arrangement was re-created in later times, when peasants provided the haulage needed to support hilltop monasteries and Lhasa government facilities. The soldiers required to defend the ancient strongholds must have been called up from the population at large as well. Having an active fighting force at their disposal was essential if the citadels were to exert any credible authority over their territories.

There were only enough castles and temples to accommodate but a small cross section of the population. Most of the farmers, shepherds, and artisans of prehistoric and early historic times resided in caves, portable shelters, and rudimentary stone houses. In Ruthok, crude domiciles of the common folk were pieced together at the edge of fields and pastures well below the castles. Some of these roughly built stone shelters may have had roofs made of animal hides or woven animal hair. In the badlands of Guge, many of the ancient residents lived in shallow caves carved from the earthen escarpments. In most of the Changthang, the pastoral way of life necessitated mobility and the use of portable structures such as the yak hair tent rather than permanent housing.

I have surveyed 140 archaic era castles right across the breadth of Upper Tibet. Only four of these are located in the eastern Changthang, a territory associated with the culture, language, and dominion of Sumpa. Like references in Tibetan historical literature to its smaller administrative and military units, this archaeological evidence indicates that Sumpa was politically weaker and probably subservient to Zhang Zhung.

In the last chapter, we examined the famous Eternal Bon historical and pilgrimage text *Tisei Karchak*, which mentions eighteen Zhang Zhung kings who resided in ten different locations. The ten places noted in this nineteenth-century CE account are mostly found in far western Tibet. As we learned, some of these ancient strongholds have not been identified by name, despite there being many candidates among the ruins. Eternal Bon texts note two main Zhang Zhung capitals: Khyunglung Ngulkhar in Gar and Khyung Dzong at Lake Dangra. My surveys of these sites indicate that, while they are likely to have played a prominent role in governance, neither installation was sufficiently large to have been an undisputed capital of all of Upper Tibet. Rather, a loosely bound confederation of clans and tribes is better imagined.

In the harsh, resource-poor environment of Upper Tibet, sundry political groups may have been at loggerheads more often than not. As there seems to be no individual castle that could act as a kingdom-wide crossroads, bottleneck, or breadbasket, many centrifugal forces were probably in operation. The disbursed natural resources of Upper Tibet appear to favor the rise of disparate political blocs. This decentralized temporal power scenario fits well with the sheer number of castles discovered and the mention of ten capitals in *Tisei Karchak*.

How many of the 140 strongholds surveyed were active at any given time can only be guessed. We can surmise however that some operated contemporaneously, as individual settlements vied with one another for political and economic domination. This democratization in castle construction probably fostered a high degree of localized autonomy. In western Tibet most major agricultural villages had their very own castle, with the biggest concentrations found in Gar, Guge, and Ruthok. Seventy percent of all archaic strongholds in Upper Tibet were located in just these three major agrarian regions. Wealth generated by surplus agricultural production and trade must have been instrumental in the construction of these installations.

The predominance of fortified installations in the ancient architecture of Upper Tibet reflects the existence of a society in which martial values and warfare were prominent. It appears that communities were organized around their local fortresses. These focal points of society formed the military rudder of Zhang Zhung, endowing it with a formidable defensive posture. In the early historic period, when imperial Tibet embarked on the conquest of much of Central Asia, the viable castles of Upper Tibet must have been used as launchpads for northern and western campaigns.

The military function of Upper Tibet's ancient strongholds is illustrated in the ramparts, parapets, massive revetments, and other defensive features constructed at many sites. Protective walls are staggered in the crags or encircle castles, furnishing secure positions from which they could be defended. Unapproachable cliffs surround many summit installations, adding to their redoubtable qualities. In certain Changthang strongholds, there is no evidence of buildings, just networks of ramparts for military use.

The strategic value of ancient castles and fortresses as lines of defense is clear to see, but who was the enemy? Conflicts within Upper Tibet or from neighboring territories are both likely scenarios. Either way, the very existence of so many protected sites alludes to a shaky security environment.

The warlike nature of the highlanders, as revealed by Tibetan literature and the rock art record, indicates that internal rivalries could have played a critical role in citadel construction. Meager natural resources and a deteriorating climate may well have conspired to keep tensions simmering between respective regions. That no less than ten royal centers are mentioned in Eternal Bon histories hints at strong provincial divisions in Zhang Zhung as well. In recent centuries, internecine conflict was endemic in the Changthang, a historical carryover perhaps from earlier times.

Domestic strife aside, there is compelling literary evidence indicating that some Upper Tibetan strongholds were established to repulse foreign enemies. In chapter 4, we saw how the ethnic mosaic of Zhang Zhung was enriched by the Mu, Bru, and Hor, tribes originating in the mountainous lands north and west of the Tibetan Plateau. In Tibetan literature, invaders entering ancient Upper Tibet from the north and west are portrayed in legendary accounts of battles between the kings of Zhang Zhung and those from the countries of Takzik and Hor. These references to ancient armed struggle find expression in the plethora of ruined strongholds. While we do not know which fortresses were used in specific military campaigns, the overall picture is one of conflict on a grand scale. Tibetan literature eloquently describes this state of strife and war, which is so often set in larger-than-life circumstances.

An Eternal Bon ritual text detailing the construction of tiered tabernacles known as *lhaten* for the chief god of Zhang Zhung, Gekhö, documents one such legendary war between prehistoric Upper Tibet and a foreign nation.[14] The main characters of the story are King Trimen of Zhang Zhung and King Troto Gyalwa of Takzik (possibly tantamount to cultural Tajikistan). The text explains the historical backdrop of the *lhaten* shrine as a prelude to the account of war:

> Accordingly, [building the *lhaten*], it was practiced by Zhang Zhung King Trimen, the holder of the iron horns of the bird. He practiced this tradition of paying homage, in that the circle of Zhang Zhung gods would be his armies and defeat the Takzik king. Consequently, the stature of the Zhang Zhung king was exalted. Later, the Zhang Zhung king of Taknailha obtained this tradition from King Trimen, and he erected the *lhaten*. The people of Zhang Zhung became powerful and wealthy. They were victorious in nine types of battles, and the circle of Gekhö gods became fulfilled and happy.

The *lhaten* text maintains that King Troto Gyalwa of Takzik had ten divisions under his command. At the height of his power he attacked Zhang Zhung and made off with a woman named Trishur Odem, the wife or sister of King Trimen. The Zhang Zhung king and his subjects were harried by the Takzik army, bringing the kingdom to the brink of defeat. Unable to defeat the Takzik army militarily, King Trimen resorted to supernatural means. King Trimen and his priests prepared a barrage of magical rituals directed against Takzik, destroying their king, army, and property.

Another Eternal Bon ritual text entitled *Drawa Nakpo* narrates the story of a prehistoric Tibetan priest (*bonpo*) named Khata Drengyuk.[15] Khata Drengyuk was from a tribe known as *dud* and a practitioner of a primitive form of religion known as Dudbon, in which blood offerings played an important role. An individual from Hor (a Central Asian nation) known as Dzum Mulsampa Lakring stole the flagship black horse of the *dud* from Khata Drengyuk, setting the stage for a showdown between them. The preparation for the battle and the actual fight itself are vividly described in the text:

> The Dudbon Khata Drengyuk tied the black turban of the *dud* lineage on his head. On his body he wore the black cloak of the *dud* lineage. On his body he held the great ax of the *dud* lineage. He rode astride the dark brown horse of the *dud* lineage. On his wrathful face he applied blood and charcoal. He butchered the black sheep with white on top of its head of the *dud* and the bay-colored yak of the *dud*. He supplied provisions to his black *dud* army. He blew the whelk of the *dud* in the sky. He dispatched the chough, the bird of the *dud*, the killer of birds. He mobilized the posse of the *dud* god "Pouring Out Bloody Head." The Dudbon Khata said to the god, "Dzum Mulsampa Lakring has challenged the black *dud*. They are opposing me the *bonpo*. The enemy and thief have risen up against the *bonpo*. Send the bird of bad omens to the enemy."
>
> Having spoken these words, Pouring Out Bloody Head set out. He landed at the castle of the Hor, Dumdum. From his mouth he flung fierce thunderbolt missiles and struck the heart of the Hor Dzum Mulsampa Lakring. He consumed the root of his life force, the trophy of the *dud*. He drank his heart blood, the heroic beverage of the *dud*. The *dud* ravenously devoured his head. With his skin they made the regimental banner of the *dud*.

The oral traditions of Upper Tibet also speak of invasions from the north and west, giving ample cause for the construction of citadels. It is said that the Central Asian general Shenpa Merutse became a follower of the Tibetan epic hero King Ling Gesar. Shenpa Merutse is attributed with deeply imprinting the culture and architecture of the northwestern Tibetan district of Ruthok. A legend around a stronghold known as Nam Dzong, or "Sky Fortress," holds that the epic hero King Ling Gesar came to the Droshö region of Upper Tibet to battle a king of Takzik named Norgyi Gyalpo (King of Wealth).[16] Norgyi Gyalpo is believed to have been as ferocious as a tiger and, because the water spirits were his patrons, extremely rich. It is said that Norgyi Gyalpo and his army were routed in a surprise attack launched from Sky Fortress. Other legends speak of the ancient Hor having strongholds in the southeast periphery of Upper Tibet.[17] According to one oral tradition, the Hor king Gurser Gyalpo invaded Tibet from the northwest, and his armies lingered there until they were finally defeated in the eighth century CE by Tibet's greatest Buddhist personality, Guru Rinpoche.

Zhang Zhung's legendary struggles with foreign powers chronicled in the oral and textual traditions dovetail with the archaeological record. The widespread use of mortuary pillars in Upper Tibet, Mongolia, and southern Siberia indicates that cultural and technological currents circulated among these regions in ancient times. Widely diffused burial customs in Inner Asian cultures suggest that warfare, trade, and intellectual exchanges were once common in the ancient heart of Asia. We will return to the fascinating tale told by the mortuary pillars of Upper Tibet in the next chapter.

Cultural linkages are also attested in rock art, indicating that intercourse between the constituent parts of ancient Inner Asia was both sustained and rigorous. The vibrant depiction of animals in the Eurasian "animal style" is a predominant genre of rock art in Inner Asia. Eurasian animal-style rock art associated with Scythians of the Iron Age shares stylistic and thematic features with the petroglyphs and pictographs of Upper Tibet. The chariot and human mask rock art of Inner Asian Bronze Age cultures are also represented in Upper Tibet.[18] Small copper alloy objects of the Scythians and a Metal Age Mongolian people known as the Slab Grave culture have significant similarities with ancient Tibetan artifacts as well.

Clearly Upper Tibet was not isolated in antiquity. Tibetan texts describing tribal origins and ancient conflicts in the region, together with the archaeological record, demonstrate that it received seminal inputs from other parts of Inner Asia. As a more benign agency, these infusions helped to draw highland Tibet into a wider cultural and geographic orbit. The hard-edged flip side to this cultural interconnectivity was the use of armed conflict to enforce the will of contending nations. That military encounters between rival groups provided the justification for the establishment of a good many citadels in ancient Upper Tibet seems assured. But how often and in what contexts Upper Tibetans met foreign peoples are unanswered questions. The extent of these cosmopolitan tendencies in early highland civilization will only be gauged through further exploration.

In the 1930s, the famous Italian Tibetologist Giuseppe Tucci explored citadels in the Guge villages of Nu, Changtang, and Luk.[19] According to the oral tradition, the citadels of Nu, Luk, and Changtang are associated with that shadowy ancient tribe known as the Mon.[20] The remains of these rambling strongholds very much impressed Tucci. The great building complexes seemed out of place when compared to the small villages in which they stood. The ruins of Nu, Changtang, and Luk and those of other Guge fortresses indicate that the ancient population of the region was probably significantly larger than it has been over the last few centuries. The proliferation of defunct agricultural fields in the region also alludes to a more populous Guge in the past. A case in point is Nu with its two large castles that must have housed hundreds of people, not to mention the farmers who resided in a nearby village, now a stone-strewn tract. Today, Nu has a total population of just seventy-five souls, hardly enough to have undertaken such ambitious construction projects. At Changtang, Khartak, Sharlang Khar,[21] and many other Guge locations, ancient strongholds presided over cave settlements. It was in these troglodytic communities that the bulk of the population found refuge.

The badlands of Guge boast a variety of early castle types. They come in stone and earth and an assortment of architectural designs and ground plans. This architectural wealth set the technological precedent for the grand Buddhist installations of later times.[22] Taken together, the archaic and Lamaist era edifices of Guge are highly noteworthy for their sheer diversity.

One of the strangest types of stronghold in Guge is found at three different locations: Hala, Kharchung, and Manam.[23] Each of these sites comprises a single, highly eroded mud brick structure accommodating longitudinal rows

The earthen hulk of Hala Khar

of tiny rooms. The windowless walls and little cells of the Hala, Kharchung, and Manam hulks recall basic design features of all-stone corbelled edifices. The purpose of these installations is unknown, but use as garrisons or religious centers comes to mind.

As in Guge, civilization in Ruthok reached its zenith in the time of Zhang Zhung. Nowhere in Upper Tibet has the loss of agriculture and population been more pronounced than in Ruthok. Many of its ruined castles rise above valleys in which not a soul now stirs. Desertification plunged this northwestern region into utter obscurity. The heart of ancient Ruthok, Dzong Ri, supported a huge stronghold that local folklore attributes to the ruler Shenpa Merutse.[24] Circa 1000 CE, sizable Buddhist monasteries appeared on Dzong Ri. Today the site is completely blanketed in ruins.

Like spokes of a wheel, the Ruthok tributary valleys and basins of Recho, Ochang, Zaphuk, Derok, Khulpa, and Rabang radiate from the Dzong Ri environs.[25] In each of these locations, water was once much more plentiful, supporting a sequence of strongholds and farming villages. Many of these sites are now largely deserted, consigned to a time when northwestern Tibet was one of Zhang Zhung's principal quarters. For those coming from Central Asia and the northern Indian Subcontinent, Ruthok was the gateway to the Tibetan Plateau. Its patchwork of agricultural enclaves and fortified settlements would have been the envy of those accustomed to the vacuous deserts and steppes of Central Asia. Ultimately, this vanguard zone of Tibet shared the same environmental fate when its finely tuned settlements came undone with the diminution of the water supply.

South of Ruthok, no fewer than eight fortresses ringed the ridgetops overlooking the Gar Tsangpo River, a northern tributary of the upper Indus.[26] The lofty strongholds of Gar were stationed on summits and steep acclivities far above the Gar valley. They may have been armed sanctuaries to which local inhabitants retreated in times of duress and invasion. At the relatively low elevation of fourteen thousand feet, the wide and well-watered agrarian Gar valley has been a magnet for human settlement for millennia.

After the fall of the Guge Buddhist kingdom and the purging of the armies of Ladakh from western Tibet in the 1660s CE, the Tibetan general Ganden Tshewang, an ethnic Mongol, established his military headquarters in the Gar basin. Since that time, all the villages of Gar have been situated in the bottomlands. Nevertheless, the ruins of older villages on benches and esplanades above the valley floor reveal a different pattern of settlement. They show that earlier inhabitants preferred the high ground for their residences, as did people in virtually all parts of ancient Upper Tibet. Clearly the occupation of higher terrain would have had strategic value in a world unsettled by war and strife. Many of the farmlands attached to the elevated villages of

Gar were left fallow centuries ago. According to the local oral tradition, these derelict plots were once cultivated by that enigmatic tribe, the Mon.

In the uncluttered Changthang, castles monitored prime pastures and farming enclaves, protecting the inhabitants and their wealth from any manner of threats. The densest collection of ancient strongholds in the Changthang was established on the east shore of Dangra Yumtsho, one of the only agricultural regions on the high plains of Upper Tibet. Ombu Dzong, Gyampai Dzong, and Gyangpai Tsuk Dzong, among others, constituted a chain of lakeside installations.[27] These all-stone corbelled castles were raised on rocky outcrops towering high above sacred Lake Dangra. Similarly constructed temples and hermitages also dot the east side of Lake Dangra. Dating to Zhang Zhung times and perhaps to the early historic period as well, these indomitable centers of political prestige and cultural advancement thrust Lake Dangra into a position of great prominence.

As we have seen in chapter 4, Eternal Bon sources maintain that the last outpost of the sovereign Zhang Zhung kingdom was Khyung Dzong, the home of King Likmikya (his name is spelled in a variety of other ways as well). The ruined Khyung Dzong, the "Horned Eagle Fortress," is poised on three ivory-colored limestone mounts overlooking the inviolable waters of Lake Dangra.[28] The buildings of this storied site have been reduced to a mass of disintegrating walls and footings. Interestingly, Khyung Dzong, its identity anchored in local tradition, is among the smaller citadels of Lake Dangra. If this was indeed a capital of Zhang Zhung, it appears to have been a royal residence and not a major troop garrison. The security of the site was probably ensured by the surrounding citadels of Dangra Yumtsho. The largest of the three complexes at Dangra's Khyung Dzong comprises building foundations poised on three different levels of a limestone formation. In addition to these razed structures, there are the remains of a buttressed stairway that accessed the three tiers of buildings. Poorly preserved wall footings of what appears to have been another small building are found on the highest point of the site, a 16,100-foot-high outcrop known as "Vulture Nest Rock." The third complex at Dangra Khyung Dzong, a series of breastworks, is situated nearby on a small pass called "Horned Eagle." These breastworks were damaged in 2013 when a road was cut around the Lake Dangra shoreline.

HERMITAGES AND TEMPLES OF THE GODS

The ancient strongholds of Upper Tibet stood conspicuously on summits, but what of the less obvious residential installations? These are the hermitages and temples of archaic civilization, all-stone corbelled structures built in secret locations. Concealed in isolated hanging valleys and on steep rocky slopes at high elevation, these structures constituted the warp and weft of elite religious life in prehistoric and early historic Upper Tibet. Some of these buildings may have been used by more contemplative members of ancient society as centers of retreat.

In Tibetan parlance, the archaic era hermitages and temples are called either "house of the gods" (*sekhang*) or "castle of the gods" (*sekhar*). According to Eternal Bon tradition, the inhabitants of Zhang Zhung and Sumpa performed esoteric rituals and explored the deepest recesses of the human mind in these abodes of the deities. In league with their gods, the ancient Upper Tibetans constructed *sekhar* as an outward sign of their enviable religious understanding and spiritual attainment.

Eternal Bon texts tell us that various priests known as *shen*, *bonpo*, and *pönse* operated in the dark confines of the *sekhar*. Unlike the conventional monks of Tibetan Buddhism and Eternal Bon, these ritualists were frequently depicted as married and actively involved in day-to-day life. The *sekhar* of Zhang Zhung and Sumpa, therefore, are probably best seen as residences where a wide range of cultural and economic activities occurred, rather than as cloisters for the ordained. This is not to say that ascetics engaged in demanding spiritual practices did not control certain archaic temples and hermitages. Some all-stone corbelled edifices may have been given over to them, especially those located above 16,500 feet in elevation, a height that is impractical for ordinary living. Children and other vulnerable members of early society are likely to have gravitated toward more amenable slopes and basins at lower elevation.

A ritual text dedicated to the chief god of Zhang Zhung, Gekhö, composed by an Eternal Bon abbot named Tshultrim Gyaltsen presents the *sekhang* as the setting for esoteric practices in which the deities of the elements and the heavens were invoked.[29] This account affirms that at a secret cave palace *sekhang* in the very middle of Zhang Zhung, the Eternal Bon founder Tönpa Shenrab Miwo and the Zhang Zhung King of Existence Triwer conducted an offering ritual to win the favor of Gekhö and his entourage. In this *sekhang*, a blazing jeweled tray was piled so high with offerings that it resembled a snow mountain. Excellent foods and beverages, grains, edible sculptures, cakes, three dairy foods, and three sweets were amassed. A mountain of meats was heaped high. Libations and a blood-red beverage inspired images of an eddying lake. A golden tree, transformed nectar, medicines, and incense smoke swirling like clouds were also presented to the gods.

Many of the so-called *sekhar/sekhang* of the archaic era were built with corbels in the same fashion as the all-stone citadels. Long pieces of stone protruding from the walls were stacked in such a way that they overarch the rooms. With notable exception, stone members teetering on disintegrating walls are all that usually remain of the all-stone roofs. *Tisei Karchak* states that the Zhang Zhung sage Dzutrul Yeshe propagated the Eternal Bon doctrine to several thousand adepts at a complex of stone houses, possibly a reference to corbelled constructions. These types of structures are still referred to as *dokhang*, or "stone houses," by local people. The complex of Dzutrul Yeshe is said to have been established in Lamor, a location on the east side of Mount Pöri Ngeden. This may refer to one of the archaeological sites nestled in the Brak Tsangpo gorge near the foot of Pöri Ngeden, southeast of Mount Tise, Tibet's holiest mountain.

It is the all-stone corbelled edifices situated away from summits, sites that do not possess strategic geographic value or defensive features, that can most readily be connected to the *sekhar* of the Tibetan literary tradition. The ruined *sekhar* of Upper Tibet are perceived as the dwelling places of elemental spirits and local protector deities. The present-day herders and farmers tend to avoid them, anxious to escape the wrath of their supernatural denizens. Gods and long lost tribes are credited with their construction in the oral tradition, if anything at all is known about them. Many *sekhar*, however, have been almost entirely forgotten. Their lofty aspect isolated from regularly used paths has loosed them from the collective memory.

Tibetan texts suggest that *sekhar* and *sekhang* were established alongside mountaintop citadels. They are supposed to have existed in parallel with the military and administrative facilities of the castles. Tibetan historical texts trumpet a close relationship between the priests and kings of Zhang Zhung. This king-priest nexus seems to indicate that both royalty and their religious guardians occupied the same summit strongholds. This combining of religious and political functions is also said to characterize protohistoric Central Tibet, where the Purgyal kings constructed *sekhang* as their primary residences. Similarly, Buddhist temples were almost invariably integrated into castles of later times.

A number of historical texts speak of a series of *sekhar* established by the protohistoric rulers of Central Tibet, beginning with the second king, Mutri Tsenpo. These *sekhar* appear to have been the chief royal residences. Tibetan historical literature stresses that the kings of Zhang Zhung and Central Tibet were heavily dependent on priests for their personal well-being and for the prosperity of the kingdom. The archaic officiants, the *shen* and *bonpo*, are depicted as the prime guarantors of temporal strength. These ancient priests are supposed to have magically empowered the kings and to have conducted rituals ensuring success on the battlefield. It is written that at large convocations it was the priests who uttered the first three words.[30] Only after their benediction would the king address the gathering and commoners sing and dance.

An ancient text devoted to the architectural design of the *sekhang/sekhar* has been preserved in an Eternal Bon text attributed to its legendary founder, Shenrab Miwo.[31] Entitled *Palace of the Shen*, it explains that the *sekhar* were divided into three rows of rooms directly opening onto one another. The archaeological evidence from Upper Tibet confirms this general description, although the fine details noted in the text are in question. According to *Palace of the Shen*, each of the nine or ten rooms in a *sekhar* had a different purpose. There was a shrine in the southwest corner; storerooms for grain, firewood, and ritual objects; and spaces for sleeping, working, and meetings.

My survey work reveals that the ancient *sekhar* were indeed partitioned into two, three, or four rows of small windowless rooms with tiny doorways. On steep slopes the rows of rooms form tiered structures. These rooms must have served a variety of purposes, like those specified in *Palace of the Shen*. Rather than large contiguous complexes, the *sekhar* were usually divided into discrete units and placed at a fair distance from one another as if their residents highly valued privacy.

Illustrative of an archaic era temple construction is Menla Phobrang, a sizable *sekhar* complex at sacred Mount Tise.[32] Menla Phobrang rests on boulder-strewn slopes high above the circumambulatory trail that rings snowy

The interior of an all-stone corbelled residence. This building is unusual in that it has a relatively large central space, which may have been used for ceremonial functions. The standing stone in the rear of the structure is not an original feature.

Mount Tise. This was a well-built center with two large core buildings and more than a dozen ancillary structures. At one time Menla Phobrang must have been the preserve of dozens of residents, but it has been entirely forgotten by pilgrims who nowadays circle the holy mountain. Many of Menla Phobrang's buildings were built partly underground, as are other edifices of this architectural genre. In fact, it is not unusual to find the rear roofline of a *sekhar* flush with the slope. The placement of buildings partly underground enhanced their structural integrity and made them easier to heat. There also appear to be religious reasons for the semi-subterranean style of construction.

Large underground recesses in some *sekhar* have the appearance of sanctums, which may have been used in the propitiation of subterranean spirits. According to Tibetan literary accounts, the ancients maintained close relationships with spirits believed to dwell in the earth and water. It would seem that with the advent of Buddhism, this connection to the chthonic denizens became more uneasy, and Tibetans lost their taste for living underground. The temples constructed by the Lamaist practitioners of later times stand well aboveground.

The largest underground sanctum surveyed to date was built into a mountainside at a temple complex attached to the Gekhö Kharlung citadel in Ruthok. Here twin stone-lined chambers accessed via corbelled passageways open directly toward the sacred mountain Gekhö Nyenlung. This orientation suggests that Zhang Zhung's chief god, Gekhö, may have been worshiped from this subterranean sanctuary.

A few Upper Tibetan *sekhar* exhibit architectural features associated with Buddhist temples, or *lhakhang*, and can be dated to the early historic period. At Riu Gonpa in northern Ruthok, the site of an elaborate all-stone corbelled edifice, courtyards within the structure and ornamental doorframes and cornices constructed with small blocks are attributable to Tibetan Buddhist architecture, which first appeared in the imperial period.[33] The folklore of Riu Gonpa connects the site to an uncle of the Tibetan epic hero Ling Gesar, also suggesting that it was originally founded as a Buddhist temple. At the Zimphuk and Chilbu *sekhar* sites there are old Buddhist inscriptions and carvings, indicating that these all-stone complexes may also have been founded as Buddhist centers sometime before 1000 CE.[34]

While some *sekhar* were freestanding buildings, others were placed in or around caves. The limestone and earthen formations of upland Tibet are pockmarked with natural cave complexes. When these cave systems were located near springs and streams they made ideal choices for human settlement. With the beginnings of Upper Tibetan civilization some three thousand years ago, these caves were built up and transformed into full-blown residential centers. Rock art and inscriptions positively identify some of these troglodytic sites as religious in nature, while others may have functioned as general-purpose villages.

A view of the interior of Riu Gonpa. All architectural elements in this photograph are made of stone.

The cave of Gyam Phuk, which is believed to have functioned as a Zhang Zhung temple. Its facade was rebuilt about twenty years ago.

Masonry facades barricading the mouth of caves afforded residents adequate protection from the weather. At larger caves these facades could be of monumental proportions. Massive ten-foot-tall walls enclosed Garsöl Drakphuk, a cathedral-like grotto with archaic pictographs in the Changthang region of Shentsa. Gyamchung Phuk, a gigantic mountaintop cavern in Gar, is another sanctuary with a big masonry front more than seven feet thick and sixty-five feet in length.[35] Either as habitations or for ritual purposes, these large caves must have once hosted sizable congregations of people.

At some archaic religious centers, anterooms were built around the mouth of caves. These outer structures ranged from single rooms to multi-roomed all-stone corbelled complexes. At Dzong Karpo in Gertse, ruins of all-stone buildings litter the foot of a bright white limestone mount.[36] Tiny rooms throng the caves of Dzong Karpo, the "White Fortress," telling of an outstanding installation long since abandoned. The many anterooms appear to be where the residents of Dzong Karpo lived, the caves behind them being where they worshipped.

Extensive cave systems modified for early human occupation mark many Lake Nam Tsho rock formations. Sites such as Bird Headland, Excellent Horse Goose Headland, and Good Luck Headland are rich in caves. The long peninsula on the southeast side of Nam Tsho, Upper Tibet's largest lake, known to the *drokpas* as Good Luck Headland and as "Sky Lake Headland" in Eternal Bon literature, was an important assembly point for the masters of yore. Among the most famous personalities supposed to have resided here was Tonggyung Thuchen, a sage of the eighth century CE credited with translating many Zhang Zhung–language scriptures into Tibetan. Eternal Bon scriptures avow that Tonggyung Thuchen was working against time. Buddhism was washing over Tibet, and he is thought to have had a limited window of opportunity in which to preserve the ancient teachings from the rising tide of the new religion.

The highly eroded earthen formations of the Guge badlands boast a veritable treasure trove of caves. These many thousands of caves were used as residences, storerooms, ritual spaces, and artisanal workshops. At many sites, large networks of caves are interconnected by way of tunnels, ledges, and galleries. In certain locations there are clusters of grottos forming subterranean labyrinths. In the well-known village of Khyunglung, there are several hundred caves alone, but that pales in comparison to Guge Piwang where around three thousand caves are burrowed into a single formation.[37]

As in the Changthang, some of the caves of Guge were enclosed by stone walls. These troglodytic centers were probably inhabited by the full spectrum of Zhang Zhung society, those fully dedicated to religious purposes a special subset among them. A small fraction of the Guge caves occupied in prehistoric times were redeveloped for Buddhist occupation during and after the establishment of the Guge-Purang kingdom in the tenth century CE. Scores of sacred grottos chosen for use as chapels were beautifully enrobed in Buddhist murals, the region's best-known artistic legacy.

The *sekhar* of the archaic era were geographically removed from the nodes of agricultural and pastoral production. They were home to an elite corps of those who could command the labor and produce of others. Given the moral authority believed to have been invested in the sages of Zhang Zhung, this is not surprising. They are regularly depicted in Tibetan literature as enjoying the finest privileges ancient society had to offer.

The exclusive aura enveloping the *sekhar* is particularly pronounced on the island settlements of Upper Tibet's great lakes. Considerable planning and manpower were required to supply these insular communities. The islands of Upper Tibet are small and rocky and could not possibly have produced more than a tiny fraction of the food and other vital provisions required by residents. Others must have been assigned with the tasks of production and transport. Traveling by boat in summer or over frozen lake surfaces in the wintertime, food, household items, ritual materials, and other supplies had to be ferried to the islands.

So far, I have identified fifteen insular settlements, though a drop in water levels over the centuries has turned some of these islands into headlands. Temples and residences grace the islands of Nam Tsho, Teri Nam Tsho, Darok Tsho, Nangla Ring Tsho, La Ngak Tsho, and several other lakes. Taken together, these ritual epicenters constituted a sacred axis running across the breadth of Upper Tibet.

On the island of Semo Do amid the abysmally deep blue waters of Nam Tsho, virtually every cave with a southern exposure was developed for habitation.[38] In the archaic era, sizable stone buildings grew around these caves, the residences of dozens or perhaps hundreds of people. Semo Do hosted one of the greatest prehistoric residential concentrations in what was once Sumpa territory. Later, when individual Buddhist saints ventured onto Semo Do, they used stones from the older structures to build their humble cave shelters.

In the facade of a Semo Do cave associated with the eleventh- and twelfth-century CE Buddhist saint Galo Lotsawa, a round of indigenous scrub juniper came from a tree that radiocarbon dating shows died sometime between 780 and 900 CE. Galo Lotsawa spent several years at Lake Nam Tsho. If indeed it was this saint who built the Semo Do cave retreat that bears his name, he used a piece of wood that was already 225 to 400 years old. Perhaps the dated rafter (approximately four inches in diameter) was taken from an older structure, but it is also possible that the cave facade was constructed at an earlier date. If this round of wood was used in the construction of the facade shortly after it was cut down, it would indicate that the lesser residences associated with Buddhist masters were established as early as the imperial period. This is in line with Buddhist texts that claim their saints such as Guru Rinpoche were reaching Nam Tsho and Semo Do by the late eighth century CE.

While the commodious prehistoric buildings of Semo Do have been almost entirely effaced, the islands of Lake Darok Tsho and Lake Teri Nam Tsho still shelter relatively well-preserved all-stone corbelled residences and temples. Buddhist settlers took a keen interest in Semo Do, and this is likely a key factor in the island's complete makeover. The insular centers of Darok Tsho and Teri Nam Tsho supported some of the finest ancient residences anywhere at the great lakes of the Changthang.[39] These island installations boast dramatic views of the water and surrounding countryside. Looking abroad from the ancient structures, it is as if they are totally engulfed by water, flawless gems ornamenting aqueous garments of epic proportions. The islands were unquestionably extremely high-value real estate, a venue for the machinations and magic that kept Zhang Zhung and Sumpa alive for centuries.

The Tibetan textual and oral traditions refer to the islands of Upper Tibet as the omphali of the sacred lakes, places of geomantic perfection and absolute sanctity. As mentioned in chapter 3, the lakes themselves are perceived by the *drokpas* as the abodes of magnificent lake goddesses. It appears that these very same fertility and protective figures were held responsible for the well-being of the ancient insular communities. The existence of derelict shrines on many of the Upper Tibetan islands seems to confirm the essential role played by these lake goddesses.

Save for brief periods of habitation by isolated mediators, the islands of Upper Tibet were not the object of subsequent occupation by Lamaist settlers. The increasing salinity of the waters and a drying climate, together with an ideological shift away from nature-dwelling spirits to more abstract forms of religion, partly account for the dereliction of the island centers. Economic and political factors also figure into their abandonment. With the fall of archaic civilization, the material and logistical wherewithal to support these high-maintenance communities fell by the wayside. Like so many other ancient sites of upland Tibet, not a soul lives permanently on the islands anymore.

In the next chapter we shall explore the final resting places of the inhabitants of Zhang Zhung and Sumpa, another key to unlocking the seal of early civilization in Upper Tibet.

• 6 •

Penetrating the Earth:
The Burial Grounds of Zhang Zhung

TERRITORY MARKED IN STANDING STONES

The architectural counterpoint to the dwelling spaces of the living is the burial places of the dead. To mark the passage of death and to dispose of mortal remains, a panoply of mausoleums, crypts, reliquaries, and pillars were raised in archaic era Upper Tibet. These tombs and funerary ritual structures match in size and complexity the ancient castles and temples of the region.

The geographic compass of Upper Tibet's first civilization can be circumscribed by plotting the distribution of its monuments and art. Specific types of structures and aesthetic forms spread across the highlands, but not to lower-lying areas of the Plateau. These special archaeological assets document the existence of a civilization squarely based in the Tibetan upland.

Among the most eye catching of the ancient funerary monuments of highland Tibet are standing stones, somber-looking monoliths erected in sundry configurations. These miniature menhirs, or pillars, watch over ancient cemeteries like soldiers keeping vigil. They rise up in desolate places where only tombs and the corpses they contain are present. These mute stone sentries are conspicuous reminders of a people who viewed death very differently than the Lamaist practitioners of later times with their doctrine of reincarnation. For the inhabitants of pre-Buddhist Upper Tibet, death was the threshold to a parallel existence of alter egos. Counterpoised by the world of the living, the world of the dead was the realm of the divine ancestors. The ritual activities carried out at the menhirs served to bridge these two existential spheres.

There are two common types of pillar monuments in Upper Tibet: pillars erected inside masonry enclosures and pillars standing in rows next to mortuary buildings.[1] These signature pillars, as part of a peculiar suite of archaeological monuments showcasing upland civilization, set it apart from India, Central Asia, and other parts of the Tibetan Plateau. The walled-in pillars and arrays of pillars appended to temple-tombs define a distinctive cultural territory unified through commonly held funerary customs and beliefs. This geographical expanse can be associated with Zhang Zhung of the Tibetan literary tradition.

According to a much-cited but highly exaggerated Eternal Bon geographic notion, Zhang Zhung was divided into outer, middle, and inner divisions, constituting a colossal chunk of Central Asia. The actual territorial extent of Zhang Zhung ascertained through the distribution of its signature pillar monuments was roughly one-ninth of this popular ascription. In Eternal Bon literature, the outer division of Zhang Zhung was itself subdivided into three parts, known as *go*, *bar*, and *phuk*. The *go* subdivision was again cut into three pieces, each of which contains one of the three major mountain-lake dyads circumscribing Upper Tibet. Inner *go* corresponds with Mount Tise and Lake Mapang, middle *go* with Mount Targo and Lake Dangra, and outer *go* with Mount Nyenchen Thanglha and Lake Nam Tsho.

The walled-in pillars and temple-tombs with arrays of pillars appeared in Upper Tibet from the eastern district of Namru to Guge in the west. These signature pillar monuments are not found in the Changthang east of the 90th meridian. The pillars are telltale territorial markers because they are located in every major area within their overall range, signaling the existence of a unique culture that flourished in the Tibet upland for centuries. The delineation of Zhang Zhung by its distinctive pillar monuments is buttressed by another defining architectural feature: quadrate funerary enclosures. These prevalent ritual and burial structures are also distributed in Upper Tibet west of 90° east longitude.

Although a few mortuary pillars grace the famous burial ground of Lebri in Central Tibet,[2] they accompany a very different suite of archaeological structures indicative of a cultural makeup foreign to that of Zhang Zhung. There are also several sites in the eastern Changthang with isolated pillars, but nowhere with the arrays of standing stones found further west. Much simpler upright stones as well as different kinds of quadrate mounds define the mortuary monuments of Upper Tibet's eastern margin. These stark differences in the assemblages of burial monuments on either side of the 90th meridian herald a cultural watershed of sorts.

Tibetan historical texts make an allowance for the geographically ordained differences that distinguish the funerary monuments of Upper Tibet. This literature records the existence of two major ancient cultures, languages, and nations in the highlands: Zhang Zhung and Sumpa. The eastern Changthang is identified with Sumpa, a smaller dominion lying east of Zhang Zhung. Tibetan texts suggest that for much of its history Sumpa was under Zhang Zhung political influence if not outright domination. As we have seen, Zhang Zhung was administratively divided into "divisions of ten thousand," while Sumpa was partitioned into "divisions of one thousand." Curiously, the lesser stature ascribed to Sumpa in Tibetan literature appears to be reflected in the archaeological record, with far fewer ancient monuments detected in the eastern Changthang than in areas to the west.

Despite there being substantial archaeological differences between regions that seem to correspond to the Zhang Zhung and Sumpa of Tibetan literature, many cultural links joined them together. This makes it permissible to speak of an Upper Tibetan civilization under which both were subsumed. The Tibetan literary tradition tells us that Zhang Zhung and Sumpa shared an archaic culture and religion, which it calls *bon*. More specifically, ancient temple and cave sites throughout Upper Tibet exhibit a similar set of morphological and situational traits. While all-stone corbelled structures have not been positively identified in the eastern Changthang, there is structural evidence suggesting that they may have been built there also. Moreover, ancient pictographs sprinkled along the shores of Lake Nam Tsho, in what appears to have been Sumpa territory, bear strong similarities to rock art in western Tibet. The hunting techniques, ritual traditions, costumes, armaments, and symbolism depicted in Nam Tsho art are represented across the entire Tibetan upland. These motifs and icons chronicle commonly held cultural traditions.

The size of ancient Sumpa has not been established, but it seems to have been centered in what is now the eastern half of Nakchu prefecture. Based on the archaeological record, only the western border of Sumpa in the vicinity of the 90th meridian can be drawn with any degree of confidence. Far to the east, an important geographic divide appears to have been Sumpa Langgi Gyimshö, a region known nowadays as Tengchen. Eternal Bon histories state that Sumpa Langgi Gyimshö was the political border of Zhang Zhung. As Sumpa may have been a vassal state of Zhang Zhung, it is possible that her territory extended as far east as Tengchen. This eastern demarcation of ancient states seems to make sense geographically, as Tengchen straddles the boundary between the parallel alpine mountain ranges and valleys of Kham in eastern Tibet and the northern highlands of Nakchu. If we take Sumpa to have extended as far as Tengchen, then together with Zhang Zhung it covered an area upwards of 350,000 square miles, stretching across the western half of the Tibetan Plateau for more than a thousand miles.

Archaeological sites with pillars and pictographs have not been reported in regions east of Lake Nam Tsho. A three-hundred-mile-wide swath of the far eastern Changthang and a network of lower valley systems lie between Nam Tsho and Tengchen. The rather scant archaeological evidence suggests that this area may have possessed a different cultural configuration than the bulk of the Changthang. It is possible that the western periphery of Sumpa was more strongly influenced by the funerary traditions of adjacent Zhang Zhung than regions further east.

The Sumpa of Tibetan sources is related to the Su-p'i of Chinese texts written during the Sui (581–618 CE) and Tang (618–907 CE) dynasties, a people of Ch'iang origins who still occupy the Sino-Tibetan marches. As explicated by the French polyglot Paul Pelliot, Chinese accounts indicate that Sumpa was centered in the northeast of the Tibetan Plateau, well east of Tengchen.[3] Sui dynastic sources as studied by scholars such as Jennifer W. Jay and R. A. Stein mention both an eastern and western kingdom of women associated with the Su-p'i.[4] In these kingdoms, women held dominant social and political roles, and there was a matrilineal royal succession. Men had no major political responsibilities and were primarily engaged in war and agriculture. It is not clear how the two kingdoms of women recorded by the Chinese correspond with the Sumpa of Tibetan literature. That there is a connection between them seems certain, but historical details are woefully lacking.

Perhaps the western kingdom of women corresponds with the archaeological culture (defined through its material remains) of the eastern Changthang. Be that as it may, the existence of a matriarchy in the eastern Changthang is encapsulated in the folklore of the region. Herders believe that this area was once ruled by a female warrior and huntress of great power named Atak Lumo.[5] According to their legends, Atak Lumo magically manifested in the middle of Lake Nam Tsho as a beautiful maiden dressed in rainbows. Initially she was the shepherdess of Dud Lutsen, the demonic monarch of the region. When first encountering the Tibetan epic hero Ling Gesar, she threatened him with her bow and arrows. After a long military campaign, Ling Gesar finally won the friendship of Atak Lumo, and she was appointed to rule over the eastern Changthang. An ancient pillar site called Palmo's Weaving Stakes is said to have been part of her back-strap loom.[6] A number of topographic features in the Changthang are also associated with Atak Lumo.

According to Eternal Bon texts, Sumpa possessed its own language, *bon* priests, and ruling dynasty. The main tribe of Sumpa was called Tong, and its protective divinity was Female Yak Hybrid Long Horns of Iron. The Tibetan text *Fully Illuminated View of the Paternal Tribes* relates that the Tong tribe descended from the heavens and was divided into four noble clans and eight clans of commoners.[7] It is written that the tribal emblem of Sumpa was a white mountain of silver.[8] As noted in chapter 4, the capital of Sumpa may have been situated near Namra, a sacred mountain in the eastern Changthang. According to oral tradition, an area in the shadow of Namra known as Rigö was the nucleus of early settlement in this locality.[9] A number of ancient cliff shelters are located there.

Archaeological and textual data both agree that the southeast border of the Zhang Zhung cultural sphere should be fixed south of the Transhimalayan range around the 85th meridian. The walled-in pillars and temple-tombs with arrays of pillars extend down the Brahmaputra River valley to just beyond this point. The eastern limits of these pillar monuments constitute clear-cut archaeological evidence of an ancient cultural demarcation, which is supported by the literary record. According to the fourteenth-century CE Eternal Bon historical text *Khrowo Wangchen*, written by Kyabtön Rinchen Özer, a region known as Tsang Kharak formed the boundary of Zhang Zhung and the Purgyal state of Central Tibet.[10] Tsang Kharak is centered around the mountain Tsanglha Phudar, the abode of a celebrated Central Tibetan royal divinity. Mount Tsanglha Phudar divides the Brahmaputra and Rakha Tsangpo drainage basins, twenty-five miles southwest of the town of Sangsang. The typical pillar monuments associated with Zhang Zhung begin just thirty-five miles northwest of Tsanglha Phudar, verifying that its southeastern frontier as delineated in *Khrowo Wangchen* is based on firm cultural intelligence.

The walled-in pillars and temple-tombs with arrays of pillars extend four hundred miles north and west from the environs of Mount Tsanglha Phudar to the western fringes of Upper Tibet. However, they do not occur in the badlands of Guge or the Purang valley of far western Tibet, indicating that these regions were subject to somewhat different funerary traditions than the tablelands of the Changthang and the headwaters region of southwestern Tibet. Lower-elevation Guge and Purang are marked by much narrower and deeper valleys. Their dissimilar geographic complexion may help to account for differences discernible in the archaeological record. Nonetheless, Guge and Purang do have various lone pillars, and all-stone corbelled architecture and rock art of the highland genre are found in Guge. These archaeological features as well as Tibetan texts tie Guge and Purang to the Zhang Zhung cultural world. According to Eternal Bon's foremost scholar, Lopön Tenzin Namdak, Guge may have been part of Khayuk, a region that was culturally or administratively differentiated from the rest of Zhang Zhung in relatively minor ways.[11]

The signature pillar types of Zhang Zhung are not distributed in Ladakh, Baltistan, or other Himalayan districts lying to the west of Upper Tibet.[12] The ethnic and cultural composition of these regions differed significantly from that of Upper Tibet. Whether they ever came under the political sway of Zhang Zhung as Eternal Bon tradition maintains remains to be determined. Although the early archaeology and ethnohistory of the western fringe of the Tibetan Plateau is still obscure, we know that Ladakh and Baltistan were impacted by prehistoric waves of Indo-European migrants. Likewise, in historic times the western rim of the Plateau was more open to Indian, Persian, and Turkic influences than Upper Tibet.

CITIES OF THE DEAD

The walled-in pillars and temple-tombs with arrays of pillars that define Zhang Zhung territory are a strange sight to behold. These upright stones loom over the grounds of the dead like gatekeepers to the other world. They stand on waterless, open terrain as magical beacons commanding the widest of panoramas. All around them lie tombs. These are the cities of the dead.

The character and complexity of the two hallmark monument types have taken the scholarly community by surprise, for virtually nothing was known about them before I undertook to survey highland Tibet. I have tallied around one hundred sites with walled-in pillars ensconced in the plains and valleys of the region. They are not easily found, engulfed as they are in the immensity of the landscape. How many more remain to be discovered can only be surmised; surely some must have escaped detection. The arrays of pillars appended to temple-tombs also proved highly elusive. In 2005, quite by accident, I came upon the twenty-ninth of these sites at Drarong in Drongpa.[13] I had previously surveyed a hilltop citadel in the vicinity and had not expected to find anything else. The barely noticeable traces of the Drarong necropolis lie in a plain at the foot of the ruined castle.

According to a widespread Upper Tibetan myth, the walled-in pillars miraculously sprung up with primordial existence. Referred to as *sridpa chakpai doring*, the pillars are thought to have emerged with the heavenly bodies and living beings of the universe. This folk belief clearly reflects the antiquity of the monument. It is also popular to associate the walled-in pillars with that mysterious ancient tribe, the Mon. Another myth pronounces the pillars hitching posts used by the Tibetan epic hero Ling Gesar to secure his magical horse, Ta Kyangwo. Of all the local tales connected to the walled-in pillars, the most plausible one simply states that they were built as commemoratives for ancient luminaries who had passed away. Local Tibetans believe that the gods invested these pillars with special powers. Their protean qualities are seen as beneficial but potentially destructive as well. Thus the walled-in pillars are assiduously avoided by farmers and herders unless they are specially visiting to supplicate the divinities with butter and incense.

Several dozen walled-in pillars at Rokhung

A quintessential example of walled-in pillars with many satellite graves is found at a place aptly called Rokhung, or "Tombs."[14] Located in Gertse, this site is elevated above the sea-green waters of Tong Tsho, an important regional lake. Here, smack in the middle of a barren valley, the ancients chose to raise long stones and bury their dead. Different types and colors of rocks were carefully selected to build Rokhung. The effort and skill that went into its construction highlight the importance of such funerary sites to the inhabitants of Zhang Zhung.

Two masonry enclosures were constructed of parallel courses of stones at Rokhung. One of these enclosures is square and boasts approximately fifty menhirs planted inside. The second enclosure is rectangular and has a row of four standing stones closely paralleling the west wall. However, at many sites there is just one menhir erected inside a stone enclosure. The pillars of Rokhung are securely fixed in the ground and rise one foot to three feet above the surface. These unhewn pillars are tabular, four sided, and irregularly shaped. At other sites, such as Gyateng Bur in upper Purang[15] and Namalung in Tshakha,[16] much more massive menhirs reach eight feet in height.

To ensure that the interior of the Rokhung enclosures was level, one or more of the perimeter walls was elevated above adjoining slopes. Parallel courses of smaller stones embedded into the ground were used to build the walls of the two enclosures. These structures measure thirty-three feet by thirty-three feet and thirty feet by twenty feet. The masonry enclosures housing other Upper Tibetan pillars are up to 5,400 square feet, with two of the largest located at the Palmo Doring site in Naktshang.[17] Some enclosures have curious design variations. In certain examples there is an opening in the east wall of the enclosure, a kind of ritual portal. At other sites, slabs of stone and small cobbles were embedded in the ground in parallel rows to create linear patterns.

There are four quadrate tumuli in close proximity to the standing stones of Rokhung. These are either tombs or venues for the performance of mortuary rituals. A little further to the west is a row of thirteen square masonry structures that was also built for funerary purposes. Interestingly, the number thirteen figures in many ancient cultural and religious traditions of Tibet. While this particular set of matching structures is unique in form, tombs and other types of funerary structures are commonly situated in close proximity to the walled-in pillars.

The regular association of walled-in pillars with tombs confirms that they were erected with death and burial in mind. The pillar monuments do not appear to contain human remains. Rather, they were used for ritual purposes, the details of which are still obscure. Perhaps the stone pens enclosing the pillars contain sacrificial animal bones, metal tools, ceramic vessels, or ashes from sacrificial fires, as is found in funerary ritual structures throughout Inner Asia.

By virtue of their conspicuous presence, the walled-in pillars seem to announce the locations of cemeteries in an act of veneration and remembrance. Eternal Bon texts mention objects called *tho* that were erected to celebrate the passing of a soul to the afterlife. Minor stone constructions of various kinds, *tho* may be represented among the menhirs of Upper Tibet. In fact, in the oral tradition, the pillars are sometimes called the "*tho* of the Mon."

Lone stelae in the Lamaist era were erected at the cornerstone of buildings to mark territory and pacify the earth spirits. We might also surmise that the walled-in pillars were put up to suppress the demons of death. In archaic funerary traditions, infernal beings are portrayed as routinely haunting the deceased. They attempt to keep the dead in their hellish thrall, preventing them from reaching the ancestral afterlife. The walled-in pillars may have had a regulatory function, acting as conduits to the celestial otherworld for the souls of the dead. Archaic death rituals enshrined in Eternal Bon texts speak of pillars called "long stones," or *doring*, which functioned as secure receptacles for the souls of the deceased. With a soul safely harbored in the long stones, pacification rites could be carried out. After the soul was ritually stabilized, it was freed from the long stones and commended to the heavens.

While Rokhung is somewhat of an exception, most walled-in pillars have wide eastern vistas. Sweeping views in this direction can extend for dozens of miles. This orientation hints at a solar dimension, whereby the rising sun was an integral part of the religious symbolism associated with the pillars. It may be that regeneration of the dead in the afterlife was recapitulated in the rising of the sun. The affinity of the walled-in pillars to the sun and perhaps other heavenly bodies is underscored by the alignment of the enclosures in the cardinal and intermediate directions. This orientation in the compass points suggests that the sun's movement was carefully tracked from the monuments during mortuary operations.

While none of the walled-in pillar sites have been directly dated, a mausoleum abutting a similarly constructed enclosure at Khyinak Rong has been fixed to the fourth or fifth century CE.[18] This suggests the time frame in which at least some of the walled-in pillars of ancient Upper Tibet are to be placed, conferring a Zhang Zhung chronology upon them. Others are liable to be much older, dating to the Iron Age and the early phase of civilization in Upper Tibet. It is not likely that they were still being constructed in the historic era. After 650 CE, some menhirs were selected for the carving of swastikas and shrines called *chorten*. These *chorten* mark the introduction of the Lamaist religions in Upper Tibet. They appear to have been etched on the pillars in order to bring them within the ambit of the new religious order springing up all over the Plateau.

Less common, but even more mystifying than the walled-in pillars, are the temple-tombs with arrays of pillars. In barren and isolated locations, masses of pillars and other stone constructions earmark the cities of the dead. These impressive necropolises of Zhang Zhung feature neatly ordered rows of standing stones extending from the east side of a prominent windowless building. Nowhere else in Inner Asia did such large numbers of menhirs appear at a single site.

Like a phalanx of soldiers on the battlefield, the lines of standing stones form compact units deployed across level ground. At their head is a temple-tomb, an imposing structure that must have been the final resting place of members of Zhang Zhung's high society. These all-stone mausoleums were the venue for elaborate mortuary rites and ceremonial observances, the character of which is still obscure. The superbly constructed temple-tombs are a fine tribute to the manual skills of the ancient Upper Tibetans. Like the arrays of pillars, these edifices are aligned in either the cardinal or intermediate directions, suggesting that they may have been used for astrological and/or astronomical readings.

An oral tradition circulating widely in Upper Tibet attributes the pillars appended to temple-tombs and many other archaic era funerary sites to the Mon. The enigmatic Mon tribe is thus credited with much more than merely the construction of temples and castles in the Tibetan upland west of the 90th meridian. This important component of the Zhang Zhung ethnos appears to have been particularly industrious.

The pillars appended to temple-tombs vary greatly in size and complexity. The most modest examples consist of several rows of miniature menhirs erected adjacent to a temple-tomb measuring ten to fifteen feet across. On the other hand, some of the necropolises are far more ambitious in scale. Among the most prominent are those at Kangchen Doring, Khangmar Dzashak, and Shasha Palkhang.[19] These once spectacular monuments now lie in shambles.

The largest pillar arrays and temple-tombs in all of Upper Tibet are located at Yul Khambu in the Rishi region of Drongpa.[20] This fabulous Zhang Zhung site boasts fields of pillars and mammoth stone hulks, ranking it among Inner Asia's greatest archaeological wonders. Nevertheless, Yul Khambu is so forgotten that the few *drokpas* living nearby mistakenly believe it to be the ruins of an old Buddhist monastery and nunnery. It was not until my 1999 expedition that this site was surveyed for the first time.

Situated sixteen thousand feet above sea level, Yul Khambu is suspended above Lake Ratshang Tsho, a circular expanse of jade-green water. The completely abandoned site is overgrown with alpine brush, but this can hardly dampen its magnificence. In addition to six giant complexes of pillars and buildings, Yul Khambu vaunts a sprawling group of outlying tombs. The site was plundered long ago, and none of its main burials have survived intact. In total, there were approximately ten thousand menhirs at Yul Khambu, ranging from eight inches to over three feet in height. Astoundingly, some six thousand of these colorful stones remain standing.

The largest of Yul Khambu's six complexes, coined the "Lower North," has a concourse of four thousand standing stones covering an area of 250 feet (east–west) by 90 feet (north–south). Most of these uncut pillars are tabular, with the thin sides oriented east and west and the broad sides facing north and south. To the east of the standing stones, many of which are tilted at radical angles, there is an adjoining concourse of slab walls running parallel to one another. Long rock slabs were laid in the ground edgewise to produce an intricate grid pattern. The temple-tomb of the Lower North complex is L-shaped and measures 180 feet (north–south) by 65 feet (east–west), a large structure by Zhang Zhung standards. The other five complexes of Yul Khambu are just as formidable, with the temple-tomb of the "Central North" complex being even longer.

The tall temple-tomb of the "Tower" complex of Yul Khambu is the best preserved funerary edifice at the site, its walls still reaching sixteen feet in height. Given that the outer walls are a full seven feet in thickness, this building may originally have been substantially taller. The walls of the Tower complex were meticulously constructed of coursed sandstone blocks with intervening layers of thin bond stones. Clearly, this structure was built to withstand the ages and elements. Although the veneer covering the bare stone walls has not survived, we can surmise that they were once encased in clay plaster, as was common with ancient residential structures. This plaster may

The "Tower" complex at Yul Khambu

have been painted with brightly colored mineral pigments, like the Lamaist reliquary shrines of a later period.

The bulky walls of the Tower complex edifice enclose highly insulated aboveground tombs. In addition to the thick outer walls, there are inner walls of finer masonry that add at least three feet to the bulk of the temple-tomb. The open center of the structure is bisected by a hefty partition wall into two halves (the larger temple-tombs of Yul Khambu were subdivided into four or more sections). The relatively small size of these internal chambers and the absence of windows and doorways demonstrate that they were used for ceremonial purposes and not habitation. Moreover, the inhabitants of Zhang Zhung were not inclined to construct their residences on open slopes where defense would be problematic. There are no signs of roofs in any of the temple-tombs of Yul Khambu, but they were probably of an all-stone corbelled composition, a characteristic form of construction in ancient Upper Tibet. The stone fabric of the walls and small interior spaces strongly hint at this style of architecture.

Only the highest of Zhang Zhung society would have been chosen for burial in the Yul Khambu mausoleums. Among those possibly selected for this honor were its chieftains and head priests (and their families). The aboveground aspect of the Yul Khambu necropolis facilitated the performance of highly elaborate mortuary rites and commemorative observances. Pieces of red sandstone and milky quartz strewn around the area may be the remnants of some of the site's ritual constituents. Unfortunately, Tibetan texts detailing the existence of Upper Tibet's necropolises have not surfaced. At this juncture, we can only conjecture about how they might have been conceived and used.

The sheer scale of Yul Khambu and other grand necropolises of Zhang Zhung indicate that they were built and maintained by large, highly organized groups of people. According to an Upper Tibetan oral tradition, each pillar of an array represented one soldier belonging to an ancient army. This folklore stresses the collective aspect of the monuments, perhaps as assembly points where Zhang Zhung celebrated its stricken military heroes. The joining of the arrays of standing stones depicting ordinary soldiers to the temple-tombs of the most revered may have typified the inclusive or communal nature of Zhang Zhung, a society welded together into the most disciplined of fighting forces by tribal convention in life and in death.

The preeminence of Yul Khambu is accented by the fact that I have not documented any ancient castles or hermitages in the area. As a memorial to the dead, Yul Khambu was deliberately placed away from major residential centers. Invasions and other destabilizing forces notwithstanding, we might expect that installations like Yul Khambu were used by many successive generations of chieftains and priests, those involved in funerary rituals perceived of as indispensable to the ancient way of life.

As noted in chapter 5, chronometric data obtained from the Khangmar Dzashak site indicate that burials associated with the arrays of pillars appended to temple-tombs appeared some fourteen hundred years before the birth of the Tibetan empire in the seventh century CE. This antiquity in itself may suggest that these necropolises were used and maintained by the inhabitants of Upper Tibet for many centuries. Despite evidence for trade with neighbors, geographic isolation appears to have aided in the preservation of distinctive social and cultural traditions over a long period of time. The merciless high-elevation environment kept the bringers of alien cultures at bay and discouraged the adoption of foreign practices, at least of a kind that would leave a permanent mark on the landscape.

It is not likely that the temple-tombs and concourses of pillars, overt symbols of Zhang Zhung cultural glory, were built after the annexation of

One of the arrays of pillars at Khangmar Dzashak

the region by the Tibetan empire. With the demise of Upper Tibetan central authority, the political security and high degree of social organization required to properly maintain the necropolises probably ebbed away. Their usage as a cultural relic, however, may have continued until the collapse of the Tibetan empire in the middle of the ninth century CE. The death knell for any vestigial cultural activities carried out at the necropolises was the emergence of Buddhism as the dominant religion in Upper Tibet between 950 and 1200 CE.

The use of standing stones at Upper Tibetan burial sites is a cultural trait shared by various Eurasian peoples in the first millennium BCE and first millennium CE.[21] Various configurations of standing stones are found at funerary sites in Kashmir, Mongolia, southern Siberia, Central Asia, and regions farther west. The raising of menhirs in Upper Tibet can therefore be viewed in the light of technological and cultural innovations that diffused across Inner Asia and beyond, irreversibly transforming the physical profile of civilizations.

Although many ancient peoples erected stones, by no means were they all created equal. Rather, disparate belief systems and behavioral patterns are incumbent in their use. The standing stones of Inner Asia were raised in conjunction with varying sets of burial monuments, environmental niches, ideological compulsions, and political imperatives. While drawing from the same overarching technologies and abstractions, the menhirs of Inner Asian cultures differ significantly in size and form. These morphological differences are indicative of important cultural and economic distinctions.

The Upper Tibetans had their own distinct style, preferring small menhirs erected in neat grids beside slab walls, tombs, and other funerary structures. The ancient cultures of the steppes, be it the pre-Scythians (1200–800 BCE), Scythians (800–300 BCE), Tashtyk people (0–500 CE), or Turks (450–700 CE), also developed their own architectural canons, raising stones in patterns that reflected their respective cultural realities.

The precedent for the raising of stones in the steppes can be traced to the Okunev culture of Bronze Age Siberia, circa 1500 BCE, and not well studied Bronze Age peoples of Mongolia. Later, the pre-Scythians and Scythians of Mongolia and the Altai set up lavishly carved pillars known as deer stones.[22] These were placed beside circular funerary structures called *khirigsuurs* and quadrate stone mounds, or the so-called *kurgans*. The Scythic pillars tend to be larger and are arrayed very differently than the Upper Tibetan examples, but they too mark the locations of cemeteries.

The Tashtyk culture of southern Siberia favored multiple uncarved standing stones in conjunction with timber-frame tombs. These pillars were sited at the foot of mountains and were often generally oriented with the two wider sides facing north and south, as were their Upper Tibetan counterparts.

The Turks for their part put up rows of menhirs appended to low-lying funerary enclosures. These funerary structures share many design and construction features in common with the pillars appended to temple-tombs of Upper Tibet. Like the Upper Tibetans, the Turks erected smallish stone slabs in long parallel rows, with the two broad sides of each pillar oriented north and south. On the west side of the networks of pillars, the Turks constructed rudimentary quadrate funerary structures, recalling the relative placement of the Zhang Zhung temple-tombs.

The Turks and Upper Tibetans were part of the same Inner Asian pancultural sphere, a world known for pillars and slab-wall monuments since the Bronze Age. A shared ideological and technological patrimony is likely to have informed the funerary customs of these two peoples. The ancient Turk homeland bordered on Upper Tibet, and common structural features in mortuary monuments are readily understandable in historical terms. In the fifth and sixth centuries CE, exchanges such as trade were probably taking place between these neighbors. As we know from historical accounts, in the seventh and eighth centuries CE, Turk and imperial Tibetan armies vied for control of eastern Central Asia. Turk soldiers defeated in battle sometimes joined victorious Tibetan armies in their ongoing military campaigns, providing ample scope for cross-cultural interaction. In fact, a Tibetan manuscript discovered in the Dunhuang grottos records that the Tibetans and the Turks kept the same kinds of funerary horses.[23] Referred to as *doma*, these horses were used to ritually transport the dead to the afterlife.

In addition to the temple-tombs and concourses of pillars, there are one-of-a-kind examples of pre-Buddhist mausoleums in far-flung corners of Upper Tibet. In Selephuk, a large archaic era mortuary temple was constructed with specially hardened bluish mud bricks and white clay seams. This unique edifice and subsidiary funerary structures stand completely alone in the middle of a vast basin. Called Bumo Lhakhang, the "Women's Temple," the stately central building is supposed to have been inhabited by three female chieftains. They are said to have met their demise when its roof caved in on them. According to local *drokpa* folklore, these three women were buried underneath the floor of Bumo Lhakhang.

I discovered another one-of-a-kind mortuary temple in Zhungpa Matshan, a region in the western Changthang. This is Khyinak Rong, an intriguing addition to the rocky landscape of an extremely remote mountain vale. An enclosure is appended to the east side of this mortuary temple, and small square structures run in rows along its west side. The limestone-block mortuary temple was at least twelve feet in height and apportioned into two chambers. These chambers seem to have functioned as both tombs and funerary ritual venues. A window opening is still partly intact in one of the cham-

The mausoleum of Khyinak Rong. Wood for scientific dating was extracted from the cavity in the middle of the structure.

bers. It may have provided ventilation for the desiccation of human remains and for the funeral priests who officiated over Khyinak Rong.

Two wood samples extracted from thick chunks of tamarisk that formed the substructure of the walls of the Khyinak Rong temple-tomb have been radiocarbon dated to the fourth or fifth century CE. This shows that this funerary site was actively used in the protohistoric period of archaic highland civilization. Evidence from Tibetan literary sources and a typological analysis of other temple-tombs suggests that this date is no exception. Already late in the history of Zhang Zhung, the necropolis at Khyinak Rong may have had a millennium of cultural and architectural precedents behind it.

UNDERWORLD TOMBS TO THE HEAVENS

Monuments for burial and ritual purposes are sprinkled all over the Tibetan upland. Their presence is most strongly felt in otherwise barren areas. In many locales, tombs are the only palpable signs of archaic era civilization. For anyone wandering around at length in Upper Tibet, these emblems of the dead are inescapable. They rise out of the ground like phantoms demanding their due of awe and respect. This is very likely how it was planned: the ancients would have wanted those passing by their tombs to pause and consider the purpose behind these great works of construction.

Besides walled-in pillars, temple-tombs with arrays of pillars, and other types of mausoleums, ancient Upper Tibetans produced many other types of funerary structures. These burial mounds, terraces, masonry pens, and stone crypts are a study in contrast to the Buddhist-inspired monuments of later times.[24] The Lamaists left only limited traces of their dead behind in the form of charnel grounds, reliquary shrines, and clay figurines containing the ashes of the departed. According to the Buddhist eschatological view, the body after death is nothing but a useless shell. The corpse can be chopped up, burned, or left for wild animals to devour because it has no intrinsic spiritual value. Only in the case of certain high-ranking monks did Lamaism concern itself with the careful preservation of dead bodies.

On the other hand, the people of Zhang Zhung and Sumpa saw burial as an essential part of their cultures and demanded funerary monuments on a much grander scale. The Upper Tibetans were probably practicing burial even before the founding of their Metal Age civilization. The interment of human remains in the region appears to have stemmed from Stone Age practices that were widespread in Inner Asia. From the Neolithic onward, large numbers of tombs appeared throughout the core of Asia, including central and eastern Tibet. With the architectural advances introduced in the Metal Age, bigger tombs and more complex funerary ritual structures were established in Upper Tibet. These monuments betray a vivid preoccupation with matters concerning death and the disposal of mortal remains.

The ancient Upper Tibetans avoided locating their funerary sites near wet ground or open water. The celebrated circa tenth-century CE ritual text *Lubum Nagpo* describes how the water spirits retaliated against an ancient sage named Mucho Demdruk who happened to perform funerary rituals near their watery abodes.[25] He became afflicted with leprosy, and because of his infirmity he could no longer work and became a social outcast. With the help of his spiritual father, Tönpa Shenrab, Mucho Demdruk eventually recovered his health.

The complex mortuary monuments of Upper Tibet allude to fancy funerary rites being the norm in Zhang Zhung. Fortuitously, some details of these esoteric procedures have been preserved in Tibetan historical and ritual texts. These written sources began to be composed in the early historic period and were first studied by Tibetologists such as Giuseppe Tucci, Frederick William Thomas, Erik Haarh, and R. A. Stein.[26] Tibetan texts indicate that embalming was practiced, and organs and other soft tissues were replaced with imitations made from precious materials. The object of these mortuary rites was to restore the corpse to as lifelike a condition as possible. This was done in order to alleviate the suffering of the deceased, portrayed in Tibetan death rituals as still being attached to his or her body. Offerings of tools and weapons were made so that the dead would be protected on their perilous journey to the afterlife. Tibetan sources also report that prepared corpses were deposited in copper vessels, stone boxes, or other types of sarcophagi before burial. Burials in caves and on high mountains are documented in both the textual and archaeological records.

The battery of death rites described in Tibetan funerary texts parallel discoveries made in Upper Tibet by local residents. I have investigated claims that well-preserved corpses buried with gold foil coverings and artificial body parts of wood and metal have been informally unearthed by Tibetan highlanders over the last half century. These finds seem to mimic the restorative rites detailed in ancient texts. Committed treasure hunters have also found mummies, effigies, tools, and weapons in graves. The underlying functions of these mortuary objects correlate quite well to the soul-calling and evil-banishing rites of liberation described in ritual texts. Sadly, when objects with monetary value are discovered, they are disposed of on the international art and antiques market before they can be properly cataloged and studied. Objects without economic value such as bones and ceramic shards are discarded mindlessly by thieves.

The large variety of funerary structures in Upper Tibet recounts the descriptions of tombs and sarcophagi found in Tibetan literature. Taken together, archaeological and textual data depict a level of sophistication in the funerary arena that we are only beginning to appreciate. Archaic era and early historic civilization in upland Tibet through its mortuary achievements attained a standard of architectural and technological excellence commensurate with neighboring civilizations in India, China, and Central Asia.

There is still much to learn about the ancient funerary monuments of Upper Tibet. Their specific social applications, ritual functions, subsurface architecture, methods of corpse disposal, the nature of grave goods, and many other critical questions have barely begun to be addressed.

The most important excavations of tombs in Upper Tibet to date have been carried out by the Sichuan University archaeologist Huo Wei and his colleagues. In the late 1990s, they discovered three cemeteries dating to the second half of the first millennium BCE in the Dungkar-Piwang region of Guge.[27] The recovery of a broad spectrum of material objects from both burial and funerary ritual structures demonstrates that the Upper Tibetans of that period were armed with state-of-the-art technologies. The presence of bronze and iron weapons and other instruments in the tombs of Dungkar-Piwang indicate that a well-developed Iron Age culture had taken root in Upper Tibet before 300 BCE.

The objects found in the graves of Guge articulate the intricate eschato-logical beliefs of their builders. In the Dungkar-Piwang cemetery of Gyaling, large burial chambers connected to the surface by short passageways were un-earthed. In one tomb, birch bark, stone arrowheads, and sheep head fragments were discovered in two niches cut into the burial chamber walls. Red ochre was sprinkled on the floor of this chamber, and human bones and a bronze dag-ger were placed upon it. The handle of this handsome one-foot-long dagger has delicate hatching and traces of gilding. In form and function it compares favorably with bronze daggers produced by Chinese and Central Asian peoples of the same period. A piece of birch bark inscribed with attractive geometric designs of lines and triangles deposited in the same tomb gives some insight into the aesthetic traditions of ancient Upper Tibet. In another tomb at Gya-ling, a piece of an iron sword blade was retrieved, reflecting the builders' aware-ness of Iron Age materials. In the Dungkar-Piwang cemeteries, fragments of fifteen ceramic amphorae were also collected. These vessels are characterized by rounded bottoms, slightly flared mouths, and small lug handles. They are cord-marked and yellow, red, and gray in color. The maximum height of an unbro-ken amphora would have been around fifteen inches. These ceramic containers must have contained a variety of funerary offerings, including edible ones.

Another tomb excavated at Gyaling held three lengths of bamboo with bamboo fiber wrappings, which were once part of a larger object. Since bamboo grows only on the south side of the Himalaya up to a height of approximately ten thousand feet, this discovery indicates that trade connections over the Himalaya were already established more than two millennia ago. Despite the loftiest mountain range in the world separating them, the two slopes of the Himalaya boast complementary natural resources. Upper Tibet produces salt (an essential nutrient), borax (needed in gold and iron making), gold, and a variety of animal products from musk and meat to hides and horns. The moist southern slopes of the Himalaya are a botanical treasure trove, the source of many plants used in traditional Tibetan medicine. Grains, precious stones, pig-ments, plant fibers, and many other commodities are also produced in Hima-layan valleys. Thus there were many good economic reasons for the inhabitants of Zhang Zhung and cis-Himalayan regions to breach the mountain barrier between them and exchange with one another. Even further afield, materials from tropical India such a cowries and spices found their way to Tibet. These exotic goods indicate the existence of larger, more complex trading systems.

The spectacular discovery in 2006 of a piece of silk in one of the tombs of Gurgyam demonstrates that Zhang Zhung's trade also extended to northern lands. This tomb was accidently opened by local monks after a truck driven on it caused the roof to collapse. The burial has been radiocarbon dated to circa the third century CE.[28] The woven silk has an indigo blue background decorated with pairs of tan aquatic birds and carnivores set inside elaborately designed flowing frames. What seem to be tiny Chinese ideograms were also woven into the material. It appears that this precious textile was made by Chinese of the Han dynasty (206 BCE–200 CE).[29] Such silks were highly coveted in many corners of ancient Inner Asia, Upper Tibet being no different, as we now know. The silk is likely to have reached Gurgyam through Iranian or Tocharian trading partners in Xinjiang. As so little excavation has taken place in Upper Tibet, trade items recovered thus far are probably only a small indication of the extent of Zhang Zhung trading networks.[30]

The development of a Transhimalayan web of trade signals the extension of Zhang Zhung cultural influences into Himalayan regions. This is in keeping with Eternal Bon biographical and historical accounts. For instance, the cotton-clad Zhang Zhung saint Harachipar of the Mon tribe is recorded as living in a grass hut beside a Himalayan forest.[31] His female disciple, Takliwer, is said to have ridden on the backs of leopards and tigers while making her rounds of the forest.[32] Takliwer is supposed to have protected her devotees from wasp stings and snakebites. Tombs cut from soft limestone south of the Himalayan crest, in the village of Malari in Uttarakhand, India, have turned up a variety of ceramics.[33] Almost identical redware jars and spouted pots were unearthed from cut chamber tombs in Gurgyam, Upper Tibet.[34] These funerary ceramics dating to circa 100 BCE to 400 CE are a strong indication of cultural ties between Zhang Zhung and adjoining regions of the Indian Subcontinent.

The golden mask discovered in a tomb in Chuthak, Guge. Photograph courtesy of Li Linhui.

The most incredible grave objects discovered in recent years, which tie the Himalaya, Tibet, and north Inner Asia together culturally, are golden death masks. Solid gold and gilt death masks have been found in Gurgyam and Chuthak in Guge, Malari in Uttarakhand (India), and Samdzong in Mustang (Nepal).[35] These masks appear to be the "golden visage" (*serzhel*) of archaic Tibetan funerary texts. The golden visage, a likeness of the deceased, was employed to enshrine and protect the dead during the evocation rites.[36] The two-piece mask of Chuthak with its embossed wild sheep, trees, and tiered shrines is especially impressive. These embossed features can be correlated to apotropaic and valedictory rites found in archaic funerary literature.[37] Golden death masks are also known from the Bomi cemetery in Xinjiang and the Shamsi cemetery in Tajikistan, among other places in Central Asia.[38] Other golden death masks were found in the Balkans, Greece, and the Black Sea region. Earlier examples from Egypt and Mycenae notwithstanding, the golden death masks of Eurasia were produced for around a thousand years, from circa 500 BCE to 500 CE. While they differ significantly in each region, these masks document the existence of common concepts and customs relating to death and the afterlife that spanned the continent. This legacy may have been spread organically, reaching far-flung peoples through a web of subtle interactions, as well as through the conventional vehicles of trade, diplomacy, war, and ideological exchanges.

Big differences in the size and intricacy of funerary structures betoken the existence of highly stratified societies in ancient Upper Tibet, societies in which wealth was unequally distributed among its various rungs. The most ambitious tombs and necropolises must have been built for the same elite elements that occupied the castles and temples. Conversely, the indigent, if they even warranted interment, were consigned to small, crude graves, some of which may not have been marked with stones on the ground surface. A fascinating variety of funerary structures lies in between these two extremes. Presumably these are where the majority of the ancient population were put to rest.

Quadrate burial mounds known as *bangso* appeared all over Upper Tibet, as they did in central and northeastern Tibet. The burial tumuli of the lower portions of the Plateau are up to three hundred feet in length, larger than those found in Upper Tibet.[39] As in Central Tibet, some of the mounds of Upper Tibet were certainly built during the time of the Tibetan empire; others are probably much older. Some of the biggest burial mounds are found on the edge of Upper Tibet just south of Mount Nyenchen Thanglha. Among these are the thirty tombs of Deuruk, which were built in long rows along sandy slopes on the edge of the spacious Damshung basin.[40] The name of this site, "Jostling Hills," is derived from the way in which the burial mounds appear at a distance to rub up against one another.

The exteriors of the Upper Tibetan funerary mounds are usually partly lined with masonry walls, but the most interesting parts of the structures lie concealed. Evidence from pilfered tombs shows that they house stone chambers for burial as well as sundry compartments for ritual purposes.

The Upper Tibetans of the archaic era applied themselves with much vigor to building stone funerary enclosures west of the 90th meridian. Along with the walled-in pillars and arrays of pillars appended to temple-tombs, these elementary structures best define the Zhang Zhung cultural zone. It appears that many of the stone enclosures are superstructures, that portion of a tomb that lies above the ground. Some were also used in funerary rituals. Informal excavation by *drokpas* reveals that some enclosures contain the bones, horns, and skulls of sheep and other hoofed animals. According to the oldest Tibetan funerary texts, the sheep, horse, and female yak were very important sacrificial animals. They are depicted as guiding and carrying the deceased through the hellish geographic obstacles that obstruct the way to the afterlife.[41]

The funerary enclosures of Upper Tibet are a highly diverse group of structures characterized by one or more lines of uncut stones embedded into the ground to create a perimeter. Sometimes uncut stone blocks lie flat in the earth to form the outline of the structure. Some perimeter walls were built to very high standards and resemble the footings of buildings. In other examples, thin stones were inserted into the ground edgewise to create upright slab walls. While most of the funerary enclosures of Upper Tibet are quadrate or sub-rectangular in form, they can also be oval or irregularly shaped. The more elevated specimens resemble burial mounds, to which they are functionally related. Occasionally stone grave markers and other structural elements are found inside the perimeter walls. At some sites, two to more than a dozen enclosures were built next to each other to create composite structures.

Funerary enclosures litter the Tibetan upland west of Namru, the largest nearly the size of a football field. The biggest one I have documented is situated at Tsitsi Monrai Thangkha, in the Naktshang district of the Changthang.[42] This giant white limestone pen sits in the midst of many smaller enclosures that fill an entire valley. Rows of tiny square masonry structures also grace Tsitsi Monrai Thangkha. These appear to be a type of *tho*, funerary ritual monuments noted in Eternal Bon and Old Tibetan texts that were employed in elaborate ritual performances.[43] The *tho* were intended to suppress the demons that plagued the dead and their surviving kinfolk.

Another extensive archaic era burial ground is situated on the opposite bank of the Drak Tsangpo River from the celebrated Zhang Zhung fortress of Mapang Pömo Khar.[44] Spread out on a sandy flat over a distance of roughly a thousand yards, there are no less than sixty well-built quadrate enclosures beside the Drak Tsangpo. Some of the larger enclosures are subdivided by

Measuring the superstructure of a tomb on the Changthang

walls into halves, quarters, and other configurations. They are composed of neatly built double-course white cobble walls and range in size from nine hundred square feet to thirty-six hundred square feet. The cobbles of the eighteen-inch- to over three-foot-thick perimeter walls protrude slightly above ground level. What might be concealed underneath the Drak Tsangpo enclosures remains to be discovered.

There is a subclass of funerary enclosures with perimeter walls made of stones heaped up to a maximum height of seven feet. A particularly large example of this genre is known as Dzongchen, or "Great Fortress."[45] Located near Lake Dangra, it was excavated by local *drokpas* for stones used in house and corral construction. These excavations exposed subterranean chambers constructed with massive stone slabs. Fragments of human leg bones I recovered from Dzongchen have undergone AMS analysis, demonstrating that these burials date to circa 700 CE. This is the first firm indication that heaped stone funerary enclosures were being used as burial monuments during Tibet's imperial period.

Those Upper Tibetan funerary enclosures made with upright slabs somewhat resemble enclosures of the so-called Slab Grave culture of Mongolia and southern Siberia.[46] Since George Roerich reported finding slab enclosures in the Yakpa and Naktshang regions of Upper Tibet in the 1920s, Soviet and Russian archaeologists have speculated on their affinity with the slab graves of eastern and central Mongolia, Transbaikalia, and Buryatia. By virtue of their contiguous distribution, the slab graves of north Inner Asia appear to have formed an interrelated cultural domain in the first millennium BCE, thus the appellation "Slab Grave" culture.

Like the upright slab enclosures of Zhang Zhung, those of the Slab Grave culture were both burial and ritual in function. Moreover, the funerary enclosures of these respective cultures are often aligned in the cardinal directions and exhibit shallow grave pits overlain with stone slabs. The funerary slab enclosures of Zhang Zhung, however, can be much larger than their steppe counterparts, while the upright stones of the perimeter walls tend to protrude from the ground far less. Also, the Upper Tibetan variants do not have piles of rubble shoring up the walls as is typical of the northern tombs. These and other crucial differences in design signal that the respective structures of the Tibetan upland and steppes were constructed by different peoples, despite sharing some ethnic and/or cultural traits in common.

The use of stone pillars and slabs to produce funerary structures had wide currency in the Metal Age cultures of Inner Asia. They were employed in the construction of a great variety of monuments. The slab enclosure–building cultures of Zhang Zhung and Mongolia relied upon similar technological knowledge applied to the same purpose, in grassland environments suited to herding and hunting. Given these morphological and ecological parallels, it is certainly possible that the slab enclosures of Upper Tibet and the Inner Asian steppes originated in the same general time frame. Robust cultural exchanges between the northern steppes and the Tibetan Plateau appear to underpin these affinities. This is supported by the discovery of sacrificial funerary offerings consisting of horse and sheep bones in both geographic settings. Furthermore, as noted in chapter 5, copper alloy objects excavated from the tombs of the Slab Grave culture have strong stylistic affinities to Tibetan copper alloy artifacts known as *thokchak*. Among these common classes of objects are three-sided arrowheads, hemispherical buttons with heavy attachment loops, and small ritual mirrors with eyelets.

Cultural intercourse between Upper Tibet and the steppes in the first millennium BCE, as reflected in similarly constructed tombs and cognate grave goods, is likely to have fostered interrelated eschatological beliefs and funerary rituals. Though the chronology of funerary practices in Upper Tibet is unclear, archaeological parallels with north Inner Asia provide some clues. Slab graves in Mongolia and Siberia that have undergone radiometric analysis have yielded dates from the sixteenth to the fourth century BCE. This huge span of time suggests that foundational cultural structures were very long lived in the eastern steppes. This degree of cultural perdurability is also a trait of archaic era civilization in Upper Tibet, with its ancient monumental groundwork enduring for many centuries. The geographic isolation of the Tibetan upland, its unique high-elevation environment, and its special brand of pastoral, agricultural, and hunting economy appear to have reinforced the preservation of fundamental cultural traits in the region over a very long period of time.

Hidden cave burials also exist in Upper Tibet, most of which are probably still undiscovered. A Victorian era Sinologist named Stephen W. Bushell translated excerpts from a Chinese text written in 801 CE which states that divination was used to augur the location of secret caves used for Zhang Zhung burials.[47] Finding them has been one of my preoccupations. Changlatak in Götshangme, an extensive limestone cavern, is one such site. The narrow, unassuming entrance to Changlatak punctuates a high mountain slope. From the mouth of the cave a narrow ledge circumvents a deep sinkhole. A dark passageway leads sixty feet inside the cave to where human bones are scattered about, the remains of what were once probably orderly interments. Human bone samples taken from the site have yielded a calibrated radiocarbon date of circa 370–470 CE, squarely placing Changlatak in the protohistoric period.[48]

In the 1990s, a German-Nepalese archaeological team discovered a number of cave burials in Mustang, a Himalayan region associated with Zhang Zhung in Eternal Bon literature.[49] These interments in inaccessible caves revealed a Himalayan rimland culture of startling sophistication. Before their discovery, it was completely unexpected that a remote Himalayan population could have attained such a high technological and cultural standard in the first millennium BCE.

Ancient Mustang appears to have been poised on important east–west and north–south trade routes, just as the region is today. If so, this would have brought it into direct contact with Upper Tibet. Drongpa, a region rich in Zhang Zhung archaeological sites, is situated immediately north of Mustang. It can well be imagined that items like bamboo, grains, medicinal plants, and textiles moved north from Mustang into Upper Tibet, while hides, meat, wool, gold, salt, and other minerals reached the Mustang trade nexus from the north. In any event, this was the pattern of trade in later historic times.

Twenty-one corpses dating to circa 500 BCE were discovered in three caves at the Chokhopani site in Mustang. These individuals were buried with musk deer tooth necklaces, copper earrings, shell pendants, and beads of bone, faience, and carnelian. Numerous ceramic vessels probably used to contain food offerings for the dead were also deposited in the grave chambers.

In 1995, a breathtaking community burial was discovered in the Mebrak cave system of Mustang by the Germans and Nepalese.[50] Dated 400 BCE to 50 CE, the remains of around thirty naturally mummified bodies were found resting in wooden coffins ornamented with carvings and elaborate paintings. Several types of wild herbivores were vividly depicted on the coffins. Grave goods consisted of personal jewelry, utilitarian objects, and the remains of domestic animals. Bamboo mats woven with variegated patterns served as burial shrouds. The corpses were attired in textile garments made of cotton, wool, linen, and other plant fibers and in fur garments. The cotton textiles display a wide variety of weaving styles and the adroit use of dyes, including madder, indigo, lac, tannin, flavonol, chemical composites, and still unidentified compounds. A wooden bow and a wooden lute were also discovered in the Mebrak cave burials. While a number of scholarly articles have appeared, a comprehensive report detailing the discoveries made in Mustang has yet to be published.

In addition to its uniquely designed mausoleums, enclosures, and mounds, there is another peculiar funerary monument in Upper Tibet. This is the small cubic tomb built from long slabs of stone perched on mountaintops.[51] By scaling dozens of summits in search of cubic tombs, I have been able to locate thirty-two different mountains hosting them. They are all distributed in the western Changthang, on both sides of the Transhimalayan Kangkar Range.

These masonry boxes are poised on prominent peaks and ridgelines, talus-strewn summits with commanding views of the surrounding countryside. They are positioned in the most open locations possible at elevations usually exceeding the heights of neighboring mountains. This highest-altitude monument of Zhang Zhung stands up to 18,500 feet above sea level.

The cubic tombs measure ten to thirteen feet on each of their sides and were five to seven feet in height. They are usually set in the cardinal directions, implying that they were designed with special astrological and/or astronomical alignments in mind. In the center of each cube there is a small, quadrate hollow, a depository for mortal remains. It appears that bones from human corpses stripped of their flesh were deposited inside. Like the reliquary shrines of the Lamaists, these more ancient secondary burials might have been perceived as instilling a holy presence in the landscape. Remaining structural evidence indicates that the central depositories were covered with slabs and probably sealed with clay and other weatherproofing materials. Nowadays, all the cubic tombs have raw stone surfaces, but we can conjecture that their veneers were originally painted with various mineral pigments. In any event, the later reliquaries of Eternal Bon and Buddhism were colorfully decorated. The radiocarbon dating of various bones I have recovered by chance from the central depositories of the cubic tombs have yielded erratic results. Thus the age of these archaic era structures is still a matter of debate.

The stone walkways, pads, barriers, and enclosures that exist in conjunction with some cubic tomb sites intimate that they were the focus of extensive ritual activities. The archaic funerary rituals enshrined in Tibetan texts stress

Mountaintop tombs and other funerary structures

the celestial nature of the afterlife. This belief is also held by contemporary tribes related to the Tibetans, such as the so-called Bhotias and Gurungs of the Central Himalaya and the Nakhi of the Sino-Tibetan borderlands.[52] The deployment of cubic tombs on mountaintops, therefore, probably aimed at getting the dead as close as possible to the upper world. These aboveground graves appear to have been conceived of as ritual launchpads for ejecting departed souls into the heavens.

Unfortunately, virtually every cubic tomb was vandalized in the distant past. These conspicuously placed monuments appear to have become a target for plunder after Lamaism and its signature monuments came to dominate the Upper Tibetan landscape. An intolerance for archaic funerary cult practices can easily be envisaged. In a likely parallel, historical accounts speak of the desecration of the great burial mounds of the Purgyal kings after the collapse of the Tibetan empire in mid-ninth century CE.

THE LOOTING OF THE TOMBS

A lack of effective measures on the part of the People's Republic of China (PRC) is leading to the destruction of archaeological treasures all over the country. Faraway Upper Tibet is no exception. Traditionally, Upper Tibetans did not much disturb tombs or other kinds of ancient monuments. They were left alone out of respect and fear. Local people were habitually wary of supernatural beings believed to lurk in archaic era sites. Now a deterioration of traditional values combined with an unquenchable thirst for building materials is putting more and more archaeological sites at risk. Stones are needed to construct homes, pastoral camps, and other facilities, which are popping up all over Upper Tibet. Archaeological sites, especially where there are no other rocks of suitable size, are proving too much temptation. The situation is grim and demands resolute action on the part of Chinese authorities to protect the native heritage of Tibet before more of Zhang Zhung and Sumpa is lost forever.

Sadly, in the last half century, many of the surviving funerary monuments of the Tibetan upland have been desecrated by thieves. In Damshung, a hundred miles northwest of Lhasa, treasure hunters have become so bold as to bulldoze entire mounds. The ancient tombs of Chumikdo and Deuruk have particularly suffered at the hands of thieves, but other funerary sites in Damshung have been hit heavily as well.[53] Organized gangs of looters coming from the Chinese mainland and the Tibetans themselves have destroyed countless funerary structures in the region, causing irretrievable scientific losses.

The grave robbing of the last quarter century is a deep blow on top of the politically inspired damage wrought to archaeological sites by the Chinese Cultural Revolution. During that tumultuous time in the 1960s and 1970s, archaeological sites used in the worship of local divinities were singled out for destruction. For example, the marvelous walled-in pillar monument of Shang Doring in Shungpa was razed to make room for a now defunct government complex despite there being ample room in the plain to locate it elsewhere.[54]

Another case in point is Kyangtsado Gyangro, the site of what may have been the largest pillar array in all of Upper Tibet.[55] Many of the imposing structures here managed to survive the Chinese Cultural Revolution, a major feat in itself. However, around twenty-five years ago, local *drokpas* tore the pillars from the ground en masse and razed the large temple-tomb. The stones thus recovered were used to build many houses and corrals (most of which have since been abandoned). The wreckage of Kyangtsado Gyangro is a huge loss to the heritage of Upper Tibet, a loss that makes us all a little poorer culturally.

In 2001 and 2002, a road was cut right through the middle of Kekar Mondur, an array of pillars appended to a temple-tomb in the Tshakha region.[56] With just a little government oversight, this site could have been spared from destruction. The new road crosses a large open plain, and rerouting it would have been easy. Another egregious example of government unconcern pertains to large stone-lined tombs of Gyamnak in Saga, which were mined to build culverts under the main road. In the process, the deftly built burial chambers of Gyamnak were scoured clean of their contents.[57]

Important Buddhist monuments and art in western Tibet are also vulnerable to the predations of present times. Priceless cave frescoes and artifacts enshrined inside *chorten* have been looted and destroyed in huge numbers, as thieves systematically target one valley after another.

Unless a clarion call to action is sounded soon, we must brace ourselves for many more archaeological sites to fall victim to greed, ineptitude, and apathy. The PRC working closely with international conservation organizations such as UNESCO can halt this destruction, if only the political will is marshaled.

· 7 ·

Flesh, Blood, and Bones in Stone: The Artistic Treasures of Zhang Zhung

INSCRIBING HISTORY IN CARVINGS AND PAINTINGS

*M*onuments built in stone are not Upper Tibet's only lasting ancient legacy. The imaginations and aspirations of her inhabitants have also been preserved in paintings, carvings, and castings. As with the monumental and literary testimonies, the art of Zhang Zhung eloquently recounts the story of an exceptional civilization. Artists who left behind symbolic messages and pictorial narratives illuminate a way of life that has otherwise receded into the murk of times past.

Among the most prolific forms of ancient art in the Tibetan highlands are rock paintings, rock carvings, and metallic objects. Rock carvings, or petroglyphs, consist of pecks, engravings, and abrasions made on stone surfaces to create a host of different symbols and figures. Rock paintings or pictographs are composed of a variety of mineral pigments applied to stone surfaces for the same purposes. A heterogeneous group of small copper alloy objects known as *thokchak* comes in many forms and designs. This class of artifacts includes talismans, jewelry, horse tack, implements, armaments, insignia, and various other things.

The folklore of Upper Tibet acknowledges that rock art was made by the ancient inhabitants of the region but also attributes it to supernatural agencies.[1] It is commonly believed that rock art was magically self-formed without human intervention. Other stories speak of it being the handiwork of spirits who wanted to make their presence and power known to the Tibetans.

Rock art was the most inclusive of aesthetic pursuits. Created by a wide assortment of people over no less than three millennia, it appears to have been the domain of the masses and elites alike. The adornment of rocks in

167

Upper Tibet with drawings and etchings traces the development of upland civilization through the ages. Archaeological and stylistic data indicate that this art began around 1500 BCE or 1000 BCE and continued to be produced throughout the prehistoric and historic epochs.

Most rock art of the upland is elementary in form, the expressions of individuals painting and carving for a variety of personal and cultural reasons. By virtue of its simplicity and candor, rock art unabashedly chronicles the highland way of life. A pictorial index of the culture, economy, religion, and society of Upper Tibet, this art encapsulates a wide range of subjects in sundry styles made using a variety of techniques. Many rock art compositions have a comely appearance that more modern artistic mediums do not capture. Their peculiar brand of charm lends images a quality that is at once enchanting and down to earth. Those with excellent artistic skills, using relatively primitive tools, created veritable masterpieces on stone. Other compositions, however, are rough and awkward, the work of less gifted or less motivated individuals.

In the 1980s and early 1990s, rock art was discovered in about twenty-five locations dispersed across Upper Tibet, opening up a new field of archaeological exploration. A number of Chinese and Tibetan scholars have cataloged and studied these rock art sites, the most notable among them being Huo Wei, Li Yongxian, and Sonam Wangdu.[2]

From the mid-1990s, I too have cataloged unknown rock art, almost tripling the number of sites documented in Upper Tibet. In the Changthang these have been discovered at Nam Tsho, Yakpa, Naktshang, and Gertse. However, the largest concentration of rock art in Upper Tibet is in Ruthok where no fewer than twenty-five different sites have been recorded. Much rock art is also found in the badlands of Guge. Rock art theatres have not been discovered in the upper reaches of the Brahmaputra River valley, the Transhimalayan ranges, or the western districts of Gar and Purang, or on the eastern fringes and far north of the Changthang. In some cases rock art may not have spread to these regions because of the unavailability of suitable rock surfaces.

Pictographs and petroglyphs bedeck large numbers of caves, cliffs, and boulders, their canvas the rock itself. Unlike most other media, rock withstands the ravages of time admirably well. No other aesthetic endeavor has proven as durable. Ancient artwork was probably also created on more perishable materials such as leather and wood, as in more recent times, but few examples have come to light. In tandem with structural remains, rock art constitutes the hard-wearing core of early civilization in Upper Tibet. Its study, therefore, is extremely important in understanding the prehistoric cultures of Zhang Zhung and Sumpa.

A large proportion of Upper Tibetan rock art is concerned with hunting activities; hence it is often located in what were important hunting grounds and near old encampments. Since early times, the Changthang has been a plentiful source of big game, inspiring itinerant hunters to compose pictures at their places of refuge. Their petroglyphs and pictographs mark rock shelters among ample sources of freshwater. These basic necessities furnished artists with the wherewithal needed to put their ideas and visions on stone.

Ancient citadels and cemeteries stand in the vicinity of certain rock art theatres. For example, the petroglyphs of Ratroktrang and Sherang Kharlung in Ruthok are situated near archaic strongholds.[3] Rock art at the Changthang sites of Rigyal and Khampa Racho was wrought near tombs[4] and on the actual stones used to build funerary structures in some places. The interweaving of ancient monuments and rock art in the same localities reflects the holistic nature of the ancient way of life, a tapestry of craft, construction, and ritual.

Rock art made after buildings were forsaken as a kind of graffiti also garnishes certain ruins. Red ochre symbols and inscriptions came to be drawn on the walls of Gobdak and Lhakhang Marchak, long abandoned hermitages overlooking the great lakes.[5] Probably scrawled by Eternal Bon pilgrims in remembrance of an august past, symbols such as swastikas and the endless knot began to appear on these ruins after 900 CE.

To locate pictographs and petroglyphs, most of which are only a few inches in size, is not an easy task. It entails combing countless expanses of rock and boulders. The largest rock art theatre in Upper Tibet is the famous Tashi Do headland at Lake Nam Tsho, which boasts paintings in fifty different caves and fissures spread over ten miles.[6] Tashi Do hosts no fewer than two thousand discrete compositions made up of many thousands of individual elements. Over a dozen sojourns to this headland, I continued to locate pictographs concealed in tiny crannies or camouflaged on walls pullulating with paintings. At other rock art sites, such as Sholo Phuk and Lopön Phuk in Shentsa, there are only a small handful of pictographs, making documentation a relatively straightforward process.

In order to create rock art, we can infer that the Upper Tibetans devised an assortment of tools and pigments. The most elementary implement for carving stone was a chunk of hard rock such as quartz or chert with a sharp edge. Petroglyphs also appear to have been made with stone adzes and celts, as well as with metal knives and chisels. Stone and metal tools were used to chip, scratch, grind, score, or flake away rock surfaces in order to produce the outlines or full silhouettes of figures. The type of tool used, together with the carving technique employed, determined the depth, clarity, and character of petroglyphs. Pictographs were produced using bare fingers, tufts of wool, and possibly pieces of wood or animal horns. Applied mineral pigments appear as fine lines, bold strokes, smudges, and dabs. These various methods of application have a strong effect on the finished qualities of pictographs.

The most commonly used paint in Upper Tibetan rock art was ochre (iron oxides). The ochre of the region comes in a variety of hues, ranging from yellow and orange to bright red and magenta. Tibetan texts tell us that in ancient times ochre was used in burial rites, medicines, and body paint. Given the vital functions of this substance, it was in all probability invested with sacred and magical properties by the creators of pictographs. At Tashi Do, the highest-quality red ochre originates in a local pit mine that is equated with the blood of the presiding tantric goddess of the region, Dorje Phakmo.[7]

Black pigments (charcoal and manganese oxides) and white pigments (calcium oxides) were also used for pictographic art. The mineral pigments of Upper Tibetan rock art have not undergone chemical or spectrographic analysis, so it is not known if they were mixed with other ingredients. The use of plant resins, animal blood and bones, and other organic substances to temper mineral pigments and as binding agents is attested in rock art from other parts of the world.

STROKES OF TIME

Upper Tibetan rock paintings and carvings are highly diverse in nature, typifying the culture and environment of the region from prehistoric times to recent centuries. Basically speaking, the form assumed by an artistic work was determined by the cultural universe, personal compulsions, and environmental exigencies of the maker or makers. Themes that were universally relevant or sacred to the Upper Tibetans account for a good many compositions. The upland environment, with its alpine steppes, deserts, lake basins, and mountain ranges, furnished the ecological backdrop for most rock art scenes. Prehistoric art includes sacred animals, fertility figures, priests, and supernatural beings. On the opposite end of the chronological spectrum are Buddhist-inspired motifs such as tiered shrines and ritual thunderbolts. Yet some depictions transcend time to find a place in the rock art of both the archaic and Lamaist eras. These include the swastika, solitary wild herbivores, and vivid hunting scenes. The technical and stylistic traits of these catholic themes, however, varied considerably over time. The historical development of rock art in Upper Tibet is especially tangible in the depiction of religious monuments, beginning with the simple stepped tabernacles of prehistory and extending to the elaborate tiered *chorten* shrines of later times.

We will never completely understand the motivations and imperatives that compelled the ancients to fashion narratives, portraits, and symbols on stone. From the finished products, we can only hypothesize about the possible meanings and functions paintings and carvings may have had for their creators. Their significance is best deciphered by appreciating the overall cultural, historical, and environmental setting of rock art, but the results are never wholly conclusive. The identification of subjects, whether they are animals or human figures, biological versions of species or shape-shifting magicians and deities, is not an easy prospect.

Like the burial monuments of Upper Tibet, rock art indicates that vigorous cultural exchanges with north Inner Asia were taking place in the Metal Age. This interconnectivity was the product of ever-flowing currents of humanity washing over the middle of Eurasia in antiquity. The numerous thematic and design parallels between the rock art of Upper Tibet and other Inner Asian regions including Qinghai, Mongolia, and Siberia partly stem from similar economic structures.[8] Throughout ancient Inner Asia, stock rearing and hunting were carried out in steppe and montane habitats. These basic economic pursuits helped mold the great rock art traditions of Inner Asia, with their multiple ethnic, cultural, and linguistic branches. The vibrant depiction of large wild herbivores best captures this interregional artistic phenomenon. The main arena of activity was the hunt, portrayed in a bold and forceful manner, the headline act of ancient Inner Asian art.

By sifting through the various categories of physical, cultural, and historical evidence, Upper Tibetan rock art, like monuments, can be divided into two broad chronological and cultural divisions: the archaic era and the Lamaist era. Rock art of the archaic era was produced from no later than 1000 BCE until around 1000 CE, and that of the Lamaist era in the last millennium. Some old-style scenes continued to be painted and carved even after the early historic period; these belong to what is best called a vestigial period.

The application of direct dating techniques to rock art, such as the radiocarbon assaying and chemical analysis of pigments and the assessment of microcrystalline structures of carvings, can be very costly and unreliable. Technical obstacles related to sampling and the calibration of test results have led to scientific controversies worldwide. Until reliable and cost-effective chronometric techniques can be applied to Upper Tibetan rock art, the actual age of compositions will not be determined with any assurance.

It is possible, however, to estimate the age of rock art by subjecting it to painstaking physical and cultural analyses. We can infer approximate age by examining the material condition, subject matter, and artistic style of compositions individually and collectively. A relative chronology can be built up in this way, a system that gauges which paintings or carvings are older than others. There are many different criteria that go into assembling a relative chronology of rock art. One important index of relative age is the hue and texture of pigments. As pictographs age, they wear down, brown, and absorb moisture, bacteria, and soluble minerals present in the rock and atmosphere. The brushing, daubing, dabbing, or chalking techniques used to make pictographs aid in pinpointing basic styles and might also highlight relative age. Likewise, the manner in which petroglyphs have eroded says something about their antiquity, as does the color and thickness of the patina that forms over them. The techniques used in rendering petroglyphs, be they pecked, abraded, roughly cut, or sharply incised, may also reflect relative age.

Identifying the elements of a composition and how these associate with one another distinguishes basic genres and may be important in computing when rock art was made. Similarly, appreciating the underlining geometric principles and methods of execution is useful in estimating the age of rock art. The physical position of art on rock surfaces is yet another indicator of relative age, with younger compositions superimposed on older ones. Comparing ethnographic, historical, and archaeological data from adjoining regions and countries can also be harnessed in understanding the chronology of Upper Tibet rock art.

SYMBOLS OF LIFE AND MARKS OF FAITH

Much can be said with a symbol. In Upper Tibet, sacred symbols were drawn or carved on rock surfaces, articulating the yearnings and beliefs of the ancient population. Swastikas, sunbursts, conjoined sun and moons, flaming jewels, circles, and trees are the icons of the Tibetan upland. These seminal forms are represented in rock art sites all over the region.

The swastika is Upper Tibet's most emblematic symbol. It was carved and drawn on numerous rock faces for spiritual protection, for staking sectarian and territorial claims, and as an esoteric religious cue. Oriented in both directions, swastikas were made in isolation or along with other art. The counterclockwise swastika, the symbol par excellence of the Eternal Bon religion, is suffused with cosmological and ritual significance. Eternal Bon texts aver that the highly auspicious swastika was employed by the priests and deities of Zhang Zhung as a symbol of cosmic stability and long life. In Tibetan it is called *yungdrung*, literally meaning "unborn, undying."

Originally a solar sign, the swastika was known to many ancient Eurasian cultures. Native origins notwithstanding, the swastika may possibly have entered Upper Tibet with the Indus River civilization or with the steppe-dwelling Andronov cultures of the Bronze Age. The painted pottery

A red ochre counterclockwise swastika painted in one of the many caves of Lake Nam Tsho. Pilgrims have put a dab of butter on it as a mark of its holy status. Tibetans traditionally believe that such ancient swastikas were magically self-formed.

of these two groups was regularly decorated with swastikas. Swastikas also occur in the rock art of Mongolia and other regions of north Inner Asia. In prehistoric times, Upper Tibetan swastikas faced both ways and had arms of equal or unequal length. However, in the early historic period the direction of a swastika took on a sectarian meaning. Like its Indian counterpart, the Tibetan Buddhist swastika generally faces clockwise, while Eternal Bon swastikas are oriented counterclockwise.

Typical examples of swastikas occur in Drakkhung Dzepo, the "Handsome Cave," of the Naktshang region.[9] Here three counterclockwise swastikas in brownish red ochre and one in yellow ochre were painted on a wall opposite the main entrance of this small Zhang Zhung sanctum. A much more unusual example of a left-turning swastika was painted at Nam Tsho's Tashi Do, the largest rock art theatre in Upper Tibet, in what seems to have been Sumpa country. Tibetan letters representing mystic themes were drawn within the ambit of the swastika's four arms. This enigmatic magical diagram appears to have been painted by adherents of archaic cults sometime between the eighth and thirteenth centuries CE.[10] Also at Tashi Do, another counterclockwise swastika marks the transition from prehistory to the historic epoch.

This red ochre swastika was superimposed upon an older wild herbivore pictograph painted in black, perhaps to symbolically bring the animal under the auspices of a more literate form of religion.[11]

At various rock art sites, swastikas hover over animals in lieu of the life-giving sun. The life-generating symbolism of the swastika is most evident in composite depictions of wild animals. At the Drakdong rock art theatre in Ruthok, a west-facing rock panel features shallow relief carvings of a counterclockwise swastika among fifty or so yaks and other wild herbivores.[12] There are also what appear to be several hunters on horseback depicted on this panel. The spatial arrangement of the figures on the rock panel accentuates the centrality of the swastika. The uniform wear and stylistic traits of these carvings suggest they were created as an integral composition by the same protohistoric period hand. Similarly, at Lhari Drakphuk in Shentsa, wild yaks and other herbivores, birds of prey, plants, a sun, a crescent moon, and other motifs are clustered around counterclockwise swastikas.[13] The core position of swastikas in this red ochre painting also alludes to its life-giving powers.

Using swastikas, archaic and Eternal Bon practitioners on one side and the Buddhists on the other tried to erase each other's religious presence. The placement of swastikas and other symbols on caves and cliffs signaled spiritual control and territorial occupation for these contending religious groups. Rivalries between the old religion and Buddhism began in the seventh or eighth century CE and continued unabated until the twelfth or thirteenth century CE, by which time virtually all upland communities had been converted to Lamaism either under the banner of Eternal Bon or Buddhism.

The historic struggle between the archaic religious and Buddhist communities in Upper Tibet is graphically depicted in the vandalism of pictures and inscriptions at various rock art theatres.[14] In Lhadre Phuk, a number of ancient swastikas painted in different red ochre pigments were destroyed when a thick chunk of the cave's ceiling was forcibly removed. Another counterclockwise swastika was drawn on the raw surface of the ceiling by followers of the old traditions in a gesture of defiance and reoccupation. Nearby at Tara Marding, tensions between archaic religionists and Buddhists were also played out. Here an eighteen-inch-tall counterclockwise swastika inscribed on a cliff was nearly obliterated using the same beige pigment, while nearby Buddhist inscriptions were left unmolested.

As elsewhere, conflicts between the ancient cults and Buddhism erupted on the island of Semo Do, an important early cultural center in the middle of Lake Nam Tsho. In one cave, a deliberate attempt was made to efface a red ochre counterclockwise swastika. In another Semo Do cave, grit was rubbed into a panel of pictographs and inscriptions that were probably created by adherents of the old religious regime. In front of Galo Phuk, a red ochre endless knot symbol belonging to the preexisting religion was defaced by a Buddhist mantra being carved over it. This superimposition, an expression of either fear or disregard of the other, documents the usurping of Semo Do by Buddhist practitioners. Likewise, at the Kabren Pung Ri site in Ruthok, a carving of a five-tiered shrine from the archaic era was obscured by a Buddhist mantra in another show of Lamaist religious force.[15]

The sunburst, a universal symbol of light and life, is an especially evocative facet of the Upper Tibetan rock art tableau. At the base of the formation sheltering the Zhang Zhung cave sanctuary of Chu Khargyam Drubphuk, there is a group of red ochre pictographs including a tree, two counterclockwise swastikas, and three sunbursts.[16] Like the swastika, the sunburst is sometimes depicted above wild yaks and other herbivores. One such prehistoric example from Rigyal, or "Monarch Mountain," depicts a solitary wild yak with a sunburst of twelve rays overhead and a crescent moon below.[17] The sunburst with its protective, procreative, and cosmological aura also occurs in the rock art of north Inner Asia. Most notably, the elk (maral) and sun in petroglyphs and other art forms were one of the key cosmological themes of ancient cultures in Siberia.[18]

A solar disc cradled inside a crescent moon is a fundamental Eternal Bon and Buddhist tantric sign, symbolizing the union of the male and female archetypes. Known as *nyida*, this motif adorns Upper Tibetan rock art sites active after the eighth century CE. The adoption of the conjoined sun and moon by Eternal Bon was inspired by Indian Buddhism. However, through archaic cultural sources, it may also owe its existence to prehistoric Inner Asian cultures. This same symbol occurs on textiles deposited in Scythian tombs of the Altai dating to the fifth century BCE, which was discovered by the famous Soviet archaeologist Sergei Ivanovich Rudenko.[19] A remarkable example of a prehistoric sun and moon at the Shaksang petroglyph site consists of a hornlike crescent moon resting upon a sun divided into nine parts with a dot in the middle.[20]

Trees are a common motif in rock art of all ages in Upper Tibet. According to Tibetan texts, the tree is an important cosmological symbol that functions to connect the three vertical spheres of the universe. At the Metal Age Ngondong site in Naktshang, trees resembling cornstalks were scraped on a boulder along with swastikas, sunbursts, and crescents.[21] In a much later period, red ochre trees in a similar style were painted in twin pyramidal niches of Tashi Do.[22] From the early historic period onward, tongues of mystic fire emitted by three bulbous jewels have embellished rock surfaces in Upper Tibet. This Eternal Bon and Buddhist religious symbol is known as the flaming jewels, or *norbu mebar* in Tibetan, and represents the treasures of the doctrine. Among the large numbers of pictographs at Tashi Do are particularly fine examples of the Eternal Bon *norbu mebar*, with and without accompanying inscriptions, painted prior to 1250 CE.[23]

Ancient examples of the eight auspicious symbols of Eternal Bon and Buddhism also occur in rock art. Traditionally these ubiquitous symbols include the wheel, white parasol, endless knot, golden fish pair, vase, lotus, victory banner, and conch. However, there are examples from the early historic and vestigial periods that deviate from the standard design of the eight auspicious symbols. An anomalous representation of the eight auspicious symbols was drawn in the Felt Tent Formation cave at Tashi Do.[24] In this rendition there is just one fish identifiable as a scaleless carp of Nam Tsho, and a five-pointed star replaces another standard symbol. Among the most intriguing symbols are those that cannot be readily identified. A case in point is two elaborate circular forms and a parasol-like figure at Rigyal in Gertse.[25] There are many such mysteries in Upper Tibet remaining to be solved.

THE ANCIENT HUMAN FIGURE IN ALL ITS GLORY

Anthropomorphic rock art provides one of the most intimate views of Upper Tibet over the long trajectory of time. For at least three thousand years, human figures in sundry poses and activities have graced the rock art theatres of the upland. There are great variations in the human form and the social, cultural, and economic contexts in which they appear. Some figures may be self-portraits or those of the maker's community. In other instances, anthropomorphic figures appear to be divine manifestations, the very gods and goddesses as envisaged in ancient times.

Among the quaintest of rock art compositions are pairs of figures, probably male and female, some hand in hand. The bonds of family and love come through in this genre of composition. These kinds of depictions inspirit the Gokra site in Ruthok and Che Do on the shores of Lake Nam Tsho.[26] Sometimes couples appear to be involved in symbolic or ritual activities. A human figure in a petroglyph of Gokra sports a prominent phallus, while his partner does not. This naturalistic portrait may have been made as a fertility-ensuring instrument. At the Thakhampa Ri site in Ruthok, a male figure with raised arms stands directly below a squatting female, in what appears to be an intimate tribute to the maternal qualities of fertility and procreation.[27] The female figure is in the classic position of giving birth. Her head, torso, and breasts are boldly rendered as prominent triangular forms. The male figure has an elongated torso and stands with his feet spread apart as if he is supporting the weight of the female above him. A prehistoric petroglyph at Ratroktrang in Ruthok depicts two squatting figures that may chronicle the giving of birth as a cosmic act of creation.[28] These two human-like forms are arrayed feet to feet with large objects emerging from between their legs. Analogous figures are well represented in Inner Asia, particularly in Mongolia, albeit not in pairs.[29] One such example found at Ust'-Tuba has been interpreted as a birth-giving female and dated by the French archaeologist Henri-Paul Francfort to the Bronze Age.[30] Such parallels in style and symbolism between Upper Tibet and north Inner Asia supply us with tantalizing but hard-to-define evidence of wide-ranging prehistoric cultural contacts.

What appear to be prehistoric dancing figures with legs and arms bent in an elegant show of motion make their presence felt in Upper Tibetan rock art. At the Tashi Do headland of Nam Tsho, there are groups of human figures pictured in long robes and possibly turbans with their left arms raised and right arms held akimbo in an orchestrated fashion.[31] These depictions of what look like dancers seem to narrate a ceremonial theme. According to Eternal Bon texts, in ancient times priests would open royal convocations with a formal dance. Regal ceremonial functions notwithstanding, dancing was an integral part of the highland way of life in marriage celebrations, military victories, and festivals.

An anthropomorphic figure mounted on a wild yak in an extraordinary showing of what might be the divine

Certain rock compositions appear to be portraits of religious adepts or deities configured in various ritual attitudes. These date to both the archaic and Lamaist eras. At the Shaksang site in Naktshang, an anthropomorph with five protuberances on its head stands over small round ritual objects, while a figure, part bird, part swastika, soars overhead.[32] This composition probably dates to the early historic period and seems to document a religious performance. At the Kyildrum site in Gegye, there are also two anthropomorphs mounted on animals reminiscent of deer or wild sheep, suggesting that the riders are gods and not humans.[33] In Eternal Bon literature, there are many examples of divine priests and deities riding wild herbivores.

A highly whimsical Lamaist era pictograph at Tashi Do depicts an acrobatically balanced anthropomorphic figure standing on the back of a horselike animal.[34] This individual grasps the reins of his mount in one hand while holding a hornlike object near his mouth in the other. Although this pictograph appears to have been drawn in a later period, it has the feel of an archaic cultural composition. In the vastness of the Tibetan upland, old styles and customs were more easily preserved than in the relatively densely populated lower regions of the Plateau. Sharp protuberances or lines radiating from the heads of anthropomorphs in rock art may represent feathers or horns. Forked headdresses are common among the pictographs of Che Do on the shores of Lake Nam Tsho, a small cave packed with prehistoric paintings of hunters and animals.[35] In Tashi Do's Felt Tent Formation cave, there are two anthropomorphs sitting with their legs folded in the manner of religious masters, which seem to sport either horns or elaborate coiffures. In another cave at Tashi Do, an archaic era figure on horseback has four thick lines extending above its head in a crownlike display. A most impressive headdress is also worn by a prehistoric anthropomorph at Thakhampa Ri in Ruthok. This carving consists of a symmetrical array of long lines extending from the head of a powerfully configured figure.[36]

In a cave hidden behind dwarf willow trees at Lake Nam Tsho's Tashi Do, a red ochre pictograph portrays an individual sitting cross-legged with the right arm held in a gesture of benediction.[37] The attitude of this historic epoch figure identifies it as a religious personage or deity. A human figure encircled by a thin line painted in the same cave appears to be shown walking.[38] This pictograph is reminiscent of a *drubthob*, the divine madmen of Vajrayana Buddhism that wandered all around Tibet and India in the Middle Ages. Another fascinating painting in a small nook at Nam Tsho shows an individual prostrating before an idol or shrine. In front of the bowing figure, a larger individual dressed in a long robe and pointed hat stands with arms outstretched as if directing the activity.

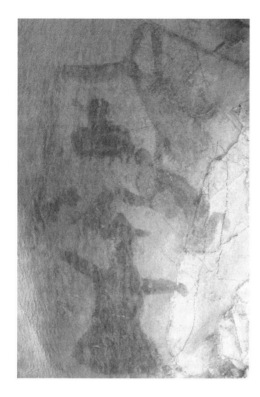

*A red ochre pictograph that appears
to show worshippers at a shrine,
Lake Nam Tsho*

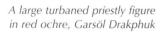

*A large turbaned priestly figure
in red ochre, Garsöl Drakphuk*

An extraordinary portrait of an archaic religious figure is situated deep inside the cave sanctuary of Garsöl Drakphuk.[39] This unusually large (three and half feet in height) red ochre composition portrays a standing male figure in a tight-fitting shirt and what appears to be a tiger-skin loincloth. On his head a large turban is wound around a very prominent topknot. Large hoop earrings hang from his drooping ears, and he has a semicircular mouth and eyes. The man wields a ritual hook in his right hand, and a lasso appears to be coiled around his left wrist. He wears either low-slung footwear or what might be anklets. A counterclockwise swastika and possibly a scepter are drawn nearby. Taken as a whole, the clothing and coiffure of this turbaned male is that of a Brahmin, the guise in which the famous eighth-century CE *bonpo* master of Nam Tsho, Tonggyung Thuchen, appeared. This pictograph and others in Garsöl Drakphuk were probably painted subsequent to the abandonment of this archaic era refuge, circa 800 to 1100 CE. These paintings are all concentrated on one wall of the cavern in memory of an august past.

Rock art reveals that the ancient inhabitants of Upper Tibet merged conceptions about humans, animals, and the divine. The transformation of humans and deities into animals, a phenomenon known as bestiovestism, is a mythological motif ingrained in many ancient cultures of Inner Asia. One of the most charming portrayals in the upland is of winged anthropomorphic figures. This rock art was inspired by the many species of eagles, hawks, falcons, and vultures native to the region. Upper Tibet is an ethereal land in which birds seem close at wing.

In Drolma Phuk at Tashi Do, a supernatural representation of this kind was painted in a black pigment.[40] This figure exhibits outstretched wings, a round head, and a human-like body and legs. There are also two red ochre bird-man figures along Tashi Do's White Formation.[41] They have disproportionately small heads, long thin necks, rectangular wings, and elongated bodies and legs, a style reflective of considerable antiquity. Similarly, at Barking Old Dog Headland, on the north shore of Nam Tsho, there is a bevy of gracefully executed red ochre bird-men with hourglass bodies and triangular wings.[42]

Bird-men and bird-women are associated with ancient *bonpo* masters who are supposed to have transformed themselves into eagles and vultures. It is written that upon her death at 360 years of age, the Zhang Zhung saint Takber Liwer turned into a horned eagle near the top of sacred Mount Tise and disappeared into space.[43] Central Tibet's second king, Mutri Tsenpo, and his four consorts are also thought to have manifested as horned eagles in the course of their religious duties.[44] Ornitho-anthropomorphic rock art may also represent deities. An ancient Eternal Bon invocation describes a god that gave rise to the territorial deities of Upper Tibet as having the body of a man and the wings of a horned eagle.[45]

A natural pillar of rock with many intriguing sub-jects probably dating to the protohistoric period, Ratroktrang. At the top of the pillar there is a sun and crescent moon flanking a counterclockwise swastika. Below these motifs are two shrines with trident-like finials. In the center of the pillar there is a horned eagle and two bird-men. Flanking these fig-ures on the right is a tree and on the left a standing archer with a prominent headdress. Directly below the bird-men is a wild ungulate and at the bottom of the image a tiger.

A sensational rock art composition of men and birds is located at Ratroktrang in Ruthok.[46] On a vertical rock slab, in descending order there is a horned eagle with spread wings, a composite figure with winglike arms and an avian head, and a fully anthropomorphic figure with what might be feathers on its head. Dating to the protohistoric period, these carvings may depict the descent of Zhang Zhung's Khyung clan from the horned-eagle progenitor to a divine intermediary and finally down to a fully human lineage. Other fine examples of rock carvings combining avian and human features are located at Thakhampa Ri.[47] Some of these figures seem to have bird feathers on their head and body, while others have bird beaks. Costumes consisting of bird feathers are associated with early adepts and deities. The Eternal Bon historical text *Rigdzin Rigpai Thukgyü* records that the Zhang Zhung sage Pebon Thoktse wore a robe of vulture feathers.[48] Similarly, an incense-offering text states that the goddess Daryarse Men of Lake Darok Tsho wears a robe of vulture feathers, while Trede Chenmo of Lake Teri Nam Tsho is attired in peacock feathers.[49]

The bird-man motif is characteristic of other regions of Inner Asia, albeit varying in style and context from that of Upper Tibet. Carvings and paintings of anthropomorphic figures in Mongolia and southern Siberia dated to the Bronze Age are not unlike eagles and falcons with outstretched

A pair of highly stylized human faces with arms and legs, from the Metal Age

wings.[50] The rock art experts Jakov Sher and Olga Garyaeva have studied petroglyphs produced in the Central Asian Kyzylkum Desert that also depict birdlike anthropomorphs.[51]

Among the most enigmatic human figures of the Metal Age are the so-called mascoids, highly stylized faces carved on boulders and cliffs. In Upper Tibet this type of art is only found in Ruthok, where about fifty different faces have been documented. Some of these mascoids have arms and legs and wield weapons. Similar mascoids are known in Ladakh, a Tibetan Plateau region west of Ruthok. Ladakh appears to have acted as a cultural bridge in the Metal Age, for its mascoids have features of both Upper Tibetan examples and those of the steppes and boreal forests of north Inner Asia.[52] The iconographic resonance existing between these human figures supports other evidence for the interregional fusion of religious and aesthetic concepts, which drew the steppes and the Plateau into the same transcultural orbit of the Late Bronze Age and Iron Age.

While livestock herding scenes are very uncommon in Upper Tibetan rock art, geometric shapes that may represent corrals and tents occur in some compositions.[53] In others, large parties appear to be in transit between hunting or pastoral camps. At the prehistoric Draktsuk and Thakhampa Ri sites

Two dueling figures with shields and weapons, Thakhampa Ri. This petroglyph appears to date to the protohistoric period.

in Ruthok, there are rock panels with long lines of anthropomorphs, each of which is carrying a packlike object on its back.[54] Yaks and other herbivores, sunbursts, and giants are interspersed between the rows of moving people, lending a lively aspect to the scenes.

Warriors and implements of war are well represented in Upper Tibetan rock art. Pairs of standing figures or ones mounted on horseback are shown engaged in martial sports or locked in mortal combat. Armaments depicted include pikes, spears, knives, swords, snares, lassos, shields, clubs, and bows and arrows. The wielding of these weapons in battle and in martial contests starkly illustrates a bellicose propensity among the ancient highlanders, helping to account for the extensive networks of citadels in Upper Tibet.

I chanced upon four pairs of dueling figures at Chulung in Ruthok.[55] In one of these compositions, two figures in long robes face one another with bows and arrows, while a third figure in a similar attitude stands some distance away. In another scene at Chulung, pairs of figures are locking shields, leaving little doubt that they are engaged in combat or a contest. In Tashi Do's Zhamar cave there are two poorly preserved ancient pictographs of horsemen confronting each other.[56] They brandish long objects, possibly spears with regimental banners (an ancient Tibetan standard), underscoring the seemingly confrontational nature of the encounters. The face of war is poignantly shown in a Tashi Do pictograph of the protohistoric period. Several figures on foot and horseback with bows, arrows, and other weapons are joined in battle.[57] This conflict pits a cavalry in slimmer-profile dress or armor against foot soldiers attired in bulky robes. This electrifying scene seems to chronicle a struggle involving two different tribes or factions.

At the Ngosok site in Ruthok, four carved anthropomorphs with hourglass-shaped bodies and triangular heads stand in a row.[58] One of them holds a bow and arrow and another figure a rectangular shield. All four figures seem to grasp swords or batons used to touch one another in what appears to be inoffensive contact. This probable protohistoric scene may chronicle a ritual empowerment convened for military purposes.

The salience of hunting to the ancient Upper Tibetan way of life is brilliantly reflected in rock art. Hunters in pursuit of wild herbivores such as blue sheep, argali sheep, antelopes, deer, and particularly wilds yaks are commonly encountered at rock art theatres. There are many stylistic variations to the basic hunting scene, parading humans and animals in highly imaginative or realistic ways. The ferment of these displays conveys the exhilaration and triumph of the hunt.

The celebration of the hunt in rock art was the province of a proud and vibrant people. Hunting spectacles reveal an exuberant lot who did not shy away from the gory details of their venatic way of life. This reveling in the open slaughter of animals is very much at variance with Lamaist morality, declaiming how different the Zhang Zhung and Sumpa cultural ethos was from Eternal Bon and Buddhism and their central ethic of nonviolence.

Until the introduction of animal husbandry in Upper Tibet three thousand or more years ago, hunting was the linchpin of survival. As inferred by the stone projectiles they left behind, the Neolithic uplanders customarily hunted wild herbivores. Even after the introduction of pastoralism and agriculture as the primary means of livelihood, hunting remained a very important corollary activity in the Tibetan upland. The hunting weapon of choice, as in all of Inner Asia, was the recurve bow, a form of this weapon made with composite materials for extra strength and draw.[59] Spears and lassos were also used to bring down game. The customs governing early historic period hunting expeditions to the wilds of northern Tibet are detailed in Tibetan manuscripts of the Dunhuang collection.

Hunting as a vital economic and social activity was captured with great regularity in the rock paintings and carvings of the Tibetan highlands. Typically one or more hunters descend upon their prey for the final kill. When there is a group of hunters, they take up tactical positions around an animal. In a complex hunting scene of much vitality at the Gokra site, four mounted archers aim at more than half a dozen wild yaks.[60] These horsemen coursing quarry exemplify the drive technique of hunting used in Upper Tibet. As in Central Asia and the Arctic, hunters drove large animals into natural constrictions or traps in order to get into close range.

Archers on foot coming in for the final kill of two wild yaks. This pictograph dates to the Metal Age, perhaps even predating the arrival of the domestic horse in Tibet. The mustard- and magenta-colored yaks have already been struck by arrows. The wild yak on the right raises its tail in alarm.

Many hunters are portrayed mounted on horseback, but substantial numbers of compositions feature archers on foot, some of which are in a stalking attitude. Some hunters carry swords and slings at their sides. In certain rock art compositions, projectiles protrude from the haunches of doomed animals, and blood spurts out from wounds and body orifices, unambiguously signaling their demise. Wild yaks are often portrayed larger than life, emphasizing their awesome power and the dangers inherent in bringing them down. Hounds sometimes accompany hunters and are limned harrying prey. Where discernible, hunters are attired in robes of various lengths and in waist-length jackets. The *lokpa*, the animal-hide greatcoat still used by *drokpas*, appears to be well represented in Upper Tibetan hunting rock art from prehistoric times onward.

Probably a variety of reasons inspired the inhabitants of Upper Tibet to chronicle their hunting exploits in graphic detail. Some scenes are likely to celebrate the bravery and success of those who took part in the hunt. Perhaps great hunters felt impelled to record their exploits in the rock art theatre as a demonstration of their social standing. The desire to give thanks and tribute to the animals slaughtered is another motivation likely to underlie the creation of ancient hunting vignettes. The Minaro people of Ladakh still carve ibexes on boulders in gratitude for a successful hunt.[61]

As the viability and prestige of ancient highland communities was dependent on hunting, it is very likely that an ensemble of magic rites was developed to secure game. Rituals still practiced by hunters in Upper Tibet revolve around mountain gods and other members of the indigenous pantheon. The propitiation of these deities relies on figurines or drawings of wild animals, which are offered to win the deities' favor in ensuring successful hunting expeditions, as well as to enhance the well-being of people, livestock, and the environment. The portrayal of the hunt in some rock art may well be an ancient corollary to these types of ritual activities.

Some wild herbivores depicted among hunters or as solitary creatures may represent zoomorphic guardian spirits, which were supplicated in order to ensure productive hunting expeditions. This type of religious theme seems to be represented in a protohistoric petroglyph of a hunter with a bow and arrow facing in the same direction as the herbivore stationed behind him.[62] Carved at Ngosok in Ruthok, the hunter is obviously not in pursuit of this probable male antelope, which is shown more in the attitude of a special mascot or divine guardian. To this day, among the Dards and Brusho of northern Pakistan, it is believed that fairies take the form of ibexes and markhors to assist hunters.

ANIMALS AS CREATURES, PERSONS, AND GODS

The Tibetan literary and oral traditions tell us that animals have played a crucial role in the culture of the upland since remote antiquity. This reflects their indispensable position in the economy, mythology, and religion of Upper Tibet. Accordingly, many rock carvings and paintings focus on animals. It has been estimated that 80 percent of Tibetan rock art is zoomorphic, spanning some twenty different species.[63] Although it is difficult to know how many species are actually represented as anatomical details are often absent, we can surmise that all the large herbivores and carnivores native to Upper Tibet made their mark in the rock art tableau. Many species of raptors and aquatic birds are also simulated.

In the archaic era of the highlands, zoomorphic rock art extended to both the ordinary and the extraordinary qualities of animals. The multifaceted identity of animals gave rise to an extremely rich rock art canvas in terms of the attitudes of portrayal and modes of association, with anthropomorphic figures sometimes depicted alongside them.

Wild yaks, followed by deer and wild sheep, alone or in small groups, are the most commonly depicted terrestrial animals in Upper Tibetan rock art. Animals shown either in outline form or fully silhouetted vary greatly

A rock portrait of a solitary stag

from highly stylized stick figures to impressionistic compositions and images with accurately rendered anatomical details. Yaks are distinguished by their bushy tails, prominent belly fringes, humped withers, and short curved horns. Deer are frequently portrayed with branched antlers, antelopes with spiraling horns, and wild sheep with thick rounded horns. Lone horses, the main transport animal of Tibet, are well represented in rock art; the native wild ass less so. Gazelles and especially antelope also turn up in Upper Tibetan rock art with a fair degree of frequency.

The solitary portrayal of wild herbivores and birds of prey is a ubiquitous theme in Upper Tibetan rock art. Why terrestrial and flying creatures were so often carved and painted in isolation cannot be known conclusively, as such information was not explicitly recorded in documents and inscriptions. We can reasonably assume that solitary animal depictions take in ordinary creatures as well as adepts and deities transformed into the zoomorphic.

Depicted in magnificent isolation, wild herbivores with large horns or antlers are shown in all their greatness. Similarly, raptors glide over rock faces just as easily as their real-life counterparts do across the sky. At its most mundane, the making of solitary animals may have simply been an amusement or adornment. Given the importance of animals in Upper Tibet, it can also be readily imagined that some were drawn or carved in appreciation of their vital assets.

Pairs of mating wild yaks at the Brakdong and Thakhampa Ri sites in Ruthok convey a special fertility theme.[64] Likewise, a petroglyph at Gokra, also in Ruthok, seems to be wrapped up in beliefs pertaining to procreation and the continuance of life. The central figure among three or four elongated animals in this composition has the branched antlers and sexual organ of a stag.[65]

Complex motives are implicated in the creation of zoomorphic compositions. We know that the use of animals as clan and power symbols and as the mounts and servants of indigenous deities are enduring aspects of culture in Upper Tibet. According to Eternal Bon biographical texts, Zhang Zhung adepts exploited wild animals as servants, in the way the uninitiated used domestic animals. These legendary personages are recorded as riding on wild yaks, wild asses, deer, wild sheep, and other animals. Like the native deities, Zhang Zhung saints are supposed to have kept tigers, lions, black bears, and brown bears as if they were yak calves or sheep. Furthermore, it is believed that these saints could appear in the guise of carnivores. For example, the twelfth-century CE text entitled *Rigdzin Rigpai Thukgyü* observes that the Zhang Zhung master Shebu Rakhuk chose to manifest as a tiger or lion to eliminate evil activities and as a vulture to fly in the sky.[66] The solitary depiction of raptors is a hallmark of Upper Tibetan rock art of all time periods. At many a site, these proud birds are shown with outstretched wings soaring across the sky or hovering overhead. Many mountain gods of Tibet are said to have divine raptors in their retinues. As in Zhang Zhung, the eagle was a totemic animal and protective cultural hero of the ancient Mongolian tribes. The Soviet archaeologist Aleksey Pavlovich Okladnikov, commenting on petroglyphs of soaring falcons, eagles, and vultures with spread wings, notes that they were a salient feature of Scythian art.[67]

In some rock art of Upper Tibet birds of prey resemble swastikas and other geometric forms. A particularly beautiful prehistoric carving of a horned eagle with partially folded wings and a broad tail is located at Rigyal.[68] There are also archaic era petroglyphs portraying horned eagles (*khyung*), the chief zoomorphic emblem of Zhang Zhung, at Gongra in Ruthok.[69] A large and well-executed rock painting of the horned eagle perched above the Buddhist deity Vajrapani was painted at Tashi Do sometime between 800 and 1200 CE.[70]

A red ochre pictograph in Tashi Do's Drolma Phuk convincingly embodies the theme of a divine emissary of the dead. This archaic era composition was first documented by the Tibetan archaeologist Sonam Wangdu in the early 1990s.[71] It portrays a supine human figure, legs dangling, being led by a raptor that gestures upward with its left wing. The decisiveness of the activity and the symbiotic posture of the human and bird figures are in keep-

A horned eagle hovering over a wild herbivore, protohistoric period

ing with ancient concepts pertaining to the ritual transference of the dead by winged deities to the afterlife.

SHRINES BRIDGING THE GAP
BETWEEN PREHISTORY AND HISTORY

The only architectural forms widely depicted in Upper Tibetan rock art are ceremonial monuments. Stepped shrines and the architecturally related but more complex *chorten* of Lamaism are well accounted for in the rock art of the highlands.[72] The oldest and most elementary shrines comprise three to five graduated platforms topped by a spherical structure and/or a simple mast. These tiered structures are regularly portrayed in paintings and carvings of the protohistoric and early historic periods. The rendering of tiered shrines on sundry rock walls suggests construction on a regular basis in ancient Upper Tibet. I have surveyed a number of ruined examples at temple and citadel sites, indicating that they did indeed lace the landscape.

At Tashi Do there are many pictographs of stepped shrines, and such images were carved at rock art sites in Ruthok as well. Occurring on opposite ends of Upper Tibet, stepped shrines are a powerful indicator of upland civilization's embrace of both the Zhang Zhung and Sumpa cultures.

The elementary stepped shrines of Upper Tibetan rock art are related to the similarly conceived *lhaten* of Eternal Bon literature. As we saw in chapter 5, *lhaten* are tabernacles traced back to Zhang Zhung's legendary war with the northwestern country of Takzik. These stepped structures were built for the sky god Gekhö and his large entourage of celestial and meteorological deities, each tier of the shrine featuring different gifts for them. Eternal Bon tradition holds that during religious ceremonies, the *lhaten* functioned as a model of the universe and as a residence of the deities.

Shrines known as *lhatho*, *tenkhar*, and *sekhar* (related to the ancient temples of the same name) are also architecturally and historically related to the stepped structures depicted in rock art. They are still constructed as sanctums for indigenous deities in all regions of Tibet. *Tenkhar*, *lhatho*, and *sekhar* range from simple piles of rocks to ornate structures large enough to enter. In Purang, in southwestern Tibet, a still maintained giant stepped structure made of cobbles resembles ancient rock art counterparts.[73] Known as Guru Bumpa, it is said to have been magically created by the eighth-century CE Vajrayana master, Guru Rinpoche, in the time it took for his disciples to cook a pot of rice.

A red ochre pictograph at Tashi Do depicting a highly unusual shrine with a tricuspidate finial, accompanied by a counterclockwise swastika and five-pointed star, made during the protohistoric period or early historic period

A uniquely designed rock art shrine from the protohistoric or early historic period at Nawo Lung resembles a simple pagoda.[74] A counterclockwise swastika and star accompany another one-of-a-kind ceremonial structure at Tashi Do.[75] This strange structure features a half-circle middle section set on a narrow pedestal and topped by three hornlike protuberances.

The architectural complexity of stepped shrines in Upper Tibetan rock art increases until they become full-fledged *chorten*, the well-known ceremonial structures of Eternal Bon and Buddhism. Referred to as *stupa* in India, *chorten* are cosmological and doctrinal monuments epitomizing a range of advanced religious teachings. Generally speaking, Tibetan variants have quadrate bases, graduated tiers, rounded midsections, and circular spires crowned by decorative finials. The Upper Tibetan rock art *chorten* of circa 700 to 1200 CE exhibit squat or pyramidal spires rather than the long spire of subsequent periods. These early *chorten* often have sinuous banners draped near the top of the spires and finials resembling the three-pronged "horns of the bird, sword of the bird" adopted by Eternal Bon, rather than the conjoined sun and moon popular among the Buddhists. Counterclockwise swastikas accompanying these *chorten* indicate that they were made by practitioners of archaic cults and their Eternal Bon successors.

At the Brakdong site in Ruthok, around twenty early historic period *chorten* were carved in various styles.[76] These five-tiered structures are crowned by an orb flanked by prominent points resembling horns. Another *chorten* at Brakdong has a flaglike finial. The variable carving techniques used in rendering these petroglyphs, combined with nonuniform levels of wear, divulge that they were produced over a fairly long period of time as part of a well-developed artistic and architectural tradition. Among the only polychrome pictographs in Upper Tibet are depicted early-style *chorten*. Painted in red, yellow, and white, these *chorten* were discovered on the shores of Nam Tsho and at Drakkhung Dzepo in Naktshang.[77]

It is not easy to differentiate non-Buddhist and Buddhist rock art *chorten* from one another prior to the complete conversion of Upper Tibet to Buddhism circa 1200 CE, as there was much overlap in their design. Close sociocultural links (both positive and negative) between Tibet's two major religious traditions seems to have stimulated this practical interplay, obscuring sectarian-based architectural traditions.

The early historic period *chorten* of Upper Tibet find resonance in the rock art of Ladakh and northern Pakistan. In Pakistan's Indus Kohistan and Gilgit, many such specimens dating to the second to ninth centuries CE were documented by the German archaeologists Karl Jettmar and Volker Thewalt and by the Pakistani archaeologist Ahmad Hasan Dani in the 1980s.[78] Some of the carved *chorten* of northern Pakistan are accompanied by Sogdian and

Kharoshti inscriptions, which are indicative of Central Asian cultural influences. There are also *chorten* with Tibetan inscriptions assignable to the invasion and occupation of northern Pakistan by imperial Tibetan armies in the eighth century CE. As in early historic Upper Tibet, a non-Buddhist cultural presence in northern Pakistan and Ladakh is reflected in mystic formulae written in the Tibetan alphabet. The most popular of these mantras reads *a ma*, syllables that in Eternal Bon symbolize the male and female aspects of existence respectively.

The characterization of a class of northern Pakistan and Ladakh rock art *chorten* as comparatively unrefined by archaeologists can be generally applied to their early historic period counterparts in Upper Tibet. These too display simple stylization, the handiwork of highlanders before the Tibetan system of writing and Buddhism gained widespread acceptance. The more elaborately designed and finely executed rock art *stupas* associated with Buddhism in the Western Himalaya seldom occur in Upper Tibet.

At the turn of the twentieth century, the German missionary August Hermann Francke documented a number of ancient rock art *chorten* on the western fringe of the Tibetan Plateau.[79] A pioneer in Ladakh studies, Francke opined that these *chorten* distinguished by flags, "tridents," and counterclockwise swastikas represented rudimentary shrines probably carved by an illiterate people. The French archaeologist Henri-Paul Francfort classifies these types of *chorten* in Ladakh as "primitive" or "folksy." So too the German archaeologist Karl Jettmar, who attributes the roughly rendered *chorten* of Indus Kohistan rock art to a "folk religion" that may have coexisted with Buddhism. The existence of cognate rock art in the Western Himalaya is indicative of Tibetan archaic cultural influences infiltrating the region during the early historic period and perhaps even earlier.

Tracing the historical development of the primitive *chorten* of Upper Tibet, Ladakh, and northern Pakistan is a difficult task. In some measure, they owe their inspiration to the stepped shrines of Zhang Zhung. Another major cultural influence affecting the design and distribution of *chorten* in Upper Tibet, Ladakh, and northern Pakistan originated in north India. The refined engravings of *stupas* in northern Pakistan reveal styles of ornamentation and architecture derived from Gandhara and Kashmir when Buddhism reigned supreme. The rudimentary stepped shrines of Zhang Zhung appear to have cross-fertilized with the intricate Buddhist *stupas* of the Western Himalaya to produce the early historic period *chorten* of Upper Tibet. However, multilingual inscriptions associated with northern Pakistan and Ladakh rock art have not been discovered in Upper Tibet. This suggests that after the second century CE, Zhang Zhung was largely cut off from the bigger cultural forces buffeting Ladakh and north Inner Asia.

Upper Tibet's increasing isolation from the roiling cultural activities of lands to the north and west meant that Buddhism did not reach there in any appreciable way before the seventh century CE. Prior to the establishment of the Tibetan empire, Buddhist inscriptions, art, and monuments do not appear in Upper Tibet. Nonetheless, the inhabitants of the Tibetan upland may have been aware of Buddhism and its followers. Ancient Indian literature suggests that sacred sites such as Mount Tise and Lake Mapang were magnets for pilgrims from the Subcontinent before the seventh century CE. The prospect of cross-cultural contacts is supported by Eternal Bon literature, which claims that Sanskrit mantras were introduced in Zhang Zhung in the prehistoric epoch. Nonetheless, the absence of Buddhist archaeological signposts in Upper Tibet prior to the seventh century CE indicates that her people were largely content with their own preliterate religious traditions.

Of north Indian inspiration, the Tibetan script was devised in the seventh century CE and is traditionally credited to Thonmi Sambhota, a minister of King Songtsen Gampo. Although Eternal Bon alleges that an alphabet known as *maryik* was used to write the Zhang Zhung language long before the invention of the Tibetan script, I have not discovered any archaeological evidence in the rock grottos of Upper Tibet to support this assertion. Had a Zhang Zhung era script really existed, it should be found on stone surfaces, just like the early historic period Tibetan inscriptions drawn and engraved at various rock art sites in Upper Tibet. Moreover, the *maryik* script is suspiciously ornamental, a characteristic quality of Tibetan calligraphy after 1000 CE.

The archaeological evidence thus indicates that early civilization in highland Tibet conducted its affairs mainly through the spoken word. Tallies in the form of knotted cords and notched boards may also have been used to keep records in prehistoric times. Both types of objects are mentioned in Tibetan ritual literature. It was only after the Tibetan empire annexed the Zhang Zhung kingdom that its inhabitants began to adopt the Tibetan script with varying levels proficiency. In the early historic period, Upper Tibetan scribes working on rock surfaces experimented with a number of writing styles, some crudely scrawled, others made with a more cultivated hand. This epigraphic evidence shows that the introduction of literacy in the Tibetan hinterlands was a long and convoluted process.

LONG-LOST CULTURAL LINKS

Sundry encounters between ancient Upper Tibetans and Inner Asian neighbors to the north are witnessed in rock art. The rock paintings of Tashi Do contain several such testimonies, documenting contacts with other lands.

One Tashi Do pictograph shows six individuals uniquely attired in tight-fitting caps and short-sleeved robes, at least one of which is marked with lines simulating a textile design.[80] These costumes are not in keeping with the types of garments usually pictured in Upper Tibetan rock art, possibly suggesting foreign origins. One scenario is that these six figures represent Central Asian Sogdian traders or emissaries of the early historic period. Another Tashi Do artist sketched an individual leading two Bactrian camels, an animal not native to the eastern Changthang.[81] This portrayal is probably that of a trader or pilgrim from north Inner Asia painted in either the protohistoric period or early historic period. In close proximity to the camel herder is a genre of pictographs that appears to portray Jurchens or Khitans, people of Altaic origins who dominated northern China from the early tenth century to the early thirteenth century CE.[82] Each human figure wears a hat reminiscent of north Chinese or Manchurian fashion. One figure stands at the window of a house with a peaked roof inspired by Chinese architecture. Undeciphered symbols resembling characters used to write the Khitan or Jurchen languages were created nearby. These highly unusual inscriptions are the only ones of foreign persuasion discovered on the rock surfaces of Upper Tibet to date.

In prehistoric rock carvings of Upper Tibet, wild yaks are sometimes depicted with small curved horns that join to form a circle. The circle-horn motif is commonly employed in bovine petroglyphs of Ladakh and north Inner Asia as well.[83] Some wild yaks in these regions are portrayed with club-like tails. Wild yaks with these traits in Upper Tibet and Ladakh belong to what can be termed the "Western Tibetan Plateau Style." In both the Plateau and steppe contexts, the circle-horn and club-tail motifs appear on bovines with a decidedly rectangular form. This underlying body structure or schema upon which analogous motifs were affixed heralds a meeting of sorts between the north Inner Asian steppes and the Tibetan highlands deep in the Metal Age. The widespread distribution of zoomorphic rock art in Upper Tibet conceived on a rectilinear framework or schema alludes to any such artistic or ideological transfers as being far reaching and fundamental. The ebb and flow of early cultural traditions and technologies between north Inner Asia and Tibet are likely to have passed through the northwest and northeast corners of the Plateau, great vortices of humanity since time immemorial.

It is generally accepted that in the second millennium BCE, the Andronovs and Tocharians, peoples with Europoid racial characteristics, left their western homelands and migrated to eastern Central Asia. The Chinese archaeologist Han Kangxin reports that twenty-one human skulls recovered from graves in the Yanbulaq cemetery of Xinjiang, dating to 1300–500 BCE, resemble in structure those of Tibetan populations.[84] This craniometric evidence may possibly indicate that Upper Tibetan contacts with northern peoples such as Tocharians were an ongoing feature of the Late Bronze Age and Iron Age.

A chariot rock carving from western Tibet

The existence of more than two dozen carvings of wheeled vehicles in Upper Tibet is one of the most vivid signs of cultural intercourse between Zhang Zhung and north Inner Asia.[85] Petroglyphs of chariots were first discovered in 2002 at the central Changthang sites of Shaksang and Gyaling by the Lhasa art historian Lobsang Tashi. I discovered many more examples in 2010 and 2011. These petroglyphs depict vehicles with two cross-shaped or multispoked wheels on either side of the central pole. These chariots are pulled by a pair of horses. The box of the chariot is rendered as a circle or square, and sometimes a human figure holding the reins is shown inside. These same types of two-wheeled vehicles are also popular in the rock art of the steppes of the second and first millennium BCE. The surprising discovery of chariots in Upper Tibetan rock art has very significant historical and cultural ramifications. It demonstrates as much as any other evidence that the ancient Plateau was linked in technological and ideological terms to the rest of Eurasia. Whether depicting a form of transport, military platform, vehicle for transporting the dead, or symbol of conquest and power, chariots, like mascoids, indelibly marked the cultural fabric of diverse peoples, a prehistoric cosmopolitanism perhaps as persuasive as any since then.

Clashes between settled societies in the south and roving steppe nomads in the north were played out again and again across Late Bronze Age and Iron

Age Central Asia. Hence, an intrusion of steppe nomads into agricultural regions of Upper Tibet and Ladakh is in keeping with the general migratory trends of those times. It is also possible though that chariots and mascoids reached the Tibetan Plateau through a long chain of cultural intermediaries, each putting its stamp on them to suit specific needs and conditions. An alinear model of diffusion can account for the transformation of seminal objects and art as they move through time and space from one people to another, imbuing more and more cultures with a common bequest.

The rock art of the steppes and Tibetan tablelands share other important artistic affinities, the result of long-acting but still poorly understood prehistoric interconnections. I have documented petroglyphs of bounding wild sheep with spiraling horns at the Pung Ri site in Ruthok.[86] Wild herbivore petroglyphs crowned with more elaborate spiraling horns have been discovered in Mongolia and are thought to date to the Iron Age.[87] Another geometric template used for the bodies of wild yaks and deer in Upper Tibet and north Inner Asia consists of two triangles arranged point to point.[88] This bi-triangular style is well known in the rock art of Mongolia, southern Siberia, and Kazakhstan. In both Upper Tibet and north Inner Asia, it was composed over an extended period of time.

A highly ornate deer engraved on a limestone rock formation at Khampa Racho in Ruthok has been the object of study by various rock art researchers.[89]

Two wild herbivores (probably antelopes) representative of the Upper Tibetan variant of the Eurasian "animal style" of the Iron Age

This technically sophisticated petroglyph was carved with scroll-like horns and a body adorned with curling lines. This style of deer with its intricate curvilinear embellishments recalls the so-called animal art of the steppes.[90]

In the rock art theatres of Ruthok, wild herbivore petroglyphs are often adorned with scrolls or volutes as part of an S-shaped schema.[91] The most popular recipients for this artistic treatment were deer and antelope, but wild yaks and sheep were occasionally rendered in this fashion as well. The S-shaped schema imparts great fluidity and vitality on rock art animals. The symbolism behind S-shaped bodies and markings is difficult to ascertain, but it may possibly simulate the life force of animals. Wild herbivores, boars, and other animals in rock carvings and decorative arts attributed to the Scythians and other tribes of the steppes of the first millennium BCE were also devised on a curvilinear schema. These animals exhibit clean-cut lines and a dynamism based on the scroll and volute. As in Upper Tibet, S-shaped lines are repeated several times to make animal compositions distinguished by considerable gracefulness and flair. While the repertoire of stylistic elements developed in Zhang Zhung and among the steppe tribes varies considerably, it builds upon the same basic geometry. This shared design canon is cogent evidence of ancient cultural interplay between north Inner Asia and Upper Tibet, for artistic correspondences extend to the very way in which animal art was conceived and created.[92]

Petroglyphs predicated on an S-shaped schema in Upper Tibet occur only in Ruthok, indicating that this region was a prime conduit of cultural interaction between the steppes, deserts, and forests of north Inner Asian and the Tibetan upland. Immediately north of Ruthok is East Turkestan, a vast territory where Scythian cultural impacts on local agrarian cultures in the first millennium BCE are well documented. By the middle of the first millennium BCE, the Scythians were pursuing an unfettered nomadic existence, whereas Ruthok was host to a highly developed agricultural society. In contrast to ancient Ruthok with its many citadels and temples, Scythian archaeology in Inner Asia is distinguished by a noteworthy absence of permanent residential structures. In the rock art of Upper Tibet, carnivores such as the wolf, tiger, and bear are less frequently depicted than wild herbivores. Scenes of ungulates being pursued by wolves and tigers, however, do occur at Ratroktrang, Shaksang, and other rock art sites in highland Tibet.[93] Predators chasing and attacking wild herbivores also show up in the petroglyphs of Yinshan and Helimu in Inner Mongolia, as documented by Tang Huisheng of Nanjing University.[94] Similar types of predatory tigers, lions, and wolves are widely distributed in rock art sites of the steppes.[95] The springing feline depicted with pointed ears, gaping jaws, and the tail curled over its body is a subject common to the rock art of Zhang Zhung and other Inner Asian territories.[96]

The widespread geographic distribution of this feline iconography further evinces far-ranging cross-cultural contacts between Iron Age Upper Tibet and her northern neighbors.

THE ALLURE OF ANCIENT ART IN METALS

In addition to rock art, there were portable objects of artistic merit manufactured in ancient Upper Tibet. Sadly, few of these more easily transported artifacts have been available for scientific study. Most of the more desirable examples have been spirited out of Tibet to mainland China and other countries by traders in art and antiquities. With few practical safeguards in place to protect Tibet's ancient heritage, a wide web of dealers have conducted their business with impunity. Enjoying patronage in powerful places, there are few signs that the illicit trade in Tibetan antiquities will end anytime soon.

The extremely cold and dry conditions of Upper Tibet are well suited to the long-term preservation of material objects. The intense ultraviolet radiation enhances the sterility of the environment, strongly retarding the decomposition of artifacts. It is not unusual for organic substances such as bone and wood in upland Tibet to exhibit a remarkable degree of structural integrity even after two millennia or more.

An ancient stone model of a stepped shrine kept in a western Tibetan village

Metal and stone figurines of animals and anthropomorphs from Zhang Zhung and Sumpa and the early historic civilization succeeding them have come to light in the Tibetan art market. Some of these sculptures functioned as funerary effigies; others appear to have had alternative uses. I had the opportunity to inspect one such object in bronze in the form of an extremely well-cast antelope or ibex. In the mid-1990s, a Tibetan dealer showed me a beautifully made stepped shrine fashioned from iron. In form, it was just like those carved and painted on rock surfaces in Upper Tibet. A smaller and simpler example of an ancient stepped shrine sculpted in stone is kept in a western Tibetan village by local residents.

The most ubiquitous objects of hunting and war from ancient Upper Tibet are arrow points and spearheads.[97] Buried in the ground or hidden in rock formations, these are regularly turned up by farmers and shepherds. Ancient weapons in copper and iron, including knives, swords, and pikes, have been discovered in various places in the upland as well. The earliest examples of metallic armaments date to the time of Zhang Zhung. While these constitute an extremely important resource for better understanding the scope and character of ancient civilization in Upper Tibet, very few examples have been formally exhibited or studied.

Chinese historical records from the Tang dynasty (618–907 CE) extol the quality and refinement of Tibetan weaponry from the early historic period. Molded gold ornaments of animals probably dating to the protohistoric period were recently salvaged from looted burials near Central Tibet's Lake Yardrok Yumtsho.[98] These lovely objects reinforce the impressions held by ancient Chinese that Tibetans were superb metalworkers. Even in more recent times, Tibetans were renowned for exceptional skill in casting statuary, tempering steel, and manipulating sheet metal.

Plain and decorated vessels of the archaic era made from metal, stone, and clay, in many different sizes and styles, have been found in Upper Tibet. These vessels were used for all manner of ritual and utilitarian needs. As noted in chapter 6, thin-walled amphorae with long bodies and lug handles dating to the second half of the first millennium BCE have been documented at funerary sites in Guge.[99] Most metal and stone vessels, being more durable than ceramics, have been whisked away by antiquities dealers. Upper Tibetan textile and wooden remnants of considerable antiquity have also surfaced. Some of these objects were inadvertently unearthed during construction projects, while others were looted from *chorten* by treasure hunters.[100]

One early metallic object that will hopefully be preserved for posterity in Tibet is an extremely important horse bridle.[101] This rare metal artifact was being offered for sale by a petty dealer in 2003, and with the help of two Western aid workers I arranged for its purchase. The bridle was donated to the Tibet Provincial Museum to augment their paltry showing of Metal Age objects. As of 2009, it languished ill-conserved in a storeroom of the museum. According to the dealer who sold it, this bridle was recovered from a tomb in Nakchu, in Upper Tibet. It consists of thirty-five molded copper alloy components, including a bit, cheek pieces, and embossed rein covers. Two larger, slightly curved plates may have ornamented the neck of a horse. This bridle demonstrates that ancient Tibetans were producing horse tack as sophisticated as any of their neighbors. Dating to the archaic era, it has design elements recalling bridles produced by the Scythians of the first millennium BCE.

A highly varied assortment of ancient copper alloy objects called *thokchak* are still worn by Tibetans for protection and good fortune.[102] This relatively common class of artifacts is chronologically and stylistically related to rock art. *Thokchak*, or "primordial metal," were produced in Tibet from the Metal Age until around 1500 CE. Some were designed as charms, while others originally functioned as insignia, ritual items, medical implements, small tools, clasps, or ornaments. These objects came to acquire talismanic value with age and the mystique that comes up around appealing ancient things. Their simple but striking designs have long fascinated Tibetans.

Thokchak are traditionally believed to be fashioned from primal metal falling from the sky. According to popular Tibetan folklore, when molten metal carried in thunderbolts strikes the ground, it gradually reacts with moisture in the soil to form *thokchak*. It is also said that these amulets were disgorged from the mouths of celestial dragons or wrought from the forges of divine blacksmiths.

Traditionally, *thokchak* were handed down over the generations from father to son, from mother to daughter, and from guru to disciple. Many now lie in foreign collections, sold off over the last three decades by impoverished or complacent Tibetans in a fast-changing world. A number of books and articles focus on *thokchak*, the most famous being Giuseppe Tucci's *Transhimalaya*.[103] Unlike larger and rarer objects, even the most humble of farmers or herders could own one or more *thokchak*, especially if they were lucky enough to find them in the countryside. Given its diversity, no other single group of material objects is as emblematic of Tibet's ancient history as *thokchak*.

Produced in different regions of Tibet over a great span of time, *thokchak* come in a dazzling array of zoomorphic, anthropomorphic, and geometric designs. Like rock art, some *thokchak* represent ancient mythological and religious themes, but these are difficult to pinpoint. Certain amulets in animal and human form are liable to be likenesses of ancestral and protective deities. In western Tibet, small figurines in the form of tiny deer, blue sheep, argali sheep, yaks, and wild asses are occasionally unearthed by local

A fibula discovered on the summit of a holy mountain by a reincarnate lama. Among its motifs are anthropomorphic and zoomorphic figures, as well as tiered shrines.

inhabitants.[104] Typically, these zoomorphic *thokchak* have attachment loops or holes so that they could be tied around the neck or to clothing. Another kind of amulet discovered in Upper Tibet is the anthropomorphic mask. Perforations in these rare miniature masks indicate that they were designed to be displayed on one's person.

One of the most impressive types of copper alloy artifacts regularly discovered in Upper Tibet is the fibula. Circular ornamental objects, fibulae were produced in the protohistoric and early historic periods.[105] That they almost exclusively come to light in Upper Tibet and Ladakh strongly suggests that these are places where they were manufactured. However, the foundries in which fibulae were made have still not been identified. Upper Tibetan fibulae may have been used to fasten clothing or as a broach to designate an individual's political rank or religious standing. They consist of one or more flat rings adorned with lions, birds, stepped shrines, vases, flowers, and divine figures. Fibulae appear to have been conceived as models of the cosmos, the animals and other decorative elements representing the gods of the clans and the structures of the natural world. The high level of proficiency that went into casting them and the adroit modeling of the decorative motifs speak well of the artisans who created them. They range in size from one inch to ten inches in diameter, with larger specimens exhibiting particularly intricate motifs. The largest and fanciest fibulae must have been owned by elite members of Zhang Zhung and early historic period upland society.

Some Upper Tibetan fibulae display the centrally positioned bust of a deity, the identity of which is not certain. In fibulae dating to the early historic period, this figure may represent Thukjechenpo, the patron god of Buddhist Tibet. The incorporation of *dorje*, the ritual thunderbolt of Buddhism, into some fibulae is a telltale sign that this type dates to the early historic period. The manufacture of fibulae in both protohistoric and early historic times is an excellent example of how certain Zhang Zhung cultural and technological traditions were conserved in the upland even after its incorporation into the Tibetan empire.

Another small but highly regarded class of ancient objects periodically uncovered in Upper Tibet are patterned agates known as *zi*.[106] According to Tibetan folklore, *zi* beads are the fossilized larvae of water spirits. These baby spirits are said to dwell in springs, but when captured they turn instantly to stone.

Zi stone patterns are characterized by lines, circles and other geometric designs in light colors inscribed on a contrasting dark background. The *zi* of Tibet are unrivaled for their elegant shapes, clarity, and the excellence of their patterns, speaking highly of its ancient past. Among the most coveted *zi* are those with nine "eyes," a polka-dot pattern suffused with cosmological symbolism. *Zi* beads were bored out by hand so that a cord could be slipped through them. Much more technically challenging was the engraving of beads in desired patterns. The scored lines were filled with a mineral paste and annealed in ovens to harden it to a rocklike consistency. It was only in the 1990s, after many years of experimentation, that Taiwanese technologists succeeded in duplicating this ancient process.

Patterned agate, onyx, and carnelian beads are also known from the ancient civilizations of India, Persia, and Mesopotamia, but the most technically advanced types seem to have been manufactured in Tibet, for these are found nowhere else in the world in any appreciable numbers. The actual location for the production of *zi* stones appears to have been Zhang Zhung, but this remains to be confirmed by further archaeological research.

The rock art and artifacts of Upper Tibet tell us much about the culture of Zhang Zhung. These material manifestations of ancient beliefs and customs overlie fervent religious traditions, which did much to shape civilization in uppermost Tibet. It is appropriate then that we turn next to the history and nature of religion in Zhang Zhung, the part of its ancient way of life that has proven most enduring.

Father Sky Eagle and Mother Earth Serpent: The Religion of Zhang Zhung

THE HISTORIC BEGINNINGS OF ETERNAL BON

*W*e have seen how the legacy of Zhang Zhung is preserved in historical texts, ruins, and art. Another splendid source of information about Zhang Zhung lies buried in the traditions of the so-called Yungdrung, or "Eternal" Bon, religion. These matters of faith have been kept alive and well by its writers for a thousand years. In this chapter, we turn to those traces of Zhang Zhung discernible in Eternal Bon literature and in related Old Tibetan texts.

Over the last millennium, the word *bon* in Classical Tibetan literature has become a catchall term for the entire native cultural heritage of Tibet. Although antediluvian forms of Tibetan religion long predate Eternal Bon and folk traditions, all have come to assume the label *bon*. This broad understanding of *bon* as the sum total of non-Buddhist culture and religion over the ages is in keeping with the literal meaning of the word. According to Eternal Bon, *bon* denotes the totality of human endeavor, the universe, and the essence of truth. As a verb, it refers to the chanting of holy words and the transmission of sacred knowledge, the instrument by which ancient wisdom was transferred to the Tibet of today.

It was with good reason that the two Lamaist religions chose to retrospectively lump together virtually every indigenous custom and tradition under the rubric of *bon*. They were responding to the well-rooted sense of the word in the archaic era. In Old Tibetan–language documents of the early historic period, the word *bon* appears as part of the proper names of priests who carried out a variety of rituals for the living and the dead. In this literature, the *bonpo* along with the *shen* were priests involved in rites of healing, prosperity, propitiation, and death. The biggest difference in the way the term *bon* is employed in the obsolete and classical senses is institutional in nature. In the archaic era, *bon* did not designate a singular religion; rather it signified sundry ritual systems propagated by various regional cults. According to Tibetan historical records, these religious parties operated in Zhang Zhung, Sumpa, Central Tibet, and surrounding prehistoric nations. With the coming of the Tibetan empire in the seventh century CE, the various regional factions began to find a common religious idiom.

Eternal Bon emerged from the ever-growing pressure Buddhism exerted upon the native cults of the early historic period.[1] As such, two major streams of spiritual waters, Indian and indigenous, merged to create Eternal Bon, one of the most eclectic of world religions. Like Buddhism, it spread across the Tibetan Plateau and to adjoining regions of the Himalaya and Central Asia. As a Lamaist faith, Eternal Bon boasts a highly sophisticated philosophy, ethics, and praxis derived from Buddhism, while at the same time preserving vestiges of the ancient traditions of Upper and Central Tibet. With all its borrowing, Eternal Bon inherited a huge volume of wisdom teachings, rituals, and esoteric practices from Buddhism. By reassembling the archaic using the tools of Buddhism, Eternal Bon juxtaposed the prehistoric with the historic, the mythic with the prosaic, to create a grand edifice of Tibetan intellectual life.[2]

The adherents of Eternal Bon are not inclined to see the syncretistic side of their faith, nor do they entertain that they are largely a by-product of Buddhist thought. To the contrary, a cornerstone of Eternal Bon is the conviction that its basic doctrines have remained unchanged for many thousands of years. This belief is epitomized in the use of the swastika as the prime symbol of Eternal Bon, a sign of eternity. Like religions everywhere, Eternal Bon assigns its ultimate origins to the ethereal realm of the divine.

A great deal has been written about the introduction of Buddhism into Tibet. Tibetologists such as Mathew Kapstein, Per Sørensen, David L. Snellgrove, Hilda Diemberger, and Pasang Wangdu examine the rise of Buddhism on the Plateau from many different angles.[3] From the seventh century CE, Buddhism was in the ascendance in Tibet as it slowly but surely won converts among the population. Genuine attractions notwithstanding, the embrace of Buddhism by some Tibetan noble families may have been politically motivated. In the political calculus of the time, the *dharma*, or "religion," of India appears to have served as a counterweight to noble factions still professing archaic forms of Tibetan religion. But the old ways would not die easily. The continued interment of the Tibetan kings in the large tombs of the Chonggye burial grounds in Yarlung demonstrates that archaic traditions remained culturally and institutionally relevant throughout most of the imperial period.[4]

Buddhism, however, was to prove a revolutionary force that would eventually topple the old religious order. It gained a foothold under Tibet's first emperor, Songtsen Gampo, who established lavish Buddhist temples in Central Tibet and beyond. The most famous of his Buddhist sanctuaries was the Jokhang, the holiest of holies erected in the middle of Tibet's capital city, Lhasa. Two celebrated early historic Buddhist temples in Upper Tibet were Tradun in Drongpa and Palkye near Gurgyam. In the edict of Samye, King Trisong Deutsen made Buddhism the state religion of Tibet circa 780 CE.[5] He also instituted a thriving Buddhist monastic system in the years to follow. This was a turning point in Tibet's religious history, marking the beginning of Buddhist domination in that country.

After the fall of the Tibetan empire in 846 CE, the Plateau entered an unsettled period lasting 150 years. In those troubled times, Buddhism consolidated its hold over the spiritual life of Tibet. By 1000 CE, the bulk of archaic religious cults had succumbed to the inexorable tide of Buddhism washing over Tibet. In the new zeitgeist they lost much of their political punch and economic energy. But so ingrained were indigenous traditions in the Tibetan way of life that they could not simply be discarded en masse; rather, many found accommodation in the new religious system. By imbibing a Buddhist worldview and morality, moribund religious traditions reappeared in new and vigorous forms. While most Tibetans openly accepted a Buddhism tailored to their particular cultural needs, those who clung to a patriotic notion of their native heritage came to found the institution of Eternal Bon.

Eternal Bon internalized Buddhist philosophical tenets, mind-training exercises, and the ethic of nonviolence with great competency. Simultaneously, revisionism brought the surviving archaic traditions in line with Buddhist teachings and sensibilities. So well amalgamated have archaic and Buddhist ideas and activities become in Eternal Bon, it is sometimes hard to tell one from the other. Beginning in the early historic period, Buddhism also adopted many indigenous cultural elements. Although it did not absorb these as enthusiastically as did Eternal Bon, many older customs and practices were taken up by it. The weaving of the archaic into the fabric of Buddhism is epitomized in the purification of deities with aromatic smoke and water, a *bon* practice it readily embraced. The Buddhists also inducted the native gods into their pantheon by placing them under oath and tinkering with their names.

While it drew inspiration from Zhang Zhung culture and history, Eternal Bon borrowed heavily from Buddhist doctrines and practices in order to remain relevant to the spiritual life of Tibetans. *Bonpo* and *shen* religious figures were made over in the guise of monks, embracing the ethics and worldview of Buddhism. The most telling example of this cultural manipulation is none other than the putative founder of Eternal Bon, Tönpa Shenrab.

Eternal Bon holds that Tönpa Shenrab was a Buddha just like Sakyamuni of the Buddhists. In Tibetan literature, the activities of these two

Buddhas share a common narrative pattern. They renounced the world, took monastic vows, and taught a doctrine in which enlightenment was the goal. The philosophical and moral teachings of the Buddha of Olmo-lungring and the Buddha of India are very well matched. Tönpa Shenrab's higher teachings, the Bon of Effects, are preserved in religious texts known as sutras and tantras, many of which have Buddhist counterparts. An excellent example of shared doctrine is the Prajnaparamita, the epitome of Mahayana Buddhist philosophical teachings, a body of sutras that was duly appropriated by Eternal Bon.

A key ideal of Eternal Bon adopted from Mahayana Buddhism is the way of the bodhisattvas, individuals who defer achieving full enlightenment in order to help other sentient beings attain liberation. The bodhisattvas accomplish this noble task through the perfection of wisdom and all-embracing compassion. Sapient beings dwelling beyond the sphere of worldly activity; two types of reality, unconditional and conditional; and the three spiritual bodies of the Buddha are other major doctrines that define the two Lamaist religions.[6]

While some religious masters of Zhang Zhung may have been deeply involved in mystic practices, they bore little resemblance to Lamaist monks of later times. The prehistoric temple remains of Zhang Zhung are not architecturally related to the Buddhist monasteries of India or the cloisters established in imperial Tibet. Moreover, the ritual functions conducted inside the installations of Zhang Zhung were part and parcel of a different religious universe. They existed within a culture that stressed honor as one of the highest of values and mastery of natural phenomena as the greatest social good. In contrast, the loftiest goal of Eternal Bon and Buddhism is escape from an endless round of rebirths, an existence seen as fraught with pain and suffering.

Eternal Bon and Buddhism claim what was borrowed from the archaic religious traditions as their very own without explicitly recognizing their debt to them. Eternal Bon, by artificially projecting its history on the distant past, obscured the ancestry of archaic customs and traditions, while Buddhism heavily marginalized the contributions of past phases of Tibetan civilization. This reengineering of the historical record is readily understandable in doctrinal terms. The accretion of more recent structures onto older ones is the norm in world religions, especially when they spread to new places and in new times.

The largely unremarked borrowings of Eternal Bon and Buddhism from an earlier fund of cultural and religious traditions as well as from one another seem to constitute a long chain of mutual deceit. But one cannot lose sight of the immense practical benefits of this give-and-take to the adherents of both religions. By assuming a Buddhist air, Eternal Bon was able to find its rightful place in Tibetan society and still maintain a cultural heritage that otherwise would have been lost. Similarly, the Buddhists, by absorbing native rituals and deities, succeeded in stamping an authentic Tibetan imprint upon their faith, making it more palatable to the population at large.

THE MYTHIC BEGINNINGS OF ETERNAL BON

For practitioners of Eternal Bon, their religion begins with Tönpa Shenrab, a personality first mentioned in Old Tibetan sources. An intricate mythology that entwines indigenous and Indian lore has come up around him as the centerpiece of Eternal Bon. By disregarding aspects of Tönpa Shenrab's archaic identity incompatible with Buddhist teachings, he was re-created in the image and likeness of a Buddha. Also known as Shenrab Miwo, he is called the Omniscient One of the present world age.[7]

Tönpa Shenrab, literally "Excellent Shen Teacher," is named for the *shen*, a paramount class of priests active in prehistoric Tibet. It is written that Eternal Bon was propagated by a long line of primal deities before being conferred upon the holy figure of Tönpa Shenrab. As with the founders of other religions, he acted as the spiritual bridge between the divine and humanity. Tönpa Shenrab is recorded teaching in Olmolungring and other heavenly realms, as well as here on the earth. According to traditional Eternal Bon chronological conceptions, his edification of deities, humans, and demons took place some eighteen thousand years ago. It is said that in the previous world age Tönpa Shenrab's brother Dakpa ruled as the presiding Buddha, and a few thousand years henceforth Tönpa will be succeeded by another brother, the Buddha Shepa.

According to Eternal Bon, Tönpa Shenrab divided his teachings in various ways, the most common being nine branches, or vehicles. The first four of these vehicles are known as Gyui Bon, or the "Bon of Causes," the ritual and healing systems of the religion. The last five vehicles, Drebui Bon, or the "Bon of Effects," are primarily devoted to monastic and philosophical teachings. This all-encompassing classification of Eternal Bon doctrines was brought to the attention of the world by David L. Snellgrove in his landmark book, *The Nine Ways of Bon*.[8]

It is believed that when Tönpa Shenrab and his immediate successors instructed the inhabitants of Zhang Zhung and other regions of the Tibetan Plateau, they spread the four vehicles of the Bon of Causes. It is said that this corpus of exalted knowledge was specifically propagated by Tönpa Shenrab to alleviate the sufferings of all living beings. He is thought to have taught his disciples how to propitiate spirits with offerings of incense and alcoholic libations, how to make ransom offerings to win back the health of the ill, and how to carry out the death rites, as well as giving instructions on many other ritual procedures with practical benefits. These ritual functions, while being systematized in a different fashion, are also ascribed to Shenrab in Old Tibetan literature. In the archaic cultural context, they belong to religious traditions that long predate the establishment of Eternal Bon.

The first vehicle of Eternal Bon teachings is called the "Shen of the Basis of Good Fortune." It comprises divinatory, astrological, and healing rites for the welfare of living beings. The second vehicle, the "Shen of Phenomenal Existence," contains a battery of rites for protection and exorcism. The third vehicle is the "Shen of Magical Power," a collection of rites for the destruction and redemption of evil beings and antagonistic forces. The fourth and final vehicle of the Bon of Causes is known as the "Shen of Existence," containing the body of funerary rites.

In Eternal Bon literature it is written that Tönpa Shenrab first revealed the magnificent Bon of Causes to a divine convocation on the summit of Rirab Lhunpo, a mythic peak in the center of the world that connects heaven to earth. This revelation of the Bon of Causes is richly narrated in the fourteenth-century CE *Drime Zijid*, the longest of Tönpa Shenrab's biographies.[9] *Drime Zijid* records that an assembly of sages offered a jeweled mandala to Tönpa Shenrab, entreating him to divulge the holy teachings. It is said that the great master was one priestly year old at that time, the equivalent of a hundred human years. This encounter between Tönpa Shenrab and his disciples in *Drime Zijid* is expressed in the same portentous style of language used in Buddhist scriptures:

> "Sacred teacher, the lamp who protects and sees to the welfare of living beings, holy prince, the laudable one, venerated by gods and men, the Bon teachings of the swastika are extremely wide and innumerable. From the middle of your mind, reveal the essence of the relevant teachings to all us disciples." They thus made their request. Then with a smiling countenance, Prince Tönpa did thus speak: "Listen Chashen Tsukphü and other disciples, the time in which you have requested the teachings is eminently appropriate. The Bon teachings of the swastika are indeed extremely wide and innumerable; however, they can be summarized and aggregated into nine vehicles. . . . Ultimately, the essence of the doctrine can be distilled into one highest truth, which unequivocally is the actual basis of reality, the infinitude of the all-compassionate mind."

Another celebrated myth set in the period when Tönpa Shenrab taught the early sages concerns his subjugation of the unruly spirits and human inhabitants of the Tibetan Plateau. It is said that by defeating this motley group of beings, Tönpa Shenrab ensured that they would uphold the Eternal Bon doctrines. This theme of subjugation parallels a Tibetan Buddhist tale whose protagonist is Guru Rinpoche, the eighth-century CE wonder-working saint.

An animated version of superhuman Tönpa Shenrab meeting his adversaries on Mount Tise emblazons the folios of the well-known nineteenth-century CE history and pilgrimage guide *Tisei Karchak*.[10] The story begins with the proud leader of a class of spirits known as the *dud*. This problematic *dud* named Khyabpa Lakring abducted one of Tönpa Shenrab's two daughters, Shenza Neuchung, and stole the master's seven horses. Shenza Neuchung had two sons with the chief of the *dud* before Tönpa Shenrab traveled to eastern Tibet and retrieved her and his horses. We know from other biographical sources that Khyabpa Lakring tired to live with Shenza Neuchung under Tönpa Shenrab's rule, but the two men's antagonism for each other was too great and the *dud* returned alone to his own country. To avenge the loss of his lover and other perceived indignities, Khyabpa Lakring, aided and abetted by three tribes from southeastern Tibet, went to Mount Tise in western Tibet and confronted Tönpa Shenrab.

The showdown between the two sides took place at the headwaters of the four great rivers that arise near Mount Tise. According to the story, the *dud* spirits and three southeastern Tibetan tribes, the Nyang, Dak, and Kong, were reinforced by the armies of Mongolia and the Sino-Tibetan borderlands. The *dud* and their allies readied themselves for the decisive battle against Tönpa Shenrab. The omnipotent Tönpa Shenrab, for his part, was not troubled by the imminent engagement, for he was well armored with pure virtue and deep meditation practice.

From the country of Takzik, Tönpa Shenrab descended upon the corolla of an eight-petaled crystal lotus manifesting on the peak of Mount Tise. Remaining in a profound state of mediation, the radiance from Tönpa Shenrab's body, speech, and mind covered all the Tibetan Plateau and eighteen surrounding countries. The earth quaked, the mountains shook, and the ocean frothed and foamed. Rainbows and clouds covered the earth, and flowers fell down like rain. Then the battle began. The first to take on Tönpa Shenrab were the native deities of the Tibetan Plateau. They had quickly assembled their forces and thirsted for the fight:

> Altogether, Mount Tise, the leader, and his orders of Zhang Zhung gods; Mount Thanglha, the leader, and his orders of Tibetan gods; Mount Pomra, the leader, and his orders of eastern Tibetan gods; and all 990,000 assemblies of Tibetan goddesses and twelve earth goddess protectors of the world conjured up a terrible army being called to action. With their wrathful mien, they displayed a fiery hurricane, thunderbolts, magic bombs, black clouds, thunderous sounds, and as many other evil occurrences through sorcery as they could.

The body emanation of the victorious one, Shenrab, manifested in the form of "Great Fierce Secret Conqueror of Demons." He revealed this destroyer manifestation with sharp arrows, magic bombs, magic missiles, and spells to the assembly of deities of the upper and lower worlds. All at once, the magical manifestations of each of the deities were neutralized. The deities then vowed not to transgress the commands of Shenrab and not to renounce their oath. . . . He conferred upon the deities the name "Oath-Holders with the Wisdom Eye." As the inhabitants of Trom and Gesar (countries in Central Asia), Mongolia, the Sino-Tibetan borderlands, and the red-faced Tibetans and some of the demons could not oppose him, they gathered around Tönpa bowing their heads.

Eternal Bon holds that the Bon of Causes was the historical prelude to the higher teachings of Tönpa Shenrab, which would be revealed by later lines of illustrious masters. The five branches of higher teachings are the Drebui Bon, or the "Bon of Effects." In content and organization these teachings resemble those of the Nyingmapa, or so-called Red Hats, the oldest living sect of Tibetan Buddhism. The vehicles of the Bon of Effects are devoted to lay and monastic ethics, tantric practices, and the consummate mind-training system known as Dzogchen.

According to Eternal Bon mythology, after teaching the gods, Tönpa Shenrab passed the doctrine on to his eight sons in the land of Olmolungring. Under the tutelage of his most accomplished son, Mucho Demdruk, six scholars translated the Eternal Bon teachings from the language of the gods into their native tongues. Hailing from Zhang Zhung, Takzik, Sumpa, India, China, and the Central Asian country of Trom, these men were known as the "Six Ornaments of Learning." After receiving the divine transmissions, the six translators returned to their respective countries to disseminate the Eternal Bon teachings in their own languages. Later, in Zhang Zhung and then in wider Tibet, the spread of Eternal Bon was undertaken by six great religious lineages: the Mu, Bru, Zhu, Pa, Meu, and Khyung.[11] At this point in the story the mythic blends nicely with the historic, as members of these clans are still active today in the doings of Eternal Bon.

As part of its mythic history, Eternal Bon maintains that its doctrines traveled to Zhang Zhung from the country of Takzik, located somewhere to the northwest. According to the Eternal Bon historical text *Treasury of Good Sayings*, scriptures totaling 16,500 chapters were packed into sacks made from the skins of tigers and leopards and transported to Zhang Zhung on the backs of vultures, cranes, and other animals.[12] It is thought that the Eternal Bon teachings were propagated in Zhang Zhung before spreading to Central Tibet. Eternal Bon claims that translation of scriptures from the Zhang Zhung language into Tibetan occurred over a very long period of time, culminating in the eighth century CE. However, as we learned in chapter 7, there is no known archaeological or epigraphic evidence for an indigenous system of writing on the Tibetan Plateau before the seventh century CE.

THE SECRET TEACHINGS OF ETERNAL BON

While more prosaic religious teachings are preserved in the Bon of Causes, the higher spiritual principles are enshrined in the Bon of Effects. The quintessence of the Bon of Effects is Dzogchen, the "Great Perfection," the highest form of wisdom in the Eternal Bon religion.[13] The sublime Dzogchen philosophy asserts that an all-encompassing primordium underlies all existence. This fundamental reality is envisioned as being as vast and empty as infinite space. The primordial ground is equated with the foundation of the mind, which is conceived of as a boundless and unchanging matrix, the source of all consciousness. The basic state of the mind in each individual is luminous self-awareness. However, this intrinsic luminosity is only recognizable to a human or divine being when the shroud of ignorance that obscures it is rent. According to Dzogchen teachings, apprehension of the true nature of the mind is dependent on the purification of unvirtuous deeds and the relinquishment of discursive thought processes.

Like Tibetan Buddhism, Eternal Bon says that a primordial Buddha named Kuntu Sangpo, or "All Goodness," exists in a state of absolute perfection in the timeless sphere of all-pervading ultimate reality.[14] It is written that in very ancient times, Kuntu Sangpo passed the mantle of Dzogchen teachings to Shenlha Ökar, a profoundly compassionate god whose existence transcends both nirvana and samsara. It is this resplendent white deity who is believed to have bestowed the Dzogchen doctrine to Tönpa Shenrab. At that time, Tönpa Shenrab is supposed to have manifested as a blue cuckoo bird, the symbol of an all-knowing teacher. Tönpa Shenrab is said to have been followed in the transmission of Dzogchen by six primal masters known by the epithet "Conqueror."

Eternal Bon avers that the original line of divine Dzogchen masters was followed by three teachers who instructed the gods, demons, and humans in the ways of this marvelous doctrine. These three teachers are considered part of a lineage of twenty-four Dzogchen sages, most of whom came from Zhang Zhung. This lineal tradition is appropriately known as the "Oral Transmission of Zhang Zhung." It is written that each Dzogchen sage entrusted the secret teachings to just one disciple, the next in the line of twenty-four. Some of these legendary Zhang Zhung masters belonged to the Gurub and Rasang, clans that still occupy Upper Tibet.

The spiritual mastery of the twenty-four Dzogchen masters of the Oral Transmission of Zhang Zhung is reputed to have been unparalleled. Their physical bodies are alleged to have dissolved into light at the time of death, leaving no mortal remains behind. This attainment of a so-called rainbow body is one of the distinguishing characteristics of realized Dzogchen practitioners. Even recent saints such as Shardza Tashi Gyaltsen (died 1935), author of the authoritative history of Eternal Bon, *Treasury of Good Sayings*, are reputed to have attained rainbow bodies.

The last of the twenty-four masters of the Oral Transmission of Zhang Zhung was Tapihritsa, a native of Upper Tibet. Inasmuch as he can be historicized, Tapihritsa lived in the eighth century CE. Although the chronology, indeed the reality, of his twenty-three predecessors has not been established, if taken literally, the number of sages in the lineage may suggest that the Oral Transmission of Zhang Zhung dates to the early centuries of the Common Era. A number of theories about the origins of Dzogchen exist. The scholar John Myrdhin Reynolds opines that Dzogchen may have come to Zhang Zhung under the influence of Indian and Central Asian Buddhist masters sometime before the seventh century CE.[15] As have some Eternal Bon scholars before him, Reynolds holds that a member of the Oral Transmission of Zhang Zhung named Zhang Zhung Garab was one and the same as Garab Dorje, a Dzogchen master of the Nyingma school of Buddhism. Garab Dorje hailed from Uddiyana, a land that may have bordered on Zhang Zhung to the west. Their sharing of the same name and Garab Dorje's geographic proximity to the heartland of Eternal Bon's Dzogchen encourages the view that he is identical to Zhang Zhung Garab. If so, this strengthens the case for the Dzogchen of Upper Tibet as having been aligned with Buddhist traditions during the rise of imperial Tibet.

Some fifty years ago, David L. Snellgrove theorized that the "Bon of Zhang Zhung" owed much of its existence to Buddhist missionaries reaching western Tibet before the seventh century CE.[16] Such contacts could possibly explain why Dzogchen teachings are common to both Eternal Bon and Buddhism. Nevertheless, we now know from the archaeological record and more detailed philological studies of Eternal Bon literature that Snellgrove's understanding of "Bon" is an oversimplified characterization of prehistoric religion in Upper Tibet. While Zhang Zhung may well have had vibrant contacts with early Buddhist masters, its highly developed civilization was the product of native innovation as well as interactions with a wide range of cultures over more than a millennium. Early Buddhist inroads into Zhang Zhung are at most one strand in its rich cultural tapestry.

Its religious source in the sphere of primordial reality notwithstanding, there is cultural historical evidence to suggest that certain elements of

Dzogchen teachings may be of native Tibetan origin. Archaic cosmogonic concepts of the primordium are similar to those used to explicate the nature of mind in Dzogchen. The qualities imputed to space as the generative principle in archaic religious traditions may have been amalgamated to the more rigorous philosophical perspective of Dzogchen. As Dzogchen tenets owe much to Buddhism, any such cross-fertilization would have transpired after the introduction of this religion to Tibet.

The primordium plays a seminal role in early Tibetan origin myths, and the ideas underpinning it appear to have taken shape in prehistory. The archaic origin myths typically begin with a vacuous state in which space, light, moisture, warmth, and the other agents of existence eventually appear. The voidlike fountainhead of these narratives is reminiscent of the ontological ground espoused in Dzogchen, yet it occurs in a cultural context devoid of Buddhist influences. Rather, the old origin myths share cardinal motifs, such as the cosmic egg and a sky father and earth mother, with creation tales that circulated around other regions of ancient Inner Asia. This is yet another indication of how archaic era civilization in Upper Tibet was tied to much more broadly distributed cultural patterns.

The Dzogchen masters of Zhang Zhung are believed to have had supernatural capabilities. Take Sene Gau for example, a native of Lion Fortress at Lake Dangra Yumtsho. This protohistoric figure is credited with founding a religious center known as Yubun, or "Turquoise Mist," on the shores of Lake Dangra.[17] Yubun is an active Eternal Bon monastery, and if there is a solid basis for the legend of Sene Gau, it is one of the longest continuously occupied religious sites in Upper Tibet. The geomantic heart of Yubun is the cavern of five carnivorous goddesses. Suspended in cliffs that tower above the lake waters, this large cave with odd rock formations is where Sene Gau is thought to have resided. Viewed as the mystic nucleus of Lake Dangra, it is considered the repository of the life force of the lake's chief goddess, Dangra Lekyi Wangmo.

Sene Gau is attributed with walking on the open waters of Lake Dangra, healing the sick of incurable diseases, repulsing hostile armies, and other miraculous feats. A short biography for him was slipped into the fourteenth-century CE text *Magyü Drubkhor*, composed by the lama Shen Nyima Gyaltsen.[18] True to his fabulous character, Sene Gau is recorded as cavorting with the goddesses of Lake Dangra as only a great sage could:

> At the secret cave of Dangra Turquoise Mist, Sene Gau had a resplendent white complexion. On his body he wore aquatic silk with a golden finish. The lake goddesses offered him the treasure vase of water. He cast the magic missile of stone to banish the lake demons. He raced on the lake riding on his drum. He circumnavigated the underwater *chorten* of crystal.

Like Dzogchen, the monastic traditions of Eternal Bon are traced to the teachings of Tönpa Shenrab. It is said that after finishing his worldly duties as a great prince, Tönpa Shenrab took the vows of a monk. Clearly, this projection of a Buddhist-like monastic way of life onto the ancient Tibetan cultural-scape is an innovation of later times. While some Indian and Central Asian Buddhist monks may have been known to prehistoric Zhang Zhung and Central Tibet, monasticism did not fully take hold on the Tibetan Plateau until the early ninth century CE. The first great Buddhist monastery built in Tibet was Samye in the Brahmaputra valley of Central Tibet, completed by King Relpachen in 825 CE.

The rules governing Eternal Bon monks and monastic life are part of the Bon of Effects. These monastic strictures known as Dulwa are said to have been propagated by the original translators of Eternal Bon, that cosmopolitan group known as the "Six Ornaments of Learning."[19] The Dulwa were supposedly passed on for thousands of years by a long line of Zhang Zhung and Central Tibetan masters. Some figures in the apocryphal Zhang Zhung monastic lineage are associated with the bird-horn holding kings described in chapter 4. Passing from Dzutrul Yeshe to Yeshe Tshultrim, then Yungdrung Tshultrim, and finally to Tsukphü Tshultrim, this latter figure is attributed with spreading monasticism throughout Zhang Zhung. According to the *Treasury of Good Sayings*, Tsukphü Tshultrim and two disciples then carried the monastic tradition to Central Tibet during the reign of its first seven kings, the protohistoric dynasty known as Tridun.

Based on the genealogy of Tibet's legendary kings, the transfer of the monastic tradition from Zhang Zhung to Central Tibet would have occurred around the beginning of our Common Era. These protohistoric monks are portrayed as leading a religious way of life not differing much from their Eternal Bon and Buddhist counterparts of the Lamaist era, but this is hardly possible. The hyperbole built into Eternal Bon's historical discourse may enhance its stature in the eyes of believers, but it obfuscates the actual nature of archaic religious activities.

As appealing as a vision of prehistoric Eternal Bon monks mediating and praying in a manner not unlike those of today is, it is squarely contradicted by the archaeological evidence. The prehistoric *sekhar/sekhang* of Upper Tibet are in no way, shape, or form like the monasteries of later times. These cavernous spaces were constructed by Tibetans for archaic religious and cultural activities. While Buddhism coming from Central Asia and the Indian Subcontinent may have touched upon Zhang Zhung in the first half of the first millennium CE, its influence could not have been very strong, for it is not reflected in the Upper Tibetan artistic, epigraphic, or monument records of that time.

THE SPREAD OF ZHANG ZHUNG
RELIGION TO CENTRAL TIBET

According to Eternal Bon texts, Shenrab Miwo and many other saints resided in Zhang Zhung, but their legacy was to spread to the entire Tibetan Plateau. Buddhist historians acknowledge a key cultural role for Zhang Zhung in some of their writings as well. Old Tibetan literature of the early historic period also honors Upper Tibet as a cradle of Tibetan civilization and propagator of religious culture.

The transference of critical religious traditions like funerary rituals from Zhang Zhung and two other western countries to Central Tibet is recorded in a text composed by the renowned twelfth-century CE Buddhist lama Jikten Gönpo.[20] This passage is set in the aftermath of the assassination of Tibet's eighth king, Drigung Tsenpo. It touts the power and knowledge of the western priests, two qualities their protohistoric Central Tibetan counterparts seem to have lacked:

> The *bonpo* of Tibet did not know how to do the funeral ritual of King Drigum Tsenpo, so three *bonpo* were invited from Kashmir, Brusha, and Zhang Zhung to conduct the funeral ritual of violent death. One of them, as a consequence of the worship of Gekhö, the horned eagle and the god of fire, demonstrated his ability to go into the sky astride a drum, handle red hot objects, cut iron with a bird feather, and so forth. One of them could distinguish the good and bad by the performance of divination through knots, divination through the pronouncements of the deities, and scapulamancy. One of them knew the various components of the funerary rites, the eradication of the distress of the dead, and the subjugation of the violent causes of death.

According to Tibetan literature, Central Tibet had its own lineages of archaic era priests and deities, setting it somewhat apart from the religious traditions of Zhang Zhung. The religious differences between ancient Central Tibet and Zhang Zhung alluded to in Tibetan texts have a clear archaeological basis. A dramatic contrast in the monumental assemblages of these two Tibetan regions shows that they did indeed host their own special cultural traditions. To call these all by the same name, *bon*, is derived from a retrospective view of history. How archaic Tibetan religions were actually labeled and classified by their followers is still a mystery.

Traditionally, it is the first king of Central Tibet, Nyatri Tsenpo, who is credited with establishing civilization in that country, circa 150 BCE. According to Eternal Bon sources, he accomplished this with the aid of three primal *bonpo* and *shen*. These priests are thought to have been holders of the

Eternal Bon doctrine, but given the period in which they were supposedly active, they could only have been practitioners of archaic religious traditions.

A historical text attributed to the eighth-century CE sage Drenpa Namkha entitled *Drakpa Lingdrak* relates the mythic origins of King Nyatri Tsenpo and his three sacerdotal brothers.[21] These four siblings are said to have appeared in the celestial abode of the ancestral gods as the offspring of Lharab Nyenrum Je and Mucham Drama. Each of the four brothers possessed the special qualities of an animal associated with maternal or terrestrial clan origins: a crystal scorpion, a golden frog, a turquoise fish, and a conch tadpole. According to the *Drakpa Lingdrak*, these four beings descended to earth at Tsemo Chunggyal in Yarlung Sokka, the first royal center of Central Tibet:

> The mother and father said, "You are the four wonderful sons." They said, "For what purpose do you have a beautiful appearance and ornaments?" The holy man of crystal said, "Dear father and mother, we four are the sons of the divine lineage and lords of the mighty spirits. I am Nyatri Tsenpo. For what reason am I called Nyatri Tsenpo? For nine months and ten days, I stayed on the nape of the neck of the mother, and that is why I am called Nyatri. My commands over the deities and demons of tangible existence are irresistible; for this reason I am called Tsenpo. This golden man is the *bonpo* of existence, Ya Ngel Shak. He can defeat the retribution from sullying springs and the hearth and from rancor, these three retributions of the demigods. This Tshe Man of turquoise is the holy man, keeper of life of the gods and mighty spirit lineages. This holy man of conch is the one called Cho Man Chanter Melodious Song of the Cuckoo. These manifestations emanated like this from the celestial gods because we are going to be the king and *shen* of the earth. Father, please advise us." Thus Nyatri Tsenpo said.
>
> The father said, "Celestial gods, to go to the earth is to go to the human country of great contamination and defilement, so Ya Ngel Shak, guide Nyatri Tsenpo from the front and do fumigation, ablutions, and the purificatory rites. There are very many obstructions and sudden calamities, so Tshe Man, support his body from the right, and empower and bless him. The gods and demons of tangible existence are wildly hostile, so Cho Man of conch, support his body from the left and make the body ransom offering that liberates from demons. Nyatri, grasp the white celestial cord as the hand support. Keep on the consecutive celestial steps as the foot support. Four goddesses support his body from all around." Thus the father spoke and commanded.
>
> Then the four miraculous goddesses from within the realm of space caught four cloud horses with the power of the wind. Placing a miraculous throne on the back of the neck of one of the horses, they made it Nyatri Tsenpo's conveyance. He held the celestial cord in his waving hand. Plac-

ing his left foot on the celestial stairs, he went amid the southern clouds and mists. He beheld the pure land Yarlung Sokka. He descended to the pure holy place of Tsemo Chunggyal.

After the descent of King Nyatri Tsenpo, Eternal Bon claims that its teachings were passed on to his son Mutri Tsenpo, the second king of Central Tibet. It is held that Mutri Tsenpo received the Eternal Bon doctrine from the royal priest Nangwa Dokchen, a divine personality. The main teaching Nangwa Dokchen conferred on Mutri Tsenpo was Chipung, an ancient mystic tradition held to have been first propagated by the primal priests Ludrub Yeshe Nyingpo and Milüsamlek. The text *Magyü Drubkhor* describes the fantastic activities of Nangwa Dokchen in obligatory mythic language:

> On the mountain peak of King of the Mountains, inside the good house of gold, the one known as Nangwa Dokchen was rotating a dark blue and golden lasso overhead. He was sporting with dragons, horned eagles, and lions. He was sending out a multitude of star-like magical bombs and bursts of fire. He bounced savage celestial iron thunderbolts like a ball.[22]

According to Eternal Bon, King Mutri Tsenpo was instrumental in the spread of this religion to Central Tibet. He is also attributed with helping to found one of the most prominent lines of Eternal Bon priests, some of which were from Zhang Zhung. Those from Zhang Zhung included Sene Gau, whom we have already met; his teacher, Anu Trakthak; and a disciple, Dami Theke. A biographical account of Mutri Tsenpo is provided in the *Rikdzin Rigpai Thukgyü*, a text attributed to Drenpa Namkha of the eighth century CE and "rediscovered" in the twelfth century CE:

> The royal priest Mutri Tsenpo had a radiant golden complexion. He wore a turban of a special type of silk and a robe of antelope skin trimmed with brocade made from the threads of precious metals. In his right hand he held a crystal staff and in his left another symbol of sovereignty, the white copper scepter. He sat in a regal and stern fashion. His four mates were the consort of existence Choma Yesang, his consort of power Trima Tongcho, his consort of sexual union Nammen Karmo, and his consort of activity Yemen Chukmo. Their colors were white, yellow, red, and blue-green respectively. In conjunction with his consorts, Mutri Tsenpo received spiritual transmissions from his master Nangwa Dokchen.
>   Their common attainments were that they could fly in the sky like birds; swim in the water like fish; manifest as dragons, horned eagles, and lions; make flowers grow in hot wastelands; create water sources in dry places; and make fire with their saliva. They could also destroy the demons by hurling meteoric iron missiles, bring the spirits of the sky and earth under their control, and make the goddesses of the four seasons

part of their retinue. Their special attainments were that they did not need ordinary food. They obtained inseparability from the pacific and wrathful aspects of the Lamp God of Sight, a manifestation of Kuntu Sangpo, the primordial deity.[23]

In numerous Tibetan historical texts, King Mutri Tsenpo and those who acceded to the throne after him are depicted as key patrons of archaic religious traditions. Each king of Central Tibet's Tridun and Purgyal dynasties is said to have had his own royal priest and ritual bodyguard, among other types of *shen* and *bonpo*. These priests used ritual means to protect the monarchs and ensured that they were victorious in battle and their kingdom strong. Although a few downturns in the fortunes of the ancient *shen* and *bonpo* are recorded in Eternal Bon literature, it is thought that they continued to dominate the religious-scape of Central Tibet until the defeat of Zhang Zhung and the rise of Buddhism in the seventh century CE.

THE ZHANG ZHUNG GODS OF THE SKY AND EARTH

Tibetan literature tells us that Zhang Zhung was a land full of gods and goddesses. They resided overhead in the sky, below the earth, and in all places where humans and animals lived. Seen as regularly intervening in the affairs of society for good and for ill, it was necessary to propitiate them in all kinds of ways. No one could escape the fate the gods had in store for them. The most one could hope for was to befriend the deities in order to win their support and protection.

According to Eternal Bon sources, of all the deities of Zhang Zhung, the mightiest was Gekhö, a god invested with the power of the atmosphere and heavenly bodies. Gekhö is said to mean "Demon Subjugator" in the language of Zhang Zhung. His Zhang Zhung identity is corroborated in the prestigious Buddhist history of Tibet *Gyabö Kyi Chöchung*.[24] The Gekhö of Eternal Bon embraces both archaic religious traditions and those of Buddhism. In his primitive form he is portrayed as a zoomorphic mountain god, the ruler of the elements and heavens. With the advent of Buddhist influences, this sky god was transformed into a multiarmed paragon of wisdom and compassion.

The genesis of Gekhö in his form as a mountain god is described in an Eternal Bon ritual text written by an unknown author.[25] This theogony is of a type that may have first circulated around Zhang Zhung as an oral tradition; hence its authorship is lost. In what appears to be his prehistoric persona, in which there is not even a hint of Buddhist doctrine, Gekhö is the primary deity for the ritual production of magical bombs and missiles. The anonymous text maintains that the first priests of Zhang Zhung offered Gekhö yaks, sheep, and gold as compensation for his participation in rites carried out to destroy demons. The origins of this mighty god have a lyrical quality about them and were probably derived from the bardic tradition of ancient Tibet:

> In the beginning existing, yes, you appeared in the primordium and virtu-ous universe. Descending, yes, you descended from radiance and light. Manifesting, yes, you manifested on a snow mountain and lake. Emerging, yes, you emerged from a precious egg. Emanating, yes, you emanated in the wild yak. Landing, yes, you landed in the country of Zhang Zhung.

The famous nineteenth-century CE pilgrimage guide *Tisei Karchak* con-tains a theogony of Gekhö that describes his cosmic descent in more detail.[26] The fundamental elements of this myth appear to be of considerable antiq-uity. It describes the god's manifestation as a primordial wild yak at Drira Phuk, a sacred site on the north side of Mount Tise. According to Eternal Bon, proof of this god's descent is found in hoofprints and horn prints that mark the rocks of Drira Phuk. *Tisei Karchak* couches the divine epiphany in terms of space, primal existence, and eggs, cosmogonic conceptions that can be traced back to the archaic cultural world of Tibet. The text's reference to "Zhang Zhung Bon" should be seen as an allusion to the archaic religious traditions of Upper Tibet:

> It is said that in the beginning, existence was in the space of the ultimate reality of primordial emptiness. In the second instance, descent came forth through the gods of bright light. In the third instance, the emanation was manifested through the light of Mount Tise and Lake Mapang. In the fourth instance, the source emerged from a jeweled egg. In the fifth instance, the gap opened itself automatically. In the sixth instance, the manifestation emerged as Gekhö. In the seventh instance, the transfor-mation magically appeared as the wrathful yak of existence. In the eighth instance, the landing was the descent into the country of Zhang Zhung Bon. In the ninth instance, the arrival came as the warrior gods of crystal Zhang Zhung Bon . . .
> At that time, the earth quaked in six different ways and the mountains also shook in six different ways. The swirling ocean was also upset. In the sky there was a bright light and in space melodious sounds. On the earth there were beautiful flowers and many other wonderful occurrences. At that time, the rock formations on the summit of the mountain [Tise] fell down. On the horns of the wrathful yak were sparking thunderbolts, and with the tips of his horns he took these rocks and threw them to the right and left.

While the mountain god Gekhö descended from the sky to Mount Tise in the ancient tradition, when recast into tantric form, this god is said to have originated in the nature of reality itself. Tantracism of this kind, a religious tradition of great complexity found in both Buddhism and Hinduism, was fully developed in India in the fifth and sixth centuries CE. In order to accommodate a Zhang Zhung god of the elements to a punctilious tantric pedigree, Eternal Bon merged his divine yak form with the more advanced iconography and doctrines of Lamaism. In Eternal Bon, these differing historical faces of Gekhö are thought to represent diverse aspects of an integral godhead, not the merging of disparate religious traditions. Nevertheless, the creation of a single deity from widely divergent sources is best seen as a blending of the indigenous and Buddhist strains of Tibetan religion, the syncretism upon which Eternal Bon was established.

Eternal Bon identifies Gekhö as its chief patron and protector of the royal lineage of Zhang Zhung. In the fifteenth century CE, the Eternal Bon lama Ngari Sonam Gyaltshen compiled a historical sketch of religious masters associated with Gekhö.[27] This lineage of Gekhö practitioners begins with King Tridem of Zhang Zhung, who is said to have been an emanation of the three main gods of the Gekhö circle: Walchen Gekhö, Ati Muwer, and Kuchi Mangke. From King Tridem, the Gekhö lineage passed through just seven individuals before reaching Drenpa Namkha in the eighth century CE. By this reckoning, the Gekhö tradition started by King Tridem could not much predate the fifth or sixth century CE. Despite this computation, Eternal Bon scholars believe Gekhö to be much older than this, as he must be if this god was really the main patron deity of Zhang Zhung. The truncated lineage preserved in the text of Ngari Sonam Gyaltshen can probably be attributed to the highly fragmentary nature of Zhang Zhung religious history, reduced even six hundred years ago to a paltry showing of names and biographical facts.

Ngari Sonam Gyaltshen's text refers to the miraculous preservation of ancient religious practices telescopically identified with Eternal Bon during the persecution unleashed by the Tibetan king Trisong Deutsen circa 780 CE. At that time, the saint Drenpa Namkha and several of his associates are believed to have hidden away texts dedicated to Gekhö practices and lore. According to the author, some two to three hundred years after Drenpa Namkha concealed the Gekhö textual treasures in the late eighth century CE, they were rediscovered by two well-known Eternal Bon treasure finders. These texts are said to have turned up at the soul mountain of the Central Tibetan kings, Yarlha Shampo, in the eleventh and twelfth centuries CE. Gekhö texts are also believed to have been recovered from Zhalsang, better known as Sangsang, a dramatic white limestone formation situated near the old border of Zhang Zhung and Central Tibet. From the time of their purported rediscovery eight hundred to a thousand years ago until the present day, these writings have formed an integral part of Eternal Bon commentarial literature.

Ngari Sonam Gyaltshen recounts the vicissitudes of the Gekhö tradition in straightforward language:

> Zhang Zhung Tridem, holder of the iron bird horns, the manifestation of the Three Protectors, practiced it. He protected the Zhang Zhung kings. He bestowed this Gekhö doctrine on Tri Ösel. He transmitted it to Zhang Zhung Sangwa Tingrum. He transmitted it to Sene Gau. He transmitted it to Gyungne Khöpung. He transmitted it to Hripa Gyerme. He transmitted it to Tsomen Gyerchen. He transmitted it to Thimar Punggyung. He transmitted it to Khöpung Drenpa Namkha.
>
> At that time, due to the power of poor karma of sentient beings and the jealousy of the Buddhist monks around Central Tibet, the doctrine of [Eternal] Bon declined. Tongchen Mutsha Gyerme, Blonchen Rasang Khöram, Khyeu Drenpa Namkha, and Lachen Khenen Yocha hid as treasures these Bon texts and others at Yarlha Shampo and Zhalzang. Thereafter, through the good karma of sentient beings and the effect of prayers of good aspirations made earlier, the great reincarnation Matön Shelseng and Chiltön Khyung Götsal, these two, rediscovered the Bon doctrines in the upper and lower countries.

The elaborate routine associated with the concealment of sacred texts during an even earlier persecution of "*bon*" is detailed in the famous pilgrimage text, *Tisei Karchak*. This first attack on religion was supposedly unleashed by Tibet's eighth king, Drigum Tsenpo, a legendary figure roughly dated to circa 200 CE. Drigum Tsenpo is said to have paid for his assault on *bon* with his life, assassinated by one of his closest ministers. *Tisei Karchak* asserts that at that time the texts for Gekhö were protected by the Zhang Zhung King of Existence Triwer Larje and a Zhang Zhung priest named Hritsa Muwer.[28] The Gekhö scriptures and those for the closely related god Meri were combined with wish-fulfilling jewels and aromatic herbs before being wrapped in silk of five colors. They were then placed in an octagonal receptacle made of sapphire and other precious substances, the handiwork of the blacksmith of primordial existence. It is written that the encased texts were hidden at the southern base of Mount Tise, in a secret formation with a raised swastika.

According to various Eternal Bon historical sources, in the time of the next Tibetan king, Pude Gungyal, religion again came to attain a very high status. Thus the texts concealed in the time of his father, Drigum Tsenpo, could be unburied. Eternal Bon literature abounds with tales of religious scriptures existing long before the historic epoch. As explained, no archaeological or epigraphic evidence substantiating that pre-Buddhist inhabitants of Tibet had a system of writing has come to the fore. I, for one, have searched many grottos and rock faces in Upper Tibet for inscriptions pre-dating the seventh century CE. Given the absence of hard evidence, one can only view with a good deal of skepticism the notion that Tibetans could read and write in their own languages before the imperial period. It appears that this legend developed so that Eternal Bon adherents could claim their predecessors were just as literate as the early Indian Buddhists, a case of trying to culturally best one's rivals.

One of the richest descriptions of Gekhö and his circle of deities was compiled by the great Eternal Bon abbot Nyamme Sherab Gyaltsen (1356–1415 CE) from antecedent textual sources.[29] In his work, Nyamme Sherab Gyaltsen devised a tantric mandala for Gekhö and his retinue. This mandala was designed in typical tantric fashion as two interlaced equilateral triangles set inside a circle, surrounded by an outer ring of eight lotus petals. The central space of the six-pointed star is occupied by Gekhö and his consort Drablai Gyalmo in ecstatic embrace, one of the hallmark features of tantra. Graphic sexual depictions do not appear to have been part of the iconographic traditions of prehistoric Zhang Zhung. In Tibetan literature, the union of what appear to be authentic Zhang Zhung divinities is depicted in procreative terms, not in the psychosexual vocabulary of India. Except for mating wild yaks, there do not seem to be any explicit sex scenes in the ancient rock art of Upper Tibet. From the evidence we have, a dignified confidentiality as pertains to the actual act was the norm in the archaic sacred traditions of the region.

Gekhö's depiction in Nyamme Sherab Gyaltsen's mandala is a mix of ancient native traditions and later Lamaist ones. Gekhö is portrayed as a tantric god with eighteen arms and nine heads. In contrast, the native divinities, as represented in rock art and in texts preserving archaic cultural features, are human-like, with one head, two arms, and two legs, or in the form of animals. Thus, in texts conserving the older mythology, Gekhö is shown in a conventional anatomical fashion as an invincible warrior. Despite Gekhö being depicted in the guise of a fierce tantric deity by Nyamme Sherab Gyaltsen, his mandala focuses on violent meteorological events. This appears to be an anachronistic carryover from the days of Zhang Zhung when Gekhö and his entourage were the personifications of the firmament.

In Nyamme Sherab Gyaltsen's text, powerful storm events are the result of lightning, thunderbolts, and hail issuing from the head of Gekhö. The roar of the dragon coming from his ears is the sound of thunder. These types of personification may help to explain the siting of prehistoric strongholds and religious edifices in high-altitude locations. It was probably in such lofty places that the sky-bound deities of Zhang Zhung were best propitiated. Be that as it may, in high-altitude sites, Zhang Zhung residents could feel closest to the heavens.

A horned-eagle head crowns Gekhö's heads, and he sports a turban of serpents. His celestial eagle and chthonic serpent traits symbolize his dominion over the entire dichotomous universe. Other important Upper Tibetan mountain gods such as Nyenchen Thanglha also manifest in the form of eagles and serpents. Their binary personalities are exemplified by the old Tibetan metaphors "sky pillar" and "earth stake." These great mountain gods rise up from the depths of the earth and reach down from the top of the sky, penetrating all the planes of existence. Gekhö holds demon-destroying weapons in his eighteen hands, some of which are also wielded by Buddhist tantric deities. Others such as the thunderbolt arrow, battle hammer, horn of the blue sheep, and violently boiling water appear to be of Zhang Zhung origin.

Gekhö is attired in an elephant hide, a classic Buddhist tantric costume, symbolizing the invincible power of the tutelary gods over nescience. His lower body is girt in a tiger-skin skirt, another typical Buddhist tantric garment, but it is trimmed in leopard and clouded leopard skins reminiscent of the robes worn by the ancient *bonpo* and *shen*. In keeping with his fundamental sky god qualities, Gekhö's sash is of zigzagging red lightning, but he also wears armlets, an Indian style of ornamentation. In this way, Nyamme Sherab Gyaltsen skillfully wove together native and Indian religious traditions to transform the uranic Gekhö into a great protector of Lamaist doctrine. In his work, he waxes poetic about the awesome appearance of this great demon destroyer:

Oh! From the dark blue center of the manifested mandala, from the middle of the blazing expanse, from the temple of the fixed, unchanging swastika rises the blazing figure of Wrathful Demon Destroyer, the dark blue, angry, fear-inspiring, blazing one with nine haughty, fear-inspiring heads, who subdues the black demons. With your short stout limbs you render the man-eating fiends unconscious. Your right heads are white. Your left heads are red. Your middle heads are dark blue with a fierce visage.

Your mouth is agape, your fangs bared, and your three eyes stare upward. Your ginger beard has the appearance of spreading sparks. The three wrathful furrows of your nose are contorted upward. From your eyebrows spread a thousand zigzagging lightning strikes, thunder and hail. From your opened mouth thunderbolts and hail fall down like the raining of blood. From your teeth spread thunderbolts, which slay the enemies and obstructors. From your nose bursts forth a black wind tornado. From your tongue great lightning blankets the world. From your ears emanates the great sound of the dragon.

Your eight subsidiary heads are wrathful in the manner of a man-eating fiend. Your crown is the head of the great blazing horned eagle. Your mane of hair is the clouds that cover all the innumerable worlds. From your hair spread golden sparks. The voice of the horned eagle is the tremulous pitch that agitates the ocean depths. Your turban is of the five types of great serpents, and you have a rosary of water monster skulls and giant clams. With your mouth of the great blazing horned eagle you consume the five types of water spirits. Your eight faces subjugate the savage eight orders of spirits. Your turquoise blue dragon earrings are spiraling. You have a necklace of masses of fire and thunderbolts that emit molten metal missiles and hail, which incinerate demons.

Your torso has the spreading wings of the horned eagle. At the base of your wings is a blazing conflagration that rapidly incinerates male demons. By the flapping of your horned-eagle wings three times, a tornado of thunderbolts swirls around the tips of your wings, which rapidly incinerates the black demon mountain. Your body hairs are turbulent masses of fire and the rain of weapons. They separate the apostates and oath-breakers from their guardian spirits. You depute the great kings of the four divisions to action. The first pair, right and left, of your eighteen hands feeds the father demons and mother demons into your mouths. They collapse the black demon mountain from its base. The hand tools of the eight right hands are the sword, battleaxe, wheel, thunderbolt arrow, mass of fire, scimitar, maul, and a rotating wheel overhead. They cut, chop, continuously assault, puncture, burn, hack to pieces, bludgeon, and make insane and insensate the enemies of religion and demons. The hand tools of the eight left hands are the bow and arrow, lasso, battle hammer, iron chain, iron hook, spear, horn of the blue sheep, and boiling torrential water which generated the erupting wave of violently boiling water. They shoot, strangle, beat, bind, rip the heart out, stab, deluge, and reduce to dust those of inimical activities, the evil-doing oath-breaker enemies.

Your torso is wrapped in an elephant hide with the skin of a male demon on its borders. Hundreds of thousands of masses of raging fire emanate from you. You quickly incinerate the adversarial demons and man-eating fiends. On your lower body is the great tiger skirt with the wild clouded leopard and leopard skin borders. You tie a sash of zigzagging red lightning. Your body hairs naturally shake out the rain of weapons. The eight orders of spirits are your servants. On your body spread the sparks of the conflagration. You have the necklace of the great blue serpent. You have encircling snake bracelets and anklets. Your armlet is decorated with a flaming great horned eagle. Your four feet press down the black demons of the underworld. You repose on a lion and water monster throne. Your head is ornamented with five types of great horned eagles. Your magnificence suppresses the black demons of the underworld.

In the study of Zhang Zhung, cultural links with the mountains, steppes, and deserts to the north and west are never very far off. They betoken a time when the highest reaches of the Tibetan Plateau were drawn into the whirlpool of peoples, ideas, and customs swirling around the core of the Asian continent. Gekhö and his entourage are a case in point.

Gekhö's preoccupation with the celestial sphere brings him in close correspondence with the ancient religious traditions of the Inner Asian steppes.[30] The old Mongolian and Gekhö deities are both closely connected to the sun, moon, stars, planets, and celestial dragons. The great god of the ancient Mongolians and Turks known as Tengri was also a personification of the heavens. In many ways Tengri's functions mirror those of the Gekhö circle of deities. The ancient gods of the steppes and Zhang Zhung were founded on a mythos in which a sky father and earth mother predominated. This divine dyad as the progenitor of the universe is thought to have governed the course of natural and human activities.

The religions of north Inner Asia and the Tibetan Plateau divided the universe into two tiers (heaven and earth) or three tiers (heaven, earth, and underworld). The Hsiung-nu, or Huns, of Mongolia subdivided their heaven into nine layers, as did ancient Tibetans. The Eternal Bon studies expert Per Kværne notes that a royal epithet of the ancient Turks, "heavenlike," is also used in a biographical text for Tönpa Shenrab.[31] The Tibetan expressions "blue heaven" and "heaven knows" recorded in the *Old Tibetan Chronicle* were also parts of ancient Turk and Mongol declarations.[32] The parallels between the cult of Gekhö and the gods of the steppes dovetail with other textual and archaeological findings we have examined, demonstrating manifold cultural links between Zhang Zhung and north Inner Asia.

In addition to cultural affinities with other parts of Inner Asia, Gekhö bears much resemblance to the gods of the *Rig Veda*, an Indian liturgical text first composed as an oral recitation around 1200 BCE. The *Rig Veda* was the object of intensive study by the notable Indologists R. T. H. Griffith and Arthur Berriedale Keith.[33] Gekhö is directly comparable to celestial gods of Indo-European origins: Indra, Varuna, and Mitra. In the *Rig Veda*, Varuna and Mitra are solar deities who regulate the movement of the moon and the light of the stars. They are also rain gods and regulators of the seasons and are sometimes associated with the ocean. These very same functions and motifs are found among the Gekhö circle of gods.

Indra in particular shares many traits with Gekhö. It is probably no coincidence, then, that in Indian literature, Tibet seems to be described as the heavenly abode of Indra. Just like Gekhö, Indra is the father of heaven and the wielder of the metallic thunderbolt, a god who rules over the atmosphere and does battle with the demons of drought and darkness. Indra is recorded as slaying his father, while Gekhö committed matricide. Indra was a war god, slayer of serpent demons and the bringer of rain, activities of Gekhö as well. A remarkable iconographic similarity is that both the

Indian and Tibetan gods have a reddish beard and hair. Furthermore, Indra and Gekhö assumed the form of an eagle. The *Rig Veda* speaks of a year of 360 days and the sky-earth division of the universe, cosmological concepts contained in the Gekhö literature as well.

Despite many functional parallels, the historical connections between Indra and Gekhö remain largely a mystery, as is the overall picture of cultural borrowing between ancient India and Zhang Zhung. It may be that Gekhö was partly the product of Indo-Iranian mythology, which spread widely in Eurasia in the second millennium BCE.[34] It is also possible, however, that Gekhö's resemblance to Indra is attributable to a later importation of Indian culture to Zhang Zhung. There are also fundamental differences between the Gekhö and *Rig Vedic* gods, which are indicative of discrepant cultural perspectives. In the Gekhö tradition, anatomical representations of atmospheric and celestial phenomena predominate. This kind of mimesis is hardly met with in the *Rig Veda*. The appearance of the gods in the shape of divine animals is also more prevalent in Gekhö iconography than it is in the *Rig Veda*. This tradition of rendering gods in zoomorphic form also appears to be well represented in the rock art of Upper Tibet.

It is written in Eternal Bon scriptures that there were 360 different classes of Zhang Zhung divinities, all of which were ruled by Gekhö. Only a sprinkling of the names and descriptions of this conventional quantity of gods has survived. How many of the deities were really known in Zhang Zhung and in what form is a moot question. What can be safely stated is that their names and aspects of their iconography are not Buddhist in character but of an indigenous persuasion.

The consort of Gekhö is Drablai Gyalmo, who like her mate is a deity of the heavens.[35] She is still worshipped dutifully by Eternal Bon practitioners however far from Upper Tibet they may live. Drablai Gyalmo's chief residence is Mount Tise and the lake in front of it, La Ngak Tsho. This goddess is said to possess the fiery radiance of the sun and the solar and lunar ornaments on her head. Her eyebrows are zigzagging thunderbolts and her hair a swirling tornado of golden light and thunderbolts. Drablai Gyalmo's rosary is made of the eight great planets (including the two lunar nodes), and her lacework is the twenty constellations. In her pacific form she is a white goddess mounted on a lioness and holding the draped arrow of life. In her wrathful form she is a black hag attired in a goat skin, the releaser of the white copper owl of death. In this terrifying aspect, Drablai Gyalmo is thought to command the absolute obedience of all the warrior gods of Zhang Zhung. So fierce is she that in one ancient tale preserved by Eternal Bon she destroyed her entire family except for one younger brother.

One of the most important figures in Gekhö's circle is the tiny but extremely powerful god Kuchi Mangke. His ancient credentials are established in an Old Tibetan–language document simply referred to as Pt 1038.[36] He appears in this text under the slightly different name, Kuchi Ser, a sky god ancestor of the first king of Central Tibet, Nyatri Tsenpo. In Eternal Bon literature, Kuchi Mangke is said to have a body as small as a golden spindle, a heart the size of a mustard seed, eyes as wide as the eye of a needle, and a mouth as big as a peppercorn.[37] His consort is Tingnam Gyalmo, the goddess of the ocean. The most vital function attributed to Kuchi Mangke is his ability to destroy demons believed to harm children. His small size is highly useful in protecting children, as he can unobtrusively watch over them.

The god of divination and astrology in Gekhö's entourage is Phuwer, a resplendent figure attired in white robes. The god Phuwer is mentioned in an Old Tibetan divination text designated Pt 1047, confirming that he is of archaic cultural origins.[38] According to a Classical Tibetan divination text of indeterminate age preserved in the literary collection of Ju Mipham (1846–1912), a famous Nyingma lama, Phuwer and his three female companions were worshipped with an arrow on which a mirror, lamb fleece, colored ribbons, and the dried hearts of a bat, crane, and cuckoo were hung.[39] Interestingly, the use of mead and grape wine as offerings for Phuwer in Mipham's text seems to point to early cultural influences coming from Central Asia. The text collected by Ju Mipham further states,

> From their abode invite the Phuwer deities to pass into the mandala. Envisage them revealing to you yourselves the prophecies of the three worlds and all good qualities. Signal them with mantras. From the middle of your heart radiate these mantras on rays of light directly in front of the deities. Consequently, envisage the deities revealing subterranean treasures to you yourselves. . . .
>
> Thereafter, praise the deities in this way: Listen! In a divine castle of bright turquoise mists, a palace of bright rainbows, rise up divine assembly of secret Phuwer gods. Proclaiming King Phuwer, you are a golden-colored noble man whose body is attired in white silk. In your right hand you hold a conch-white knotted cord of divination. Reveal to the *bon* priests the good and bad, the benefits and detriments. In your left hand you hold a silver mirror in which all of existence clearly appears. Reveal the good qualities of existence to us.

Ati Muwer is another principal god of the Gekhö circle.[40] His Zhang Zhung–language name can probably be translated as "Grandfather Sky King." He is clad in golden armor and brandishes a bow and arrow made of celestial iron. Ati Muwer is depicted riding on the light rays of the red planet

Mars, a classic Eurasian war god. Yet another chief Zhang Zhung god named Traphü has explicit north Inner Asian cultural connections. The Eternal Bon text *Meri Pawo Gyephur* reports that he manifested in Drugu, an ancient Turkic land, in a crystal castle surrounded by birds, moonbeams, and sun rays.[41]

According to Eternal Bon documents, the gods of the four elements, wind, earth, water, and fire, also played an important role in the religious traditions of Zhang Zhung. Part of Gekhö's retinue, they have retained names partially derived from the Zhang Zhung language.[42] In windswept Upper Tibet, the most important personification of the elements was probably the god of the air, who is depicted as riding a white deer. Recalling the iconic flying deer of the Scythians, Eternal Bon texts cite the "deer that knows how to fly" as the name of one of twelve ancient ritual systems contained in the Bon of Causes.[43] In addition to its use as a magical vehicle in Eternal Bon sources, Buddhist historical texts referring to pre-Buddhist "*bon*" practices suggest that the deer was the sacrificial animal of choice in ancient Tibet.

A Scythian cultural link to ancient Tibet is also revealed in the ritual activities of Tönpa Shenrab, the individual credited with founding the Eternal Bon religion. This intriguing figure is the next topic of discussion.

THE RIDDLE OF TÖNPA SHENRAB
AND THE PASSAGE OF THE DEAD

Tibetan textual evidence convincingly shows that the religious deeds of Tönpa Shenrab were strongly influenced by those ascribed to Buddha Sakyamuni. Nevertheless, the biographical details of their lives as well as many aspects of their teachings, especially those preserved in the Bon of Causes, are very different in character. The earliest Eternal Bon accounts of Tönpa Shenrab's life and works are preserved in texts like *Dodü* and *Zermik*, works not written before the end of the tenth century CE. These texts were purportedly rediscovered as part of a class of literature known as *terma*, or "treasures." Most *terma* are texts that support or elaborate upon the Eternal Bon canon, those teachings attributed directly to Tönpa Shenrab.

In 1017 CE, Shengur Luga of Tsang began to discover Eternal Bon treasure texts said to have been concealed when the old religion was outlawed in the 780s CE.[44] Belonging to the ancient Shen lineage, Shengur Luga, the "Crooked Shen Liked by the Water Spirits," was paramount among Eternal Bon treasure finders. He along with his disciples, who belonged to the influential Bru, Zhu, and Pa lineages, were instrumental in codifying a new generation of religious teachings. Their efforts allowed archaic religious traditions to reemerge in Lamaist garb. The Shen, Bru, Zhu, and Pa, and a fifth major religious lineage known as Meu, each of which traces its ancestry back to Zhang Zhung, were by the eleventh century CE heavily active in Central Tibet. The recasting of archaic traditions in a Buddhist mold by these lines of dedicated scholars laid the ecclesiastic and doctrinal groundwork for Eternal Bon, a religion that has endured to the present day.

If the materials enshrined in Eternal Bon literature were the only sources available to us, it would be extremely difficult to assess Tönpa Shenrab's historical background. Eternal Bon literature has built up an extravagant myth around him that is beyond the pale of history. It is said that he was an all-knowing being with disciples throughout Tibet, China, India, and Central Asia. It has long struck historians as odd, though, that such a highly esteemed religious figure did not merit even passing mention in the literary traditions of foreign peoples. The legendary imprimatur of Tönpa Shenrab, a persona with the all-encompassing powers and the wisdom of a supreme god, naturally raises questions as to his historical reality. Eternal Bon assigning his life to remote antiquity has only added to the elusive aura surrounding him.

While Eternal Bon has created a preternatural Tönpa Shenrab, a cache of ancient parchments discovered a century ago shed light on his life and influence in an earlier age. These rare writings had been deposited in the Dunhuang grottoes situated on the edge of the Gobi Desert. Nearly nine hundred years after the cave library of Dunhuang was sealed, the British Aurel Stein and the Frenchman Paul Pelliot began recovering texts from it in 1907 and 1908 respectively. Among the prolific collections of early historic manuscripts found in Dunhuang are more than a dozen texts dedicated to archaic funerary traditions. These texts were written sometime between the seventh and tenth centuries CE in the obsolete language known as Old Tibetan.

For understanding the life and times of Tönpa Shenrab, it is very fortuitous that the name and activities of his alter ego, Shenrab Nyiwo (the old spelling for Shenrab Miwo), have been preserved in six different Dunhuang manuscripts.[45] In the twentieth century, various philologists, most notably Frederick William Thomas, Marcelle Lalou, and Rolf Alfred Stein, investigated the Dunhuang funerary manuscripts in great detail. These scholars produced papers and monographs of a high order, significantly contributing to our understanding of these precious sources in the study of ancient Tibetan culture.

The Dunhuang funerary manuscripts are abstruse documents, written in an archaic form of Tibetan, a language with comparatively few extant source materials. This makes translation an extremely challenging proposition. Beginning in the early 2000s, I too dedicated myself to deciphering the funerary manuscripts of Dunhuang. Working in close collaboration with Lopön Tenzin Namdak, Eternal Bon's foremost scholar; Yungdrung Tenzin; and other Eternal Bon literati, little by little I made progress in understanding these ancient documents. Eternal Bon savants brought to my attention a corpus of texts written in Classical Tibetan containing analogous funerary traditions. One of these Eternal Bon collections known as the *Muchoi Tromdur* was virtually unknown to non-Tibetan scholars in the twentieth century. The familiar grammatical signposts of the *Muchoi Tromdur* acted as a Rosetta stone for decoding the older Dunhuang materials. Thus I was able to make headway in fathoming the cultural and historical significance of Tibet's oldest known ritual literature.[46]

In the archaic context, Tönpa Shenrab, alias Shenrab Nyiwo, is a sacrificial priest. In the Lamaist context he is a Buddha. Nevertheless, in the literature of both eras he is an embodiment of the savior archetype. In Dunhuang literature, Shenrab Nyiwo does not appear as the founder of a monolithic religion; he is rather the purveyor and guardian of the native sacred traditions of Tibet. In the Old Tibetan documents, Shenrab Nyiwo relies on sacrifices and magic to free his clients from evil. In Eternal Bon literature as Tönpa, or the "Teacher," he liberates his disciples from samsara using a regimen of moral and mental instructions. Although these two depictions of Shenrab Nyiwo are poles apart culturally, this one personality essentially fulfills the same role. Whether through esoteric rites or philosophical understanding, he remains responsible for the salvation of humanity.

It is probably because of Shenrab Nyiwo's fundamental soteriological function that religionists of the tenth and eleventh centuries CE saw fit to transform him into a Buddha figure. For those writing in that period, there may not have been any underlying contradiction, for a savior is a savior, whatever his external credentials might be. To be sure, the means to liberation changed along with changes in religious sensibilities, but Shenrab Nyiwo persisted in serving the vital needs of the Tibetans.

In the Dunhuang funerary manuscripts, Shenrab Nyiwo appears as a model funerary priest, a cultural hero instrumental in liberating the dead from their earthly bounds. There is absolutely no intimation in the Dunhuang materials that he was responsible for the creation of an entire religion. Instead, Shenrab Nyiwo is presented as an ancestral champion responsible for the propagation of prehistoric funerary traditions. The diminished role for Tönpa Shenrab in the relatively prosaic Dunhuang narratives is more in keeping with a real-life personality than the apotheosized figure of Eternal Bon literature with its Buddhist overlay. The Old Tibetan writings do not necessarily prove the historical existence of Tönpa Shenrab, but they certainly make it a more likely prospect.

References to Shenrab Nyiwo in the Dunhuang manuscripts are sprinkled in narratives read as a prelude to the performance of funerals. Known as *mang*, these declarations of origins endow the early historic funeral rituals with an august pedigree, legitimatizing their preservation and practice. Given that the Dunhuang *mang* were written eleven to thirteen hundred years ago, their characterization of Shenrab Nyiwo and the funerals in which he was involved as "ancient" is particularly noteworthy. This indicates that these tales began as an oral tradition prior to the early historic period in which they were penned. Though very ancient, the appearance of riding horses in some *mang* narratives indicates that they could not have arisen in anything like their present form before the first half of the first millennium BCE, the period in which equestrian arts developed in Inner Asia. While this is less ancient than the larger-than-life Tönpa Shenrab of Lamaism, the Dunhuang texts nonetheless establish him as a pivotal prehistoric personality.

One of the early historic funerary manuscripts of Dunhuang to mention Shenrab Nyiwo is referred to by the uninspiring title of Pt 1289, a holding of the Paul Pelliot collection in the Bibliothèque National, Paris.[47] This text describes Shenrab Nyiwo as the maker of funerals and the searcher of lost souls. He is depicted holding the great flat-bell, or *shang*, in his left hand and a bird wing in his right hand. In the archaic funerary rites, the wings of various species of birds were used to ritually guide and liberate the dead. According to another Old Tibetan text recently discovered in a derelict shrine in southern Tibet, the horse-riding Shenrab Nyiwo also carried a large drum and was attired in a long gown of silk or some other fine material. Eternal Bon documents add that he donned a turban as well, an ancient style of headgear in Tibet.

Another Dunhuang source mentioning Shenrab Nyiwo is the manuscript designated Pt 1136. Pt 1136 contains two narratives, one of which is geographically associated with the headwaters country located in the vicinity of Mount Tise, indicating that it was set in a territorial sense in Zhang Zhung. Written within two centuries after the fall of the Zhang Zhung kingdom, Pt 1136 furnishes a historical precedent for Eternal Bon claims that Tönpa Shenrab spent time in Upper Tibet. Similarly, later Tibetan literature, Eternal Bon and Buddhist, also attributes the source of archaic funerary traditions to Zhang Zhung.

The Tibetan upland as a source of funerary traditions is a recurring theme in Eternal Bon. One untitled text of considerable antiquity describes the origins of a bumblebee god called Sise Bongwa Takchung. The tale is set in Mrayul, the "Country of the Mra," Mra being an ancient ethnic designation of people from Zhang Zhung. The father noted in this tale went to hunt deer while his wife collected an edible tuber called *dro*, activities closely but not exclusively associated with Upper Tibet. While the parents were away hunting and foraging, their two beloved children were murdered by a type of fiend known as *chungsi*. Funeral rites performed after the burial of the children and the capture of the killer were the responsibility of Shenrab Miwo and two other priests, Zangte Mongthung and Sibon Muphen Beura.

In the Dunhuang funerary narratives, Shenrab Nyiwo (an older rendering of his name) is a man of great eloquence and power. In a funerary narrative of Pt 1134, formal language befitting the funeral of a high-ranking dignitary is employed. In this address, Shenrab Nyiwo and two other funerary priests, Durshen Mada and Karshen Thiuzhuk, address the deceased with hard-hitting metaphors:

> You are dead. The lord is dead, you are no more. Chipped, the turquoise is chipped, so it is no more. The degenerated son, yes, you are dead. The crane egg, yes, it is cracked. The sharp bow, yes, it is broken.

The chipped turquoise in the above passage is no other than the soul turquoise, or *layu*, a magical stone celebrated in Tibetan folklore and religion. The *layu* functioned as a receptacle safeguarding the soul of a living person and as a special vessel used in rites of evocation at the time of death. Tibetans still believe that a damaged or discolored soul turquoise presages illness and death. Likewise, the cracked crane egg and the broken bow are figures of speech that represent death in Pt 1134.

In the archaic eschatology of the Tibetans, the afterlife is often known as the "Joyous Land," or Gayul, a northern paradise that existed in the sky or on top of lofty mountains as a kind of parallel world. The Pt 1134 manuscript credits the "fathers" or venerable ancestors, Durshen Mada and Shenrab Nyiwo, with making the tomb and a square ritual superstructure, which helped to release the deceased from his mortal chains. Because of this, the expired one was able to travel to the correct position among the expansive heights, ensuring his or her arrival in the afterlife. Eternal Bon funerary texts indicate that the spirits of the dead in Gayul enjoyed the same kind of life they had on earth. They possessed farms, livestock, castles, and jewelry, as well as social networks and divine companions. This parallel afterlife is even illustrated on wooden coffins recently discovered in northeastern Tibet.[48]

It would appear that Shenrab Nyiwo was not nearly as omnipotent as Eternal Bon makes him out to be. Pt 1134 does not greatly distinguish Shenrab Nyiwo from his fellow funerary priests known as *durshen*. In this manuscript, he does not possess the social decorum or special characteristics that would indicate a significantly superior standing, let alone the aura of a Buddha, the position accorded him in Eternal Bon. The prototypic funerary priests in Pt 1134 appear to be on an equal social and ritual footing. In fact, the Dunhuang funerary manuscript designated Pt 1194 declares that Durshen Mada was the source of all funerary rites. Curiously, there is no mention whatsoever of Shenrab Nyiwo in this text.

The funerary priest Durshen Mada is known to Eternal Bon through the *Muchoi Tromdur* texts.[49] Although the *Muchoi Tromdur* was written down after 1000 CE, it retains many archaisms of early historic times. It is significant that the *Muchoi Tromdur* and the Dunhuang funerary manuscripts depict Durshen Mada as an ancestral figure of the distant past, upon which the Tibetan funerary system rested. While in the Dunhuang manuscripts Durshen Mada appears to be a peer of Shenrab Nyiwo, in the *Muchoi Tromdur* he is one of a long line of funerary priests, stemming from a lineage in which Tönpa Shenrab was the first earthly representative.

Otherwise Durshen Mada is portrayed in the *Muchoi Tromdur* much as he is in the Dunhuang manuscripts. One text, *Lhabon Shensum*, observes that the prototypic funerary priest Durshen Mada was descended from a group of nine divine funerary priest brothers, who are hailed as gods of power. As part of the account of funerary ritual origins, *Lhabon Shensum* lists the divine parents and grandparents of Durshen Mada. While his brothers went from the earth to various celestial countries, Durshen Mada stayed behind to be king of the priests and the supervisor of all original teachings. To his inner circle of *shen*, he revealed the techniques of using bird wings to subjugate infernal beings, methods of soul rescue, preparation of the corpse for burial, and other funerary procedures.

As in many ancient cultures, Tibetans believed that the corpse and the mind/soul of the dead had to be treated in a special manner; otherwise they could be a cause of misfortune for the living. In the Tibetan archaic funerary traditions, salvation was assured by avoiding the fragmentation of the soul through physical and psychological trauma while alive and the hindrances of the grim underworld after death. These various threats to the soul were personified as different types of demons. Freed from their clutches, an individual would assume a divine state in the Gayul paradise. Here the dead were joyfully reunited with their ancestors and genealogical gods. In the archaic era, Tibetans believed that they descended from the deities as part of an intrinsic patrimony only to be reunited with them after death via their ancestors. This doctrine of salvation differs starkly from the one upheld in Lamaism, which stresses an impersonal form of liberation and the transience of all phenomena. In Buddhism and Eternal Bon there is no permanent self or eternal heaven.

The Dunhuang texts and Eternal Bon sources speak with one voice in asserting that the Tibetan funerary traditions and one of its most favored practitioners, Shenrab Nyiwo, are of hoary origins. In no uncertain terms, the two etiologic tales found in the Dunhuang funerary manuscript designated Pt 1136 reflect this antiquity. The first tale in this text is set in the northern wilderness of Upper Tibet. It concerns the capture of a celestial transport horse by a man who needed it for the funeral of his best friend.

The deceased man was named Mranyite Tsunpo. *Mranyi* means the "Man of Mra," revealing his highland origins.

The second origin tale of Pt 1136 vividly recounts the travails of a noble family residing in the headwaters region of southwestern Tibet. The daughter of this family, Lady Lhogyal Gyi Changmo, distraught at being betrothed to the lord of Guge in western Tibet, took her own life. Lady Lhogyal Gyi Changmo's father and brother asked Shenrab Nyiwo to help them untie the noose with which the she had killed herself, but the master replied that he alone could not help them. Shenrab Nyiwo enlisted the help of a divine bird, which he called with the aid of a divine ibex. Tönpa Shenrab of Eternal Bon would never resort to petitioning "worldly beings" for help, illustrating how different his archaic cultural disposition was from Lamaist conceptions about him.

As in other Dunhuang funerary manuscripts, Shenrab Nyiwo is presented in Pt 1136 as a cultural hero or one of the fathers of the ancient funerary tradition, a paradigmatic personality. Still, he must depend on the gods for his power. It was the divine bird Chashen Jönmo who assisted in the ritual in which the demons of death were exorcized, thereby allowing the noose to be removed from Lady Lhogyal Gyi Changmo's neck. Shenrab Nyiwo had sent Chabon Bangpa Thangrek, a divine pheasant, to call Chashen Jönmo, but when he was unable to bring him, the great priest sent the divine ibex Kyinpo Ruthokje to summon the divine bird. It was the ibex who could travel to the great heights in which Chashen Jönmo (probably a sacred raptor of some kind) lived, a place closely associated with the dead. In addition to chanting the sacred words of *bon* ritual, sheep and goats were prepared for sacrifice in order to ransom the soul of Lhogyal Gyi Changmo. The restoration of the princess's white complexion, an allusion to the reconditioning of her corpse and mind, shows that the sacrifice was successful. Thus, the way was paved for the girl to reach the afterlife:

> Well then, although the father Tsangde Hödak and Mrabon Zingkye requested her to wake up for breakfast, she did not wake up. Although they asked her to wake up for supper, she did not wake up. The face of the Lady Lhogyal Gyi Changmo became dark. The end of the black hair rope was dangling from her neck. The father Tsanghodei Hödak and the brother Mrabon Zingkye informed the father Shenrab Nyiwo, "My daughter, the wretched man's daughter, Lady Lhogyal Gyi Changmo, died bound to a black hair rope." He requested, "Now please untie the black hair rope."
>
> The father Shenrab Nyiwo said, "I cannot untie the black hair rope. Chashen Jönmo can untie it." Well then, although he sent Chabon Bangpa Thangrek to call Chashen Jönmo, he could not bring Chashen Jönmo, so he sent Kyinpo Ruthokje to call Chashen Jönmo. He brought Chashen Jönmo. Then the black sheep of binding and the brownish goat of binding were interconnected along a rope by Chashen Jönmo. For three nights the priests

chanted the sacred rituals. On the dawn of the following day, on the black sheep of binding and the brownish goats of binding they put all the evils tormenting the deceased, and the demons were banished. The black hair noose was untied from the neck of Lady Lhogyal Gyi Changmo. Her face took on a bright white complexion and she reposed as if smiling.

With the rehabilitation of Lady Lhogyal Gyi Changmo's mental condition, the funeral rituals were able to go ahead unimpeded. As part of these activities, Pt 1136 mentions two captured horses offered by her father and brother as the celestial transport vehicles. These ritual horses, or *doma*, the pyschopomps that carried the soul of the princess, are described earlier in the text. The offspring of an aquatic mare and a mountain stallion, they were captured with the aid of snares and tethered with a magical cord.

Unmistakably, this Pt 1136 origin tale alludes to a prehistoric phase in the culture of Upper Tibet. Although its ritual precedent, or *mang*, was written for early historic funerals, it concludes with a statement that the benefit and merit of the celestial funerary transport horses are equal to those of ancient times. In the words of the text, "The *doma* is beneficial and meritorious. In ancient times it was beneficial, now it is also beneficial. In ancient times it was meritorious, now it is also meritorious." The word "ancient" here indicates that this etiologic tale was understood to have originated in a period that substantially predated the composition of the text.

One of the longest Dunhuang funerary narratives is found in a manuscript of the British India Office Library collection simply designated ITJ 731. It colorfully describes the misadventures of three primal equid brothers. These equids left more ethereal regions for places in the Changthang, which of course was part of the Zhang Zhung and Sumpa tribal unions. This text, like other Dunhuang funerary manuscripts, presents the historical roots of the funerary traditions as having a Tibet-wide geographic and cultural ambit. By the time these texts were written down, the Purgyal empire had already absorbed Zhang Zhung, Sumpa, and the other proto-nations of the Tibetan Plateau. The Dunhuang funerary manuscripts, therefore, represent a codification of tradition with relevance across the Tibetan world. These texts appear to have been composed as part of a broad historical and political movement, the aim of which was to weld the Tibetan Plateau into a unified polity with a common set of beliefs and values. The finality of death and the momentousness of funeral observances must have been particularly effective agents aiding in the cultural unification of imperial Tibet.

The hero of the origin narrative in ITJ 731 is the youngest of the three equid brothers, Khukron Mangdar, a horse. The tale relates that after he disowned his middle brother, a wild ass, for not avenging the death of their older brother, who had been impaled on the horns of a wild yak, Khukron

Mangdar went on to become the first riding horse of Tibet. The funerary origins narrative describes the symbiosis between horse and rider in terms of a solemn pact. When Khukron Mangdar's human owner Mabu Damshe died, he became his *doma*, the magical horse capable of carrying the deceased over the infernal obstacles of the underworld to the heavenly afterlife.

Although fragmentary, the last part of the ITJ 731 manuscript relates that Shenrab Nyiwo and Durshen Mada, as the archetypal priests, conducted the essential funerary practices of concealing the bounds of the tomb and making its ritual superstructure in a valley. Through the deployment of the *doma*, the deceased man, Mabu Damshe, was correctly positioned in the heights. This indicates that the soul of the deceased attained the loftiness required for entry into the afterworld. After the origin tale, the text refers to an early historic funeral ceremony, epitomizing its ancient precedent.

The last complete sentence of ITJ 731 requests the *doma*, the surrogate relative of the deceased, to be the funerary conferment for travel over the pass and the river of the dead. The pass and river mentioned separated the hellish underworld from the celestial paradise, as such topographical barriers did in the mythology of many ancient Indo-Eurasian cultures. By affirming that the *doma* traverses the mountain pass and crosses the shallow ford to the bank opposite the infernal underworld, ITJ 731 signals that the deceased goes on to a heavenly reward:

> The good turquoise was chipped. The lord died, he died. The chipped turquoise was chipped from the head. The decayed lord perished and was sadly lost; he was no more, so the fathers Shenrab Nyiwo and Durshen Mada established the limits of the tomb in concealment. They made the tomb ritual in the valley. . . . For the cherished *doma* the youngest brother Khukron Mangdar was made as the ford crosser, he who would cross the ford. The ordered position of the lord was high. In ancient times, it was perfectly accomplished. Now we have collected the ritual constituents. Today . . . you cherished *doma* be that which goes above the water and go over the pass and cross the shallow ford!

The Dunhuang funerary manuscripts Pt 1136 and Pt 1134 as well as the *Muchoi Tromdur* confirm that the horns of eagles were erected on the heads of the *doma*. This custom brings to mind the Scythians of the middle of the first millennium BCE, who placed horned headdresses in the form of birds or flying deer on their sacrificial funerary horses. The Dunhuang funerary texts and Scythian burials of the Altai also attest to the use of saddles and special treatment for the manes and tails of funerary ritual horses. Moreover, the deployment of funerary effigies, the deposition of food offerings and sacrificial livestock in tombs, the ritual functions of weapons, and the use of substitute body parts made of various materials also point to a shared eschatological heritage among the Scythians and ancient Tibetans.

The similarities between the funerary practices and customs of the Scythians and those described in Tibetan literature are strengthened by the archaeological evidence we have already examined. Analogous copper alloy objects further signal ideological as well as material parallels between the Inner Asian steppes and the Tibetan Plateau. This cultural convergence between the steppes and Tibet is most pronounced as regards Zhang Zhung, which is traditionally seen as a wellspring of Tibetan funerary rituals and a nexus of cultural transmissions. The pillar and slab-wall mortuary monuments and rock art of the Upper Tibetans and their northern counterparts also undergird the common ground between them. These intercultural links demonstrate that Zhang Zhung was a Tibetan vanguard to prehistoric Eurasia, vindicating the formative role accorded it in Eternal Bon.

The cultural interactivity between north Inner Asia and the Tibetan Plateau in the first millennium BCE highlights the antiquity of the Old Tibetan funerary traditions. While the Dunhuang manuscripts could not have been composed before the seventh century CE, they preserve Iron Age customs and traditions closely associated with Upper Tibet. This many-centuries-long cultural stream persisted until Buddhist religious inroads into the Tibetan empire cut the prehistoric links joining it to the north and west.

Another Dunhuang funerary manuscript to mention Shenrab Nyiwo is Pt 1068. This funerary narrative describes in rich detail the death rites of a female protagonist. Instead of a horse, a hybrid female yak was used to transport her soul to the celestial realm. The text tells us that the brother of a deceased girl invited Shenrab Nyiwo and Durshen Mada as well as another funerary priest named Shentsha Lungdra to officiate over her funeral. The setting of this origin tale was the Kyi valley, located in and around Lhasa in Central Tibet.

The royal couple of Kyi, Kyije Mangpo and Kyidagi, had a son and a daughter. The queen died prematurely and her children, Kyichuk Jönwa and Kyinam Nyakchikma, came under the custody of a wicked stepmother. The two siblings were left to starve, so the brother went to a northern region to hunt deer and antelope. When he returned, he found that his sister had died a terrible death in a pigsty. The great torment afflicting Kyinam Nyakchikma even in death is epitomized by her hair standing straight up and an infestation of lice. Milking a hundred female yaks and a hundred female sheep, the brother tried to use the butter obtained from them to produce an unguent that would restore his sister's corpse to an unharmed state. Kyichuk Jönwa also tried a salve compounded from the bone marrow of various wild herbivores for the same purpose, but neither of these preparations worked.

The grieving Kyichuk Jönwa invited Shenrab Nyiwo and his two associates to carry out the prognosticative and restorative funerary rituals for Kyinam Nyakchikma. If the venue for her funeral was Central Tibet, as is likely, it indicates that Upper Tibet shared some of its funerary culture in common with the middle of the Tibetan Plateau, just as Classical Tibetan texts maintain. The funerary priests advised the brother Kyichuk Jönwa to go to the country of prototypic yaks to capture a female yak called Dzomo Drangma. Dzomo Drangma furnished the butter needed for the unguent that would return Kyinam Nyakchikma's hair to its normal state and rid her corpse of lice, thus effecting a mystic renovation.

In Pt 1068, the brother Kyichuk Jönwa requested Dzomo Drangma to act as the magic conveyance that would carry Kyinam Nyakchikma across the river of the dead. Durshen Mada appointed Dzomo Drangma to ford the infernal river, thus ensuring the deceased sister Kyinam Nyakchikma's deliverance. The text concludes in a similar fashion to Pt 1136 with a declaration that the merit and benefit of having a funerary transport female yak was equal to that of ancient times, when Dzomo Drangma carried Kyinam Nyakchikma's soul to salvation. The actual custom of using a hybrid yak as a sacrificial funerary offering is represented in a tomb excavated in Malari, near the crest of the Indian Himalaya.[50]

Although Lamaist doctrine is at odds with many of the ancient eschatological traditions we have been examining, the archaic continues to cast a long shadow over Tibet. The evocation rites of Buddhism and Eternal Bon have retained potent motifs adopted from the antecedent funerary culture. The fundamental belief that ritual intervention is still possible even after death is one such anachronism. According to Buddhist conceptions, the salvation of the dead depends on their karmic debt as well as their ability to distinguish the true nature of reality in the postmortem state, not on ritual aid. Strictly speaking, rituals cannot prejudice the outcome of death, but that is precisely what lamas attempt to do in their funerary rites, just as their archaic counterparts did. The past remains alive in more sinister ways too. Historical Tibet abounds with tales of people known as *delok* who have returned from the grave, and *rolang*, or reanimated corpses, that haunt the countryside. Despite its sophisticated worldview, Lamaism could not blot out these untoward beliefs connected to death. The irrational stemming from transmogrified elements of the archaic funerary culture continues to exert an influence on the Tibetan psyche today.

In 2006, another Old Tibetan–language manuscript detailing the ritual activities of Shenrab Nyiwo was discovered in southern Tibet. When a group of villagers were preparing to rebuild a derelict *chorten* known as Gathang Bumpa, they happened upon a pile of old folios concealed within the ruins. Fortunately, those responsible had the good sense to call in Pasang Wangdu and Dhondrup Lhagyal, experts in ancient Tibetan history from Lhasa's Tibet Academy of Social Sciences.

Among the texts hidden in Gathang Bumpa was one dedicated to the origins of ransom offerings in which the main ritualist is Shenrab Nyiwo.[51] This startling discovery in the heart of Tibet independently verifies that Shenrab Nyiwo was indeed an archetypal priest, just as he is portrayed in the Dunhuang funerary manuscripts. These respective writings were discovered in places separated by fifteen hundred miles, yet they belong to the same early historic body of ritual traditions. The Gathang Bumpa text establishes that the portrayal of Shenrab Nyiwo in the Dunhuang materials is not a fluke or the product of a foreign group acting alone in the Gobi Desert. The Gathang Bumpa text, however, goes further in its description of Shenrab Nyiwo. He emerges not as a funerary priest, but as a practitioner of all types of archaic rituals: those to diagnose, heal, and ransom the lives of individuals enthralled by angry spirits.

The Gathang Bumpa Shenrab Nyiwo text is composed in a somewhat later style than the archaic funerary manuscripts of Dunhuang, but its grammatical structure reveals that it was written before circa 1000 CE. With the aid of my friend Yungdrung Tenzin, I managed to produce a translation of this abstruse composition in its entirety. This text contains several narratives, the longest of which is set in the Changthang territory known as Mrayul Thanggye. This riveting tale is full of romance, passion, and adventure. It begins with Lurab Sangto and Mracham Silema, a young couple deeply in love. Angered over Mracham Silema having taken a lover among another tribe and her neglect of farmwork, her brother Mra Thenwa slew Lurab Sangto. Learning of his son's death, the aggrieved father of Lurab Sangto, Luje Tsenpo, sought to take revenge against the perpetrator. Allied with all manner of demons, Luje Tsenpo, the king of the water spirits, pursued his son's murderer to the ends of Tibet.

Mra Thenwa appealed to the gods for help, arguing in his defense that he had killed Lurab Sangto in a fit of passion and not for criminal gain. As it was an honor killing, the gods spared Mra Thenwa's life but imposed an impossibly large fine on him. Being more than he could ever possibly pay, he sought a ritual remedy from Shenrab Nyiwo. Shenrab Nyiwo appealing to a chief god of the otherworld, Lhawo Lhase, eloquently recounts the plight of his client:

> In Mrayul Thanggye, Mra Thenwa killed Lurab Sangto, so all the gods acted as the arbitrators. For the blood money of the water spirits seven hundred and seventy thousand pieces of gold was ruled. Mra Thenwa could not accept that. . . . Mra Thenwa was nearly taken like a bird in a snare. He was nearly snatched like a fish in a trap. He was nearly seized like a sheep by the scruff of the neck.

Finally, after several attempts to save his client's life, including the most lavish offerings imaginable, Shenrab Nyiwo and his colleague Müpal Trokrol were able to devise a ransom ritual that had the intended effect. It was used as a substitute for the *srang*, or pieces of gold, that Mra Thenwa was supposed to have paid to the king of the water spirits. The narrative ends by reiterating that the ransom ritual for Mra Thenwa was performed in ancient times, a thousand-year-old reference to the earlier age in which Shenrab Nyiwo is reputed to have lived.

Another origin tale of the ransom ritual inscribed in the Gathang Bumpa text graphically describes how Shenrab Nyiwo carried out the sacrifice of a sheep. It is written that this slaughter was instrumental in saving the life of Yabla Daldruk, the divine ancestor of the Purgyal kings and emperors of Central Tibet. Yabla Daldruk had fallen foul of the king of bad omens Gangpar Geber, and it was up to Shenrab Nyiwo and three other priests to rescue him. The heart of a sacrificial sheep was removed and wrapped in silk ornamented with gold and turquoise. In this way, the text states that the beating sheep heart was exchanged for the beating heart of Yabla Daldruk.

The taking of life is anathema to Buddhism and Eternal Bon. The two Lamaist religions do not condone its practice whatever the purported benefits. As reprehensible as the sacrifice of animals is to Lamaism, it appears to have been a stock ritual practice in ancient Tibet. Perceived as highly effective in bringing about positive outcomes for those in need, this practice flourished until Buddhist ethics came to have a superior influence in Tibet.

Nothing illustrates the unfathomable gulf that exists between the archaic and prevailing religions of Tibet better than the ritual killing of animals in the Gathang Bumpa text. This is especially true when one of the officiants is Shenrab Nyiwo, the holiest figure in Eternal Bon. This heretical view of its founder, as adherents would see it, could not stand if Eternal Bon was to have even a modicum of legitimacy in a Tibet dominated by Buddhism. Thus, Eternal Bon effaced the old Shenrab Nyiwo, the sacrificial priest, replacing him with Shenrab Miwo, the Buddha. Eternal Bon has been largely successful in its bid to re-create the past, but it came at the cost of an accurate rendering of the ancient religious complexion of Tibet.

The portrayal of Shenrab Nyiwo in the Dunhuang and Gathang Bumpa manuscripts hits upon another fundamental difference between the archaic religious traditions and the prevailing Lamaism of Tibet. Lamaism was founded on a religious model with clearly defined biographical, temporal, and geographic frameworks. Its foundations are unambiguously ascribed to Tönpa Shenrab of Olmolungring and the Buddha of India. The archaic religious traditions of Zhang Zhung, Sumpa, and Central Tibet were much more amorphous, the product of sundry cultural inputs over a long time period rather than the output of a single founder acting in a specific time and place.

In the next chapter, we look into other facets of ancient culture in Upper Tibet, a collective way of being in which holiness and honor were the highest of values. Through their cultural legacy Zhang Zhung and Sumpa achieved a greatness that would outlive most other ancient civilizations.

· 9 ·

Horned Heroes and Turquoise Maidens:
The Cultural Life of Zhang Zhung

MYTHS OF THE BEGINNING

$\mathcal{O}$ver the last millennium, the Buddhist-inspired interpretation of history and culture adopted by Lamaism resulted in many archaic traditions falling by the wayside. To bring them in line with Buddhist doctrines, native cultural foundations had to be modified, marginalized, or eliminated. Yet despite this wholesale reengineering of religion, remnants of archaic myths, rituals, and customs still manage to find a voice in Eternal Bon scriptures.

The origins of human beings and the universe is a preoccupation in virtually all cultures. The perennial questions of "Who am I?" and "Where did I come from?" appear to have been addressed with great flourish in ancient Upper Tibet. The answers to these and other fundamental questions reveal a profoundly contemplative people, one not satisfied with fairy-tale explanations and simple metaphors alone. To the contrary, the inhabitants of the uplands appear to have developed a refined speculative tradition marked by a high order of abstraction.

Eternal Bon literature boasts hundreds of different origin myths derived from various historical sources. Many of these are found in an abbreviated form as mythic precedents to various rituals. Cosmogony seems to have played a particularly important role in the archaic religions of Tibet, in which the establishment of origins was considered essential for the legitimization and practice of rituals. Tibetan written sources lead us to believe that a vacuous state of preexistence as the ultimate source of all things was the cornerstone of ancient cosmogony in Tibet.[1]

A lavish Eternal Bon origin myth of significant antiquity is found in the well-known ritual text *Lubum Trawo*. It tells in epic language the tale of a serpent goddess of cosmic proportions.[2] In this myth, all the physical, biological, and divine constructs of the universe emanate from a female serpent known as the "Queen of the Water Spirits." Cosmic serpents giving birth to the universe are found in the mythology of indigenous peoples throughout the world. The Tibetan variant of the myth promotes highly refined cosmogonic conceptions pertaining to the nature of the primal void.

The possible prehistoric origins of the Tibetan serpent mother myth are reflected in its ascribing the origins of existence and living beings to a Gaean mother, not to a lineage of male gods like many other Eternal Bon cosmogonies do. Although the parent myth may be derived from early sources, the surviving textual account can be attributed to a reworking of early historic materials. Reference to the languages and peoples of Zhang Zhung, Sumpa, and Central Tibet indicates that it developed to accommodate the political and cultural realities of the Tibetan empire. In order to foster a sense of unity in the imperial period, the pan-Tibetan political apparatus required myths of origin pertinent to the entire Plateau. By citing the languages of Zhang Zhung, Sumpa, and Central Tibet, we can assume that this *Lubum Trawo* narrative originally came from either Upper Tibet or Central Tibet. In any case, the rich celestial and meteorological imagery surrounding the Queen of the Water Spirits is comparable to the Gekhö gods, alluding to Zhang Zhung cultural influences.

The *Lubum Trawo* myth attributes all elements of the universe to various parts of the Queen of the Water Spirits' body, which appeared from rainbow light. After describing the intricate mind-sky nexus over which the Queen of the Water Spirits presides, the text turns to the corporeal elements of existence. As in many other ancient Eurasian cultures, the sun is equated with the swastika. After the birth of the heavenly ornaments of the sun and moon, the four male planets appeared from the Queen of the Water Spirits' upper fangs and the four female planets from her lower fangs. In addition to the personification of comets and eclipses, these are the "seven planets" of the classical world widely known in Eurasian and North African cultures.

With the celestial vault in place, the serpent mother myth enumerates thunder, lightning, clouds, fog, rain, and hail, which appeared from the goddess's mouth and eyes. These natural forces acted as the basic engine of life. From the nostrils of the Queen of the Water Spirits spread various types of life-nourishing winds. From her blood came the five oceans and from her nerve channels all the watercourses. The light of the great goddess's flesh formed the golden earth, the sustainer of all life.

The animal world is held to have manifested from the Queen of the Water Spirits' limbs, while the front and back of her gigantic bulk were responsible for the day and night, illustrating her pantheistic nature. The spirit world was actualized from the light of her organs. The myth concludes by referring to the cosmic serpent lady's begetting of cultural foundations:

> In the beginning of existence there existed absolutely nothing, abiding in the nature of emptiness. Thereafter, in the sphere of emptiness there existed not even a particle of the vapor of existence; everything was not wrought and nothingness was not wrought as well. From the sphere of blissful moisture a rainbow-like form came into being. The very attractive and brightly colored rainbow-like form, an inapprehensible entity, came into being. It also formed something concrete and likewise had bright colors. From its essence an entity as large as a sesame seed came into being. From the essence of the spontaneously self-opening entity as large as a sesame seed, the figure of a woman one hand in height came into being.
>
> A woman, a female with a one-hand-high body and robust limbs was born. She was born as one with differing speech coming from her mouth. Her mind covered the worlds of the innumerable world systems. Her miraculous body and beneficent mind, which covered everything, was born. She was given names. In the language of Zhang Zhung: *Sang Karate Kuntu Khyab*. In the language of Sumpa: *Molzhi Kunkhyab*. In the language of Tibet she was known as "Queen of the Water Spirits Organizer of Existence." From the vapor on the crown of her head the turquoise-colored blue sky came into existence. Although it was visible, the existence that emerged from the vapor was not tangible.
>
> There was absolutely nothing that could not be covered by the sky. In the language of Zhang Zhung, that is known as the "all-covering emptiness." In the language of Sumpa it is known as "uniformly covering." In the language of Tibet it is known as "sky." In the language of Eternal Bon it is known as the "sky" or the "inapprehensible and intangible space quiddity." There was absolutely nothing not covered by the light. Therefore, it was called the highly resplendent all-covering. It unremittingly looked over existence; so there was absolutely nothing that was invisible.
>
> From the light rays of the right eye of Queen of the Water Spirits Organizer of Existence, the bright moonlight came into existence. Thereafter there was absolutely nothing that was not illuminated. From the light rays of her left eye the sun, the maker of warmth, came into being. Its warmth came down upon the innumerable world systems, and there was absolutely nothing that it did not cover. It had no egocentricity; therefore, in the language of Zhang Zhung it was known as the "great uniform covering." In the language of Sumpa it was known as the "impartially affectionate mother of all." . . . In the language of Tibet it is known as the "sun." In the language of Tibet it is also known as the "unsurpassable swastika."
>
> The sun and moon were kept as the ornaments of all visible existence. Thereafter, from the four upper fangs of Queen of the Water Spirits Organizer of Existence there appeared the four male planets. They are the moon, Jupiter, Venus, and that called eclipses and comets. . . . From her

four lower fangs came the sun, Mars, Saturn, and Mercury. These are the four female planets. When Queen of the Water Spirits opened her right eye, night appeared. When she opened her left eye it was daytime. Thereafter, from the twelve upper teeth of Queen of the Water Spirits Organizer of Existence the male stars appeared, and from her twelve lower teeth, the female stars appeared. By the planets, the seasons and time cycles were controlled. Also, the stars likewise controlled the time cycles.

From the speech of Queen of the Water Spirits thunder sounded in the innumerable world systems. There was absolutely no one who could not hear this. From the light rays of her tongue, the lightning strikes that illuminated the innumerable world systems came into being. From the vapor of her mouth, clouds and fog appeared. From the tears of her eyes, rain appeared. If her tears are copious the rain is great. If her tears are scant there is less rain. From the saliva of her tongue, hail appeared.

From the breath of her right and left nostrils the breezes and winds in the cycle of the seasons came erratically. If her breath is heavy the wind is great. If her breath is light there is less wind. . . . From the breath of the Queen of the Water Spirits Organizer of Existence appeared the currents of wind. From the wheel of the wind the four great wheels of wind appeared: the wind blowing in the sky, the wind that brings down hail and warmth, the wind that cleanses the channels of living creatures, and the wind that induces growth. Such are the four.

From her blood the four great oceans were produced. Along with the central ocean, these five appeared. Thereafter, from her three hundred and sixty subtle energy channels each of her streams, thousands of rivers, came into being. From her thousands of streams the plants consumed by animals came into being, and there was absolutely nothing not produced by animals. Thereafter, from the light rays of her flesh the all-supporting golden earth came into being. There was absolutely nothing not included in it. There was absolutely nothing not growing from it. There was absolutely nothing not sustained by it.

From her light rays of warmth the epochal light came into being from primordial times, so there was absolutely nothing that was not sustained by this warmth. From the light rays of her bones the mountain [in the center] of the world also came into being. The rock formations of existence and the stones came into being then. Thereafter, from each strand of body hair and each strand of hair on the head of Queen of the Water Spirits Organizer of Existence, the trees, plants, forests, and so forth came into being. Thereafter, from the light rays of her four limbs the animal world came into being. . . . From her front and back the sunny and shady places came into being. From the light rays of her organs and from the light rays of her throat hundreds of thousands water spirits came into being. . . . From the light rays of her heart the gods and demons of visible existence bestowed with names came into being.

> The inconceivable "*bon*" and "non-*bon*" religions that bring happiness to sentient beings came into existence. Also, all the musical traditions and so forth of the gods came into being. From the light rays of her brain all the great lakes and small lakes came into being. From the light rays of her abdomen all the marshes and ponds came into being. Her intestines created the thoroughfares. The physical countries and castles came into being. From her womb the continuous path of birth came into being. There is absolutely nothing that does not exist from her.

In the archaic mythology of Tibet, the cosmic egg is a prevalent theme. A generative egg, source of all life, had pride of place in the mythologies of many ancient peoples. In some Eternal Bon cosmogonies, there are actually two eggs: a luminous white egg from which the primal virtuous being, "Illuminating Resplendence," emerged and a murky black egg that produced the original evil being, "King of the Negative Realm." All the good and bad in the universe are supposed to have descended from these two beings.

There are many variations in the Tibetan cosmic egg myth. An abbreviated version is found in a funerary text of the *Muchoi Tromdur* collection.[3] It upholds that in the beginning there was nothing but space. Thereafter, the agencies of light and water gave rise to three cosmic eggs from which the gods and humans appeared. Although this cosmogony was not placed in writing before the eleventh century CE, its basic elements appear to be much older than that:

> In the language of Zhang Zhung: "the primordium of all-encompassing space." In the language of Tibet it obtained the name "existence, light itself, the light of the planets and the light rays of the gods." In the language of "Bon": "the womb of the space of emptiness, the primordium without qualities." . . . Thereafter primal light came into being. After that, light and rays appeared. After that, moisture and dampness came into being. After that, a precious lake came into being. A film appeared on the lake. Furthermore, the lake film rolled into eggs. Three wonderful eggs rolled, the eggs that are greatly wondrous. One was a globule of the white light of conch, one was a globule of the red light of copper, and one was a globule of the black light of iron. From inside the opened eggs the lineages of the gods of purity and humans appeared, the lineages that appeared from light and miracles.

According to Eternal Bon sources, the *bonpo* and *shen* priests of Zhang Zhung and Central Tibet would recite the origins of the universe as a prelude to their ritual activities. The sponsors of the rituals had to demonstrate considerable hospitality and offer gifts to these priests if they were to carry out their vital religious duties. A fine account of these activities and the words uttered in the recitation of origins has been preserved in a text devoted to the Gekhö circle of deities.[4] This account prefaces the *walchu*, an elaborate ritual performance of total purification, believed to have originated in Zhang Zhung. According to the main *walchu* text, this ritual tradition was first practiced by the Zhang Zhung King Tridem, holder of the iron horns bird crown.

The text of the Gekhö origin myth is read in the first person; reputedly it was uttered by a Zhang Zhung priest belonging to the *walchu* ritual tradition. The modes of transport, headdress, and ritual objects used by this priest are mentioned before the actual myth of origins is given. Among the gifts given to the priest is a turquoise, Tibet's most important precious stone.[5] Ancient strings of turquoise were discovered in 2013 in the burials of Gurgyam, confirming the hoary status accorded this substance in Tibetan literature. Like the generative egg cosmogony of the *Muchoi Tromdur* above, the Gekhö text affirms that the gods and human beings share the same divine parentage:

> Tonight, on the best day of existence for subduing the wrongdoing enemies and demons, I the *walbon* was invited by this sponsor and benefactor. From beyond a big pass, I was escorted here on a horse and wild ass. From the other side of a big river, I was brought here on a boat and ship. Under me a precious textile carpet was spread. Above me a brocade tent was set up. On my neck a turquoise was hung. I was offered a nectarous libation to drink. On my head a white turban was tied. A precious gift was offered to my hands. In front of me bright butter lamps were lit. An arrow was erected as the good body tabernacle of Gekhö. I am the great *wal* priest for subduing enemies and obstructors. I will explain the source of the great *wal* that insulates from heinous defilements.
>
> In the absolute nothingness of the beginning there appeared the element of wind. There arose the enveloping fire. There arose the enveloping water. There arose the circle of the earth. There existed darkness and oscillations. There existed a little dampness and a little moisture. From the miraculous combination of warmth and moisture, a lake as large as a mirror came into being. In the lake a bubble as large as a tent whirled up. The essence of that bubble existed as an effulgent holy man. He bestowed a name upon himself: he was known as "King of Primordial Existence." From the manifestation of his mind three miraculous eggs appeared. Inside the opened eggs appeared a man from the primordium, "Primordial Aspiration Black-Headed One"; he of existence came into being. He was the eldest brother, primordial priest of consummate power. There appeared a woman who was the epochal "Queen Lady of Water." The gods, humans, and priests, these three, appeared from them.

In the mythic epoch of the first human beings, all living creatures, spirits, and natural objects residing on earth are believed to have been joined in one great society. According to Tibetan legend, in very early times, the celestial and terrestrial spirits existed in close association with humans. This is said to have been so in the period before weaving and woodworking, when Tibetans lived in stone huts, caves, and cavities in the ground. Tibetan literature also professes that in the first epoch there were six successive stages in Tibet ruled by nonhumans, during which the deities, demons, and humans were not separated. According to a history of Eternal Bon by its greatest contemporary scholar Lopön Tenzin Namdak, as time went on the kinship between humans and the spirits of the earth and sky diminished. Thus he writes,

> In the subsequent era, the territories of Zhang Zhung and Tibet were gradually separated, and humans gradually learned [technological] activities. The orders of the celestial spirits and terrestrial spirits and others resided in the mountains, rocks, and rivers and were miraculously born from the same extraction. They did not actually have corporeal forms and were invisible to humans. The humans and deities and demons had less and less cooperative association. They could not see each other, and their residences and existences were disassociated.[6]

An Eternal Bon text probably of the twelfth century CE, *Dulwa Lingdrak*, also recounts the first epoch in which universal comity prevailed.[7] Such accounts of halcyon days are common in world mythology and religion:

> The celestial spirits and terrestrial spirits were not separated in the time when humans, celestial spirits, and terrestrial spirits could exchange conversation. The stones, trees, and earth all spoke the language of humans. The celestial spirits, water spirits, and humans, these three, exchanged conversation.

According to the traditional view of Tibetan history, after the separation of the various hosts of spirits and humans, society evolved into more technologically advanced forms. In the countries of Zhang Zhung and Central Tibet, a great many intellectual and technological advances are thought to have occurred, spurred on by the feats of great monarchs and priests.

THE AWESOME FEATS OF ZHANG ZHUNG'S GREATEST PERSONALITIES

Tibetan literature furnishes many accounts of cultural life in prehistoric Zhang Zhung, Sumpa, and Central Tibet. Most of these tales have a spiritual or ritualistic backdrop and are disposed to couch even the most utilitarian aspects of ancient life in the language of piety. Much of what has been written about people and culture in ancient Tibet is weighted toward the extraordinary and unverifiable. In addition to incorporating the mythic, Tibetan narratives dealing with the remote past have an elite bias; the activities of great saints and royalty loom large, not those of the common man. This focus on the exceptional makes for superb storytelling as fabulous as it may be.

A liberal admixture of myth and legend distorting documented events is nothing unusual, for preternatural themes color ancient histories the world over. It is from the highly embellished and somewhat stilted Tibetan literary tradition that we must look for clues about the paleoculture of Zhang Zhung. Fortunately for the historian, the mundane does often enough intrude upon the supernatural, the two blended together like water in milk. Only through the churning of critical analysis can they be separated.

Much of what has been written about archaic culture in Tibet over the last millennium reflects the ethos of Buddhism and the mind-set of the faithful. Moreover, these writings were composed centuries after the historical fact, in a time when the collective memory had faded and physical evidence of the past was reduced. Thus Tibetan literature furnishes a rather hazy and contrived record of Zhang Zhung. When using Tibetan texts to fathom its cultural character, it is not prudent to expect them to yield the past in any positively verifiable way. This literature is better suited to an understanding of the great sweep of ancient cultural history. In essence, it is a chronicle of the cultural leitmotiv, not a registry of specific events and personalities.

Through a broad survey of recurring themes and fundamental motifs presented in Tibetan texts, we get an inkling of the archaic cultural heritage. Certain patterns in the lifestyle, mentality, and undertakings of ancient times are accorded considerable credence in these writings. It is on these points that we must build our cultural history, always poised to admit the light of empirical evidence from the field as and when it becomes available.

Although colorful accounts of archaic era personages in Eternal Bon literature are clearly mythic or legendary in character, a certain amount of historical lore regarding indigenous religious and cultural practices persists. Taken as a whole, the activities and appearances of the archaic masters differ from customary portrayals of Lamaist practitioners. Most importantly, many of their rituals, costumes, and implements are wedded to the Tibetan landscape, not imported from India. It is written that the *shen* and *bonpo* priests occupied special Upper Tibetan habitats such as the islands and headlands of the great lakes and resided in temples known as *sekhang* and *sekhar*. As we have seen, these habitational patterns are corroborated by the Upper Tibetan archaeological record. The intimate association of archaic era wizards with mountains, lakes, the weather, and the heavens also tends to set them apart from the monks of later times.

In Eternal Bon texts, ancient priests are depicted attired in animal-skin robes, turbans, horned headdresses, lobed crowns, and other ornaments that distinguish them from Lamaist monks. They often exhibit martial predilections and are vigorously involved in military affairs of state, qualities at variance with Lamaist ideals. The ancient *shen* and *bonpo* are supposed to have been able to magically transform themselves into wild animals or to have controlled fierce creatures. These kinds of capabilities are generally downplayed in accounts of Lamaist mystics. For ancient adepts, it appears that religious emphasis lay on the performance of rituals with practical benefits, not otherworldly speculation. Moreover, it is recorded that the *shen* and *bonpo* participated in the construction of tombs and large-scale burial rites, a clear reference to the archaic cultural milieu.

Eternal Bon texts aver that archaic religious masters had the ability to speak to the deities of heaven, earth, and water. This is supposed to have been a carryover from the golden age when human society lived in perfect harmony with the natural and supernatural worlds. The friendship of saints with mountain gods and their dalliances with lake nymphs is a common theme in Eternal Bon narratives. Lamaist texts hold that the holy men of later times also befriended spirits of the natural world, exploiting them in much the same way as their ancient counterparts did. It is believed that by forming partnerships with deities, religious adepts were able to regulate the natural world, using it for their own purposes. While this seems to have been a means to an end in the archaic era, in Lamaist times such practices were subordinate to transformative processes of the mind superintended by tutelary gods.

According to Eternal Bon, a sign of the great power of archaic priests was their ability to rear wild animals, exploiting them like ordinary people do horses, cattle, and other livestock. The *bonpo* and *shen* are said to have kept tigers, lions, bears, wolves, and other fierce carnivores as their minions. The Central Tibetan adept Pebon Thoktse is recorded as being served by wild yaks and crocodiles.[8] It is claimed that another Central Tibetan, Khubon Thongdrak, rode around space on a dragon.[9] It is also purported that these ancient masters magically transformed themselves into wild animals in pursuit of special aims. The twelfth-century CE *Rigdzin Rigpai Thukgyü* tells us that the prehistoric saint Zingpa Thuchen manifested as a wolf in order to retrieve the wandering souls of patients.[10] This foretells the tradition of spirit-mediums turning themselves into wolves to recall the errant souls of clients in contemporary Upper Tibet. Supposedly, other ancient savants became vultures and flew around space, a mystic theme that has also persisted among spirit-mediums to the present day.

To be sure, the *shen* and *bonpo* of Zhang Zhung, Sumpa, and other parts of Tibet are credited with many sensational abilities. The supernatural powers ascribed to the ancient priests in Eternal Bon texts are intended to accentuate their sacred authority, establishing them as fit objects for religious devotion. Their various fantastic activities also have much metaphorical significance. In literature, this is expressed in archaic cultural themes and in Buddhist-style philosophical and moral exercises.

A provocative selection of priestly feats is found in a text of the Eternal Bon Mother Tantra tradition composed in the fourteenth century CE.[11] For instance, it states that the royal priest Nangwa Dokchen bounced savage celestial thunderbolts as if they were a ball. This outlandish proposition puts Nangwa Dokchen in close functional correspondence with the Gekhö circle of deities and its focus on the sky. The Mother Tantra records that Anu Trakthak of Mount Tise in western Tibet flew in space on wings of white clouds, another allusion to ancient sky-bound religious phenomena. The Mother Tantra alleges that Sadne Gau of Lake Dangra navigated the water on his drum, while Namra Tseku mounted his drum to fly in the sky. Zingpa Thuchen of eastern Tibet is thought to have ridden on the corona of the moon as if it were a horse. The Mother Tantra also purports that Shephu Rakhug, who hailed from Drum Kyi Taktshal west of Lake Nam Tsho, prayed with a string of beads made of lightning. In the same vein, Libon Mucha is said to have scattered hills with his fingertips at the base of Mount Tise, while Mucho Bar of Sumpa collected clouds and made rain fall. Not to be outdone, Khubon Thongdrak of Central Tibet, flying in the sky, connected the peaks of mountains with his fiery lasso. Another Zhang Zhung master of the Mother Tantra, Nangzher Löpo, is thought to have been able to pass through all types of mountains.

Far-fetched powers are also attributed to Zhang Zhung *bonpo* in *Drakpa Lingdrak*, a historical text that was probably compiled in the twelfth century CE. The Zhang Zhung master Long Muwer is recorded as wrapping up Lake Mapang in his skirt, while Libon Chosang (probably the same personality as Libon Mucha) carried Mount Tise on his small finger.[12] Other *bonpo* of Sumpa and Kashmir are said to have ridden on drums, just like the shamans of the Himalaya and Inner Asia of more recent times are reputed to have done.[13]

Eternal Bon descriptions of early saints illustrate that they were created in the image and likeness of the gods or vice versa. There is nothing unusual here, this theme being repeated in religions all over the world. In world mythology the human embodying the divine constitutes a fundamental archetype. In Tibet, the archaic luminaries and gods shared many things in common, including their activities, costumes, and ritual tools. As we saw in the etiologic myths, humans are generally assigned divine origins. As the kith and kin of the gods, they are their mortal representatives on earth. The divine pedigree of humans is a Tibetan cultural formula that has every appearance of being extremely ancient. It can be traced to Old Tibetan ritual narratives, many of which are set in the prehistoric epoch.

The Eternal Bon historical text *Rigdzin Rigpai Thukgyü* is packed with descriptions of primal and prehistoric saints of the heavenly and terrestrial realms.[14] These figures illustrate the principle of the gods and humans being genealogically related to one another. Let us look at some of these mythic personalities to see how Tibetan authors have portrayed this fundamental relationship. The mother of the heavenly priest Chime Tsukphü, Zangza Ringtsun, is said to have held a golden vase in her hand, as do a variety of pacific deities. In Tibetan religions, the vase fashioned from various metals is a symbol of long life and prosperity. Chime Tsukphü himself wore a tiger-skin loincloth, a style of dress popular with native and Buddhist gods. Chime Tsukphü's consort is recorded holding a victory banner, which in various forms is a common attribute of deities as well.

Rigdzin Rigpai Thukgyü relates that the mythic tantric master Sangwa Dupa wielded a sword and bow, as do many of the fierce gods of Tibet. His consort, Senthubma, held a thunderbolt arrow, a specific attribute of the Gekhö gods. It is thought that with these ritual weapons this couple subdued the enemies of religion and removed the life force of demons, functions popularly conducted by protective deities as well. The ancient *bonpo* Menyak Chetsha Kharbu wielded an ax in his right hand, the weapon of choice for the *dud* spirits. He and his consort Lucham Barma are perceived as responsible for increasing the wealth-attaining capacity of people, a vital function of many deities too.

In *Rigdzin Rigpai Thukgyü*, the Zhang Zhung saints Mutsha Gyerme and Rasang Khöram, like the gods, have tiger-skin and leopard-skin costumes and play drums and flat-bells. Another early priest, Lhabon Yongsu Dakpa, is depicted with a bright white color and a turban on his head, just like many of the mountain divinities of Tibet. The primordial priest Milüsamlek is said to have worn a red turban and a red-striped cloak, popular attire of the *tsen* warrior spirits. Reputedly the consort of the *bonpo* Ngampa Chering, White Lioness Face, was attired in a mantle, the priest Debon Gyimtsha Machung in a robe of feathers, and Hripa Gyerme in a tiger-skin greatcoat, types of dress well represented among the indigenous divinities of Tibet. Also according to *Rigdzin Rigpai Thukgyü*, the primal saint Ludrub Yeshe Nyingpo and his consort Chamgyung Nerok were appareled in aquatic silk, a material used by indigenous deities, both male and female. This couple is recorded subduing all troublesome water spirits, as are the mountain and lake deities.

Biographical vignettes about the adepts of Zhang Zhung grace a variety of Eternal Bon ritual and historical texts. One of these saints was the celebrated female Takber Liwer, who is portrayed as a tantric practitioner and yogini in the Buddhist vein of hagiography. She is said to have resided on the shores of sacred Lake Mapang in southwestern Tibet.[15] *Rigdzin Rigpai Thukgyü* furnishes a short biographical account of this archetypal female figure of Zhang Zhung.[16] Here Takber Liwer assumes a mythic character, making her a fit object for supplication. The biography tells us that after Takber Liwer left the earth, she became one with her mediation deity, a religious tradition borrowed from Vajrayana Buddhism. Her physical appearance and worldly activities are related as follows:

> She had a red complexion and kept her hair in a topknot. She wore a handsome cloak of white silk. In her right hand she held a banner of the wind and her left hand a lotus bowl. Her common attainments were that she could keep tigers, leopards, bears, and brown bears as if they were sheep. The water spirits, mountain spirits, and spirits of the soil were her servants. After teaching for three hundred and sixty years she turned into a horned eagle below the peak of Mount Tise and disappeared into space.

One of the best-known Zhang Zhung masters is Tonggyung Thuchen, a man thought to have lived in the eighth century CE. According to Eternal Bon history, this was the time when Zhang Zhung was conquered by the Central Tibetan Purgyal dynasty and the native religion was persecuted by the Tibetan empire. Tonggyung Thuchen resided at Nam Tsho, and the goddess of this lake, Nam Tsho Chukmo, is supposed to have been his consort. A detailed hagiographic account in the *Rigdzin Rigpai Thukgyü* likens him to a peripatetic Buddhist saint, conferring Mahayana- and Vajrayana-style teachings on his disciples in various parts of Tibet.[17] His ascetic appearance and religious activities recall that of an Indian yogin. If this textual depiction is historically accurate, it shows that certain archaic cults were already heavily Buddhacized by the late eighth century CE. Nonetheless, Tonggyung Thuchen's ritual tools and the identity of his lover point to the persistence of older customs:

> Tonggyung Thuchen, the holder of the [religious] lineage, obtained realization at Nam Tsho Chukmo. Dressed as a Brahmin, he had a dark brown complexion, a wrathful visage, and his hair in a topknot. On his body he wore bone ornaments. In his right hand he held a sharp sword and in his left a weapon resembling the claws of an eagle. He stood in an animated and regal fashion. His consort was the Lake Queen with a bright blue turquoise complexion and her hair in tiny turquoise braids. She was attired in a magical battle cloak made with aquatic wool. In her right hand she had a shell filled with nectar for offering and in her left hand a snake skull with blood. [Tonggyung Thuchen's] ordinary attainments were his ability to throw mustard seeds in order to expel enemies and obstructors,

wrap up Nam Tsho in his lap with his clothes, and throw a magical missile in the form of a mountain.

Another pair of Zhang Zhung practitioners featured in the twelfth-century CE *Rigdzin Rigpai Thukgyü* is similar in appearance to the indigenous protective deities of Tibet. The male adept's attributes are those of mountain gods, and his consort has attributes common to lake goddesses. This pair, Shebu Rakhuk and Ödenma, lived in Drum Kyi Taktshal, a Changthang locale. Like the gods and other archaic saints, this pair are portrayed as masters of wild animals and spirits:

> Shebu Rakhuk obtained enlightenment as Drum Kyi Taktshal. He had a radiant white complexion, and flowing hair covered the upper part of his body. He was dressed in clothes of aquatic silk. In his right hand he held a regimental banner made of aquatic silk and in his left hand a silver vase. Feet turned upward, he displayed a terrifying mien. His consort was Ödenma with the white complexion. She had flowers in her hair bun and wore a mantle of aquatic wool. In her right hand she had a golden flat-bell and with her left she offered a lotus bowl of nectar. [Shebu Rakhuk's] ordinary attainments were that he could manifest as a tiger and leopard, eradicate obstructions, and transform himself into a vulture and fly in the sky. . . . He could dispatch the spirits of the sky and earth as his servants, he could put the female lake deities to work, and he could display multifarious manifestations.[18]

THE ANCIENT WARRIORS AND PRIESTS OF ZHANG ZHUNG AND CENTRAL TIBET

Tibetan tradition is unambiguous: the archaic era priests were warlike and actively participated in military campaigns in support of the Zhang Zhung and Central Tibetan kings. The martial predisposition of the *shen* and *bonpo* is reflected in the arms they bore and in the destructive magic they perpetrated for political ends. While much of the relevant literature presents highly exaggerated accounts of the glories of battle, a cynosure of priests and rulers stands behind the myths.

The religious and political institutions of the various prehistoric nations of Tibet appear to have been mutually supporting. The priests and sages gained political patronage from royalty to ensure their prosperity and social standing. In turn, the kings acquired religious legitimacy and ideological authority from the priests, essential for maintaining their mandate to rule. The close link between the ruling and sacerdotal classes in Zhang Zhung and

Sumpa are mirrored in the archaeological monuments of Upper Tibet. The temples and citadels of the region share the same styles of construction and patterns of residency.

A passage found in an Eternal Bon text probably composed in the eleventh century CE, *Rigdzin Düpai Khogbub*, relates how the Zhang Zhung master Dami Theke single-handedly defeated the armies arrayed against him.[19] The various militaries mentioned in this account appear to have been regiments from various parts of the Zhang Zhung kingdom. Why Dami Theke was at war with his own people is not explained in the text. This incident seems to point to a particularly strife-torn period in Zhang Zhung history, real or imagined. Nevertheless, the great proliferation of citadels throughout the region intimates that such internecine conflict was a historical reality. *Rigdzin Düpai Khogbub* incorporates archaic cultural motifs of friendship between gods and saints and the magical transformation of humans into animals. The account also includes Buddhist-style concepts of meditation and enlightenment, betraying the Lamaist hand that composed it. The epic battle between Dami Theke and his foes unfolds at Mount Pöri Ngeden in southwestern Tibet:

> While the master Dami Theke meditated at Pöri Ngeden in pursuance of the doctrine of *bon*, he was [confronted] by the army of Zhang Zhung Sede, the army of Detrin, the army of Tsede or the divine army, the army of Dami, the army of Shudkyi, the army of Mangde, the army of Guge, and others, which at that time altogether numbered sixteen thousand [troops]. By a manifest demonstration of his spiritual realization, all these armies were simultaneously rendered unconscious. Throwing his hat in the sky, it was transformed into an eagle that struck the enemy, and his boots emanated as a donkey that destroyed the mischievous spirits. He was able to use the celestial and terrestrial spirits as his servants. His special attainment was that at two hundred and seventy years of age his body manifested as a dragon and dissipated like clouds in the south or like a rainbow disappears, and he attained enlightenment.

The centuries-old Eternal Bon text known as *Yungdrung Bon Gyi Gyübum* contains accounts of various Tibetan military campaigns against nations to the north, east, and south, which are reputed to have taken place in the protohistoric period. Among these accounts there is an archaic priest from Zhang Zhung and one from Sumpa who aid in the conquest of territory and the protection of Central Tibetan Purgyal monarchs.[20]

Penegu of Sumpa is supposed to have invoked the gods during a campaign against a Turco-Mongolian land known as Hor. This legendary event appears to be attributed to the reign of Trinamtsen, the twenty-fifth king of the Purgyal dynasty. Datable to roughly 400 CE, this tale is important because it seems to corroborate the impact that north Inner Asian regions had in protohistoric Tibet. Whether based on historical fact or not, it preserves a collective recollection of Tibet's long-standing connections to northern lands. In order to guarantee Purgyal's victory over the Hor, Penegu had to rally the warrior gods known as *dralha* and neutralize the murderous spirits of the enemy, the *sri*. In recognition of his services, Penegu was awarded a number of highly valuable objects, two of which can no longer be accurately identified. Known as the *sesang/sezen* and *menshö*, in the Eternal Bon religion they are kinds of edible ritual sculptures. However, in the protohistoric setting of the *Yungdrung Bon Gyi Gyübum*, these two articles seem to refer to more permanent things. An arrow and spindle made of precious substances were also given to the Sumpa adept Penegu. The arrow and spindle, symbols of manhood and womanhood respectively, have been used in the worship of clan and protective spirits and as tabernacles of the deities for untold centuries. Their possession must have accorded Penegu much glory:

> The *bonpo* of Sumpa, Penegu, invoked the warrior spirits and suppressed the homicidal spirits of the enemy; hence the Hor were attacked and the Hor kingdom brought thus under the jurisdiction [of the king of Tibet]. For that great accomplishment, [Penegu] was awarded the golden *sezen* and *menshö* of turquoise as the insignia. The gold arrow and turquoise spindle were presented as the trophies. Therefore, the erection of *sesang* and *menshö* as supports of the gods [by] the *bonpo* and the erection of the arrow and spindle also began from that time.

The *Yungdrung Bon Gyi Gyübum* account of a priest from Zhang Zhung takes place during the reign of Lhatho Thori Nyenzhel, the twenty-eighth king of the Purgyal dynasty. Through sorcery, a yak of the *srin*, a class of vexatious terrestrial spirits, stole the soul turquoise of the monarch. The soul turquoise, or *layu*, was thought of as a vital talisman that safeguarded human life. The usage of the *layu* continues to the present day although in a much reduced form. In addition to turquoise, Tibetans have availed themselves of boulders, trees, lakes, and other natural objects to enshrine the soul or animating force. As the loss of his soul turquoise imperiled the life of King Lhatho Thori Nyenzhel, a Zhang Zhung *bonpo* named Shele Mikmar was called to retrieve it. Overjoyed with Shele Mikmar's success, Lhatho Thori Nyenzhel offered him a number of overcoats and headgear made from the hides of valuable animal species. These animals were seen as divine beings in their own right, and those privileged to wear their skins did so as a mark of honor and prestige:

> Also, the soul turquoise of Lhatho Thori Nyenzhel was stolen by the bay-colored yak of the terrestrial spirits. The Zhang Zhung *bonpo* Shele Mikmar

generated [powerful visualizations] at the yak of the terrestrial spirits and removing the soul turquoise from the mouth of the yak of the terrestrial spirits, offered it to the lord. As a consequence [the Lord] was delighted. He presented [Shele Mikmar] a marmot robe, a lynx robe, and a wolf robe, these three, and a tiger greatcoat, a leopard greatcoat, and a clouded leopard greatcoat. As the badge of valor, he conferred a tiger helmet on him. The present-day wearing of the tiger greatcoat, tiger headgear, and the lynx and snow leopard robes by the *bonpo* began from that time.

The mythic origin of the soul repositories, namely turquoise and gold nuggets, is related in a text of the *Muchoi Tromdur* collection of Eternal Bon funerary literature.[21] This soul stone, or *lado*, tale appears to be of considerable antiquity, part of a ritual tradition that long predates its written form. In this origin myth, or *mang*, the progenetrix of humanity is a *sri*, a type of being that is usually demonized in Tibetan religious literature. The fundamental role she plays in the narrative seems to hark back to a formative period in the development of Tibetan religious traditions. This is supported by a comparative linguistic study conducted by Paul K. Benedict, which shows that the term *sri* and its various Tibeto-Burman cognates were derived from the same prehistoric root.[22] According to the *Muchoi Tromdur* myth, a turquoise stone (female) and a gold nugget (male) served as the soul receptacle of a primal sister and brother. The text states that these two were the children of the gods, touching upon the seminal theme of humans and divinities sharing a common genealogy. In the Lamaist religions this interrelationship is greatly diminished, as the gods and humans belong to discrete orders of sentient beings, neither of which has an intrinsic existence. For the ancient Tibetans, however, they and their deities existed in a more permanent sense within the great wheel or womb of existence. Descending from the gods, Tibetans once believed that at death they would be reunited with them in the afterlife. According to the *Muchoi Tromdur*, the soul turquoise and golden nugget were the foundation of good fortune for the living. During the intermediate state after death, they remained the vessels of the soul and mind. It was the funerary priests through the correct performance of the death rites who jettisoned the consciousness principles to the other world. The soul stone origins myth begins with the descent of the divine *sri* lady to earth:

> In the beginning, from the lofty and pristine country of the gods, [the *sri* lady] came down to earth to supplement the source of humans. She appeared upon the swastika happy rock formation. When she looked upward she saw the high pristine country of the gods. When she looked downward she surveyed the verdure of naturally occurring grain. She said, "Here is a boulder." And so the rock formation also replied in human language, "Yes, there is." On the rock formation are also the souls of sentient be-

ings. The lady *sri* cut the peak of the swastika rock formation with a very sharp-edged instrument, and at this gold nugget stone and turquoise stone she also tied the souls of the brother and sister, progeny of the gods. . . . During their lifetimes they were the receptacle of the basis for good fortune and good fortune capability. At their death they were the receptacles of the soul and mind.

Another royal priest of Zhang Zhung origins selected for special honors by a Purgyal king was Khyungpo Rasang. The Eternal Bon historical text *Drakpa Lingdrak* affirms that Khyungpo Rasang liberated Takri Nyenzik, the thirty-first king of the Purgyal dynasty, from the prison of a rival. This event, if indeed it can be historicized, must have occurred in the late 500s CE. In any event, an Old Tibetan language version of the same account exists.[23] For his pains many distinctions were conferred on the royal priest. These took the form of objects made from precious materials:

> To repay the kindness [of Khyungpo Rasang] and as a badge of his greatness, the superior distinction conferred on the royal priest was for the royal priest to remain at the head of the right row [of the royal assembly]. A throne of ivory and a brocade carpet of precious threads were given him. As the insignia, a hair tie of gold and a vase of sapphire were also given him.[24]

As we have seen, Eternal Bon texts hold that the acquisition of magical power, ritual prowess, and symbols of high social standing were regarded as very desirable in the archaic era. The accounts of the Zhang Zhung *bonpo* and *shen*, however, do not permit an understanding of their society in any great depth. In the more voluminous literature germane to the *bonpo* of Central Tibet, these same basic values are also at the forefront of ancient society. Much of this cultural material regarding Central Tibet relies on stereotypic historical models that seem to have wider geographic relevance. While the archaeological record accents cultural differences between Upper Tibet and Central Tibet, this is not very much in evidence in textual materials, as generalized and paradigmatic as they are. The *bonpo* of the various parts of the Tibetan Plateau, despite speaking different languages and belonging to different political orders, are supposed to have shared much of their religious patrimony in common. This blending of religious traditions belonging to various prehistoric cultures of the Plateau in historical documents is partly the result of viewing the distant past through the looking glass of later periods. More fundamentally, these common regional links are also partly attributable to the civilization that underpinned the early cultures of the Tibetan Plateau. With an eye toward Zhang Zhung, let us examine the priestly traditions of Central Tibet in more detail.

The important Eternal Bon historical text *Drakpa Lingdrak* gives an account of four central Tibetan royal priests, or *kushen*, credited with saving the life of King Mutri Tsenpo.[25] In the *Drakpa Lingdrak*, these same royal priests accompanied Mutri Tsenpo's father, King Nyatri Tsenpo, on his descent from the heavens to become the first sovereign. As described in chapter 8, Mutri Tsenpo is believed to have been instrumental in importing religious traditions from Zhang Zhung to Central Tibet. According to the *Drakpa Lingdrak*, King Mutri Tsenpo was made ill by the demigods for hoarding the religious teachings. The four royal priests, Yang Ngel (also called Ya Ngel), Shemi, Chomi, and Tharbon Drubkyol, carried out sundry curative rites on Mutri Tsenpo. For their successful intervention, these four men received superior distinctions or awards known as *tsik* from the king. It is understood that the *tsik* became customary privileges earned by the royal priests of Central Tibet for almost all of the protohistoric period. These awards, at least as they were conceived in later times, were of three kinds: body, mind, and speech.

The *tsik* for the body included sumptuous clothes, luxurious foods, and ceremonial privileges. The magnificent clothing mentioned in the *Drakpa Lingdrak* is of a style that the masters of Zhang Zhung are also thought to have worn. The *tsik* for speech was that the royal priests would open the royal convocations with the first three words spoken. The uttering of three momentous words is related to Old Tibetan ritual performances, where it occurs in association with the priests Durshen Mada and Shenrab Nyiwo, suggesting that this tradition was also known in the Upper Tibetan cultural context.[26] The *tsik* for the mind was designed to provide for the contentment of the royal priests. It included blood money for murder equal in amount to that of the king, a vast sum. The killer of a priest was also remanded in custody of the victim's relatives to face possible execution. Other punishments are stipulated for theft and the assault of lesser priests. The traditional penal code presented in the *Drakpa Lingdrak* is based on the principle of retribution, of the "eye for an eye" kind. It appears that every crime in ancient Tibet came with a set price tag, justice being served by payment of exactly what was owed to those wronged:

> Then the two royal priests, Yang Ngel and Shemi, carried out lustration, fumigation, and the purification rites and urgently made apologies, offerings for fulfillment, and penance [to the deities]. Both Chomi and Tharbon Drubkyol made the restorative rites and body ransom offering for freeing [the king]. Therefore, the epidemic was halted and [the king's] broken oath reinstated. The dominion of the lord was equivalent to the heavens.
> Then [Mutri Tsenpo] conferred these awards upon the *bon* [and] *shen*: the superior distinction offered for the body was long unbound hair, which

was untrimmed and never cut; a white silk regal turban on which the flex-
ible feathers of the king of the birds, the vulture, were erected; and golden
bird horns with turquoise. The clothes were robes of white lynx and white
wolf, to which a collar and trim of tiger were attached, leopard and clouded
leopard, these three. They dismounted and mounted horses from a carpet.
Along the path of their travel were peacock parasols. In the area within
the range of their vision were golden victory banners. In the area within
the range of their smell was the scent of incense smoke and frankincense.
For their food they were offered dairy products, sweets, and beer in which
the medicine of sugar was added. They were given the placement at the
head of the right row [of the royal assembly]. On their thrones of ivory,
gold, and silver, sumptuous seats of brocade with precious threads were
laid down. In their hands they held scepters of gold and white cane staffs
of great authority.

The superior distinction offered for the speech was that until three
words were uttered by the priests, the king would not enter into speech
and the ministers would not enter into consultations. Until the priests had
sung three words of a song, the king and ministers would not dance and
sing, and the subjects would not sing and dance and their performances of
many melodies was not permitted.

The superior distinction for the contented, happy mind was that the
[royal priest's] blood money was equivalent to the king's "ten thousand
unlimited." The actual murderers [of priests] were given over to [their
surviving relatives for punishment]. If minor priests were clubbed, punish-
ment was carried out in the kingdom. If their possessions and wealth were
taken, they had to be compensated ninety-fold. [The priests] were offered
such [distinctions].

The provisions of justice set out in the *Drakpa Lingdrak* were underpinned by a stringent sense of honor, which appears to have formed the
bedrock of social contracts in ancient Tibet. A life taken was worth the life
of its taker. In ancient Tibet, even access to the afterlife depended on paying back before death exactly what was owed to an aggrieved party. This
cultural principle is well expressed in the archaic funerary elements of the
Muchoi Tromdur. In pastoral Upper Tibet and eastern Tibet until the modern
period, a similar system of retributive justice prevailed. Although Buddhism
and Eternal Bon have as their ethical centerpiece the concept of nonviolence,
Lamaist ethics in the Tibetan hinterland could not do away with the harsher
legal ethos of earlier times.

An imperial period hunting manuscript from Dunhuang studied by
the Tibetologist H. E. Richardson prescribes penalties for causing death
or injury to someone with an arrow in a hunting accident and for failing to
rescue someone who had fallen under a wild yak.[27] The least severe fines
were levied upon those of high status who inadvertently caused the death of

a low-status individual. However, even individuals in the highest ministerial positions could be put to death for failing to pay blood money for a death in which they bore responsibility. Likewise, high officials could be executed for not rescuing someone who had fallen under a yak, while they would be exempt for accidentally killing someone with an arrow. The extreme penalties for cowardice and the shirking of one's duty spotlight the warlike society of the Tibetan empire. Given its fortress mentality and bellicose priests, an unyielding rectitude borne of a martial tradition appears to have characterized Zhang Zhung society as well. On a wider level, honor and its place in the formulation of draconian legal measures characterized many ancient Eurasian societies.

Beyond the obvious abhorrence of cowardice and the strict hierarchal nature of society, the ancient legal picture in Tibet was one in which the discharge of debts, as part of a system of proportional justice, was essential. This fundamental reciprocity is demonstrated in the four basic laws that Songtsen Gampo, Tibet's thirty-third king, is reputed to have promulgated:

> If someone kills, they must pay blood money. If someone steals, they must repay it eight times over plus the actual stolen goods, a nine-fold [penalty]. If someone commits sexual misconduct, they must make a payment. If someone tells a lie, they must swear an oath that they will not do it again.[28]

The termination of the golden age and the headlong decline of humanity are predicted in another Dunhuang manuscript that probably dates to the imperial period. A spirited passage in this text (designated ITJ 734) forthrightly condemns the degradation of social values, which it sees as inevitable with the passing of time.[29] Lack of trust and shame leads people to renounce their oaths, an anathema in honor-bound ancient Tibet. The text affirms that people will become so brazen and avaricious that they will not even appreciate the value of their own lives. It is stated that this moral decadence will only worsen in the future. The circumstances behind the writing of this passage are unclear. It may possibly have been authored for a specific political purpose calling upon cosmological and moral themes in order to shame those to whom it was directed. As much as a prophetic enunciation, this manifesto of imperial times elevates honor above all other values:

> It will come to pass that nobody will do right, as in the salutary age of the nonseparation of men and gods. It has become the evil age of life, so gradually it will come to pass that all bipedal humans are shameless and untrustworthy. It will come to pass that they do not know shame. It will come to pass that they do not keep their oaths. It will come to pass that for wealth they do not fear their own killer of the life force. It will come to pass that in the search for wealth they will wreak all kinds of evil on

other men. Without a sense of shame and fidelity for the future, they will renounce their oaths, and by this sin, the sons will become worse than the fathers and the grandsons will become worse than the sons. Gradually, the generations of humans will become worse.

THE ANCIENT MATERIAL CULTURE OF ZHANG ZHUNG AND CENTRAL TIBET

As we have seen, Tibetan literature tells us that the ancient priests of Zhang Zhung, Sumpa, and Central Tibet possessed a special repertoire of tools, costumes, and insignia. These same kinds of material objects are supposed to have been used by the gods themselves. At present there is minimal scientific confirmation of this material culture. If and when comprehensive archaeological excavations are permitted in Tibet, more of the things detailed in the texts are likely to be discovered.

As explicated in chapter 8, one of the oldest descriptions of ancient Tibetan dress concerns none other than Shenrab Nyiwo (called Shenrab Miwo in later texts). This great master of the prehistoric epoch is reputed to have had two main ritual instruments: a flat-bell, or *shang*, and a bird's wing.[30] The *shang*, a small cymbal-shaped bell made of bronze, was the quintessential ritual tool of the *bonpo*. First rung by ancient priests, it is still played by Eternal Bon practitioners and spirit-mediums today. Its peal is said to repulse demons and attract helpful deities. The bird wing held by Shenrab Nyiwo is also a prototypic ritual instrument referred to in Dunhuang and Eternal Bon documents.[31] Birds' wings were employed in archaic funerary rites to attract the divine guardians of the dead to funerals and to magically herald the way to the afterlife. According to the funerary ritual texts, bird wings of various species were mounted on pieces of cane and embellished with sundry objects such as metal mirrors, cloth streamers, jewels, and needles. The *Muchoi Tromdur* states that bird-wing instruments were made from the lammergeyer, crane, pheasant, eagle, grouse, chough, cuckoo, lark, raven, and owl.

An eleventh-century CE Eternal Bon biography of Shenrab Nyiwo records that as an infant he wore a turban and a silk robe.[32] The hair on top of his head was kept in a bun and ornamented with various precious objects in a style known as *tsukphü*, while the rest of his hair was braided into many fine plaits. The use of turbans in early Tibet, as in many other ancient Eurasian societies, appears to have been particularly widespread. The wearing of this headgear is documented in Old Tibetan sources such as manuscripts Pt 1285 and ITJ 731, where a hundred *shen* priests of the sunny side of a mountain are attired in white turbans.[33]

One of the most remarkable lists of ancient ritual apparel is grafted onto a funerary text of the *Muchoi Tromdur* collection.[34] Although the material objects enumerated in this work are associated with archaic funerary traditions, they are applicable to a much wider range of ritual functions. As in other texts we have perused, the *Muchoi Tromdur* states that the ancient funerary priests or *durshen* wore robes fabricated from the hides of wild carnivores. In Upper Tibet, brown bears, wolves, lynxes, snow leopards, vultures, and eagles potentially provided the raw materials for this kind of ritual attire, while trade with adjoining regions may have made available other types of animal hides.

The apparel recorded in the *Muchoi Tromdur* is said to have originated with the primordial gods and priests. From what has been written, this clothing had both symbolic and practical significance for the ancient *bonpo*. As symbols of power, the costumes distinguished the priests from the general public, according them much esteem. It is also thought that priestly garb functioning as spiritual armor helped wearers prevail against demons. The sacerdotal vestments by their very beauty were designed to please the deities, giving them good cause to visit the ritual venues and assist officiants.

Like the kings of Zhang Zhung, the ancient *bonpo* priests are thought to have placed "bird horns" on their heads. Rather than horns per se, these may have been the feathery crests that dignify certain species of birds. Eternal Bon asseverates that the bird-horn crown signified the absolute dominion of the priests and kings over all living beings. As studied by Stephen W. Bushell, one of the oldest historical references to sorcerers and warriors wearing bird-shaped hats and tiger-skin skirts is found in the *New Tang Annals* in a description of the Sino-Tibetan peace treaty of 822 CE.[35] While this account does not speak for the prehistoric antiquity of these customs of dress, it does furnish an independent historical account written by a foreign people. According to the *Muchoi Tromdur*, the crowns of the *bonpo* were ornamented with tiger-skin streamers. For the ancient Tibetans, the tiger was a vivid sign of warriorship and the manifest power of the male gods. As a ritual text dedicated to the mother goddess of Lake Nam Tsho makes known, tiger-skin greatcoats and bird horns were synonymous with ancient *bonpo* garb.[36]

Two other types of crowns are documented in the *Muchoi Tromdur*: the *traphü* and *trokzhu*, both of which were ornamented with gold. The identity of these majestic symbols is uncertain. It appears that these crowns had points or lobes, not unlike those worn by kings in ancient southwestern Asia and medieval Europe. A red ochre painting of what may be a three-pointed crown is found on a cave wall in Shentsa, Upper Tibet.[37] The crowns of early Tibetan priests appear to have signaled lofty social status by highlighting their affinity to deities and royalty alike. It is thought that like bird horns, the *traphü* and *trokzhu* linked their wearers to the divine realm, whence they drew their ritual power and social authority. Earrings of gold and turquoise with flower designs and hanging silver bell are also purported to have been worn by archaic priests. If Tibetan earrings of later times are anything to go by, those of ancient times were large and showy affairs.

According to the *Muchoi Tromdur*, the hats of ancient priests were made from the skins of the lion, dragon, horned eagle, tiger, leopard, black bear, brown bear, vulture, wild yak, elephant, lynx, and snow leopard. Small metal mirrors were affixed to these hats. To this day, copper alloy mirrors decorate the headdresses of Tibetan bards and spirit-mediums. These mirrors are believed to attract deities and repel demons. Mirrors also symbolize the mystic vision of the wearer, who could equally look into the past, present, and future. The creatures chosen for producing hats are known for their strength, agility, power of flight, and other awe-inspiring attributes. We might expect that each type of hat conferred the physical qualities of that animal upon the wearer, with different priests using different hats according to personal preference and the nature of their ritual work.

The *Muchoi Tromdur* lists a number of different robes worn by ancient priests. Like other aspects of ritual costumery, these functioned to call and direct the deities during ritual performances. The mention of a regal leather greatcoat sporting a miraculous alphabet reminds us that the *Muchoi Tromdur* is the product of a literate Tibet. Whatever vestiges of prehistoric garb this literature may document, the intervening centuries have acted to depict these in the zeitgeist of the Lamaist era. Among the types of outer dress noted is the greatcoat (*lak*) of the dragon of total victory. As in China, the mythical dragon occupied a weighty role in Tibetan cultural traditions. Dragons are found in the retinue of many different deities, a symbol of the fecundity of the earth and the ferocity of the chthonic spirit realm. To this day, the *drokpas* of Upper Tibet believe that dragons live in the deep waters of the great lakes. Other priestly garb mentioned in the *Muchoi Tromdur* includes the power greatcoat of the fierce tiger and lion, the hawk greatcoat of the cutting conquerors, and the red and black textile robe (*jolber*) of power. Robes known as *thulpa* made from the skins of the tiger, leopard, lynx, and wolf are described as emanating light rays, a manifestation of their innate magnificence.

According to the *Old Tibetan Annals*, tiger skins were given as high commendations to soldiers in the imperial Tibetan armies. In ancient Tibet, the tiger, or *tak*, was an epithet for a brave warrior or male hero and formed part of proper names. Tibetan ritual texts say that the uniforms and armaments of warriors were known as the "dress of the tiger." The famous historical work *Khepai Gatön* informs us that the tiger-skin robe, along with the treasury, ensign, royal castle, temple, and royal insignia, were the six sovereign emblems of the first Tibetan emperor Songtsen Gampo.[38] As we have learned, tiger-skin clothing is traced to the prehistoric epoch in Tibetan literature. Take for instance the prototypic funerary priest Durshen Mada who is recorded as wearing a tiger-skin greatcoat. A poetic description of tiger-skin apparel set in prehistoric times is interspersed in an early historic ransom ritual text from the Gathang Bumpa collection.[39] It concerns a great god of western Tibet known as Namse Chirum who is supposed to have been active in the same period as Shenrab Nyiwo. This divine warrior is attributed with providing protection for Mra Thenwa, a man wanted by a huge army of gods for the murder of their leader's son. In the words of the Gathang Bumpa text,

> Namse Chirum's [head was covered] all around in tiger skins, so many tiger skins. He was with a tiger-skin helmet. [His body was clad] all around in iron, so much iron. He was with a *phunu* (a type of armor) of iron. He wore a greatcoat of iron. In his right hand he held a chain lasso nine hundred and ninety spans long.

The *Muchoi Tromdur* alleges that the ancient priests wore shawls and clothing made from human skins. The use of flayed human skins is also part of the wrathful deity traditions of Vajrayana Buddhism, where it is a highly charged symbol of the absolute emptiness of all phenomena. Whether such skins were really donned by the fearsome fighters of archaic Tibet remains to be established.

The rock art record of Upper Tibet and Tibetan literature reveals that the most popular arms of ancient times were the spear, bow and arrow, and sword. As we saw in chapter 7, these instruments of war and hunting feature prominently in the prehistoric and early historic pictographs and petroglyphs of the Tibetan upland. In old Tibetan parlance, the bow and arrow and sword are collectively referred to as the *khorsum*. Most references to them in Tibetan literature concern use by deities. For example, it is written that those divine denizens of the central Changthang, the Targo mountain gods, brandished the *khorsum*.[40] The *khorsum* was not just the prerogative of males, for the great female warrior of Tibet's epic, Atak Lumo, is said to have brandished a bow and arrow and sword.[41] This huntress and combatant is reckoned to have roved around the eastern Changthang in ancient times.

Reliance on the bow and arrow is regularly mentioned in Old Tibetan ritual narratives set in the prehistoric epoch. In a prototypic hunting vignette of the Dunhuang manuscript ITJ 731, a man called Mabu Damshe wields his bow and arrow to slay an evil wild yak.[42] In other funerary manuscripts of Dunhuang, the broken bow is a metaphor used to express the condition of death.[43] In the Gathang Bumpa ransom ritual text, the bow is one of the offerings given to buy off demons.[44] The bow and arrow is also employed in the same text to slay the effigies of demons. These types of ritual functions involving weapons have been preserved in the exorcistic rites of the Lamaist religions as well. In another Old Tibetan–language text of the Gathang Bumpa collection, *Origin Tales of the Deer Horns Showing the Way*, the primal sky and primal ocean, before being reconciled with one another, almost went to war with the bow.[45]

The arrow is an even more popular instrument in Tibetan rituals than the bow. The ritual arrow, or *dadar*, is draped with silken cloth and ornamented with various objects. In the ransom ritual text of Gathang Bumpa, an arrow with a dark blue strip of cloth and a black nock is one of the objects used to liberate the divine progenitor of the Purgyal dynasty, Yabla Daldruk, from a host of malicious demons.[46] The cane shaft of this arrow is specified as having three joints and being decorated with sheep skin. Similar arrows are employed to appease the demons of death in other texts of the Gathang Bumpa collection.

The arrow's most important ritual function is as a tabernacle for the male ancestral and territorial gods. During ritual performances, the invoked deities are encouraged to take up residence in the arrow so that they can be feted. Many Tibetan families still keep a draped arrow enshrined on their altars for this purpose. An Eternal Bon text for the territorial deities, or *yulha*, describes the draped arrow in this way:

> Ho! We erect the support of the mind [arrow] for you mighty *yulha*. The bamboo with three joints is sought in the forest groves of the south. [The arrow] is adorned with the feathers of the lammergeyer. It is decorated with beautifully colored vermilion. Its tip is of a very sharp and hard celestial iron. On the shaft five types of colored cloths are tied. It is ornamented with decorative hangings of tiger skin and leopard skin and a mirror.[47]

In a more than thousand-year-old allusion to the draped arrow and other ritual articles in Dunhuang manuscript Pt 126, a messenger of the Cha tribe requests a member of the Mu tribe to allow him to pay respects to the Mu tribal deity Kula Nyithur.[48] The Mu tribe and Kula Nyithur (also called Kula Muthur) god are closely connected to Zhang Zhung. The man of the Mu asks the Cha messenger what things he has brought for their god, touching upon the draped arrow, foodstuffs, and animals still used by Tibetans to propitiate deities:

> Do you have or not bamboo offerings from the lower regions, the divine arrow decorated by a perfect lammergeyer feather? Do you have or not the constituent of the divine arrow, a small piece of patterned cloth to suspend from it? Do you have or not unworked gold? Do you have or not a greatcoat with decorations of turquoise? Do you have or not nine measures of prized blue grain? Do you have or not liquid offerings of blue grain beer? Do you have or not a globular mass of cheesecake as large as a pheasant? Do you have or not meat roasted in butter as large as a partridge? Do you have or not cream as thick as a measuring tray? Do you have or not a divine sheep with a red face? Do you have or not a divine horse with white ears?

Do you have or not a divine female yak of variegated color? Do you have or not a divine male yak with the long belly fringe?

Another popular armament of great antiquity is the spear. It is the weapon of choice for many indigenous protective gods. The most common spear for ritual purposes has a banner or ensign attached to it and is called *dungdar*. According to Tibetan lore, in ancient times each regiment possessed its own banner. As ritual tools, *dungdar* were in regular use in Tibet until the Communist period. Like the draped arrow, the spear and standard functioned as a tabernacle for deities during religious rituals. During travel the *dungdar* was affixed to one of the stirrups of a horse and held upright. The spear offered to the Zhang Zhung god Gekhö had a long shaft, and various types of clothes and grains were tied to it. In one Eternal Bon invocatory text, the spear of the well-known red warrior deity Draktsen Marpo, a resident of Upper Tibet, is praised in spirited language:

Accompany us [spear] receptacle for a long time without parting. The spear point with the face of the wrathful female earth spirit is joined to the magnificent awe-inspiring very pointed long spear [shaft]. It is decorated with jewels, red cloth, and a piece of [yak] tail. A soul-stone and life-force circle are placed on it. We erect this support for the circle of oath holders.[49]

We have already encountered the lasso in rock art and as an attribute of religious masters and deities. In Tibetan texts, lassos made of fire, wind, lightning, iron, copper, rawhide, snakes, and human intestines are noted. In ancient times the ritual usage of lassos and snares appears to have been a trait common to both India and Tibet. In the ritual traditions of both countries it is utilized to seize and strangle enemies of religion and demons of all stripes. According to the great contemporary Tibetan bard Samdrup, the epic villain Dud Lutsen ruled with terror over his ancient eastern Changthang kingdom, deriving his power from a magic lasso that had been given to him by his mother.[50] This lasso functioned as a wish-fulfilling instrument by which Dud Lutsen could obtain anything he wanted. It also functioned as a horse and could transport him at will to any of the three realms of the universe.

Other armaments mentioned in Tibetan texts as attributes of the gods and ancient sages include clubs, staffs, batons, slings, battleaxes, and battle hammers. An unusual weapon said to have been wielded by Zhang Zhung personalities is the *barshe*, which resembles the claws of an eagle. Among the most intriguing of ancient weapons are those that magically operate themselves. The self-thrusting spear called the "equipment of the gods" can be traced to the Dunhuang manuscript Pt 250. In his masterful study, Erik Haarh also refers to the self-cutting sword, self-dressing armor, and self-deflecting shield of Pt 250.[51] These implements of great magical power were supposedly granted by Central Tibet's eighth king, Drigum Tsenpo, to his future assassin, Longam Tadzi. The historical text *Khepa Deu* enumerates a self-thrusting spear and similar magical articles given to Nyatri Tsenpo before he descended to earth to become the first king of Tibet.[52]

The fourteenth-century biography of Tönpa Shenrab entitled *Zijid* relates how, having warded off a demonic attack, he obtained the weapons and armor needed to invoke the *dralha* warrior spirits.[53] It is testified that to benefit his disciples Shenrab taught them how to propitiate the *dralha* with incense and offering articles. These spirit warriors are forthrightly described in *Zijid*. One squad of *dralha* that Tönpa Shenrab is said to have invoked is the nine Drama brothers, invincible patrons of nine important types of weapons and armor. In the text Tönpa Shenrab specifies the activities of these supernatural warriors and exactly what he and his followers expect from them. This *Zijid* ritual invocation set in mythic times epitomizes the cult of warrior gods and arms that persisted in Tibet until modern times:

> The wisdom army of *dralha*, the nine *dralha* of radiant men and beautiful horses: The *dralha* of the helmet is Hero Holder of the Iron Horns of the Bird. The *dralha* of the blue coat of mail is Hero Holder of the Bronze Armor Skirt. The *dralha* of the razor-sharp sword is Hero Holder of Razor Sharp Weapons. The *dralha* of the self-drawing bow is Hero Holder of Sparking White Molten Steel. The *dralha* of the self-shooting arrow is Hero Holder of the Pointed Arrow and Bow. The *dralha* of the self-thrusting spear is Hero Holder of the Fiery Banner. The *dralha* of the self-surrounding shield is Hero Holder of the Shield Fringe of Wind. The *dralha* of the self-twirling lasso is Hero Possessor of Lightning Speed. The *dralha* of the self-hooking battle-ax is Hero Holder of the Magical Hook. These are the nine Drama brothers of the *dralha*.
>
> From the birth of primordial existence until the present day, the wind could not strip away [the weapons] of the Drama. They are the *dralha* of the undamaged razor-sharp [weapons]. They reside, dwelling in the armory. They stay, reposing on the peak of the celestial mountain. They protect, fond of *bon*, they are protecting. They help, venerating the *shen* priests, they are aiding. They escort, accomplishing for the oath holders. They assist, accomplishing for the vow holders. They despise, hating the enemies who hate us. They fulminate, raging against the noxious obstructive forces. . . .
>
> Today upon this divine foundation, I call the gods, the nine Drama bothers. Lo! I offer to and praise the very great *dralha*. From ancient times you have been offered to and praised. Presently, I am offering to and attending the gods of the lineage of existence, do not stray from me. I am raising you up in homage, do not begrudge me. I am calling forth, do not pretend that you cannot hear me. I am signaling and striding toward you, do not pretend that you cannot see me.

I make offerings to you. I offer with the first part of the three white foods and other dairy products. I offer with the three red foods and other fresh organs. I offer with the three sweets and other sweets. I offer beer made from the juice of the nine grains. I offer a very sharp three-pointed ritual cake. I offer with yaks, sheep, and goats. I offer with deer, wild asses, antelopes, and gazelles for riding. I offer with tigers, leopards, black bears, and brown bears as escorts. I offer with lynx skins, wolf skins, and silk vestments. I offer with artemisia, juniper, rhododendron, and flowers [incense]. I offer with whatever is your preference, the ingredients of the oath and ritual supports.

Mighty *dralha*, do not be ambivalent [toward me]. Mighty *dralha*, do not be malevolent [toward me]. Mighty *dralha*, do not defile me. Mighty *dralha*, do not pollute me. If you are contrary, I will straighten you with a support of white cane. If you are malevolent, I will win you over with offering cakes and whatever else you prefer. If defiled, I will purify you with lustration and incense. If polluted, I will wash you in pure ablutions. If thirsty, I will offer you consecrated beer. If hungry, I will offer you the warm hearts of the enemy to eat.

I erect the support of nine types of armor and armaments. Mighty *dralha* stay in this support. Stay around this helmet. Stay around this coat of mail. Stay around this razor-sharp sword. Stay around this self-drawing bow. Stay around this self-shooting arrow. Stay around this self-thrusting spear. Stay around this self-surrounding shield. Stay around this self-retrieving lasso. Stay around this self-hooking battle-ax.

I, the *bonpo* of the lineage of existence, call upon the deities that have been offered to by my lineage. Mighty *dralha*, don't do small favors. When I am in residence, shore up my fortune. When traveling, may I be accompanied by a gathering of heroes. During the daytime, keep watch. During the nighttime, let a lamp illuminate. If I am traveling abroad, carry out my wishes. If I am crossing bad roads, defend me from terror. If I send you to the enemy, destroy them. If there is a dispute, let me triumph. When authority is exerted in the kingdom, guard the royal law. When the religious doctrine is spread, give assistance.

The manufacture of metallic ritual objects, armor, and weapons in ancient Tibet is also detailed in *Zijid*, the most extensive of Tönpa Shenrab's biographies.[54] This description of religious and military equipment is attributed to the founder of Eternal Bon himself. The inclusion of steel as an important material for the fabrication of armor and weaponry indicates that the *Zijid* deals with highly sophisticated manufacturing traditions. Cross-cultural comparisons with India and Persia suggest that the production of steel in Zhang Zhung may have originated as early as the second half of the first millennium BCE. The metal crafts and armaments noted in the text, however, are likely to represent a fourteenth-century CE reworking of imperial period technological and military traditions. Nevertheless, the presence of Zhang Zhung words in this *Zijid* account of material goods does suggest that it preserves a glimmer of prehistoric lore.

According to *Zijid*, there are three types of beating and working metal that produce beautiful, magnificent, and desirable articles. The types of metals mentioned include gold, silver, copper, iron, brass, bronze, bell metal, and white metal. The origins of these metallurgical traditions are still obscure, but the limited art historical and archaeological data available suggest that most if not all of these metals and alloys were known by the early historic period. The *Zijid* states that objects made by working metals included various religious symbols and implements, flat-bells, transverse flutes, percussion instruments, ritual mirrors, architectural components, and food containers.

Steel is said to have a silvery cast and to be of two main types: that produced to manufacture armor and that for weapons. The text observes that through a tempering process five classes of steel were made. In descending order of quality, they are used to fabricate armor, helmets, weapons, implements, and the foundations of pillars. According to *Zijid*, there were two main classes of swords: those of virtuous existence and those of unvirtuous existence. The virtuous-class swords are divided into three subtypes with Zhang Zhung–language names: *yatsa* (jewel-shaped point), *kyagam* (leaf point), and *shanglang* (point angled like a stylus).[55] The unvirtuous-class swords are also divided into three subtypes that have Tibetan names: *raltri* (spatulate), *chutri* (pointed on one edge only?), and *putri* (worked to resemble a bird feather). The *raltri* and *putri* swords are also noted in Old Tibetan texts of the Gathang Bumpa collection.

Zijid also describes eight types of helmets fashioned from different metals and with varying designs. The steel egg-shaped helmet worn by kings known as *zhunkar keru* recalls the style of helmet used by Scythian and Kushan warriors.[56] *Zijid* also lists eight types of laminar armor thought to have been worn in the time of Tönpa Shenrab. The armor worn by kings was associated with various elemental spirits and lavishly decorated. The armor of queens is thought to have been created after divine girls were injured while watching a battle between their respective armies. The armor of warriors is associated with the primal battle between the gods of virtuous and unvirtuous existence. *Zijid* also describes armored boots that are supposed to have had wings, not unlike those of the Greek god Hermes.

To comprehensively assess textual references to material culture in ancient Upper Tibet requires more archaeological exploration. Archaeology aside, the collective memory of the herders and farmers of the upland is another promising source for understanding the character of Zhang Zhung. In the final chapter, we turn full circle to the present day and its guardians of the ancient ways.

My Ancestors, My Gods: Zhang Zhung Reigns in Contemporary Upper Tibet

THE KEY TO THE PAST AND PRESENT

*U*pper Tibet's shepherds and farmers continue to embrace ancient traditions. These masters of the fields and pastures are torchbearers of a way of life first established in their world of towering mountains and high-altitude valleys long ago. The past is their bond with the present, the two tied together through the ever-changing march of the generations.

The most graphic signs of collective remembrance in Upper Tibet are seen in the traditional dress and ornamentation of the people. A case in point is the wearing of *zi* and *thokchak*, patterned stone beads and copper alloy amulets respectively, a significant portion of which date to prehistoric and early historic times. Some of these precious objects have been diligently handed down over many generations from father to son and mother to daughter. The *drokpas* in particular have also retained personal names that existed before Buddhism came to dominate the culture and religion of Tibet. Timeworn appellations include Lhatse (Divine Mountain Peak), Jo-gö (Brave Lord), Lhalu (God and Water Spirit), Tshomo (Lake Woman), and Druk Tsho (Dragon Lake), among many others.

In chapter 4, we looked at the historical picture of Upper Tibet through its clan traditions. That the descendents of the ancient inhabitants still occupy their ancestral territory says reams about the link between today's residents and the ancient past. The clan identity of the highlanders runs very deep, this having persisted in the face of repeated migrations of people to the upper reaches of Tibet. Eternal Bon literature holds that early clans such as Gurub and Nyel had much impact on highland society. Additionally, the oral tradition has preserved examples of what are believed to be the autochthonous clans of Upper Tibet.

The ancient heritage of Upper Tibet encompasses many areas of the way of life of her people. Take celestial lore, a field of study that has been barely explored by researchers. Traditionally, pastoral migrations were regulated through the observation of the constellations using mountains and other topographical features as baseline sighting points. This kind of astronomical tradition is first recorded in a text written in the Old Tibetan language.[1] Important mountains such as Tise and Targo were observed to determine the date of the winter solstice celebration. In western Tibet, the old winter solstice New Year is celebrated one month before the Lamaist New Year. In the 1990s, I discovered a primitive observatory at Lake Nam Tsho.[2] A cave here named "Dancing Pad of the Sky-Walkers" contains a cairn that marks the approach of the summer solstice. This cairn is fully sunlit through a big hole in the roof on the longest day of the year.

Ancient botanical and geological lore is also widespread in Upper Tibet, another area of study in its infancy. The use of plants and minerals for medicines and pigments stretches far back in time. As the rock art record testifies, the mineral iron oxide, or red ochre, has been used as paint for several millennia. The exploitation of wild plants for food and knowledge of the grasses and herbs upon which livestock depend have every indication of being bona fide examples of ancient knowledge too. As we have seen, high-altitude plants commonly used as incense such as juniper, rhododendron, and artemisia are mentioned in ancient texts, the historical aspect of ritual traditions being especially strong to the present day.

As rock art unambiguously divulges, the hunting of antelope and wild sheep for food is yet another hoary practice. Traditionally, Upper Tibetan hunters have a rich vocabulary with which to describe their game. The Tibetan researcher Norsam brings attention to a number of cultic terms used exclusively by hunting parties.[3] For instance, wild yaks according to the color of their fur, the shape of their horns, and other distinctive physical traits have their own special names. Hunters have special patron deities, which are propitiated to guarantee a safe and successful hunt. When an animal is brought down, hunters are obliged to offer its gallbladder and other body parts to the helper deities.

The customs and traditions of the upland reflect a cultural conservatism that is probably more pronounced than anywhere else in the Tibetan cultural world, with the notable exception of the mountainous periphery of the Plateau. With an eye on the past, the shepherds and farmers of the highlands continue to find strength in their culture as did their parents and grandparents before them. This adherence to the old ways provides a rudder with which to navigate the sea of modern social, economic, and environmental transformation. In addition to what has been handed down by word of mouth, the

Upper Tibetans have a rich body of literature at their disposal, which edifies ancient cultural models. These textual exemplars pertain to royal and priestly celebrities and deities, proud reminders of what the highlanders once were.

DIVINE MOUNTAINS AND LAKES OF SHEPHERDS AND FARMERS RECALL ANCIENT TRADITIONS

The customs and traditions of today's highlanders when compared to Tibetan writings reveal the vibrant interplay between the past and present. For more than a millennium this literature has chronicled special ritual activities revolving around sacred mountains and lakes of the upland. In the guise of ancestral and protective deities, these topographical features are considered essential to the well-being of shepherds and farmers, overshadowing many aspects of everyday life. Today, as in ancient times, this native pantheon is regularly petitioned for prosperity, happiness, health, and victory.

The worship of mountain and lake spirits in Upper Tibet is derived from religious customs and traditions originating in Zhang Zhung and Sumpa. The liturgies for Upper Tibetan mountains and lakes were first propagated by ancient bards and priests. After the seventh century CE, this oral tradition was put to writing by clerics and scribes. Ancient praises, invocations, and petitions to the gods and goddesses may have been first recorded verbatim, but over the centuries many were modified to assume a Lamaist mantle and to embody more modern grammatical forms of the Tibetan language. The single biggest Lamaist innovation was to impel the gods and goddesses of Zhang Zhung and Sumpa to take oaths upholding Buddhist and Eternal Bon doctrines. Secondly, the iconography of the deities was redrawn to bring it into conformance with the appearance and personality of Indian deities.

Despite these and other wholesale changes to the native pantheon, certain aspects of archaic era religion have changed little since the introduction of Lamaism to Upper Tibet fourteen centuries ago. Foremost among these cultural relics is an environmental ethic that stresses the desirability of sound physical surroundings. The shepherds and farmers of the highlands still go to great lengths to ritually protect the integrity of the land, water, and atmosphere. In the harsh, high-elevation conditions of the Tibetan upland, living in an ecologically sensitive manner assumes special significance.

Contamination of the environment through burning and dumping waste is considered a particularly good way to anger guardian deities. It is also traditionally believed that indiscriminate slaying of wild animals, digging holes, and other inappropriate actions cause the gods to retaliate by unleashing sickness and reducing the grain harvest. The appeasement of angry gods by rectifying the harm done to them and the habitats they rule over remains central to the relationship between the Upper Tibetans and their native gods. Tibetan environmental taboos have long influenced the inhabitants, for they are cited in a litany to the territorial deities found in an untitled ritual text attributed to four sages of the eighth century CE, but which was redacted at a later date.[4] Among the four men to whom the untitled ritual text is attributed is Tonggyung Thuchen of Zhang Zhung. In attempting to reconcile the gods, the authors cover many ways in which the balance between humanity and deities is thrown off by unwholesome activities. The proscriptions found in this ancient text are acknowledged to the present day in a remarkable assertion of the traditional environmental ethic.

In a cosmogonic preface to the untitled text, the ultimate source of the territorial and ancestral gods is primordial radiance. Thereafter, from the union of a female lake and male wind, a conch white egg magically appeared. From this egg emerged a being with the body of a man and the wings of a horned eagle, the prototypic god of ancestors and territory. After three more generations of divine progeny, five chief mountain gods were begotten, including three from Upper Tibet: Tise, Thanglha, and Gekhö. The other two, Yarlha Shampo and Lha Nyen Sengge, hail from the lower reaches of the Tibetan Plateau. The debut of these chief mountain gods was followed by the spawning of the remainder of the indigenous pantheon, including the water spirits and owners of the earth.

Like contemporary rituals carried out for the spirits of the air, earth, and water, the four masters of the eighth century CE are recorded offering them precious substances and delicious foods. In a decidedly mercenary exchange, the assistance of the deities is purchased with many presents of their liking. Pedestrian negotiation and bribery still characterize dealings between the native gods and humans. Like unpredictable wild animals, it is believed that these deities can turn on human beings, so one must defend against provoking them. The indigenous gods have to be ritually purified with incense and water, a practice done on a daily basis in Tibetan households. The so-called higher gods of Lamaism are also invoked using water and aromatic substances, but this is done for less "worldly" purposes. Once it is felt that the gods of the environment have been satisfied with the treatment meted out to them, lamas and laypeople alike ask for their support, as do the ancient masters in our text:

> Assembly of water spirits, mountain spirits, masters of the earth, and territorial deities, listen to our speech, that of the *bon* priests. The sponsors, benefactors and us, have not dug at your palace residence. In the event there was digging let us be peacefully reconciled. We reconcile you by offerings of jewels and incense. We did not upset your mighty stones. In the

event that we did upset you let us be peacefully reconciled. We reconcile you by offerings of jewels and incense. We did not divert your mighty waters. In the event there was diversion let us be peacefully reconciled. We reconcile you by offerings of jewels and incense. We did not cut your mighty trees. In the event that there was cutting let us be peacefully reconciled. We reconcile you by offerings of jewels and incense.

> If we screamed on the mountaintops,
> And irrigated with water channels and reservoirs,
> And excavated at your mighty springs,
> And set big fires on mountains,
> And killed your mighty deer and hunted your wild ungulates,
> And destroyed your palaces and dwellings,
> And spread flesh and blood at your mighty places,
> And inadvertently sullied the hearth with dairy and meat products,
> And slept in the middle of your palaces,
> And went naked at your mighty places,
> And mindlessly made harsh sounds,
> And startled you with drum and conch,
> And showed the light of the fire in the evening,
> And poured out hot steaming liquids at your mighty places,
> If we molested the mighty territorial deities, rendered them
>   unconscious, ravaged them, startled them, made them ill, or
>   injured them, whatever transpired;
> We offer, by the benediction of the gods of the void,
> These offerings of various kinds of herbs and medicines.

You are the mighty territorial deities, and if you have any ill will for both us and the sponsors we will now reconcile it. If you are angry may you be pacified. If you are quarrelsome, we will reconcile the contention. If you are malicious may you be pacified. We give you offerings of incense, and pacific offerings to the mighty territorial deities. May all your grudges be pacified. May all our infectious diseases and ailments be pacified. May your hatred and malice be pacified. May all harm be pacified. Consummate our and our social circle's happiness. Propagate good luck and the *bon* doctrine. May our merits increase.

The shepherds of Upper Tibet are heirs to an economic way of life several thousand years old, dating to a time when yaks, sheep, goats, and horses were first domesticated in the region. Their self-assured bearing, itinerant lifestyle, and tent homes set them apart from their more sedentary neighbors. The idealized pastoral world of olden times is captured in an ancient hymn to Pholha Shelgyung, one of the most important ancestral figures, or "father gods," of Upper Tibet.[5] Residing on a lofty snow mountain in the Transhimalaya, Pholha Shelgyung personifies a *drokpa* patriarch in all his magnificence.

Eventually, this poetic account of a nomadic sovereign with a fair complexion and magnificent white attire living in a sumptuous tent came to be written down and a Buddhist oath added to it. This was the work of the founder of an Upper Tibetan monastery called Dargyeling, which lies in the shadow of Pholha Shelgyung. Nevertheless, much of the content of the archaic era hymn was preserved, fostering the ancient pastoral traditions of the upland:

> At the rock formation cave of the vulture on the pyramidal white snow mountain, at the rock formation cave of the white snow mountain, an erected white silk tent rippling in the wind, golden pillars pointed like spears and arrayed in rows, guy lines of turquoise taunt like bowstrings, and jewel stakes in all directions. Inside such a tent there is a white silk curtain moving rhythmically. Behind that curtain, on a blue turquoise throne, is the avuncular god of all the people of Upper Tibet, the father god of all the regions of Upper Tibet.
>
> Hark! Diminutive white crystal man, on your head is tied a regal white silk turban. In your hand you hold a white silk regimental banner. On your body you wear a white silk robe. As your mount you ride a goose-orange horse with a white muzzle.

Until being brought under the Communist Chinese, the *drokpas* of Upper Tibet were a high-spirited and sometimes a pugnacious lot. Conflicts between contending groups of shepherds were not unusual, and banditry was a serious problem. Thus the adroit use of arms and expert equestrian skills were highly valued traits. Even today horseback riding and archery contests are extremely popular with the *drokpas*. In the summertime each area holds its own festivities in which young men show off their strength and skills.

The martial qualities of the *drokpas* are reflected in the appearance and activities of the mountain gods, the archetypal warriors and heroes of Upper Tibet. Another text attributed to the eighth-century CE Zhang Zhung sage Tonggyung Thuchen is dedicated to Nyenchen Thanglha, the most important mountain divinity in the eastern Changthang.[6] Entitled *Honors and Praises of Thanglha*, this hymn was appropriated and revised by Eternal Bon authors after 1000 CE. The text contains a dramatic description of Thanglha, the greatest of nomad commanders. Surrounded by a vast cavalry, this noble fighting figure wears a helmet surmounted by a plume, a symbol of military and spiritual triumph. The bards and spirit-mediums of contemporary Upper Tibet also wear bird feathers in their hats, recapitulating this ancient custom. In a concession to Lamaist tradition, the explanation of the god's attributes in *Honors and Praises of Thanglha* refers to skillful means and wisdom, prerequisite qualities for enlightenment. Like a general and his army on the battlefield, the hosts of Thanglha are primed to take on the demons attacking the followers of religion. The battle cries of this huge military ring out loud and clear over the countryside:

> You Nyenchen Thanglha of Tibet ride a light orange horse. On your person you wear yellow golden armor. On your head you have a golden helmet with the bird feather of the rising sun. In your hands you hold the bow of wisdom and the arrow of skillful means. On your right side you lead a female dragon and on your left is zigzagging lightning. A white lioness follows you. Soaring overhead is a golden horned eagle. A retinue of one hundred thousand mighty spirit soldiers surround you. You send as your attendants the one hundred thousand sons of the mighty spirits, white men on white horses, holding white banners aloft. They are yelling *ki so cha*. The mountains fall down by the sound of the hoofs of their racing horses. They make the sky and earth quake. In ancient times you were the divine ally of *bon*.

Not one of the ancient castles of Upper Tibet is still used as it was originally intended. Most were abandoned and fell into disrepair centuries ago. As we have seen, the greatest castle construction occurred in the archaic era, a time when highland culture was at its zenith. In a few cases, monasteries took over early citadel sites using the ruins as foundations and building materials. While kings and priests no longer reside in fortresses, the gods are thought to inhabit their numinous counterparts, majestic edifices built with precious metals and jewels.

Another text of ritual invocations for Nyenchen Thanglha describes him as a monarch residing in a magnificent castle.[7] This text is attributed to Guru Rinpoche, the great Vajrayana master of the eighth century CE, but it is actually derived from an archaic hymn to the mountain god. In order to make it palatable to Buddhist practitioners, this hymn was modified to include the obligatory passage in which Thanglha and his cohort swear allegiance to the Vajrayana saints. In this way, a Buddhist text was created from archaic lore that once circulated around Upper Tibet:

> On the peak of the divine white snow mountain is the personal castle of the lord Thanglha shimmering in the atmosphere. The four foundations are made from black iron. The four sides are made from bright conch. The four corners are made from precious gold. The cornices are made from turquoise. The roof rafters are made from lapis lazuli. Its pillars and beams are made of crystal and coral. Its sparkling doors are of multicolored gold. The eaves are red and white. Spears and arrows are on the roof. There are flags and banners fluttering in the wind. On the flanks are rising mists. On the foundations there is limpid water overflowing. At the east portal of such a castle is a great herd of divine white yaks. At the south portal of such

a castle there are straw-colored divine horses running about. At the west portal of such a castle there are tigers, leopards, black bears, and brown bears fiercely roving around. At the north portal of such a castle birds soar overhead. Inside such a castle reposes the mighty and fierce Thanglha.

Drokpa women enjoy one of the strongest gender roles in all of Tibet. They control exactly half the tent and are directly responsible for most of a family's food production. Seen as kin to the tellurian female spirits, women are guarantors of a family's well-being. It is believed that the prosperity of a household is under the control of the personal goddesses that accompany women. Known as *molha*, or "divine mothers," these deities preside over the hearth, children, and livestock. They are entrusted with ensuring a successful outcome to all domestic economic activities. For example, it is thought that the yield of milk and wool hinges upon the relationship between a family's matriarch and her *molha*. The importance of such personal defenders of females can be traced back to an Old Tibetan language ritual text designed to save women who died during childbirth from a hellish fate.[8]

The *molha* is commonly described in her most basic or generic form. The arrow and mirror of this prototypic female spirit function to increase household good fortune and prosperity. Such objects are commonly found on altars for the personal deities in tents and in homes:

> The *molha* is a beautiful and attractive young woman. She has a white body, one face, and two hands. In her right hand is a draped arrow, and in her left hand she holds a ritual mirror. She wears a blue silk overcoat. She has a precious hair tie and is decorated with many types of ornaments. She rides on a doe and variously displays the manifestations of a mother and maternal aunt.[9]

The robust position of woman in *drokpa* society is reflected in texts for the propitiation of local female deities. One of the most famous of these goddesses is Nam Tsho Chukmo, the consort of the mountain god Nyenchen Thanglha. In her older cultural form as a great matriarch, she was perceived as the queen of existence responsible for the welfare of all living creatures in her geographic purview. In her Eternal Bon aspect, this goddess of Nam Tsho is the leader of the divine mountains that encircle her, taking precedence even over the mighty Thanglha. As the largest and holiest lake in what appears to have been ancient Sumpa, Nam Tsho encapsulates the heightened status that seems to have been accorded women in that territory. Known as Yum, or the "Mother," her proud and powerful mien is conveyed in an Eternal Bon text attributed to the eighth century CE, but which appeared in its present form only after 1000 CE.[10] In this Lamaist work, the goddess of

Nam Tsho is elevated in status to a high defender of religion, the arbiter of long life and disease:

> Mother Queen of Existence you have a dark green body color and a crown ornament of turquoise. Your peacock feather robe costume is beautifully ornamented with black tassels. In your right hand is the blue and red lasso of disease that binds the oath-breaker enemies. In your left hand is the vase of life that preserves the life and life force of the *shen* priests. You rove around the innumerable worlds riding the black female bird of the *dud* demons. You delegate the work of the worldly female deities. We are affectionately calling, come in an instant. The time has come to slaughter the oath-breaker enemies. Conquer quickly and slaughter the obstacles, enemies, and obstructers.

The lake goddesses of Zhang Zhung appear to have been formidable warriors in their own right. In Eternal Bon invocations they are girt for battle, possibly reflecting ancient customs whereby women also participated in combat. According to historical accounts and archaeological findings, it appears that Scythian and Hun females also played an active role in war.

An Eternal Bon work in which the four main holy lakes of southwestern Tibet were transformed into religious guardians may be based on a model for ancient warrior women.[11] In this text these goddesses have Zhang Zhung names and are introduced as "the sovereign females of the four mighty lakes." They are believed to have been protectresses of Zhang Zhung in the circle of the warrior queen Drablai Gyalmo, consort to Zhang Zhung's chief god Gekhö. The four lake goddesses are clad in armor and helmets and wield spears, daggers, lassos, and magic missiles:

> Cha Tsame (Lake Gongkhyung Ngultsho), you are the white lady of silver inside the white silver lake, who wears a silver helmet on your head. You wear white crystal armor on your body. You ride a black mule mount with a silver head. With your right hand you hurl a golden magical bomb. With your left hand you throw a red copper lasso. You dispatch the male and female life-force master attendants.
>
> Ting Tsame (Lake Mapang Yumtsho), you are the blue lady of turquoise inside the blue turquoise lake, who wears a helmet of turquoise on your head. You wear blue-jeweled armor on your body. You ride a turquoise hawk mount. In your right hand you hold a turquoise spear. With your left hand you hurl the magic bomb of turquoise like an arrow. You dispatch the water spirits of the lake depths as your attendants.
>
> Tsa Tsame (Lake La Ngak Tsho), you are the yellow golden lady inside the yellow golden lake, who wears a helmet of crystal on your head. You wear yellow golden armor on your body. You ride a yellow golden tiger

mount. With your right hand you ignite the red magical bomb of the great fire. With your left hand you hurl a red-blood magical missile.

Ba Tsame (Lake Zomshang Chaktsho), you are the dark blue lady of molten pig iron inside the molten iron lake, who wears a molten pig iron helmet on your head. You wear armor of blue iron on your body. You ride the celestial iron great horned-eagle mount. With your right hand you dispatch a fiery hawk. With your left hand you thrust the celestial iron dagger. You dispatch iron wolves with fiery tongues as your attendants.

THE SEARCH FOR WELL-BEING THROUGH THE AGES

To ensure family happiness, *drokpas* conduct special rituals to summon the good fortune capacity, or *yang*, of the divinities. This calling of the *yang* typically entails the caparisoning of high-quality livestock as a prelude to setting them free in the mountains as gifts to the gods and goddesses.

The *yang* and the rituals made for its increase are mentioned in the Dunhuang manuscripts, linking today's Upper Tibetans with customs known more than a thousand years old. In the text ITJ 734, archaic priests summon the *yang* in the daytime using ephedra, an herb reputedly possessing magical qualities.[12] The retaining of the *yang* of livestock used to provision the deceased for the journey to the afterlife has its precedent in another Dunhuang funerary manuscript. This funeral ritual text of royal proportions known as Pt 1042 details groups of sacrificial horses, sheep, and yaks specially sequestered so that their *yang* could be properly conserved.[13] It is still believed by Upper Tibetans that should the *yang* depart from livestock, they would become prey to bad weather, disease, and predators.

The yaks, goats, and sheep selected for the *drokpa yang* rituals must be healthy, be free from physical defects, and have well-shaped horns. Their horns are decorated with red ochre and dabs of butter, and colored strips of cloths and tassels are suspended from their ears, withers, and tails. Typically, checkerboard designs in red ochre are drawn on the backs of the animals. These ochre markings represent the saddle of the deity. In the Changthang west of Lake Dangra, the linear pattern drawn on the right side of an animal symbolizes the subjugation of enemies and obstructions, while the curvilinear pattern on the left side is drawn to attract happiness and profit to its owner. Once an animal is duly decorated, incense is burnt, and blessed barleycorn and sacred springwater are sprinkled over it.

To complete the consecration of a *yang* animal, an invocation is said over it. In the central Changthang, white wool and a wooden tablet with

crosshatches known as a *tram* are the ritual tools accompanying the consecration of *yang* animals.[14] Once offered to the deities of the heavens, earth,
and water, these gifts are left to lead out their lives undisturbed. The *yang*
livestock are conceived of as the physical station of personal and territorial
deities, showering blessings on the families that own them. *Drokpas* believe
that the recipient deities use these creatures for riding. In certain instances,
the presiding spirits are supposed to mate with *yang* livestock or take possession of them. It is said that yaks, sheep, and goats of extraordinary size
and strength and possessing unique anatomical traits such as four horns are
divine crossbreeds or vessels of the deities.

In the *yang* performances, livestock of various colors are given to the deities. The precedent for this custom of offering different livestock to different
deities can be traced to Dunhuang manuscripts such as Pt 126 and Pt 1060.[15]
Traditionally, the god of males (*pholha*) and territorial gods (*yulha*) receive all-
white male yaks, white sheep, and white horses. The red *tsen* spirits are gifted
bay-colored yaks, red goats, and white sheep with red faces. The black *gönpo*
defender spirits are bequeathed all-black yaks and sheep. The female water
spirits (*lumo*) and goddess of women (*molha*) are given bluish female yaks,
horses, goats, and sheep. In the western Changthang, a region with a high
proportion of ancient clans, the tradition of gifting specially marked animals
to the clan god (*rulha*) has also survived.

A traditional invocation accompanying the *yang* summoning ritual in
the Yakpa region of the eastern Changthang has been recorded by the researcher Sonam Dorje.[16] While red ochre was applied to the horns of the
animals, the *drokpas* declaimed,

> Sharpen! Sharpen the right copper horn!
> The cutter robber of our saddles,
> The schemer thieves of the night,
> The established armies who target us,
> The potential enemy plotters,
> Those whose speech is softer than milk but whose mind is rougher than a
> thorn:
> Sharpen! Sharpen!
> Left horn of purplish agate: Love! Love!
> Give love to the kinfolk.
> Give love to the sworn friends.
> Give love to the friendly neighbors.

Thereafter, when butter was applied to the animals as a mark of stability, the
following words were repeated:

> May the life of us humans be stable and long-lasting.
> May the *yang* of the livestock be stable and long-lasting.
> May the essence of foods be stable and long-lasting.
> May our luck and domination be stable and long-lasting.
> Join our ears to pleasing speech.
> Join our mouths to food.
> Join our hands to wealth.

An origin myth for the *yang* and a related auspicious force known as *cha* is found in an Eternal Bon text called *Muye Traphü*.[17] This ancient work relates how an ancestral god known as Lhase Gampo, or "Fully Accomplished Son of the Gods," managed to capture an island-dwelling magical conch deer with crystal horns to serve as the tabernacle or support for humans and their ancestral deities. By obtaining the deer as the foundation of the *cha* and *yang*, humans and deities were able to extricate themselves from misfortune and obtain all sorts of boons. In the text, the deer tabernacle is described by the adjective "swastika," indicating its stable and enduring nature. As in many other Eternal Bon etiologic myths, the ultimate cosmogonic principle in this text is the void in which a primal light appears. From this light all the animate and inanimate features of the universe came into being. Along with the four elements of wind, fire, water, and earth, mountains and lakes are recorded as engendering factors of existence, reflecting the importance of this geographic dyad in the origin myths of the Upper Tibetan oral tradition. According to *Muye Traphü*, in the beginning of existence, humans appeared in conjunction with their deities, reiterating their shared ontological basis in the archaic traditions of Tibet. In the narrative, the god who sends Lhase Gampo to obtain the magical deer is no other than Yabla Daldruk, the divine progenitor of the Tibetan kings.

In *Muye Traphü* the great goddess Grandmother Sky Queen directs the god Lhase Gampo to a lake island located north of the world mountain. This island and lake are the residence and soul repositories of a magic stag, Crystal Horned Conch Deer. The mythic abode of this stag underscores the geomantic centrality of islands in Tibetan geographic conceptions. Imbued with a secret or innermost aspect, the geographic source of the good fortune energies *cha* and *yang* recalls the string of early settlements on the islands of Upper Tibet. Similarly, in an Old Tibetan text of the Gathang Bumpa collection entitled *Origin Tales of the Deer Horns Showing the Way*, a sacrificial deer is associated with an island that appears to be located in Upper Tibet.[18] Only after its capture and much repartee is Crystal Horned Conch Deer enticed to return to the land of the gods and serve as the foundation for the *cha* and *yang*:

> In the time of [early] existence, in the country of Brightness Cha Land,
> in a beautiful jeweled castle, the king of the *cha* of primordial existence

gathered the *cha* gods of existence. Then the great *cha* god Yabla Daldruk [said], "Please tell us [father of existence] Sridpa Sangpo, the *cha* does not have a foundation, how significant is this defect?" . . . Sridpa Sangpo replied, "All the *cha* gods of existence listen to me . . . the father god of existence [Yabla Daldruk] does not have a *cha* foundation because the wicked sorcery of the evil demons threw the five gods of existence into the sky, and they occupied [the place] abandoned by the gods, so both the brightness and magnificence of the gods' appearance have deteriorated. Humans without *cha* have many diseases, and disease and accidents beset livestock without *yang*. Without its essence, food is very much weakened. These are the defects of not having a *cha* foundation. We will seek a support for the *yang* gods." He said, "Who can search for a *phywa* foundation?"

. . . Lhase Gampo said, "I will go to search for a *cha* foundation." . . . He went to the top of [world mountain] Rirab Lhunpo. Inside the castle of the thirty-three realms of the deities he came before Grandmother Sky Queen and asked, "The *bon* god of existence is without the swastika *cha* foundation. Goddess of existence please counsel me." Thus this much he asked. Grandmother Sky Queen replied, "On the north side of Rirab, in the middle of an upwelling turquoise lake, there is a four-sided swastika island. On top of the swastika island the father is Sky Deer Long Horns and the mother is Celestial Hind. The son of the union of these two is Crystal Horned Conch Deer. You make him the foundation of the swastika *cha*." She thus diligently instructed.

Then Lhase Gampo rode the thoroughbred of high intellect and landed upon the swastika island. He met Conch Deer with Crystal Horns. . . . The deer spoke fluently in the language of humans: "I am Crystal Horned Conch Deer. This divine lake is my soul lake and this celestial island is my soul mountain. . . . For what have you come?" Lhase Gampo replied, "Listen to me Crystal Horned Conch Deer . . . my father, the lord of the *cha*, Yabla Daldruk, does not have the foundation of the *cha* and *yang*. Grandmother Sky Queen provided me with instructions. She sent me [here] to search for the foundation of the *cha*. You are the deer of marvelous manifestation. Now please come for the *cha* and *yang*." Thus this much he asked. The deer rejoined, "Listen to me Lhase Gampo. The sun and moon reside in the middle of the sky. If you separate the sky from the sun and moon residing in the middle of the sky surely sentient beings would be covered by darkness. If you separate the lake from the fish and otters residing in the lake they would die. If you separate the island from the deer residing on the island it would perish."

. . . Again Lhase Gampo spoke, "Listen to me conch white deer. You are the deer with all the perfected qualities. The crystal horns divided into five branches on your head are a sign of the residing five divine lords. The circular jewel on top of your head is a sign of the residing *muye praphud* [gods]. The long hair on your back, the divine abode, is a sign of the residing five divine brothers of wealth. The deer speaking the language of

humans is a sign of it serving as a messenger between the gods and humans. The brighter than white color of your body is a sign of the purification of sins and defilements. Your four hoofs formed from black iron are a
sign of the drying of the four rivers of the demons. The medicinal foliage
you eat as your food is a sign of the liberation from disease. Like that you
possess in full measure all good qualities. Please let us go now for the *cha*
of the people." Thus this much speech he said.

Again the deer replied, ". . . Do not lead me to the country of humans."
Upon saying this he was ready to flee. By his miraculous power Lhase
Gampo threw the lasso of method and caught the deer by the neck. Lhase
Gampo spoke these words, "You are the deer possessing in full measure all
good qualities. Do not be angry; let your affection grow. If you turn anger
into affection it will purge the anger of others. Be wise; do not be ignorant.
If you turn your ignorance into wisdom it will purify the ignorance of
others. Do not be arrogant; be peaceful. If you turn your pride into peace
it will purify the pride of others. Do not be envious; be magnanimous. If
you turn your envy into magnanimity it will purify the envy of others. Do
not be selfish; do for others. If you completely serve others [whatever you
need] for yourself will come naturally. . . . You are the deer of the body
with knowledge. You are the son of sentient beings with the great powerful mind. The words you spoke possess much meaning. Show compassion
for sentient beings that are troubled by disease, famine, and weapons.
Swastika deer let us go quickly."

The deer then replied, "My mind is based on the four elements. The
body of the four elements [can feel] great heat and cold. Please search for
a place without heat or cold. . . . The body of the four elements [can feel]
great thirst and hunger. Please search for food so that I am not thirsty or
hungry. . . . The body of the four elements [is prone to] great fear. Please
search for a country without fear." Thus requested the deer.

Lhase Gampo spoke again, "When you come to the country of the
cha [gods] you will eat the grain crop as your food. You will drink the
extract of sweetness for your thirst. You need not worry about thirst and
hunger. You will stay in the middle of the corral of power. You need not
worry about heat and cold. Your neck will be ornamented with gold and
turquoise. Your head will be ornamented with silk cloths. Vermilion and
indigo will decorate your body. We will install you as the support of the
gods. We will lay you as the foundation of the *cha* and *yang*. You need not
worry about fear and anxiety." Thus this much he said.

Lhase Gampo and the deer went to the *cha* country of Brightness Turquoise Peak, to the secret *cha* castle of nine peaks. Lhase Gampo said to
Yabla Daldruk, "I offer to you for the foundation of the swastika *cha*, the
son of the sky deer and celestial deer couple, Crystal Horned Conch White
Deer. Bring the *yang* and human *cha* riches. Obtain the dazzling and brilliant personal appearances." Thus this much he said.

TODAY'S SHAMAN SUCCESSORS TO
THE ADEPTS OF ZHANG ZHUNG

One of the oldest vocations in Upper Tibet is that of the spirit-medium or shaman. These vehicles of the gods personify the ancestral and protective dimensions of religion in the region. For the well-being of their communities, shamans purport to call down the gods upon themselves.[19] Between 1997 and 2005, I met twenty of the greatest shamans residing across the breadth of Upper Tibet. These men and women never cease to intrigue and surprise. Even today, I am at a loss to fully explain some of the things they do, for how much is really known about the deepest workings of the human mind?

Seen as the embodiment of supernatural beings, the shamans of Upper Tibet join the worlds of gods and humans in a pact of mutual understanding and benefit. This primal impulse, of people consorting with deities, is one of the pillars upon which native religious traditions and society rest in Upper Tibet. The shamans primarily serve as incarnate forms of the region's mountain and lake deities. It is believed that when possessed by these spirits, shamans act as their mouthpiece. In this psychologically transformed state they are purported to heal the sick, insulate livestock from epidemics, exorcise evil spirits, bring good fortune, and predict the outcome of future events.

A shaman of Upper Tibet using his drum and flat-bell to suck out disease-causing impurities from a patient's body

The farmers and shepherds of Upper Tibet have depended on spirit-mediums for centuries, something that Chinese Communism could not fully eradicate. However, their numbers are now much reduced as the children of shamans move into different lines of work. Viewed as superstitious and anti-modern by secular authorities, the practice of spirit-mediumship in Upper Tibet is strongly discouraged. Conducted under the auspices of Lamaism, the ethic of shamanism in Upper Tibet revolves around a deep sense of altruism. The alleviation of pain and suffering is paramount, bringing this profession into consonance with Buddhist and Eternal Bon teachings.

In Upper Tibet, shamans are known as *lhapa* and *lhamo*, the "god men" and "god women," and carry the epithet "hero" or "heroine" for their exemplary services. They are culturally invested with the power to act and speak on behalf of the gods. As the deities are believed to come alive through the shamans, they represent one of the most tangible and immediate of Tibetan epiphanies. Highly proficient spirit-mediums are held in awe, tales of their exploits having spread far and wide. Their reputations building over time, celebrated shamans of past generations are attributed with superhuman abilities. Just like the ancient *shen* and *bonpo* priests of Tibetan literature, they are purported to have ridden wild animals and to have flown in the sky like birds.

The village- and camp-based shamans of Upper Tibet are the less prestigious counterparts of the old state oracles of Tibet, mediums for big deities such as Pehar and Chamsing. The Pehar oracle is now based in exile in the Indian hill town of Dharamsala. While the state oracles had many more resources at their disposal and conducted trances under strict monastic supervision, the basic premise of their practice is the same as in Upper Tibet. That is that deities can take over the bodies of men and women for the wider benefit of society.

Shamans of similar persuasion to those in Upper Tibet are active in other regions of the Tibetan Plateau and across the Himalayan rimland. In high Himalayan communities, they carry out therapies and rituals just like their upland brethren in the Changthang and western Tibet. In north-eastern Tibet, shamans practice their profession more freely than in Upper Tibet, participating in high-profile fortune-bestowing communal festivals. In Ladakh, shamans toil to cure illnesses, conduct divinations, and exorcise evil spirits, precisely their roles in Upper Tibet. In the western Himalayan district of Spiti, a winter solstice festival is held in honor of the various territorial deities to ensure the well-being of the community in the coming year. In the summertime, shamans of different villages of Spiti participate in celebrations to honor the household gods with food, alcohol, and the raising of prayer flags. Such public displays of shamanic power in adjacent Upper Tibet are now banned.

The Indian savant Sarat Chandra Das appears to have been the first to formally study Tibetan spirit-mediums. Writing in 1882, he describes an Eternal Bon shaman who when possessed by his tutelary deity purified a defiled hearth with a sacred arrow.[20] Das explains that when the hearth was sullied, the subterranean *sadak* spirits were angered and thus caused illness, a belief still commonly held. Another Victorian era Tibetologist, Augustus L. Waddell, details the expelling of a demon from a patient by a shaman wielding a draped arrow as a tube for sucking.[21] One end of the arrow was placed on the afflicted area of the patient's body while the shaman put the opposite end into his mouth. This sucking procedure remains unchanged. Waddell mentions that shamans wear a mirror on their breast and the five-lobed headdress of Vajrayana Buddhism, ritual accoutrements very much in evidence today. Waddell further explains that at the start of a trance ceremony, Guru Rinpoche and the Buddha are invoked, followed by the presiding deity of the trance who brings his helping spirits with him. This calling upon the higher gods of Lamaism for aid and protection before the possessing deities appear remains standard practice in the trance ceremony.

The Upper Tibetan shamans allege that during the trance their own consciousness is displaced by those of the possessing deities. Like a vessel full to the brim, when the deities occupy a shaman there is no space left for his or her own personality. The normal consciousness of the shaman is thought to be spirited away to a ritual mirror or to the abode of the gods for safekeeping. At the end of the ceremony when the gods retreat from their human host, the personal consciousness is reinstated, or so it is believed. Spirit-mediums observe that when they are fully possessed by the gods, they have absolutely no recollection of themselves. In effect, they appear to exist in a state of suspended animation.

Spirit possession in Upper Tibet is referred to as *lha babpa* (deity descent) or *lha zhuk* (deity residing) and is characterized by radical changes in the speech and comportment of the medium. Under the influence of a "deity," shamans exhibit bizarre symptoms such as profuse perspiration, great bodily strain, extraordinary physical strength, seizures, foaming at the mouth, and the disappearance of the irises in the back of the head. A 1935 *National Geographic* article by the celebrated American scholar Joseph Rock shows a photo of a sword blade twisted like a piece licorice.[22] Reputedly it was deformed in this way by one of the Tibetan monastic mediums known as *kutenpa*. Such exhibitions of superhuman strength are also supposed to have been commonplace in Upper Tibet.

Many of the remedial or helping spirits of the trance take the form of eagles, owls, bears, wolves, tigers, or foxes. Under their possession the shamans behave in a similar manner to these animals. They cry out or hiss like wild animals and imitate their movements and actions. In trance, it is routine to hear the simulated growl of tigers or bears, the snarl of wolves, or the screech of raptors.

But what is actually happening to someone purportedly possessed by deities? This is a question that exercises scientists and philosophers the world over, for shamanism and spirit possession are a global cultural phenomenon. There are many theories but few definitive answers, beyond the obvious ones of fakery and charlatanism. Psychological and sociological explanations abound as well. In earlier Western scholarship on the subject, shamans were seen as propagating psychological and social pathologies, a product of the primitive level of development in their societies. That shamans practice auto-hypnosis or induce a temporary psychosis in order to achieve the trance state are popular views among some observers. In recent years researchers tend to take a more holistic approach, seeing the shamans and their patients as part of a collective bond in which perceptions of possession constitute a potent social metaphor. Playing their respective roles, both shaman and patient act in culturally prescribed ways in pursuance of positive social outcomes.

While the social equation unequivocally has a large impact on spirit-mediumship in Upper Tibet, this is not the complete picture. The stark changes in behavior and physiological response that mark the trance are also indicative of a profound transpersonal psychology. This altered state of consciousness appears to enhance a shaman's physical and mental capabilities. For the Tibetans, however, the gods are the real possessing agents, and it is the shaman who receives them.

Without exception, spirit-mediums of the upland report that the first years of divine possession are traumatic, causing much physical and mental distress. They speak of experiencing body pains and psychotic-like symptoms so severe they seem life threatening. Typically, it is in adolescence that a budding shaman is first visited by the gods. In the beginning there is anxiety about the possessing entity over whether it might be a demon instead of a bona fide god. Traditionally, Upper Tibetan shamans were vetted by monastic authorities who traveled around pastoral communities. These lamas would test young people receiving visitations to determine if they were possessed by demons or deities. Reportedly these were rigorous examinations that forced participants to identify hidden objects and to reveal the visions they beheld in a ritual mirror. Those found to be under demonic influences were given ritual treatment and were enjoined not to fraternize with supernatural entities. Those individuals believed to be channeling authentic deities were blessed and their practice consecrated in a religious ceremony.

Typically the initiation of a shaman requires several years of tutelage by a senior member of the profession. An experienced shaman and his young charge will go into trance together so that the elder figure can give instruction about the appearances and actions of the deities. Master shamans confer various invocations, rituals, and curative operations upon their students and show them how to formulate oracular pronouncements. In order to become a full-fledged shaman, a neophyte also has to complete many Lamaist devotions and make pilgrimages to holy places.

Upper Tibet in premodern times had few doctors and not a great many monks, so local communities also relied on shamans for practical guidance and medical care. The prayers and techniques of the shamans are part of a cultural endowment that combines Buddhist religious concepts with native customs and practices. Spirit-mediumship remains one of the great oral traditions of the upland, kept alive by family lines of practitioners. It is not unusual for Buddhist shamans to trace their profession back to the eighth-century CE Buddhist religious giant Guru Rinpoche. It is said that Guru Rinpoche initiated four men from the four corners of Tibet as the first shamans. These four men are credited with establishing hereditary lineages of shamans known as the Zurshi Lhapa, which are still active today.

According to the alternative view of Tibetan history disseminated by Eternal Bon, spirit-mediumship began long before Guru Rinpoche. Eternal Bon maintains that spirit-mediums were first introduced to Tibet by its legendary founder Tönpa Shenrab. The channeling of the gods is part of an oracular tradition found in the first vehicle of Eternal Bon teachings as one of four methods of divination. According to Eternal Bon texts such as *Zijid*, it was the *dralha*, or warrior spirits, that spoke through the ancient mediums of Tibet. The *dralha* still occupy a crucial place in the pantheon drawn on by the spirit-mediums, indicating that their vocation does indeed stem in part from archaic religious traditions. The indigenous character of Upper Tibetan spirit-mediumship is also reflected in deities that dwell in localized topographical features and in zoomorphic form. The ritual tools and sacred substances used by shamans are largely based on local natural resources as well.

The earliest historical references to the gods revealing themselves through the mouth of shamans seem to be found in early historic period manuscripts. The French Tibetologist Ariane Macdonald observed that in one Dunhuang divination manuscript, there may be mention of female mediums who could predict the future and prescribe funerary rites for the deceased.[23] The Dunhuang text Pt 126 records a conversation between lordly figures belonging to the Mu and Cha, two important proto-tribes of Tibet.[24] In this text the lord of the Cha requests the directives of the Mu deity, but it is not certain if this is an allusion to an oracular event or a kingly decree. The Cha lord says, "I the humble one have seen the face of the god. I am obeying the divine directives. Please confer upon me the commands." If indeed this encounter between the Cha and Mu is based on divine prophecy, it alludes to the existence of a well-established tradition of spirit-mediumship in the early historic period.

The *melong*, or circular metal mirror, is one of the most important ritual implements of the Upper Tibetan shamans. The *melong* functions as the temporary residence of possessing deities and their retinue of remedial spirits, and as a sanctuary for a spirit-medium's consciousness during the trance. An Eternal Bon text attributed to unnamed Zhang Zhung masters says that the chief goddess Queen of Existence holds a *melong* that brightly reflects all things.[25] Ancient copper alloy mirrors kept as heirlooms or discovered by Tibetan shamans in the countryside demonstrate that this ritual implement has a long history. Some Tibetan mirrors are close in design to those recovered from Scythian archaeological sites of north Inner Asia, which date to the first millennium BCE.[26]

Another important ritual tool of Upper Tibetan shamanism is the flat-bell, or *shang*. As we saw in chapter 8, the *shang* is the prototypic instrument of archaic deities and adepts.[27] It is used in the worship of mountain gods and other indigenous spirits. According to an Eternal Bon origin myth, in ancient times the goddess Queen of Existence and other deities rang the shining, divinely empowered *shang* to suppress the enemies of religion. It is also written that the prehistoric master Tönpa Shenrab rang the great *shang* to defeat demons and heretics. Moreover, the sound of the flat-bell is supposed to avert illness, injury, mishaps, and pestilence. The magical power of the *shang* is vouchsafed by the shamans of Upper Tibet, who hold it in great reverence, despite mostly being Buddhist practitioners.

Next to the mirror and flat-bell, the drum is the most important tool in the ritual armory of highland shamans. As do other Tibetan ritualists, shamans use different types of drums, including large ones struck with an S-shaped drumstick and hourglass-shaped hand drums. Like the *shang*, the sound of the drum is thought to seat the trance venue under good auspices, attract deities, and defeat demons. The origins of the drum are related in several Eternal Bon etiologic tales.[28] It is written that in early times, *bonpo* priests discovered the juniper tree with which to construct the first drum on the world mountain. One side of this primal drum was covered by the skin of a black buck, and the other side by the skin of a horned eagle. In another origin myth, a *shen* priest of primordial times called Takla Mebar is credited with building five drums, corresponding to the four cardinal directions and the center. These drums were fashioned from different types of wood and stretched with the hides of an elephant, horse, dragon, demon, and white lioness.

Other ritual tools used by the shamans of Upper Tibet include swords, spears, daggers, tridents, conch shells, and magic missiles. Eternal Bon texts indicate that all of these objects have an ancient pedigree, often attributing them to Zhang Zhung masters of yore. As for the burning of incense and lustration with water, a Gekhö ritual text avers that the raw materials for these rituals were prepared by the people of Zhang Zhung and offered to their king, the holder of the iron horns of the bird.[29]

The tradition of spirit-mediumship in Upper Tibet shares much in common with shamanism in north Inner Asia and Siberia. Similarities between Tibetan and other Asian shamans were first studied by the Tibetologists Réne de Nebesky-Wojkowitz and Helmut Hoffman.[30] Although there are many parallels between the deities, costumes, ritual paraphernalia, and philosophy of the various shamans, the historical and ethnological factors that gave rise to these are highly obscure.[31] While it may be that some of the common rudiments of spirit-mediumship in the heart of Asia can be traced to Metal Age religious practices, there is a dearth of direct evidence to show so. As we have seen, cognate ancient monuments, rock art, and artifacts of Tibet, Mongolia, and the Altai hint at a high degree of cultural interaction between these regions beginning no later than the first millennium BCE. However, these archaeological parallels do not in themselves confirm that the shamans of middle Asia are successors to a common Bronze Age or Iron Age cultural patrimony, a legacy that continued to inform the development of shamanism in later times. Far more research and exploration is required before Inner Asian ethnohistory is known well enough to address such big questions.

Among various tribal groups of Mongolia and southern Siberia, the mirror is employed in a fashion similar to Upper Tibet. Another important ritual implement the shamans of Upper Tibet and north Inner Asia have in common is the draped arrow. This symbol of men and their personal gods is employed to attract good fortune and to expel demons. Likewise, the shamans of Upper Tibet, Central Asia, and Siberia have drums, which are often covered in the hides of wild ungulates. The mythic motif of shamans flying in the sky on drums is found in steppe and arctic mythology, and as we have seen, this same theme is connected to ancient priests in Eternal Bon texts. Other material analogies between the shamans of Upper Tibet and north Inner Asia involve the use of raptor feathers in headdresses, healing rituals, and the burning of juniper incense.

Upper Tibetans and their northern counterparts such as the Tuvans and Yakuts commonly divide their universe into three vertical spheres. Another striking similarity between the shamans of the Tibetan Plateau and boreal forests is the use of a sucking technique to remove impurities believed to cause disease from the bodies of patients. Moreover, the vocation of shamans in Mongolia and Siberia is often hereditary, as it is in Upper Tibet. Spirit-mediums in diverse corners of Inner Asia are possessed by mountain gods and have zoomorphic helping spirits. For example, Tuvan shamans imitate the voices of a variety of animals, including bears, wolves, and eagles, just as do their opposite number in Upper Tibet. The Evenk shamans have deputy spirits in the shape of bears and eagles, and Dolgan shamans have fox and wolf helpmates. These same animal helpers are personified by Upper Tibetan shamans.

Ancient rituals based on the cult of the *dralha*, or warrior spirits, are maintained by Phowo Sridgyal, one of Upper Tibet's greatest contemporary spirit-mediums.[32] Born in 1927, Phowo Sridgyal's chief possessing mountain gods are the white men and white horses of Mount Nyenchen Thanglha, the "Variegated Wild Ass," and Tsengö Namra. These three mountain gods are the field commanders of the trance, organizing and dispatching the hosts of spirits under them.

Phowo Sridgyal reports going into trance dozens of times in a year. Sometimes patients come to his house or summer camp in large groups. He has no fee schedule and treats the indigent free of charge. I had the opportunity to observe Phowo Sridgyal in trance on several occasions in the mid-2000s. In one performance, the possessing deity was Variegated Wild Ass, a fiery red god of the *tsen* class who resides on a hill in the middle of a gigantic plain. The many preliminary prayers invoked a wide range of Buddhist protectors and indigenous deities and were accompanied by offerings of incense and water. As the gods of the trance were poised to invade Phowo Sridgyal's mind, his speech became agitated and his movements erratic. Finally, with the full force of the gods bearing down on him, he sprung to his feet and danced about wildly. After several moments, Phowo Sridgyal dropped back down to his knees and announced the momentous change in his identity. He had become Variegated Wild Ass, the rider of the wild ass, a fierce red divinity:

> Hey, listen to me!
> If you do not recognize me the Tsen like this,
> Yeah, the country residence of Handsome Body,
> Yeah, the country in which I Handsome Tsen reside,
> Yeah, it is in the upper plain of Baga Thuk in the east.

After Variegated Wild Ass made his presence known, he got down to the order of the day: the healing and guidance of the people eagerly gathered around. The embodied god called upon his army of *dralha* to aid and protect those in attendance. Phowo Sridgyal's warrior spirits are in zoomorphic form, and he invoked them with a lyrical voice, the voice, it is believed, of Variegated Wild Ass god himself. Phowo Sridgyal, a Buddhist, has unwittingly preserved the archaic warrior spirit cult through an oral tradition bequeathed over the generations. While ordinary humans need to make physical offerings, the more lavish the better, to the *dralha*, Variegated Wild Ass is able to fulfill their wishes with just one sacred word: *so*.

> There are the young men [*dralha*], so, so, so!
> The mother and father territorial protectors of the *dralha*,
> The support of the good men, the males,
> Eliminate the sudden-onset misfortunes and obstacles of life.
> You defeat the diseases of the demonic spirits.
> You defeat the diseases and demonic influences of the sudden-onset obstructions.
> Be the support of the men with the one span [long] body.
> *So! So!* The sparkling snow mountain of sunrise,
> The *dralha* who is like the white lioness;
> I praise you white lioness with the turquoise mane.
> Realize their wishes whatever place they go.
> *So* to you, be the good guide whatever country they stay in.
> Yeah, I praise the protector who looks like the white vulture in the good white vulture nest on the high red rock,
> Your downy lammergeyer wings *di ri ri* [conveys a loud swooshing sound].
> *So* to you, flying flocks of birds *khro lo lo* [conveys a raucous chattering].
> *So* to you, be the *dralha* of males whatever place they go.
> *So* to you, the tiger in Nepal in the sparkling forest.
> *So* to you, the body god who is like the good red tiger.
> *So* to you, good red tiger with the six converging whorls.
> You must be the good guide whatever place they go.
> Be the protector of the good man, the one span [long] body.

Invocations to the *dralha* not unlike those uttered by Phowo Sridgyal can be found in Eternal Bon documents. An old text collected by the Eternal Bon master Brutön Gyalwa (born 1242 CE), entitled *Whirling Auspiciousness Summoning the Yang*, has verses beckoning the zoomorphic *dralha* to usher in the good fortune basis (*cha*) and good fortune capability (*yang*).[33] The temper of these verses and the divine animals they conjure echo the words of Phowo Sridgyal:

> Hey! The renowned female white conch horned eagle is on top of the wish-fulfilling tree. We take for our *cha* and *yang*, the fame *yang* of the female white conch horned eagle. The renowned blue turquoise dragon is among both the winds and clouds. We take for our *cha* and *yang*, the fame *yang* of the turquoise blue dragon. The renowned white conch lion is deep within Mount Tise. We take for our *cha* and *yang*, the fame *yang* of the white conch

lion. The renowned big striped tiger is deep within sandalwood forests. We take for our *cha* and *yang*, the fame *yang* of the big striped tiger. The renowned lammergeyer is deep within the white rock formation. We take for our *cha* and *yang*, the fame *yang* of the lammergeyer.

In the trance ceremony, Phowo Sridgyal as Variegated Wild Ass called upon many other *dralha* to assist his patients. Completing the vital work at hand, this *tsen* god commenced to make various prophecies. Fortunately for those participating in the proceedings, the deity pronounced their fate as being generally positive, so long as they remember their religious observances. The last part of Phowo Sridgyal's trance ceremony entailed the return of Variegated Wild Ass and his circle of divine helpers to their respective abodes. As in other sequences of the ceremony, the language used to signal this retreat is highly imaginative. Like any good *drokpa*, Variegated Wild Ass takes his leave on horseback:

> I Variegated Wild Ass of the world horseman,
> I Variegated Wild Ass of the east will return to my country.
> At the place of the four-petaled lotus,
> The puffed out chest of the swift moving horse.
> I go with the thunderous sound of the white-tailed horse,
> I go with the horned-eagle finial of the conch head helmet.

Another well-known shaman of the eastern Changthang is Karma Rigdzin, whom I have observed in trance a number of times.[34] Born in 1935, Karma Rigdzin is an individual of considerable personal integrity and moral authority. He has worked untiringly for his community of shepherds for many years now. His father and paternal ancestors were part of the northern lineage of the illustrious Zurshi Lhapa, the original lines of Buddhist spirit-mediums in Tibet. According to Karma Rigdzin, the Zurshi Lhapa used to accomplish great feats of magic such as riding vultures and eagles, but gradually their power diminished due to increasing spiritual contamination.

In a trance ceremony where Karma Rigdzin is purported to have become the god Dudtsen Marpo, he instructed those in attendance in the mysteries of the divine. Dudtsen Marpo is the benefactor and guardian of the Taklungpa, a subsect of Tibetan Buddhism. Many dozens of deities were invoked before and after this wrathful god took hold of Karma Rigdzin. While in trance, Karma Rigdzin recounted the divine abodes and lineages of the divinities in colorful detail. In the final portion of this spectacle of divine intoxication, Karma Rigdzin as Dudtsen Marpo imparted moral instructions on the cluster of people gathered around him:

If I was to explain clearly to you: all of you need to display virtuous behavior. Do not differentiate between those who have wealth and those who do not. Have a good heart. Do not differentiate between those of high status and those of low status. Have a virtuous heart. Have a good heart. Ah, there is no distinction between those who have false religion and those who have no religion. If from your mouth you explain religion in a false fashion, if you take whatever you can get from the hands of others, if you are [black] like charcoal, what religious activities you do are a sin. If your inside is white like this, show the way to those who do not know the path. Give whoever needs a respite, a respite. Give respect to those who are respectable. Be very good to your parents. Have a good heart for all human beings. Teach a person who does not know something valuable. Reveal that which they do not know. If you show kind regard to people that all is religion. Those all are virtues.

The exploits of Upper Tibet's shamans are many and varied. For untold centuries they have been flying on the backs of raptors and riding astride carnivores, at least in their own minds. At the confluence of the archaic and Lamaist cultural streams, these spirit-mediums are the most conspicuous example of the composite nature of religion in Upper Tibet. The aspiration to improve the well-being of communities is at the heart of spirit-mediumship in upland Tibet, however one may view the reality of the mythic. The shamans seeing the world in a wider or divine light have helped their fellow inhabitants survive in one of the most difficult lands on earth.

Conclusion

$\mathcal{W}$e have explored the uppermost reaches of Tibet from the distant past to the present day through its archaeology, literature, and people. The main focus of this book has been ancient civilization and its lasting imprint on the people of Upper Tibet. These shepherds' and farmers' view of past signposts is articulated in their customs and traditions. Of all the old legacies in upland Tibet, that which looms largest is Zhang Zhung, a traditional name for the dominant prehistoric culture, people, and polity of the region.

As this work has shown, the distribution of the all-stone corbelled residences, special types of funerary pillars, and rock art delineate the geographic extent of Zhang Zhung. Its uniform monumental and artistic composition was the product of a large and well-integrated cultural formation. The Metal Age civilization that took root in Upper Tibet continued to define Zhang Zhung and its cultural subsidiary Sumpa until the rise of the Tibetan empire in the seventh century CE.

In the steppes of Inner Asia, tribal unions also spread over wide areas in the first millennium BCE and early first millennium CE. For example, the Scythians and Huns expanded their reach to encompass large portions of the Eurasian landmass. The shared cultural links between Upper Tibet and north Inner Asia explored in this work seem to have been reinforced by the migrations and mixing of tribes in antiquity. That such interactions took place is indicated in recent studies of the genetic makeup of Tibetans, who while being predominantly related to speakers of Tibeto-Burman languages also carry central and north Asian genes. The hunting and stock-rearing traditions prevailing in the steppes and on the Plateau probably facilitated cultural transmissions as well. In the Late Bronze Age and Iron Age, it appears that religious ideas circulated widely throughout Inner Asia, carried along by the spread of new technologies such as metallurgy and the equestrian arts.

Most archaic era residential facilities in Upper Tibet were built on unassailable high ground, on inaccessible islands, or in hidden spots. This insularity indicates that defense was a preoccupation of the population. Eternal Bon historical sources speak of the martial character of Zhang Zhung society and its political nexus of kings and priests. The archaic priests are frequently depicted in this literature as possessing arms and being involved in bellicose displays of power and magic.

It is clear from the large number of citadels in western Tibet and Lake Dangra that armed struggle was a defining feature of agricultural enclaves in Zhang Zhung. It would appear that military incursions into these communities came from sources both inside and outside Upper Tibet. With the climatic degradation of the Late Bronze Age and Iron Age, Inner Asian populations became restive and large-scale conflict commonplace. Tibetan literary accounts describe the invasion of prehistoric Upper Tibet by aggressors from the north and west, and we may take this as allegorical evidence of interregional clashes.

Despite being subject to foreign threats, Zhang Zhung culture was long-lasting and relatively stable in nature. This is mirrored in its coherent monumental assemblage, rock art, systems of economic production, and its unique ecological and geographical situation. The long-term continuity of Zhang Zhung is also supported by the absence of evidence for catastrophic foreign invasions such as inscriptions in alien languages or aberrant monumental and aesthetic forms. The geographic isolation of Upper Tibet and its extreme elevation must have also conspired to conserve old ideologies and practices. Such a difficult environment would not be the first choice of most invaders seeking new territory.

The Changthang lakes belt makes up a large portion of Upper Tibet. In the time of Zhang Zhung and Sumpa, these lakes contained fresher water and were subject to a generally milder climate, making them more conducive to human habitation than they are today. Given that the rest of the Changthang is drier and higher, these bodies of water were an ideal place to preserve and propagate ancient culture. The rivers and streams feeding the lake basins constitute great reservoirs of freshwater, and pasturelands abound along these waterways. As we have learned, the rugged shorelines of the southern belt of great lakes were a magnet for the construction of archaic era fortresses, hermitages, and temples. These lakes formed an eight-hundred-mile-long east–west axis of elite settlement. For the establishment of these privileged facilities, builders favored easy-to-defend headlands, cliffs, and islands with a southern exposure. Along with the meridian ranges and the lower-elevation valleys of far western Tibet, these lakeshore sites were the prime incubators of archaic culture in Upper Tibet.

The all-stone corbelled residences with their hives of small cells demonstrate that secluded, high-altitude locations were a fundamental part of religious life in the ancient Tibetan upland. The construction of large and extremely durable citadels and burial grounds in Upper Tibet points to a people in possession of considerable technological expertise. The great variety of necropolises in the region indicates that intricate beliefs were attached to death and the afterlife.

A high level of cultural sophistication is also evidenced in the fine-quality copper alloy and iron objects attributed to archaic era Upper Tibet. The Tibetan textual patrimony that has come down to us since the early historic period describes this material culture with great flourish. Eternal Bon scriptures proclaim that the priests and rulers of Zhang Zhung were attired in sumptuous fur robes, and that they wore turquoise, patterned agates, and meteoric iron talismans, as well as brandishing many kinds of weapons. These literary accounts also hold that the ancient priesthood was very adept in the practice of astrology, divination, magic, and medicine.

The great cultural achievements of the Tibetan highlanders over the last thousand years stem from the encounter between the archaic and Lamaist civilizations. While Lamaism drew its inspiration from India, the core of the Upper Tibetan identity, its native customs, traditions, and ethos, were derived from Zhang Zhung and Sumpa. This fundamental cultural bequest still colors the lives of today's residents. Interpenetrated by Buddhist thought and practice, the archaic has evolved as a living testament, the birthright of a people who have occupied their homeland for millennia.

From prehistoric cultural origins and the historic florescence of Buddhism to the secular regime of the present day, time moves toward an uncertain future in Upper Tibet. In this period of environmental change on a scale not seen for millennia the farmers and shepherds of the highlands confront challenges of epic proportions. Reassuringly, the tools needed to meet these trials lie in their culture and religion and in science and technology. To bring the traditional to bear upon the modern is the order of the day.

Even if the promise of the present is not realized and the modern gives way to something else, the cries of livestock in the grasslands and the whir of the plow cutting through the earth will continue to ring out in Upper Tibet. Zhang Zhung has long since past, but what has been wrought from it illuminates the path ahead.

Notes

CHAPTER 1: DISCOVERING THE FIRST CIVILIZATION OF TIBET

1. For Tucci's highly informed explorations, see, for example, Tucci 1950; Tucci and Ghersi 1934. Hedin's field research and publications were epic in scope, among which is Hedin 1909; 1913; 1916–1922. For Richardson's extensive collected works, see Richardson 1998.

2. See Roerich 1996.

3. For their reviews of archaeological work conducted in Tibet, see Aldenderfer and Zhang Yinong 2004; Chayet 1994.

4. See Aldenderfer and Zhang Yinong 2004; Gelek 1993.

5. For a state-of-the-art study, see Brantingham et al. 2013.

6. For a review of the work conducted by Chinese archaeologists at Chogong and other Neolithic sites in Tibet, see Chayet 1994, pp. 36–55; Aldenderfer and Zhang Yinong 2004; Aldenderfer 2007.

7. Reportedly, Sonam Wangdu has written and edited five books on Tibetan archaeology and antiquities, all of which are in the Chinese language. These include a monograph on the Kharo site. For more information on his work, see Stoddard 1994, p. 138.

8. See Huo Wei 2001a; 2001b.

9. For his findings, see Aldenderfer 2011; 2003; Aldenderfer and Moyes 2004.

10. For a description of this archaeological exploration, see Li Yongxian 2011. Also see Wangdu 2005.

11. For a description and analysis of these recent discoveries encompassing a wide spectrum of artifacts made from a variety of metals (iron, copper, bronze, silver, and gold), wood, and stone (common and precious), as well as silk and wool textiles and ceramic vessels, see Bellezza 2012a; 2010b; Tong Tao 2011.

12. See Chan 1994; McCue 2003; Schaller 1997. Rowe does not appear to have published anything of significance concerning his explorations in Tibet.

13. For his fascinating explorations and scientific research in the region, see Prana-vananda 1949.

14. For his account, see Singh 1915.

15. See Bellezza 1993.

16. Dhondrup Lhagyal 2003.

17. As noted in the introduction, the term "Lamaism" is used in this book to de-scribe the two prevailing religions of the Tibetans and related peoples: Eternal Bon and Vajrayana Buddhism. The strong interplay between these two faiths demands a single term to describe them in tandem. In this work, "Lamaism" is applied exclu-sively as a designator of the Tibetan faith of the last millennium and must be read as possessing no connotations, be they negative or positive.

CHAPTER 2: THE GREAT SKY REALM

1. For a colorful study of the land and people of the Changthang, see Ma Lihua 1991.

2. See website and reports of the Intergovernmental Panel on Climate Change, http://www.ipcc.ch, especially "Working Group I Contribution to the IPCC Fifth As-sessment Report Climate Change 2013: The Physical Science Basis," 9.4.1.1, 4.3.3.3, http://www.climatechange2013.org/images/uploads/WGIAR5_WGI-12Doc2b_FinalDraft_All.pdf; and "Climate Change 2007: Working Group II: Impacts, Adapta-tion and Vulnerability, 10.6.2 The Himalayan Glaciers," http://www.ipcc.ch/publica tions_and_data/ar4/wg2/en/ch10s10-6-2.html. Also see Hansen 2009.

3. Cultural and religious aspects of Nam Tsho are covered in detail in Bellezza 1997a; 2005.

4. Bellezza 2005, p. 233.

5. For the cultural history and religious complexion of Dangra Yumtsho and her sisterhood of lakes and mountain mate, see Bellezza 1997a; 2005.

6. The ancient insular settlements of Teri Nam Tsho are explored in Bellezza 2001, pp. 223–46.

7. For an archaeological survey of Darok Tsho, see Bellezza 1999a.

8. For the lore of Drablai Gyalmo, see Bellezza 2008, pp. 325–29.

9. This great pilgrimage center is fluently described in Johnson and Moran 1989; Snelling 1991.

10. The archaeological sites of Mount Tise are studied in Bellezza 2002a, pp. 44, 53, 54, 62–75; in press-a.

11. For an engaging account of this legendary encounter, see Garma 1962, pp. 219–20.

12. For general studies on Tibetan wild mammals, see Schaller 1997; Environ-ment and Development Desk 2005.

CHAPTER 3: TILLERS AND HERDERS, WARRIORS AND SAINTS

1. The earliest agricultural site thus far discovered in Tibet is the fully developed Neolithic site of Kharo (3900–2100 BCE), located near Chamdo. Millet was cultivated at Kharo. The origins of Tibetan pastoralism based on keeping domesticated sheep are still unknown. Comparative archaeological evidence suggests a Neolithic time frame. See Rhode et al. 2007b, p. 609. The bones of what are believed to have been domesticated sheep and possibly domesticated yaks dating to circa 1700 to 1100 BCE were discovered at the Chogong site near Lhasa. Based primarily on genetic data, it is thought that yaks were first domesticated somewhere in northern Tibet. In Dulan County, in the northeastern portion of the Tibetan Plateau, a pen containing sheep-goat dung was discovered, suggesting that these animals were of the domestic variety. These remains date to circa 1000 BCE. See Flad et al. 2007, pp. 190–91, 193.

2. For in-depth studies of the *drokpas*, see Norbu 1997; Topgyal and Topgyal 1998; Goldstein and Beall 1990; Ekvall 1968.

3. For studies and photos of these objects, see Tucci 1973; Bellezza 1994; 1998; John 2006; Lin 2003.

4. *Zi* stones are the object of study in Ebbinghouse and Winsten 1988; Lin 2001.

5. The cosmology of the Tibetan tent and its cross-cultural characteristics are touched upon in Haarh 1969, p. 141.

6. Rhode et al. 2007a, pp. 207, 208; Xuebin et al. 2008.

7. For other accounts of Tibetan marriages, see Norbu 1997, pp. 62–66; Karmay 1998, pp. 147–53, 318; Topgyal and Topgyal 1998, pp. 46–47.

8. For general studies of Tibetan funerary practices, see, for example, Gouin 2010; Malville 2005.

9. Goldstein and Beall 2002; 1990; Miller 2008; and Miller's oral presentation given at "Meltdown: The Impact of Climate Change on the Tibetan Plateau," conference of the Asia Society, New York, January 16, 2009.

10. Klein et al. 2007; Harris 2010.

11. Oral presentation given at "Meltdown: The Impact of Climate Change on the Tibetan Plateau," conference of the Asia Society, New York, January 16, 2009 (his publications are pending after the recent completion of his PhD at the University of Colorado).

12. See website and reports of the Intergovernmental Panel on Climate Change: http://www.ipcc.ch.

13. Thompson, oral presentation given at "Meltdown: The Impact of Climate Change on the Tibetan Plateau," conference of the Asia Society, New York, January 16, 2009. Thompson was the field leader of a twenty-five-member team to collect ice cores on Nemo Na Nyi between September 9 and November 1, 2006. For his findings, see Kehrwald et al. 2008.

CHAPTER 4: FROM SKY TO EARTH

1. For a discussion of the signification of the ancient toponyms of Upper Tibet, see Bellezza 2013b.
2. For a cultural-historical overview of the clan makeup of Tibet including Zhang Zhung, see Vitali 2003.
3. See Bellezza 2013a, pp. 149 (n. 232), 169; Stein 2010 (Antiqua III), pp. 147–48, 152–54.
4. For a discussion of the localization and nature of Olmolungring, see Martin 1995; Karmay 1998, pp. 104–8.
5. Karmay 1998, p. 107.
6. Martin 1995.
7. Karmay 1972, pp. 6–8. Text: *Legs bshad mdzod*, by Grub-dbang bkra-shis rgyal-mtshan (1859–1935). Transliteration of text published in ibid.
8. Ibid., p. 7.
9. Bellezza 2001, p. 66; 2008, pp. 224–29. Text: *g.Yung drung bon gyi rgyud 'bum* (*Sources for a History of Bon: A Collection of Rare Manuscripts from Bsam-gling Monastery in Dolpo (Northwestern Tibet)*), nos. 1–46, published by Tibetan Bonpo Monastic Centre: Dolanji, 1972.
10. Bellezza 2005, pp. 283–86. Text: *Dra ba nag po lda zor bsgrub thabs ma bu tshang ba*, attributed to Hris-pa gyer-med, in *Dra ba dmar nag gi rgyud* volume, nos. 381–404, Tibetan Bonpo Monastic Centre: Dolanji, 1972.
11. Bellezza 2008, pp. 349–52. Text: *Rlangs kyi po ti bse ru rgyas pa* (fourteenth century CE), in *Gangs can rig mdzod*, vol. 1, Bod-ljongs mi-dmangs dpe-skrun khang: Lhasa, 1986.
12. Bellezza 2008, p. 524. Text: Pt 1060.
13. Bellezza 2008, p. 325. Text: *Me ri dpa' bo gyad phur gyi bskang ba*, in *Zhang zhung me ri bka' mi'i sgrub skor gyi gsung pod*, nos. 543–64, published by rMa-rtsa rin-chen rgyal-mtshan: Delhi, 2000.
14. Bellezza 2002a, pp. 23–24. Text: *Drang don sgron ma mun sel las gtam rgyud brda yi gzer bu*, in *Drang don mun sel sgron ma*, attributed to Dran-pa nam-mkha' (eighth century CE), published by Lo-ru bSod-nams 'gyur-med: Chab-mdo, 1988.
15. For a more detailed treatment of the Mon in the oral tradition, see Bellezza 2008, pp. 21–22.
16. Ibid., p. 116 (fn. 120). Text: *rGya bod kyi chos 'byung rgyas pa*, by mKhas-pa lde'u (late thirteenth century CE), *Gangs can rig mdzod*, vol. 3 (ed. Chab-spel tshe-brtan phun-tshogs), published by Bod-ljongs mi-dmangs dpe-skrun khang: Lhasa, 1987.
17. See Vitali 1996, p. 200 (fn. 287).
18. These texts are presented in Takeuchi and Nishida 2009.
19. This thesis is developed at length in Hummel 2000.
20. Ibid., pp. 8–11.
21. Driem 2001; Nishi and Nagano 2001; Takeuchi et al. 2001.
22. Hoffman 1990, pp. 374–75; Haarh 1968.

23. Driem 2001, p. 39.

24. Ibid.

25. Jacques 2009.

26. Ibid.

27. Bellezza 2008, pp. 261–62. Text: *dBu nag mi'u 'dra chags* [Appearance of the Little Black-Headed People] in *The Call of the Blue Cuckoo: An Anthology of Nine Bonpo Texts on Myths and Rituals* (eds. S. G. Karmay and Y. Nagano), Senri Ethnological Reports 32, Osaka National Museum of Ethnology, 2002, 35 folios.

28. Bellezza 2008, pp. 288–89; Karmay 1972, pp. 11–13. Texts: *Khyung rabs.*

29. Bellezza 2005, p. 204. Text: *Pha rabs mthong ba kun gsal.* On the connection of the Mra to Zhang Zhung, see Stein 1959, pp. 51–52, 54; Bellezza 2010a.

30. Ibid., pp. 201, 204.

31. Bellezza 2008, pp. 525–29.

32. Vitali 1996, p. 199 (fn. 285) (after Demiéville 1952).

33. Vitali 1996, passim.

34. For a résumé of ancient clans from the oral tradition of Upper Tibet, see Bellezza 2008, pp. 263–69.

35. Bellezza 2005, pp. 202, 205.

36. Ibid., p. 406 (fn. 222).

37. *Gu rib pha rabs kyi byung khungs mdor bsdus bzhugs so*, anonymous, 12 folios. I have prepared a translation of the first seven folios of this text, which pertain to the history of the Gurib clan in the archaic era.

38. *g.Yung drung bon gyi bstan pa'i byung khungs nyung bsdus zhes bya ba bzhugs so*, by sLob-dpon bsTan-'dzin rnam-dag, in New Collection of Bon *bka'-brten*, vol. 270, nos. 553–670, published by dKar-ru bstan-pa'i nyi-ma: Lhasa, 1998. For a translation of the materials in this text, infra, see Bellezza 2011a, pp. 60–72. Also of great importance to the cultural historical study of Zhang Zhung is Lopön Tenzin Namdak's 1997 work, *sNga rabs bod kyi byung ba brjod pa'i 'bel gtam lung gi snying po*, Delhi: Paljor Publications.

39. Norbu 1995, pp. 156–58.

40. For a systematic analysis of correlations between the textual and archaeological records, see Bellezza 2011a.

41. Ibid. Text: *g.Yung drung bon gyi bstan pa'i byung khungs*, by sLob-dpon bsTan-'dzin rnam-dag.

42. Ibid. Text: *Me ri gsang ba 'khor lo.*

43. Bellezza 2002a, p. 63. Text: *Khri rje lung bstan gyi mdo*, in Bon *bka'*, vol. 41, Sichuan edition (Si-khron Hru'u phang dpar-khang), published by Kun-grol lha-sras mi-pham rnam-rgyal, 1996.

44. The extensive references to this text in this work are derived from Bellezza 2002a, pp. 56–60; 2011a, pp. 81–89. More recently, these same textual materials have been studied by Roberto Vitali 2008. See also Norbu and Pratts 1989.

45. Yamaguchi 1977. Ancient Chinese sources also state that Zhang Zhung had eighty thousand to ninety thousand warriors, a formidable army. See Bushell 1880, p. 527 (fn. 9).

46. Bellezza 2008, p. 271. Text: *Chos 'byung mkhas pa'i dga' ston*, by dPa'-bo gtsug-lag phreng-ba (1504–1566), Mi-rigs dpe-skrun khang: Beijing, 1985.

47. Norbu 2009, pp. 131–32. In this work, Namkhai Norbu sets forth an impressive traditional historical perspective on Zhang Zhung.

48. See Bellezza 2011a, p. 67. Text: *g.Yung drung bon gyi bstan pa'i byung khungs*.

49. Bellezza 2002a, pp. 64–65.

50. This site (B-115) is surveyed in Bellezza in press-a.

51. Ibid., sites B-132, B-133.

52. Ibid., sites A-82, B-78.

53. In personal communication. This site is examined in ibid., A-52.

54. Bellezza 2002a, p. 63. Text: *Bod yul gnas kyi lam yig gsal ba'i dmig bu zhes bya ba bzhugs*, published by Bod kyi bon-dgon do-lan-ji: Dolanji, 1983.

55. This site and adjacent areas are discussed in ibid., pp. 62–75.

56. For a discussion of this important site, see Bellezza 2011a, p. 72–75; 2002a, pp. 37–43.

57. For references to this text, see Bellezza 2002a, pp. 21, 22, 39, 40; Ramble 1995. Text: *Kun 'bum khro bo bzhugs pa'i dbu phyogs legs so*, in Bon *bka'*, vol. 167, Sichuan edition.

58. Bellezza 2002a, pp. 37–38.

59. The localization of this castle according to these authors is discussed in ibid., p. 38; Bellezza 2011a, p. 72.

60. Ibid. p. 75–76, 82.

61. Bellezza in press-a, site B-98.

62. Ibid., site A-50.

63. Ibid., site A-51.

64. Ibid., sites B-128, B-129, B-130; Bellezza 1999a.

65. Bellezza 1997a, pp. 398, 399.

66. Bellezza 2002a, p. 17 (fn. 2).

67. For surveys of these sites, see Bellezza 1997a; 2001; 2002a; 2011a.

68. See Bellezza 2011a, p. 68.

69. Surveyed in Bellezza in press-a, site A-80.

70. Surveyed in ibid., site A-134.

71. These sites are examined in ibid., A-54, A-101.

72. See Francke 1914; 1926.

73. See Howard 1995.

74. Personal communication. This exploration was carried out as part of Devers's PhD dissertation, at the École Pratique des Hautes Études, Paris. On the corbelled fortresses of Ladakh, also see Bellezza 2012b; 2013b; Vernier 2012.

75. Bellezza 2001, pp. 102–4.

76. For a more detailed lore, see Bellezza 2001, p. 102–3; in press-a, site A-93.

77. Bellezza 2011a, p. 71.

78. Beckwith 1987, p. 14.

79. Hoffman 1973, pp. 39–40.

80. Bellezza 2001, p. 65; 2008, p. 228.

81. Uray 1972b, p. 40; Richardson 1977, p. 13; Dotson 2009, p. 17.

82. Uray 1972b, p. 40; Richardson 1977, p. 13. Also see Bacot et al. 1940–1946.

83. Richardson 1998, p. 133.

84. Uray 1968, p. 296; Uray 1972b, pp. 36, 37, 40, 41; Richardson 1998, p. 54; Dotson 2009, p. 82.

85. Bellezza 2008, p. 523.

86. Uray 1972b, pp. 41–42.

87. Treatment of Semarkar's songs is based on Uray 1972a.

88. Petech 1977, p. 9.

89. This account of King Songtsen Gampo's reaction to Semarkar's songs is taken from Norbu 1995, p. 32.

90. Uray 1972b, pp. 36, 37, 40, 41; Richardson 1998, p. 54; Dotson 2009, pp. 84–85.

91. Uray 1972b, pp. 41–42, 44.

92. Dotson 2009, pp. 38, 50.

93. Ibid., pp. 39, 41.

94. Uray 1968, p. 293; Dotson 2009, pp. 84–85.

95. Dotson 2009, p. 87.

96. Ibid., p. 91.

97. Richardson 1998, p. 16.

98. Beckwith 1987, p. 43; Dotson 2009, p. 92.

99. Petech 1977, p. 8; Dotson 2009, p. 111.

100. Petech 1977, p. 8; Dotson 2009, p. 114.

101. Uray 1972b, p. 33.

102. Hazod 2009, pp. 167, 195.

103. For this translation of Lopön Tenzin Namdak's account, see Bellezza 2011a, p. 71.

104. The following account of King Likmikya/Likmigyal is based upon translations in Norbu 1995, pp. 32–33, 214–16; Reynolds 2005, pp. 96–103. See also Bellezza 1999a, pp. 80–81.

105. Thompson et al. 2006.

CHAPTER 5: TOUCHING THE SKY

1. For these surveys of archaeological monuments, see Bellezza in press-a; in press-b; 2008; 2003; 2002a; 2001; 2000a; 1999a; 1997a.

2. For a global but incomplete view of western Tibetan archaeological sites, see Huo Wei 2005.

3. How long human beings have lived on the Tibetan Plateau is a matter of debate among specialists. Colonization of the Plateau may have occurred as far back as thirty thousand years ago. For a review of archaeological and genetic studies pertaining to the arrival of *Homo sapiens* in Tibet, see Bellezza 2013c.

4. The account in this work on the origins of civilization in Upper Tibet, including cross-cultural comparative elements, is adapted from Bellezza 2008, pp. 92–94, 102–4, 196–99, 545–57, 572, 573, etc.; 2002a, pp. 131, 135 (fn. 29), etc.

5. See Bellezza 2002a, p. 135 (after Sharif and Thapar 1992).

6. Bellezza in press-b, site C-160; 2008, p. 91.

7. For corbelling in world architecture, see Juvanec 2000.

8. For their findings, see Aldenderfer 2003; Aldenderfer and Moyes 2004; Huo Wei 2001a.

9. See Bellezza 2008, pp. 108–10; 2001, pp. 237–43.

10. Gekhö Kharlung is examined in Bellezza 2008, pp. 36, 37, 143 (fn. 152); Bellezza in press-a, site A-89.

11. These two sites are surveyed in Bellezza 2001, pp. 88–89; 2002a, pp. 60–62; in press-a, site A-1.

12. This site is surveyed in Bellezza in press-a, site A-141.

13. For a survey of this site, see ibid., site A-54.

14. See Bellezza 2008, pp. 255–58. Text: *Ge khod lha la rten mkhar gzugs pa zhes bya ba bzhugs pa legs swö*, attributed to sTon-pa gshen-rab, in *Ge khod sgrub skor*, New Collection of Bon *bka'-brten*, vol. 242, nos. 357–461.

15. Bellezza 2005, pp. 282–86.

16. For the folklore and physical traits of Nam Dzong, see in press-a, site A-48.

17. Bellezza 2005, pp. 282–83.

18. The Bronze Age and Iron Age cultural links between Upper Tibet and north Inner Asia, as revealed in the rock art record, are studied in Bruneau and Bellezza 2013.

19. Tucci and Ghersi 1934, pp. 198–99, 210–12, 232.

20. For a survey of these citadels, see Bellezza in press-a, sites A-119, A-120, A-121.

21. For surveys of these strongholds, see ibid., sites A-114, A-116, A-118.

22. The most comprehensive survey of secular and monastic installations in Lamaist era Guge is Guge tshe-ring rgyal-po 2006, a Tibetan-language work.

23. These sites are described in Bellezza 2008, sites A-59, A-136, B-77.

24. For a survey, see Bellezza 2001, pp. 102–4.

25. Archaeological sites in these locations are surveyed in Bellezza 2001; 2002a; in press-a; in press-b.

26. These ancient settlements are described in Bellezza 2001, pp. 107–8; in press-a, sites A-22, A-23, A-41, A-42, A-43, A-44, A-66, A-67.

27. Accounts of these sites are found in Bellezza 1997a; 2001; 2002a.

28. This celebrated site is described in Bellezza 1997a, pp. 384–87; in press-b, site A-5.

29. See Bellezza 2008, pp. 251–52. Text: *gSang drag tshogs bskang yod*, by gShen gyi drang-srong tshul-khrims rgyal-mtshan (the sixth abbot of sMan-ri), in *Ge khod sgrub skor*, New Collection of Bon *bka'-brten*, vol. 242, nos. 287–92.

30. Ibid., pp. 220–21.

31. This text is examined in ibid., pp. 294–99. Text: *gShen gyi pho brang gzhal yas bkod pa* [Design of the Palace of the gShen], 11th section (nos. 95–101) of *g.Yung drung las rnam par dag pa'i rgyud*, rediscovered by Gyer-med nyi-'od (born 1092 CE), in *bka'*, vol. 1, nos. 1–253. See also Karmay 1998, pp. 200–205.

32. Surveyed in Bellezza in press-a, site B-21.

33. See ibid., site B-25.

34. These sites are surveyed in ibid., sites B-24, B-31.

35. Surveyed in ibid., sites B-122.

36. For this site, see Bellezza 2002a, pp. 48–50.

37. For the sites of Khyunglung, see Bellezza in press-a, sites A-56, B-117; for Piwang, ibid., site A-83.

38. For survey and analysis of the Semo Do sites, see ibid., B-126, B-127.

39. The archaeological sites around these two lakeshores are examined in Bellezza 1999a; 2001, pp. 225–46; in press-a, sites B-130, B-131.

CHAPTER 6: PENETRATING THE EARTH

1. For a morphological, functional, and cross-cultural analysis of these pillar monuments, see Bellezza 2008, pp. 74–108; in press-a.

2. This site is examined in Caffarelli 1997.

3. Pelliot 1963.

4. Jay 1996; Stein 1959.

5. Bellezza 2001, pp. 68–75; 2005, p. 116 (fn. 108).

6. See Bellezza in press-b, site C-125.

7. Bellezza 2005, p. 204. Text: *Pha rabs mthong ba kun gsal*, 5 folios, manuscript from Nepal.

8. Ibid.

9. For a survey of this region, see Bellezza 2002a, pp. 25–27.

10. See Bellezza 2011a, pp. 61, 68. Text: *Khro bo dbang chen ngo mtshar rgyas pa'i rnam bshad gsal ba'i sgron ma*, sKyabs kyi ston-pa rin-chen 'od-zer (born 1353), in *Spyi Spungs Dang Dbal Phur Gyi 'Grel Pa*, nos. 31–392. New Thobgyal: Tibetan Bonpo Monastic Centre.

11. See ibid., pp. 61–62.

12. For a more detailed geographic analysis, see ibid., pp. 87–88; Bellezza 2013b.

13. Surveyed in Bellezza in press-b, site C-168. For two more recently discovered arrays of pillars appended to temple-tombs, see Bellezza 2010c.

14. For a survey of this site, see Bellezza in press-b, site C-167.

15. Ibid., site C-111.

16. Bellezza 2002a, pp. 112–13.

17. Surveyed in ibid., pp. 107–8; in press-b, site C-67.

18. Apparently also called Khyinak Bub. See Bellezza 2008, pp. 145–47; in press-b, site F-3.

19. Shasha Palkhang is studied in Bellezza 2001, pp. 128–29. For Kangchen Doring and Khangmar Dzashak, see Bellezza in press-b, sites C-157, C-160.

20. This site is examined in Bellezza 2001, pp. 179–81; 2000a, pp. 53–54; 2003; 2008, p. 85 (fn. 44).

21. The cross-cultural comparative discussion, infra, is based on Bellezza 2008, pp. 92–108.

22. On the deer stones of Mongolia, see Volkov 2002.

23. Bellezza 2008, p. 524.

24. The archaic structures are the object of study in Bellezza 2008, pp. 110–35; in press-a.

25. See Bellezza 2008, pp. 489–92. Text: *Klu 'bum nag po*, in *Gtsang Ma Klu 'Bum Chen Mo: A Reproduction of a Manuscript Copy Based upon the Tāranātha Tradition of the Famed Bonpo Recitational Classic*, vol. 4, Dolanji: Tibetan Bonpo Monastic Centre, 1977.

26. See Tucci 1950; Thomas 1957; Haarh 1969; Stein 1970; 1971.

27. For their study, see Huo Wei 2001a; 2001b. For an English-language assessment of these works, see Bellezza 2008, pp. 111–15.

28. Bellezza 2010b.

29. Ibid.

30. For further discussion on the role of trade in Zhang Zhung, see McKay 2011, pp. 192–95; Denwood 2008.

31. Bellezza 2008, pp. 210–211, 214.

32. Ibid., pp. 211, 214.

33. See Bhatt et al. 2008–2009.

34. See Bellezza 2010b; 2013d.

35. For a description and analysis of these masks, see Bellezza 2013d; 2013e.

36. See Bellezza 2008, pp. 396, 412.

37. See Bellezza 2013a, pp. 156–59.

38. For more details about these masks and a comparative analysis, see Bellezza 2013d; 2013e.

39. For the burial tumuli of Central Tibet, see Hazod 2012. On funerary structures and rites in lower-lying parts of Tibet, also see Heller 2003.

40. For a survey of this site, see Bellezza in press-b, site D-99.

41. For detailed information, see Bellezza 2008, pp. 496–542; 2013a, pp. 212–46.

42. Surveyed in Bellezza press-b, site D-125.

43. For a study of these curious structures, see Bellezza 2008, pp. 492–95; 2013a, pp. 139–41, 148–49, 196, 225, 239.

44. For these sites, see Bellezza in press-a, site A-52; in press-b, site D-41.

45. See Bellezza 2002a, pp. 87–89; 2008, pp. 127–29.

46. For this cross-cultural analysis, see Bellezza 2008, pp. 123–26. For a comprehensive study of the Slab Grave culture, see Tsybiktarov 1998.

47. Bushell 1880, p. 527.

48. For this site, see Bellezza in press-b, site E-30.

49. Their exploration of the Mustang burial sites is documented, for example, in Simons 1997; 1992; Simons et al. 1994.

50. Ibid.

51. For a description of this monument, see Bellezza 2008, pp. 135–41; in press-a.

52. For more detailed information, see Bellezza 2008, pp. 560–68. On old *bon* customs and traditions of the Gurungs, see Gurung 2003; on the funerary traditions of the Nakhi, see Rock 1955; on the funerary traditions of the Bhotiyas, see Sherring 1906.

53. For these sites, see Bellezza in press-b, sites D-99, D-100, D-101, D-102, D-103.

54. Bellezza 2001, pp. 166–67.

55. The sad fate of this site is recounted in Bellezza 2002a, pp. 118–19.

56. Bellezza in press-b, site C-154.

57. See ibid., site D-59.

CHAPTER 7: FLESH, BLOOD, AND BONES IN STONE

1. The study of rock art in this chapter is based on Bellezza 1997a; 1997b; 1999a; 1999b; 2001; 2002a; 2002b; 2004a; 2008. Also see Bruneau and Bellezza 2013 and various newsletters of the author: http://www.tibetarchaeology.com.

2. See Sonam Wangdu 1994; Li Yongxian 2004; 2011.

3. For the art of Ratroktrang, see Bellezza 1999b, pp. 211–24.

4. Rigyal is documented in Bellezza 2002a, pp. 131–35. Khampa Racho is documented in ibid., p. 145; Sonam Wangdu 1994, pp. 76–77.

5. For Lhakhang Marchak, see Bellezza 1999a, pp. 59–64.

6. An analysis of the Tashi Do site and a description of its various pictographs are found in my works on rock art. Also see Sonam Wangdu 1994, pp. 141–56.

7. Bellezza 1997a, pp. 210–11.

8. Cross-cultural comparisons drawn in this chapter are derived from Bellezza 1997a, pp. 421–25; 2002a, pp. 125–47; 2008, pp. 189–99; Bruneau and Bellezza 2013.

9. Bellezza 2002a, pp. 131–32.

10. Ibid., p. 130.

11. Bellezza 1997a, p. 182.

12. Bellezza 2002a, pp. 142–43.

13. Sonam Wangdu 1994, p. 134.

14. For graphic examples of religious struggles in the rock art of Upper Tibet, see Bellezza 2008, pp. 188–89; 2012c.

15. Bellezza 2012c.

16. Bellezza 2002a, pp. 145–46; Sonam Wangdu 1994, p. 94.

17. Bellezza 2002a, p. 133.

18. Anisimov 1963, pp. 162–63.

19. Rudenko 1960, pl. CXIX. For more information on Scythian tombs of the Altai, also see Rudenko 1953; 1970; Gryaznov 1969; Ishjmats 1994.

20. Bellezza 2008, p. 167.

21. Sonam Wangdu 1994, p. 128; Bellezza 2008, p. 167.

22. Bellezza 1997a, p. 196; Sonam Wangdu 1994, pp. 148–50.

23. Bellezza 2008, pp. 166–67; 2000c.

24. Bellezza 1997a, p. 202; 2001, p. 208; 2004a, no. 7a; 2002b, p. 392.

25. Bellezza 2002a, pp. 134–35.

26. Bellezza 2002a, p. 141; 2008, p. 178; 2002b, p. 394.

27. Bellezza 2008, pp. 178–79.

28. Bellezza 2001, p. 220; 2008, p. 179.

29. Bellezza 2001, p. 220.

30. Francfort 1998, p. 307.

31. Bellezza 1997a, p. 197; 2004a, no. 10a.

32. Sonam Wangdu 1994, p. 114.

33. Ibid., p. 106. For a variety of figures mounted on wild animals, see Bellezza 2012d.

34. Bellezza 1997a, pp. 197–98; Sonam Wangdu 1994, pp. 148–49.

35. For the art of Che Do, see Sonam Wangdu 1994, pp. 136–40; Bellezza 1997a, pp. 238–46.

36. For the extraordinary anthropomorphic figures of Thakhampa Ri, see Sonam Wangdu 1994, pp. 83–93; Bellezza 2013d.

37. Bellezza 2002a, pp. 126–27; 2000c.

38. Bellezza 2000c.

39. Bellezza 2008, p. 179.

40. Bellezza 2000b, pp. 44–45.

41. Ibid., p. 50.

42. Ibid.; Bruneau and Bellezza 2013, p. 111.

43. Bellezza 2001, p. 57.

44. Ibid., p. 56.

45. Bellezza 2005, p. 330.

46. Bellezza 2001, pp. 217–19; 2004a, no. 15a; 2008, p. 175.

47. See Bellezza 2013d.

48. Bellezza 2001, p. 58.

49. Ibid., p. 83.

50. Bellezza 2000b, p. 46 (after Martynov 1991).

51. Sher and Garyaeva 1996, p. 108.

52. For a discussion of the cosmopolitan cultural influences reflected in the mascoids of Upper Tibet and Ladakh, see Bruneau and Bellezza 2013, pp. 40–45, 68–71, 121–22, 150–56. Also see Bellezza 2000c; 2002a, p. 142.

53. See Sonam Wangdu 1994, pp. 86, 121.

54. Ibid., pp. 85–86, 90, 91; Bellezza 2013d.

55. Bellezza 2002a, pp. 146–47.

56. Bellezza 2001a, p. 201.

57. Bellezza 1997a, pp. 185–86.

58. See Bellezza 2008, p. 181.

59. For more on the Tibetan recurve bow, see Bellezza 2013f.

60. Bellezza 2002a, p. 141; 2000c.

61. Bellezza 2008, p, 173 (fn. 178) (after Peissel 1984). On the religion and culture of the Minaro, see Vohra 1989.

62. Bellezza 2008, p. 174.

63. Sonam Wangdu 1994, introduction by Li Yongxian and Huo Wei, p. 30.

64. Bellezza 2008, p. 171.

65. Bellezza 2002a, p. 141.

66. Bellezza 2001, p. 62.

67. Okladnikov 1990, pp. 88–89.

68. Bellezza 2002a, p. 134; 2000c.

69. Bellezza 2002a, p. 140.

70. Bellezza 2002b, pp. 385–86; 2004a, no. 5a. For more horned eagles in the rock art of Upper Tibet, see Bellezza 2012e.

71. Sonam Wangdu 1994, p. 144. Also see Bellezza 1997a, pp. 184–85; 2008, pp. 174–75; 2013a, p. 39.

72. This study of ceremonial monuments in rock art is based on my published works as well as unpublished field notes and photographs.

73. Bellezza 2010b; 2008, p. 145.

74. Bellezza 2008, p. 182.

75. Bellezza 2002a, p. 129; 2000c.

76. Bellezza 2002a, pp. 143–44.

77. Bellezza 1997a, p. 262; 2002a, pp. 130–31; 2000c; 2008, p. 159.

78. See, for example, Jettmar 2002; Jettmar and Sagaster 1993; Jettmar et al. 1989; Dani 2001. For a comparative study of *chorten* from Upper Tibet, Ladakh, and Indus Kohistan, see Bellezza 2002a, pp. 127–29. It is from these sources that the discussion on *chorten* in regions west of Tibet, infra, is derived.

79. Bellezza 2002a, p. 128 (after Francke 1902; 1903; 1905). The *chorten* of La-dakh have been comprehensively documented by Laurianne Bruneau and Martin Vernier but are still awaiting publication.

80. Bellezza 1997a, pp. 203–4; 2012f. See also Sonam Wangdu 1994, p. 152.

81. Bellezza 2008, p. 171.

82. See Bellezza 1997a, pp. 208–10; 2000b, pp. 49–50.

83. This paragraph is derived from Bellezza 2008, pp. 193–95; Bruneau and Bellezza 2013.

84. Han Kangxin 1998, pp. 561, 568. On the early populations of Xinjiang, also see Mallory and Mair 2000.

85. For an analysis of these far-reaching links, as typified by chariot rock art, see Bellezza 2008, pp. 195–96, Bruneau and Bellezza 2013, pp. 32–40.

86. Bellezza 2002a, p. 139.

87. Ibid., p. 139 (fn. 38). For the rock art of Mongolia more generally, see Novgorodova 1984.

88. For a discussion of this body style, see Bellezza 2002b, pp. 375–76.

89. See, for example, Sonam Wangdu 1994, p. 77; Chen Zhao Fu 2006; Bellezza 2002a, p. 145.

90. For a discussion of the "animal style" in Upper Tibet and Ladakh and its af-finities with north Inner Asian variants, see Bruneau and Bellezza 2013, pp. 45–51.

91. For an in-depth discussion of this schema, see Bellezza 2002a, pp. 136–38; 2008, pp. 190–92.

92. On volutes and other features drawing western Tibet into the artistic orbit of north Inner Asia, also see Francfort 1992; Francfort et al. 1992.

93. Sonam Wangdu 1994, p. 111; Bellezza 2000c; 2012g; Bruneau and Bellezza 2013, pp. 51–53.

94. Tang Huisheng 1993, p. 88. See also Tang Huisheng and Zhang Wenhua 2001.

95. Bruneau and Bellezza 2013, pp. 51–53.

96. This type of composition is discussed in Bellezza 2002a, p. 139.

97. For illustrations of these classes of objects, see John 2006, pp. 174–75; Bellezza 1998.

98. In personal communication with the Tibetan archaeologist Shargen Wangdu.

99. Huo Wei 2001b.

100. For woolen serge from a circa third-century CE burial at Gurgyam in western Tibet, see Bellezza 2010b.

101. See Bellezza 2008, pp. 546–49.

102. See Tucci 1973; Bellezza 1994; 1998; John 2006; Lin 2003; Ronge 1988.

103. See Tucci 1973.

104. This is of the type illustrated in John 2006, p. 131, no. R-306.

105. For illustrations of fibulae, see John 2006, pp. 95–97; Bellezza 1998, p. 62.

106. For a survey of these precious stones, see Ebbinghouse and Winsten 1988; Lin 2001.

CHAPTER 8: FATHER SKY EAGLE AND MOTHER EARTH SERPENT

1. For a comprehensive bibliography of Bon studies, see Martin 2003.

2. For a general survey of Eternal Bon literature, see Kværne 1974.

3. See Kapstein 2000; 2006; Sørensen et al. 2005; Snellgrove 1987; Snellgrove and Richardson 1980; Wangdu and Diemberger 2000.

4. On these tombs, see Tucci 1950; Caffarelli 1997; Panglung 1988; Hazod 2012.

5. Karmay 1972, pp. xxxii–xxxiii.

6. For good overview studies of the two forms of Lamaism, see Tucci 1980; Stein 1972.

7. For biographical lore, see Karmay 2005, pp. 139–210; 1998, pp. 108–113; 1972, pp. xvii–xxi; Kværne 1995, pp. 17–21; Stein 1972, pp. 242–45; Martin 2001, pp. 30–39.

8. Snellgrove 1967.

9. See Bellezza 2005, pp. 344–50. Text: *Dri med gzi brjid*, attributed to sTang-chen dmu-tsha gyer-med, rediscovered by sPrul-sku blo-ldan snying-po (born 1360), published by Bod-ljongs bod-yig dpe-rnying dpe-skrun khang: Lhasa, 2000.

10. See ibid., pp. 47–49.

11. For an account of their religious activities, see Karmay 1972, pp. 3–13.

12. Ibid., pp. 20–21.

13. For an in-depth treatment of Dzogchen in Eternal Bon, see Wangyal 1993; Lopön Tenzin Namdak 1995; 2006; Rossi 1999; Reynolds 2005.

14. For more detailed accounts of the history of Dzogchen in Eternal Bon, see Karmay 1972, pp. 51–58; 1998; Reynolds 2005.

15. Reynolds 2005, pp. 11–15, 59; Reynolds 1996, pp. 225–27.

16. Snellgrove 1967, pp. 15–16.

17. Bellezza 2001, p. 94 (fn. 9). Text: *Rig 'dzin rig pa'i thugs rgyud*, attributed to Dran-pa nam-mkha' (eighth century CE), rediscovered by rMa-ston shes-rab sengge, in *Sources for a History of Bon: A Collection of Rare Manuscripts from Bsam-gling Monastery in Dolpo (Northwestern Tibet)*, nos. 186–237, Tibetan Bonpo Monastic Centre: Dolanji, 1972.

18. Bellezza 2008, pp. 211, 214. Text: *Le'u bzhi ba (Fourth Chapter)* of *Ma rgyud sgrub skor* (manuscript copied by dPal-ldan tshul-khrims, Indian edition, nos. 45–94), by dMu-rgyal rnal-'byor nyi-ma (gShen nyi-ma rgyal-mtshan) (born in 1360 CE).

19. For more detailed information on the Dulwa, see Karmay 1972, pp. 35–39.

20. See Bellezza 2008, pp. 370–71. Also see, for example, Vitali 1996, p. 101 (fn. 16); Martin 2001, p. 191; Norbu 1995, p. 40. Text: *Thu'u bkwan grub mtha'*, in *Pan-Chen Bsod-Nams Grags-pa Literature Series*, vol. 60, published by Drepung Loseling Library Society: N. Kanara, 1992.

21. See Bellezza 2008, pp. 272–76. Text: *bsGrags pa gling grags*, attributed to Dran-pa nam-mkha' (eighth century CE). sNyan-rong manuscript, 68 folios.

22. Ibid., pp. 210, 213. Text: *Ma rgyud sgrub skor.*

23. Bellezza 2001, pp. 56–57.

24. Bellezza 2008, p. 300 (fn. 395).

25. See ibid., pp. 320–21. Text: *dBal chen ge khod kyi dug phyung tshan dkar dmar spos bsang bcas*, anonymous, in Ge khod sgrub skor stod cha, New Collection of Bon *bka'-brten*, vol. 242, nos. 81–101.

26. See Bellezza 2005, pp. 415–17.

27. Bellezza 2008, pp. 249–50. Text: *dBal chen ge khod kyi dbang khrid byin rlabs sprin dpung zhes bya bzhugs sō*, compiled by mNga'-ris bsod-nams rgyal-mtshan (fifteenth century CE), New Collection of Bon *bka'-brten*, vol. 242, nos. 1441–94.

28. Bellezza 2011a, p. 70.

29. See Bellezza 2008, pp. 305–316. Text: See *Ge khod gsang ba drag chen ldog med gser gyi spu gri'i gzhung*, compiled by Drang-srong [mNyam-med] shes-rab rgyal-mtshan (1356–1415), at bKra-shis sman-ri'i khrod, New Collection of the Bon *bka'-brten*, vol. 242, nos. 187–281. For another translation of a tantric description of Gekhö, see Kværne 1995, pp. 81–84.

30. For more detailed cross-cultural comparative data, see Bellezza 2008, p. 307 (fn. 312).

31. Kværne 1980, pp. 93, 96–97.

32. Ibid.

33. See Griffith 1973; Keith 1925a; 1925b.

34. For an overview of Indo-European cultures, including the Indo-Iranian variants, see Mallory 1994.

35. For more detailed lore on Drablai Gyalmo, see Bellezza 2008, pp. 312–13, 325–29.

36. Ibid., pp. 277–78.

37. For a more extensive description of Kuchi Mangke and his consort, see ibid., p. 313.

38. Pt 1047, ln. 016. On divination in Old Tibetan manuscripts, see Dotson 2007.

39. See Bellezza 2005, pp. 355–59.

40. Ati Muwer and his consort are described in Bellezza 2008, pp. 313–14.

41. Ibid., pp. 323–24. Text: *Me ri dpa' bo gyad phur gyi bskang ba* in *Zhang zhung me ri bka' mi'i sgrub skor gyi gsung pod* (published by rMa-rtsa rin-chen rgyal-mtshan, Delhi, 2000), nos. 543–64. Anonymous.

42. See Bellezza 2005, p. 337 (fn. 486).

43. For a description of these twelve ritual systems, see Norbu 1995, pp. 48–50.

44. The religious activities of Shengur Luga are a major focus in Martin 2001.

45. The study of these six manuscripts, infra, is derived from Bellezza 2008, passim; Bellezza 2010a; 2013a, pp. 213–20. For references to these and associated Dunhuang manuscripts, also see Stein 2003a; 2003b; 1970; Macdonald 1971; Thomas 1957.

46. The *Muchoi Tromdur* (dMu cho'i khrom 'dur) is the object of extensive study in Bellezza 2008; 2013a.

47. Transliterations of Tibetan manuscripts from Dunhuang belonging to the Pelliot tibétain (Pt) texts of the Bibliothèque nationale de France, and those of the India Office Library (IOL Tib J) of the British Library Stein Collection, can be found at Old Tibetan Documents Online: http://otdo.aa.tufs.ac.jp.

48. See Bellezza 2013a, pp. 243–47; Tong Tao and Wertmann 2010.

49. Bellezza 2008, pp. 374, 377, 383–88, 395, 414, 461, 480.

50. Bellezza 2013d. A sixth Dunhuang text mentioning Shenrab Nyiwo is designated Pt 1194. Pt 1194 relates the origins myth of the sheep that leads the dead to paradise. For an explication of this fragmentary document, see Bellezza 2013a, pp. 213–20.

51. This manuscript in full is the object of study in Bellezza 2010a. Text: *Byol-rabs*, in *Gtam shul dga' thang 'bum pa che nas gsar du rnyed pa'i bon gyi gna' dpe bdams bsgrigs* (eds. Pa-tshab pa-sangs dbang-'dus [Pasang Wangdu] and Glang-ru nor-bu tshe-ring), Bod-ljongs bod-yig dpe-rnying dpe-skrun khang: Lhasa, 2007.

CHAPTER 9: HORNED HEROES AND TURQUOISE MAIDENS

1. For another study of Eternal Bon cosmogonies, see Karmay 2003.

2. For the full translation and analysis of this text, see Bellezza 2008, pp. 343–49. Text: *Klu 'bum khra bo*, vol. 2 (*kha*), in *Gtsang Ma klu 'Bum Chen Mo: A Reproduction of a Manuscript Copy Based upon the Tāranātha Tradition of the Famed Bonpo Recitational Classic*, Tibetan Bonpo Monastic Centre: Dolanji, 1977.

3. See Bellezza 2008, pp. 352–53. Text: *sNgags kyi mdo 'dur rin chen phreng ba mu cho'i khrom 'dur chen mo las rin chen phreng ba gzhung gi nyin bon le'u gnyis pa'o* [Second Chapter of Daytime Bon of the Primary Text Scripture from the Great Funeral Ritual Multitude of Mu-cho Jewel Rosary Tantric Funeral Ritual Texts], New Collection of Bon *bka'-brten*, vol. 6, nos. 341–79.

4. Ibid., pp. 354–55. Text: *dBal shel rgyung dkar po'i dbal chu bzhugs pa'i dbu phyogs legs swō*, New Collection of Bon *bka'-brten*, vol. 242, nos. 927–1016.

5. For a study of Tibetan turquoise, see Bellezza 2013g.

6. Bellezza 2005, pp. 428–29. Text: *sNga rabs bod kyi byung ba brjod pa'i 'bel gtam lung gi snying po*. Delhi: Paljor Publications, 1997.

7. See Bellezza 2001, pp. 54–55. Text: *'Dul ba gling grags*, rediscovered by Khod-po blo-gros thog-med in 1301, in *Sources for a History of Bon*, nos. 114–40.

8. Ibid., p. 58.

9. Bellezza 2008, p. 217.

10. Bellezza 2001, p. 58.

11. The feats detailed in this paragraph come from Bellezza 2008, pp. 209–20.

12. Ibid., p. 219.

13. Ibid., pp. 219–20.

14. The hagiographic lore in this and the next two paragraphs comes from Bellezza 2005, pp. 223–24.

15. Bellezza 2008, pp. 211, 214.

16. Bellezza 2001, p. 57.

17. Ibid., pp. 59–61.

18. Ibid., p. 62.

19. Ibid., p. 63. Text: *Rigs 'dzin 'dus pa'i khog dbubs byin brlabs brgyud byang bzhugs so*, rediscovered in the eleventh century CE by Khyung-rgod-rtsal at Zhal-bzang brag, in *brGyud byang bzhugs so*, nos. 255–78, Delhi edition.

20. For these biographical accounts, see Bellezza 2001, pp. 63–68; 2008, pp. 227–29. Text: *g.Yung drung bon gyi rgyud 'bum* (*Sources for a History of Bon: A Collection of Rare Manuscripts from Bsam-gling Monastery in Dolpo (Northwestern Tibet)*), nos. 1–46. Tibetan Bonpo Monastic Centre: Dolanji, 1972.

21. See Bellezza 2008, pp. 413–17. Text: *sNgags kyi mdo 'dur rin chen phreng ba mu cho'i khrom 'dur chen mo las* [From the Great Funeral Ritual Multitude of Mu-cho Jewel Rosary Tantric Funeral Ritual Texts] *Bla rdo bal lam rten dang sprad pa bla rdo dkar po'o*, New Collection of Bon *bka'-brten*, vol. 6, nos. 167–70.

22. Benedict 1972.

23. See Uray 1972b, pp. 37–39; Richardson 1998, p. 120.

24. Bellezza 2008, p. 223.

25. The textual passage that follows is derived from ibid., pp. 272–76.

26. See Bellezza 2013a, p. 235; 2008, pp. 456 (fn. 320), 513.

27. For this text and an analysis, see Richardson 1998, pp. 149–66.

28. Bellezza 2008, pp. 391–92.

29. See ibid., pp. 222–23; Thomas 1957, pp. 61–95.

30. Bellezza 2010a. Text: Pt 1289.

31. Bellezza 2008, pp. 429–35, 506–10.

32. Ibid., pp. 226–27.

33. Ibid., p. 227; 2013a, p. 150 (fn. 232). On the symbolism of shade and sun in early manuscripts, see Dotson 2008; Chayet 2008.

34. The account of ancient ritual apparel and objects that follows is derived from Bellezza 2008, pp. 238–42.

35. Bushell 1880.

36. Bellezza 2005, pp. 318–23.

37. See Sonam Wangdu 1994, p. 133.

38. Bellezza 2008, pp. 242–44. Text: *Chos 'byung mkhas pa'i dga'ston*, by dPa'-bo gtsug-lag phreng-ba (1504–1566 CE). Beijing: Mi-rigs dpe-skrun khang, 1985.

39. See Bellezza 2010a, p. 80.

40. Bellezza 2005, p. 234.

41. Ibid., p. 117 (fn. 108).

42. Bellezza 2008, pp. 532, 536, 537.

43. Ibid., p. 513.

44. Bellezza 2010a, p. 54.

45. Bellezza 2013a, p. 210. Text: *Sha ru shul ston rabs la sogs pa.* in *Gtam shul dga' thang 'bum pa che nas gsar du rnyed pa'i bon gyi gna' dpe bdams bsgrigs* (eds. Pa-tshab pa-sangs dbang-'dus [Pasang Wangdu] and Glang-ru nor-bu tshe-ring), pp. 60–75, 180–211, 2007.

46. Bellezza 2010a, p. 52.

47. Bellezza 2005, pp. 439–40.

48. See ibid., pp. 341–42.

49. Ibid., pp. 444–46.

50. In personal communication, reported in Bellezza 2001, p. 73.

51. Haarh 1969, pp. 401–2.

52. Bellezza 2005, p. 385 (fn. 144).

53. See ibid., pp. 380–87.

54. For this inventory of material objects, see Bellezza 2008, pp. 239–42.

55. For a lexicon of Eternal Bon terms in the Zhang Zhung language, see Pasar Tsultrim Tenzin et al. 2008. On the Zhang Zhung language, also see Haarh 1968; Hummel 2000.

56. For these helmets of north Inner Asia, see Litvinsky 1998.

CHAPTER 10: MY ANCESTORS, MY GODS

1. See Bellezza 2013a, p. 208.

2. Described in Bellezza 1997a, p. 201.

3. See Bellezza 2008, p. 462 (fn. 345) (after Norsam, no date).

4. This text is discussed and translated in Bellezza 2005, pp. 325–32. Text: Untitled, attributed to Zhang-zhung sTong-rgyung mthu-chen, Se-bon Sha-ri dbu-chen, lDe-bon Gyis-tsha rma-chung, and Me-nyag lCe-tsha mkhar-bu (eighth century CE), in *gSol kha*, New Collection of Bon *bka'-rten*, vol. 87, nos. 897–902.

5. For this text, see Bellezza 2008, pp. 334–38. Text: *Shel skyongs gsol mchod*, attributed to Shri 'gro-mgon, Dar-rgyas gling, 5 folios.

6. See Bellezza 2005, pp. 173–74. Text: *Thang lha'i mchod bstod*, attributed to sTong-rgyung mthu-chen (eighth century CE) and rediscovered by rMa-lha rgod-thog at Mount Sham-po, in *gSol kha*, New Collection of Bon *bka'-rten*, vol. 87, no. 1421, ln. 3, to no. 1423, ln. 3.

7. For detailed treatment of this text, see ibid., pp. 183–93. Text: *'Dzam gling spyi bsang* [Universal World Purification], attributed to Slob-dpon padma sambha (Gu-ru rin-po-che) (eighth century CE), 4 folios.

8. Bellezza 2013a, pp. 143–44. Text: *Rnel drĭ 'dul ba'i thabs sogs*, in *Gtam shul dga' thang 'bum pa che*, 2007, pp. 33–59, 131–78.

9. Bellezza 2005, p. 311 (fn. 419). Text: *Lha lnga'i gsol mchod bsod nams dpal bskyed*, by Za-hor sngags-smyon, in *bSang mchod phyogs sgrigs* (ed. bSod-nams 'bum), nos. 68–73, Mi-rigs dpe-skrun khang: Lhasa, 2003.

10. For a full translation of this work, see ibid., pp. 317, 322. Text: *gTer bdag yum sras lnga yi dril bsgrub*, probably attributed to Dran-pa nam-mkha' (eighth century CE), in *Phyi nang gsang gsum gyi nyer mkho 'dod 'jo 'khri shing*, nos. 617–30.

11. See Bellezza 2008, pp. 329–31. Text: *Me ri bka' ma gyad phur gyi sgrub gzhung* in *Zhang zhung me ri bka' mi'i sgrub skor gyi gsung pod*, nos. 391–525, published by rMa-rtsa rin-chen rgyal-mtshan: Delhi, 2000.

12. Ibid., pp. 436–37.

13. Ibid., pp. 454–55.

14. For an account of this practice, see Bellezza 2005, 467.

15. For further information, see Bellezza 2005, pp. 341, 346, 468 (fn. 154); 2013a, p. 44 (fn. 65).

16. See Bellezza 2008, p. 454 (fn. 318) (after Sonam Dorje 1992).

17. This myth is studied in Bellezza 2005, pp. 472–79.

18. Bellezza 2013a, pp. 200–202.

19. Spirit-mediums from Upper Tibet living in exile are the focus of study in Berglie 1976; 1978; 1980. More detailed studies inside Upper Tibet include Bellezza 2005; 2011b; 2012h. For the spirit-mediums of other regions of Tibet, see, for example, Havnevik 2002; Diemberger 2005; Nagano 2000.

20. Das 1882, p. 11.

21. Waddell 1895, pp. 482–83.

22. See Rock 1935.

23. Macdonald 1971, pp. 274–75, 294–95.

24. See Bellezza 2005, pp. 11–12.

25. Bellezza 2005, pp. 437–38.

26. Bellezza 2008, pp. 99–101.

27. For the *shang* in Eternal Bon origin myths, see Bellezza 2005, pp. 419–22.

28. For the drum in Eternal Bon origin myths, see ibid., pp. 423–32.

29. Ibid., p. 447. Text: *Ge khod lha la rten mkhar gzugs*, in the first volume of the *Ge khod sgrub skor*, New Collection of Bon *bka'-brten*, vol. 242, nos. 357–461.

30. Nebesky-Wojkowitz 1956, pp. 538–53; Hoffman 1961.

31. The cross-cultural study in this work is based on Bellezza 2005, pp. 20–34.

32. This study of Phowo Sridgyal is based on Bellezza 2011b, as well as my unpublished research notes.

33. See Bellezza 2005, pp. 456–62. Text: *g.Yang 'gug bkra shis 'khyil ba*, in entitled *gZungs 'dus pod gnyis pa*, by Bru-ston rgyal-ba (born 1242), nos. 469–79, New Collection of Bon *bka'-brten*, vol. 2.

34. This study of Karma Rigdzin is based on Bellezza 2005, pp. 154–69; Bellezza 2011b; as well as my unpublished notes.

Bibliography

Aldenderfer, M. 2011. "The material correlates of Tibetan religious practice in far western Tibet: 500 BCE–500 CE," in *Emerging Bon: The Formation of Bon Traditions in Tibet at the Turn of the First Millennium AD* (ed. H. Blezer), pp. 13–33. PIATS 2006: Proceedings of the Eleventh Seminar of the International Association for Tibetan Studies, Königswinter 2006. Halle: International Institute for Tibetan and Buddhist Studies GmbH.

———. 2007. "Modeling the Neolithic on the Tibetan Plateau," in *Late Quaternary Climate Change and Human Adaptation in Arid China*, Developments in Quaternary Sciences 9 (ed. D. B. Madsen, F. H. Chen, and X. Gao), pp. 149–61. Amsterdam: Elsevier.

———. 2003. "A new class of standing stone from the Tibetan Plateau," in *The Tibet Journal*, vol. 28, nos. 1 and 2, pp. 3–20. Dharamsala: Library of Tibetan Works and Archives.

Aldenderfer, M., and Moyes, H. 2004. "Excavations at Dindun, a pre-Buddhist village site in far western Tibet," in *Essays on the International Conference on Tibetan Art and Archaeology*, pp. 47–69. Chengdu: Sichuan Remin Chuban She.

Aldenderfer, M., and Zhang Yinong. 2004. "The prehistory of the Tibetan Plateau to the seventh century A.D.: Perspectives and research from China and the West since 1950," in *Journal of World Prehistory*, vol. 18, no. 1, pp. 1–55. Netherlands: Springer.

Anisimov, A. F. 1963. "The shaman's tent of the Evenks and the origin of the shamanistic rite," in *Studies in Siberian Shamanism* (ed. H. N. Michael). Toronto: University of Toronto Press and Arctic Institute of North America.

Bacot, J., Thomas, F. W., and Toussaint, Ch. 1940–1946. *Documents de Touen-houang relatifs à l'histoire du Tibet*. Annales du Musée Guimet. Paris: Librairie Orientaliste Paul Guenther.

Beckwith, C. I. 1987. *The Tibetan Empire in Central Asia: A History of the Struggle for Great Power among the Tibetans, Turks, Arabs, and Chinese during the Early Middle Ages*. Princeton, NJ: Princeton University Press.

Bellezza, J. V. In press-a. *Antiquities of Zhang Zhung: A Comprehensive Inventory of Pre-Buddhist Sites on the Tibetan Upland, Residential Monuments*, vol. 1. Sarnath: Central University of Tibetan Studies. Online version: Tibetan & Himalayan Library (thlib.org): http://www.thlib.org/bellezza, 2011.

———. In press-b. *Antiquities of Zhang Zhung: A Comprehensive Inventory of Pre-Buddhist Sites on the Tibetan Upland, Ceremonial Monuments*, vol. 2. Sarnath: Central University of Tibetan Studies. Online version: Tibetan & Himalayan Library (thlib.org): http://www.thlib.org/bellezza, 2011.

———. 2013a. *Death and Beyond in Ancient Tibet: Archaic Concepts and Practices in a Thousand-Year-Old Illuminated Funerary Manuscript and Old Tibetan Funerary Documents of Gathang Bumpa and Dunhuang*. Philosophisch-Historische Klasse Denkschriften 454. Wien: Verlag der Österreichischen Akademie der Wissenschaften.

———. 2013b. "Gyapa Jo Khar and the historical signification of the term Zhang Zhung," in *Flight of the Khyung*, June 2013: http://www.tibetarchaeology.com/june-2013.

———. 2013c. "The origins of the Tibetan people: A review of 'Modeling the Neolithic on the Tibetan Plateau,'" in *Flight of the Khyung*, May 2013: http://www.tibetarchaeology.com/may-2013.

———. 2013d. "The golden burial mask of Shamsi" (with contributions by Christoph Baumer and Sören Stark), "More on the golden mask from Malari," and "Hunters, warriors, shamans and lovers: Chronicles of ancient life at Thakhampa Ri," in *Flight of the Khyung*, December 2013: http://www.tibetarchaeology.com/december-2013.

———. 2013e. "Visages of the past: The golden burial masks of Upper Tibet, the Himalaya and northwestern Xinjiang," in *Flight of the Khyung*, November 2013: http://www.tibetarchaeology.com/november-2013.

———. 2013f. "Curves of history: The composite bow in Upper Tibet," in *Flight of the Khyung*, March 2013: http://www.tibetarchaeology.com/march-2013.

———. 2013g. "Tibetan turquoise: Beaming stone of life," in *Flight of the Khyung* (with contributions by James Wainwright, Stephen Shucart, and Samten G. Karmay), August 2013: http://www.tibetarchaeology.com/august-2013.

———. 2012a. "A major center of civilization in Upper Tibet, circa the 3rd century CE," in *Flight of the Khyung*, April 2012: http://www.tibetarchaeology.com/april-2012.

———. 2012b. "My (Bellezza's) visit to Stok Mon Khar," in *Flight of the Khyung*, September 2012: http://www.tibetarchaeology.com/september-2012.

———. 2012c. "Palimpsests: The superimposition of images and inscriptions," in *Flight of the Khyung*, November 2012: http://www.tibetarchaeology.com/november-2012.

———. 2012d: "It may or may not be god" and "Divine riders of the unfettered," in *Flight of the Khyung*, July 2012: http://www.tibetarchaeology.com/july-2012.

———. 2012e. "The horned eagle: Tibet's greatest ancestral and religious symbol across the ages," in *Flight of the Khyung*, January 2012: http://www.tibetarchaeology.com/january-2012.

———. 2012f. "Figures from foreign lands?" in *Flight of the Khyung*, February 2012: http://www.tibetarchaeology.com/february-2012.

———. 2012g. "A brief introduction to the tiger in Tibetan culture," "Ancient tigers in Upper Tibet," and "Tigers in the rock art of Upper Tibet," in *Flight of the Khyung*, August 2012: http://www.tibetarchaeology.com/august-2012.

———. 2012h. "Spirit-mediumship in Upper Tibet: The vocation of one expert practitioner," in *Bulletin of Tibetology*, vol. 48, no. 2, pp. 7–32. Gangtok: Namgyal Institute of Tibetology.

———. 2011a. "Territorial characteristics of the pre-Buddhist Zhang-zhung paleo-cultural entity: A comparative analysis of archaeological evidence and popular Bon literary sources," in *Emerging Bon: The Formation of Bon Traditions in Tibet at the Turn of the First Millennium AD* (ed. H. Blezer), pp. 51–116. PIATS 2006: Proceedings of the Eleventh Seminar of the International Association for Tibetan Studies, Königswinter 2006. Halle: International Institute for Tibetan and Buddhist Studies GmbH.

———. 2011b. "The liturgies and oracular utterances of the spirit-mediums of Upper Tibet: An introduction to their *bSang* rituals," in *Revue d'etudes tibétaines*, no. 20, April 2011, pp. 5–31. Paris: CNRS: http://www.himalaya.socanth.cam.ac.uk/collections/journals/ret/pdf/ret_20_01.pdf.

———. 2010a. "gShen-rab Myi-bo: His life and times according to Tibet's earliest literary sources," in *Revue d'etudes tibétaines*, no. 19, October, 2010, pp. 31–118. Paris: CNRS: http://www.himalaya.socanth.cam.ac.uk/collections/journals/ret/pdf/ret_19_03.pdf.

———. 2010b "The Mon burials of Montsher: A preliminary report," in *Flight of the Khyung*, October 2010: http://www.tibetarchaeology.com/october-2010.

———. 2010c. "Recently discovered pre-Buddhist necropolises in Upper Tibet," in *Flight of the Khyung*, November 2010: http://www.tibetarchaeology.com/november-2010.

———. 2008. *Zhang Zhung: Foundations of Civilization in Tibet: A Historical and Ethnoarchaeological Study of the Monuments, Rock Art, Texts and Oral Tradition of the Ancient Tibetan Upland*. Philosophisch-Historische Klasse Denkschriften 368. Wien: Verlag der Österreichischen Akademie der Wissenschaften.

———. 2005. *Calling Down the Gods: Spirit-Mediums, Sacred Mountains and Related Bon Textual Traditions in Upper Tibet*. Leiden: Brill.

———. 2004a. "Metal and stone vestiges: Religion, magic and protection in the art of ancient Tibet," in *Asian Art Online Journal*: http://www.asianart.com/articles/vestiges/index.html.

———. 2004b. "Pilgrim's way, scientist's mind" (Chinese trans. Fu Jun), in *Tibet Geographic*, vol. l, pp. 133–38. Lhasa.

———. 2003. "Bringing to light the forgotten: Major findings of a comprehensive inventory of archaic sites in Upper Tibet (Tibet Autonomous Region, Peoples' Republic of China). Conducted between 1992–2002," in *Athena Review*, vol. 3, no. 4, pp. 16–26. Westport. Chinese-language version: Xunzhao Shiluo De Wenhua: "Xibu Xizang Qian Fujiao Shiyi Zhongyao Kaogu Yiji Diao Cha Baogau" (Chinese trans. Tang Huisheng and Tan Xiuhua) in *Essays on the International Conference on Tibetan Archaeology and Art*, pp. 1–29. Chengdu: Sichuan Remin Chuban She, 2004.

———. 2002a. *Antiquities of Upper Tibet: An Inventory of Pre-Buddhist Archaeological Sites on the High Plateau.* Delhi: Adroit.

———. 2002b. "Gods, hunting and society: Animals in the ancient cave paintings of Celestial Lake in northern Tibet," in *East and West*, vol. 52, pp. 347–96. Rome: IsIAO.

———. 2001. *Antiquities of Northern Tibet: Archaeological Discoveries on the High Plateau.* Delhi: Adroit.

———. 2000a. "Pre-Buddhist archaeological sites in northern Tibet: An introductory report on the types of monuments and related literary and oral historical sources," in *Kailash*, vol. 19, nos. 1–2, pp. 1–142. Kathmandu: Ratna Pustak Bhandar.

———. 2000b. "Bon rock paintings at gNam mtsho: Glimpses of the ancient religion of northern Tibet," in *Rock Art Research*, vol. 17, no. 1, pp. 35–55. Melbourne: Archaeological Publications.

———. 2000c. "Images of lost civilization: The ancient rock art of Upper Tibet," in *Asian Art Online Journal*: http://www.asianart.com/articles/rockart/index.html.

———. 1999a. "A preliminary archaeological survey of Da rog mtsho," in *The Tibet Journal*, vol. 24, no. 1, pp. 56–90. Dharamsala: Library of Tibetan Works and Archives.

———. 1999b. "Northern Tibet Exploration: Archaeological discoveries of the Changthang Circuit Expedition," in *Asian Art Online Journal*: http://www.asianart.com/articles/tibarchaeo/index.html.

———. 1998. "Thogchags: Talismans of Tibet," in *Arts of Asia*, vol. 28, no. 3, pp. 44–64. Hong Kong.

———. 1997a. *Divine Dyads: Ancient Civilization in Tibet.* Dharamsala: Library of Tibetan Works and Archives.

———. 1997b. "Notes on three series of unusual symbols discovered on the Byang Thang," in *East and West*, vol. 47, nos. 1–4, pp. 395–405. Rome: IsIAO.

———. 1994. "Thog lcags," in *The Tibet Journal*, vol. 19, no. 1, pp. 92–97. Dharamsala: Library of Tibetan Works and Archives.

———. 1993. "Quest for the four fountains of Tibet," in *Himal*, vol. 6, no. 1, pp. 41–44. Kathmandu.

Benedict, P. K. 1972. *Sino-Tibetan: A Conspectus.* Cambridge: Cambridge University Press.

Berglie, P. A. 1980. "Mount Targo and Lake Dangra: A contribution to the religious geography of Tibet," in *Tibetan Studies in Honour of Hugh Richardson: Proceedings of the International Seminar of Tibetan Studies, Oxford, 1979* (ed. M. Aris and Aung San Suu Kyi), pp. 39–43. Warminster: Aris and Phillips.

———. 1978. "On the question of Tibetan shamanism," in *Tibetan Studies Presented at the Seminar of Young Tibetologists* (ed. M. Brauen and P. Kværne), pp. 39–51. Zürich: Völkerkundemuseum der Universität Zürich.

———. 1976. "Preliminary remarks on some Tibetan 'spirit-mediums,' in Nepal," in *Kailash: A Journal of Himalayan Studies*, vol. 4, no. 1, pp. 85–108. Kathmandu: Ratna Pustak Bhandar.

Bhatt, R. C., Kvamme, K. L., Nautiyal, V., Nautiyal, K. P., Juyal, S., and Nautiyal, S. C. 2008–2009. "Archaeological and geophysical investigations of the high mountain cave burials in the Uttarakhand Himalaya," in *Indo-Kōko-Kenkyū—Studies in South Asian Art and Archaeology*, vol. 30, pp. 1–16.

Brantingham, P. J., Gao Xing, Madsen, D. B., Rhode, D., Perreault, C., van der Woerd, J., and Olsen, J. W. 2013. "Late occupation of the high-elevation northern Tibetan Plateau based on cosmogenic, luminescence, and radiocarbon ages," in *Geoarchaeology*, vol. 28, pp. 413–31.

Bruneau, L., and Bellezza, J. V. 2013. "The rock art of Upper Tibet and Ladakh: Inner Asian cultural adaptation, regional differentiation and the 'western Tibetan Plateau style,'" in *Revue d'etudes tibétaines*, vol. 28, December 2013, pp. 5–161. Paris: CNRS. http://himalaya.socanth.cam.ac.uk/collections/journals/ret/pdf/ret_28.pdf.

Bushell, S. W. 1880. "The early history of Tibet: From Chinese sources," in *Journal of the Royal Asiatic Society*, vol. 12, pp. 435–541. London.

Caffarelli, Mortari Vergara, P. 1997. "Architectural style in tombs from the period of the kings," in *Tibetan Art: Towards a Definition of Style* (ed. J. C. Singer and P. Denwood), pp. 230–61. London: Laurence King.

Chan, V. 1994. *Tibet Handbook: A Pilgrimage Guide.* Chico: Moon Publications.

Chayet, A. 2008. "A propos de l'usage des terms 'nyin' et 'srib' dans le mDo smad chos 'byung," in *Tibetan Studies in Honour of Samten Karmay*, part 1, *Revue d'Etudes Tibétaines*, no. 14, October 2008, pp. 71–79. Paris: CNRS. http://himalaya.socanth.cam.ac.uk/collections/journals/ret/pdf/ret_14_05.pdf.

———. 1994. *Art et Archéologie du Tibet.* Paris: Picard.

Chen Zhao Fu. 2006. *Zhongguo yanhua quanji—Xibu yanhua* (2) [The Complete Works of Chinese Rock Art—Western Rock Art Volume 2], vol. 3. Shenyang, Liaoning meishu chubanshe.

———. 1996. "Rock art studies in the Far East during the past five years," in *Rock Art Studies: News of the World I. Recent Developments in Rock Art Research (Acts of Symposium 14D at the NEWS95 World Rock Art Congress, Turin and Pinerolo, Italy)* (ed. P. G. Bahn and A. Fossati), pp. 127–31. Oxford: Oxbow Monograph 72.

Dani, A. H. 2001. *History of Northern Areas of Pakistan (up to 2000 AD).* Lahore: Sang-e-Meel.

Das, S. C. 1882. *Contributions on the Religion and History of Tibet.* Reprint, Delhi: Manjushri Publishing House, 1970.

Denwood, P. 2008. "The Tibetans in the West," in *Journal of Inner Asian Art & Archaeology*, vol. 2, pp. 7–21.

Diemberger, H. 2005. "Female oracles in modern Tibet," in *Women in Tibet* (ed. J. Gyatso and H. Havnevik), pp. 113–68. London: Hurst and Company.

Dhondrup Lhagyal (Don-grub lha-rgyal). 2003. "Introduction to the cultural heritage of the Zhang Zhong kingdom in the north of Tibet," in *Tibetan Studies*, vol. 88, no. 3, pp. 93–108. Lhasa: Tibetan Academy of Social Sciences.

Dotson, B. 2009. *The Old Tibetan Annals: An Annotated Translation of Tibet's First History.* Wien: Verlag der Österreichischen Akademie der Wissenschaften.

———. 2008. "Complementarity and opposition in early Tibetan ritual," in *Journal of the American Oriental Society*, vol. 128, no. 1, pp. 41–67.

———. 2007. "Divination and law in the Tibetan empire: The role of dice in the legislation of loans, interest, marital law and troop conscription," in *Contributions to the Cultural History of Early Tibet* (ed. M. T. Kapstein and B. Dotson), Brill's Tibetan Studies Library 14, pp. 3–77. Leiden: Brill.

Driem, G. van. 2001. "Zhangzhung and its next of kin in the Himalayas," in *New Research on Zhangzhung and Related Himalayan Languages*, Bon Studies 3 (ed. Y. Nagano and R. J. LaPolla), pp. 31–44. Osaka: National Museum of Ethnology.

Ebbinghouse, D., and Winsten, M. 1988. "Tibetan dZi (gZi) beads," in *The Tibet Journal*, vol. 13, no. 1, pp. 38–57. Dharamsala: Library of Tibetan Works and Archives.

Ekvall, R. B. 1968. *Fields on the Hoof: Nexus of Tibetan Pastoralism*. New York: Holt, Rinehart and Winston.

Environment and Development Desk. 2005. *The Endangered Mammals of Tibet*. Dharamsala: Department of Information and International Relations, Gangchen Kyishong.

Flad, R. K., Yuan Jing, and Li Shuicheng. 2007. "Zooarchaeological evidence for animal domestication in northwest China," in *Late Quaternary Climate Change and Human Adaptation in Arid China*, pp. 205–24. Amsterdam: Elsevier.

Francfort, H.-P. 1998. "Central Asian petroglyphs: Between Indo-Iranian and shamanistic interpretations," in *The Archaeology of Rock Art* (ed. C. Chippindale and P. S. C. Taçon), pp. 302–18. Cambridge: Cambridge University Press.

———. 1992. "New data illustrating the early contacts between Central Asia and the north-west of the Subcontinent," in *South Asian Archaeology 1989: Papers from the Tenth International Conference of South Asian Archaeologists in Western Europe, Musée National des Arts Asiatiques—Guimet, Paris, France, 3–7 July 1989* (ed. C. Jarrige et al.), pp. 97–102. Monographs in World Archaeology, no. 14. Madison: Prehistory Press.

Francfort, H.-P., Klodzinski, D., and Mascle, G. 1992. "Archaic petroglyphs of Ladakh and Zanskar," in *Rock Art in the Old World: Papers Presented in Symposium A of the AURA Congress, Darwin Australia, 1988* (ed. M. Lorblanchet), pp. 147–92. Delhi: Indira Gandhi National Centre for the Arts.

Francke, A. H. 1926. *Antiquities of Indian Tibet. The Chronicles of Ladakh and Minor Chronicles, Texts, Translations, with Notes and Maps*, vol. 2. Reprint, Delhi: Archaeological Survey of India, New Imperial Series 1, 1972.

———. 1914. *Antiquities of Indian Tibet*, vol. 1. Reprint, Delhi: Asian Educational Services, 1992.

Garma, C. C. Chang (trans.). 1962. *The Hundred Thousand Songs of Milarepa*, vol. 1. Reprint. Boulder, CO: Shambhala, 1977.

Gelek. 1993. "The Tibetan Plateau—one of the homes of early man," in *Proceedings of the International Seminar on Anthropology of Tibet and the Himalaya* (ed. C. Ramble and M. Brauen), pp. 73–79. Zurich: Ethnographic Museum of the University of Zurich.

Goldstein, M. C., and Beall, C. M. 2002. "Changing patterns of Tibetan nomadic pastoralism," in *Human Biology of Pastoral Populations* (ed. W. R. Leonard and M. H. Crawford), pp. 131–50. Cambridge: Cambridge University Press.

————. 1990. *Nomads of western Tibet: The survival of a way of life*. Berkeley: University of California Press.

Griffith, R. T. H. (trans.). 1973. *The Hymns of the R̥gveda*. Delhi: Motilal Banarsidass.

Gryaznov, M. 1969. *The Ancient Civilization of South Siberia* (trans. J. Hogarth). London: Barrie and Rockliff.

Gouin, M. 2010. *Tibetan Rituals of Death: Buddhist Funerary Practices*. Routledge Critical Studies in Buddhism. London: Routledge.

Gu-ge tshe-ring rgyal-po. 2006. *Mnga' ris chos 'byung gangs ljongs mdzes rgyan*. Lhasa: Bod ljongs mi dmangs dpe skrun khang.

Gurung, B. C. 2003. *Bon in the Himalaya*. Kathmandu: Uma Gurung.

Haarh, E. 1969. *The Yar-luṅ Dynasty: A Study with Particular Regard to the Contribution of Myths and Legends to the History of Ancient Tibet and the Origin and Nature of Its Kings*. Copenhagen: G. E. C. Gad's Forlag.

————. 1968. *The Zhang-Zhung Language: A Grammar and Dictionary of the Unexplored Language of the Tibetan Bonpos*. Copenhagen: Einar Munksgaard.

Han Kangxin. 1998. "The physical anthropology of the ancient populations of the Tarim basin and surrounding areas," in *The Bronze Age and Early Iron Age Peoples of Eastern Central Asia* (ed. V. H. Mair), vol. 2, pp. 558–70. Washington, DC: Institute for the Study of Man.

Hansen, J. 2009. "Survival of Tibetan glaciers," in *National Aeronautics and Space Administration: Goddard Institute for Space Studies*. December 2009, accessed December 5, 2013: http://www.giss.nasa.gov/research/briefs/hansen_14.

Harris, R. B. 2010. "Rangeland degradation on the Qinghai-Tibetan Plateau: A review of the evidence of its magnitude and causes," in *Journal of Arid Environments*, vol. 74, pp. 1–12.

Havnevik, H. 2002. "A Tibetan female state oracle," in *Religion and Secular Culture in Tibet, Tibet Studies II* (ed. H. Blezer), pp. 259–88. Leiden: Brill.

Hazod, G. 2012. *The Burial Mounds of Central Tibet*. Austrian Academy of Sciences, accessed November 8, 2013: http://www.oeaw.ac.at/tibetantumulustradition.

————. 2009. "Imperial Central Tibet: An annotated cartographical survey of its territorial divisions and key political sites," in *The Old Tibetan Annals: An Annotated Translation of Tibet's First History*, pp. 161–231. Wien: Verlag der Österreichischen Akademie der Wissenschaften.

Hedin, S. A. 1909 and 1913. *Trans-Himalaya: Discoveries and Adventures in Tibet*, vols. 1–3. London: Macmillan.

————. 1916–1922. *Southern Tibet: Discoveries in former times compared with my own researches in 1906–1908*, 12 vols. Stockholm.

Heller, A. 2003. "Archeology of funeral rituals as revealed by Tibetan tombs of the 8th and 9th century," in *Ērān ud Anērān Webfestschrift Marshak*: http://www.transoxiana.com.ar/Eran/Articles/heller.html.

Hoffman, H. 1990. "Early and medieval Tibet," in *The Cambridge History of Early Inner Asia*, pp. 371–99. Cambridge: Cambridge University Press.

————. 1973. *Tibet: A Handbook*. Bloomington: Research Center for the Language Sciences, Indiana University.

———. 1961. *The Religions of Tibet* (trans. E. Fitzgerald). London: George Allen and Unwin.

Howard, N. 1995. "The fortified places of Zanskar," in *Recent Research on Ladakh 4 & 5: Proceedings of the Fourth and Fifth International Colloquia on Ladakh* (ed. H. Osmaston and P. Denwood). London: School of Oriental and African Studies.

Hummel, S. 2000. *On Zhang-zhung* (trans. G. Vogliotti). Dharamsala: Library of Tibetan Works and Archives.

Huo Wei. 2005. "A study on the archaeology of the early civilization of western Tibet," in *Tibetan Studies*, vol. 94, no. 1, pp. 43–50. Lhasa.

Huo Wei (Chinese Institute of Tibetology, Sichuan University). 2001a. "Trial excavation of ancient tombs on the Piyang-Donggar site in Zanda County, Tibet," in *Kaogu*, no. 6, pp. 14–31. Beijing.

———. 2001b. "Survey of Gebusailu Cemetery in Zanda County," in *Kaogu*, no. 6, pp. 32–38. Beijing.

Intergovernmental Panel on Climate Change (http://www.ipcc.ch). "Working Group I contribution to the IPCCc Fifth Assessment Report Climate Change 2013: The physical science basis. Final draft underlying scientific-technical assessment," accessed December 3, 2013: http://www.climatechange2013.org/images/uploads/WGIAR5_WGI-12Doc2b_FinalDraft_All.pdf; "Climate change 2007: Working Group II: Impacts, adaptation and vulnerability, 10.6.2 The Himalayan glaciers," accessed December 3, 2013: http://www.ipcc.ch/publications_and_data/ar4/wg2/en/ch10s10-6-2.html.

Ishjmats, N. 1994. "Nomads in eastern Central Asia," in *History of Civilizations of Central Asia*, vol. 2, *The Development of Sedentary and Nomadic Civilizations: 700 B.C. to A.D. 250* (ed. J. Harmatta, B. N. Puri, and G. F. Etemadi), pp. 151–69. Reprint, Delhi: Motilal Banarsidass, 1999.

Jacques, G. 2009. "Zhangzhung and Qiangic languages," in *Issues in Tibeto-Burman Historical Linguistics*, Senri Ethnological Series 75 (ed. Y. Nagano), pp. 131–50. Osaka: National Museum of Ethnology.

Jay, J. W. 1996. "Imagining matriarchy: 'Kingdoms of Woman,' in Tang China," in *Journal of the American Oriental Society*, vol. 116, no. 2, pp. 220–31. Ann Arbor.

Jettmar, K. 2002. *Beyond the Gorges of the Indus*. Oxford: Oxford University Press.

Jettmar, K., König, D., and Thewalt, V. 1989. *Antiquities of Northern Pakistan*, vol. 1. Mainz: Verlag Phillip Von Zabern.

Jettmar, K., and Sagaster, K. 1993. "Ein Tibetisches Heiligtum in Punyal," in *Antiquities of Northern Pakistan: Reports and Studies* (ed. K. Jettmar et al.), vol. 2, pp. 123–40. Mainz: Verlag Phillip Von Zabern.

John, G. 2006. *Tibetische Amulette aus Himmels-Eisen*. Rahden: Verlag Marie Leidorf.

Johnson, R., and Moran, K. 1989. *The Sacred Mountain of Tibet: On Pilgrimage to Kailas*. Rochester, VT: Park Street Press.

Juvanec, B. 2000. *Six Thousand Years, and More, of Corbelling: Age of Stone Shelters*, accessed August 21, 2013: http://www.unesco.org/archi2000/pdf/juvanec.pdf.

Kapstein, M. T. 2006. *The Tibetans*. Oxford: Blackwell.

———. 2000. *The Tibetan Assimilation of Buddhism: Conversion, Contestation, and Memory*. Oxford: Oxford University Press.

Karmay, S. G. 2005. *Feast of the Morning Light: The Eighteenth Century Wood-Engravings of Shenrab's Life-Stories and the Bon Canon from Gyalrong.* Bon Studies 9, Senri Ethnological Reports 57. Osaka: National Museum of Ethnology.

———. 2003. "Light, ray, frost and dew: Formation of the world," in *Cosmogony and the Origins, Lungta,* no. 16, pp. 7–10. Dharamsala: Amnye Machen Institute.

———. 1998. *The Arrow and the Spindle: Studies in History, Myths, Rituals and Beliefs in Tibet.* Kathmandu: Mandala Book Point.

———. 1972. *The Treasury of Good Sayings. A Tibetan History of Bon.* Reprint, Delhi: Motilal Banarsidass, 2001.

Kehrwald, N. M., Thompson, L. G., Yao Tandong, Mosley-Thompson, E., Schotterer, U., Alfimov, V., Beer, J., Eikenberg, J., and Davis, M. E. 2008. "Mass loss on Himalayan glacier endangers water resources," in *Geophysical Research Letters,* vol. 35, pp. 1–6. https://bprc.osu.edu/Icecore/Kehrwald%20et%20al%202008.pdf.

Keith, A. B. 1925a. *The Religion and Philosophy of the Veda and Upanishads.* Harvard Oriental Series 31. Harvard: Harvard University Press.

———. 1925b. *The Religion and Philosophy of the Veda and Upanishads.* Harvard Oriental Series 32. Harvard: Harvard University Press.

Klein, J. A., Harte, J., and Zhao, X. Q. 2007. "Experimental warming, not grazing, decreases rangeland quality on the Tibetan Plateau," in *Ecological Applications,* vol. 17, no. 2, pp. 541–57. Washington, DC: Ecological Society of America.

Kværne, P. 1995. *The Bon Religion of Tibet: The Iconography of a Living Tradition.* London: Serindia Publications.

———. 1980. "Mongols and Khitans in a 14th-century Tibetan Bon-po text," in *Acta Orientalia Academiae Scientiarum Hungaricae,* vol. 34, pp. 85–104. Budapest.

———. 1974. "The canon of the Tibetan Bonpos," in *Indo-Iranian Journal,* vol. 16, pp. 18–56, 96–144.

Lalou, M. 1953. "Rituel Bon-po des Funérailles Royales (fonds Pelliot tibétain 1042)," in *Journal Asiatique,* vol. 240, no. 1, pp. 339–63. Paris: Société Asiatique.

Li Yongxian. 2011. "Archaeological survey of 'Khyung Lung Silver Castle' in western Tibet," in *Emerging Bon: The Formation of Bon Traditions in Tibet at the Turn of the First Millennium AD* (ed. H. Blezer), pp. 35–52. PIATS 2006: Proceedings of the Eleventh Seminar of the International Association for Tibetan Studies, Königswinter 2006. Halle: International Institute for Tibetan and Buddhist Studies GmbH.

———. 2004. "The discoveries of rock painting in Zhada basin and some ideas on Tibetan rock painting," in *Essays on the International Conference on Tibetan Art and Archaeology,* pp. 30–46. Chengdu: Sichuan Remin Chuban She.

Lin, Tung-Kuang. 2003. *Antique Tibetan Thogchags and Seals.* Taiwan: Liao, Yue-Tao.

———. 2001. *The Gzi Beads of Tibet.* Taiwan: Liao, Yue-Tao.

Litvinsky, B. A. 1998. "The ancient Iranian army: Xûd (Helmet)," in *Circle of Ancient Iranian Studies,* accessed August 4, 2012: http://www.cais-soas.com/CAIS/Military/xud_helmet.htm.

Lobsang Tashi (Blo-bzang bkra-shis). 2002. "Naqu Nimaxian Xiasang Jialinshan Yanhua Diaacha Jianbao," in *Xizang Yanjiu,* vol. 84, no. 3, pp. 61–64. Lhasa.

Lopön Tenzin Namdak (Sman-ri'i slob-zur bstan-'dzin rnam-dag). 2006. *Bonpo Dzogchen Teachings.* Kathmandu: Vajra Publications.
———. 1995. *Heartdrops of the Dharmakaya.* Ithaca, NY: Snow Lion Publications.
Ma Lihua. 1991. *Glimpses of Northern Tibet* (trans. Guan Yuehua and Zhong Liangbi). Beijing: Chinese Literature Press.
Macdonald, A. 1971. "Une Lecture des Pelliot Tibétain 1286, 1287, 1038, 1047, et 1290. Essai sur la formation et l'emploi des mythes politiques dans la religion royale de Sroṅ-bcan sgam-po," in *Études tibétaines dédiées à la mémoire de Marcelle Lalou* (ed. A. Macdonald), pp. 190–391. Paris: Libraire d'América et d'Orient.
Mallory, J. P. 1994. *In Search of the Indo-Europeans: Language, Archaeology and Myth.* London: Thames and Hudson.
Mallory, J. P., and Mair, V. H. 2000. *The Tarim Mummies: Ancient China and the Mystery of the Earliest Peoples from the West.* London: Thames and Hudson.
Malville, N. J. 2005. "Mortuary practices and ritual use of bone in Tibet," in *Interacting with the Dead: Perspectives on Mortuary Archaeology for the New Millennium*, pp. 190–204. Gainesville: University Press of Florida.
Martin, D. 2003. "Bon bibliography: An annotated list of recent publications," in *Revue d'etudes tibétaines*, no. 4, October 2004, pp. 61–77. http://himalaya/socanth.cam.ac.uk/collections/journals/ret/pdf/ret_04_02.pdf.
———. 2001. *Unearthing Bon Treasures: Life and Contested Legacy of a Tibetan Scripture Revealer, with a General Bibliography of Bon.* Leiden: Brill.
———. 1995. "Ol-mo-lung-ring, the Original Holy Place," in *The Tibet Journal*, vol. 20, no. 1, pp. 48–82. Dharamsala: Library of Tibetan Works and Archives.
McCue, G. 2003. *Trekking in Tibet: A Traveler's Guide.* Seattle: The Mountaineers.
McKay, A. 2011. "In search of Zhang Zhung—the 'grey and empty' land," in *Emerging Bon: The Formation of Bon Traditions in Tibet at the Turn of the First Millennium AD* (ed. H. Blezer), pp. 185–206. PIATS 2006: Proceedings of the Eleventh Seminar of the International Association for Tibetan Studies, Königswinter 2006. Halle: International Institute for Tibetan and Buddhist Studies GmbH.
Miller, D. J. 2008. *Drokpa: Nomads of the Tibetan Plateau and Himalaya.* Kathmandu: Vajra Publications.
Nagano, S. 2000. "Sacrifice and lha.pa in the glu.rol festival of Reb-skong," in *New Horizons in Bon Studies.* Bon Studies 2. Senri Ethnological Reports 15 (ed. S. G. Karmay and Y. Nagano), pp. 567–651. Osaka: National Museum of Ethnology.
Nebesky-Wojkowitz, R. D. 1956. *Oracles and Demons of Tibet: The Cult and Iconography of the Tibetan Protective Deities.* Reprint, Kathmandu: Tiwari's Pilgrims Book House, 1993.
Nishi, Y., and Nagano, Y. 2001. "A general review of Zhangzhung studies," in *New Research on Zhangzhung and Related Himalayan Languages.* Bon Studies 3 (ed. Y. Nagano and R. J. LaPolla), pp. 1–30. Osaka: National Museum of Ethnology.
Norbu, N. 2009. *The Light of Kailash: A History of Zhang Zhung and Tibet*, vol. 1 (trans. D. Rossi). Merigar: Shang Shung Publications.
———. 1997. *Journey among the Tibetan Nomads: An Account of a Remote Civilization.* Dharamsala: Library of Tibetan Works and Archives.

———. 1995. *Drung, Deu and Bön. Narrations, Symbolic Languages and the Bön Tradition in Ancient Tibet* (trans. A. Clemente and A. Lukianowicz). Dharamsala: Library of Tibetan Works and Archives.

Norbu, N., and Pratts, R. 1989. *Gaṅs Ti Se'i Dkar C'ag. A Bon-po Story of the Sacred Mountain Ti-se and the Blue Lake Ma-pan*. Serie Orientale Roma 61. Roma: Istituto Italiano per il Medio ed Estremo Oriente.

Novgorodova, E. A. 1984. *Mir Petroglifov Mongolii*. Moscow: Nauka.

Okladnikov, A. P. 1990. "Inner Asia at the dawn of history," in *The Cambridge History of Early Inner Asia*, pp. 41–96. Cambridge: Cambridge University Press.

Old Tibetan Documents Online, coordinated by I. Hoshi, accessed October 14, 2013: http://otdo.aa.tufs.ac.jp.

Panglung, J. L. 1988, "Die metrischen Berichte über die Grabmäler der tibetischen Könige. Ihre Überlieferung und ihr Beitrag zur Identifizierung," in *Tibetan Studies: Proceedings of the 4th Seminar of the International Association for Tibetan Studies, Schloss Hohenkammer—Munich 1985* (ed. H. Uebach and J. L. Panglung), pp. 321–68. Munich: Bayerische Akademie Wissenschaften.

Pasar Tsultrim Tenzin, Changru Tritsuk Namdak Nyima, and Gatsa Lodroe Rabsal. 2008. *A Lexicon of Zhangzhung and Bonpo Terms* (trans. H. Stoddard). Bon Studies 11, Senri Ethnological Reports 76. Osaka: National Museum of Ethnology.

Pelliot, P. 1963. *Notes on Marco Polo*, vol. 2. Paris: Imprimerie Nationale Librairie Adrien-Maisonneuve.

Petech, L. 1977. *The Kingdom of Ladakh*. Oriental Series 51. Rome: Istituto Italiano Per il Medio ed Estremo Oriente.

Pranavananda, S. 1949. *Kailās Mānasarovar*. Delhi.

Ramble, C. 1995. "Gaining ground: Representations of territory in Bon and Tibetan popular tradition," in *The Tibet Journal*, vol. 20, no. 1, pp. 83–124. Dharamsala: Library of Tibetan Works and Archives.

Reynolds, J. M. 2005. *The Oral Tradition from Zhang-Zhung: An Introduction to the Bonpo Dzogchen Teachings of the Oral Tradition from Zhang-zhung Known as the Zhang-zhung snyan-rgyud*. Kathmandu: Vajra Publications.

———. 1996. *The Golden Letters. The Three Statements of Garab Dorje, the First Teacher of Dzogchen, Together with a Commentary by Dza Patrul Rinpoche Entitled "The Special Teaching of the Wise and Glorious King."* Ithaca, NY: Snow Lion Publications.

Rhode, D., Madsen, D. B., Brantingham, P. J., and Tsultrim Dargye. 2007a. "Yaks, yak dung and prehistoric human habitation of the Tibetan Plateau," in *Late Quaternary Climate Change and Human Adaptation in Arid China*, pp. 205–24. Amsterdam: Elsevier.

Rhode, D., Zhang Haiying, Madsen, D. B., Gao Xing, Brantingham, P. J., Ma Haizhou, and Olsen, J. W. 2007b. "Epipaleolithic/early Neolithic settlement at Qinghai Lake, western China," in *Journal of Archaeological Science*, vol. 34, pp. 600–12. Amsterdam: Elsevier.

Richardson, H. E. 1998. *High Peaks, Pure Earth: Collected Writings on Tibetan History and Culture*. London: Serindia Publications.

———. 1977. "Ministers of the Tibetan kingdom," in *The Tibet Journal*, vol. 2, no. 1, pp. 10–27. Dharamsala.

Rock, J. F. 1955. *The ²Zhi ³mä Funeral Ceremony of the ¹Na-²khi of Southwest China.* Vienna: St. Gabriel's Mission Press.

———. 1935. "Sungmas, the Living Oracles of the Tibetan Church," in *National Geographic*, October 1935, pp. 475–86. Washington, DC: National Geographic Society.

Roerich, G. N. 1996. *Trails to Inmost Asia*. Reprint, Delhi: Book Faith India.

Ronge, N. G. 1988. "Thog lcags of Tibet," in *Tibetan Studies: Proceedings of the 4th Seminar of the International Association for Tibetan Studies, Schloss Hohenkammer— Munich 1985* (ed. H. Uebach and J. L. Panglung), pp. 405–12. Munich: Bayerische Akademie Wissenschaften.

Rossi, D. 1999. *The Philosophical View of the Great Perfection in the Tibetan Bon Religion*. Ithaca, NY: Snow Lion Publications.

Rudenko, S. I. 1970. *Frozen Tombs of Siberia: The Pazyryk Burials of the Iron Age Horsemen* (trans. M. W. Thompson). London: J. M. Dent and Sons.

———. 1960. *Kultura naseleniya Tsentralnogo Altaya v skifskoe vremya*. Izdatelstvo Akademii Nauk SSSR.

———. 1953. *Kultura naseleniya Gornogo Altaya v skifskoe vremya*. Moscow: Izdatelstvo Akademii Nauk SSSR.

Schaller, G. B. 1997. *Tibet's Hidden Wilderness: Wildlife and Nomads of the Chang Tang Reserve*. New York: Henry N. Abrams.

Sher, J., and Garyaeva, O. 1996. "The rock art of northern Eurasia," in *Rock Art Studies: News of the World I. Recent Developments in Rock Art Research (Acts of Symposium 14D at the NEWS95 World Rock Art Congress, Turin and Pinerolo, Italy)* (ed. P. G. Bahn and A. Fossati), pp. 105–25. Oxford: Oxbow Monograph.

Sherring, C. A. 1906. *Western Tibet and the British Borderland: The Sacred Country of Hindus and Buddhists*. Reprint, New Delhi: Asian Educational Services, 1993.

Simons, A. 1997. "The cave systems of Mustang—settlement and burial sites since prehistoric times," in *South Asian Archaeology, 1995: Proceedings of the 13th International Conference of the European Association of South Asian Archaeologists* (ed. R. Allchin and B. Allchin), pp. 499–509. Cambridge: The Ancient India and Iran Trust.

———. 1992. "Trial excavation of a cave system in Muktinath Valley," in *Ancient Nepal: Journal of the Department of Archaeology* (ed. K. M. Shrestha), nos. 130–33, pp. 1–19. Kathmandu.

Simons, A., Schon, W., and Shrestha, S. S. 1994. "Preliminary report on the 1992 campaign of the team of the Institute of Prehistory, University of Cologne," in *Ancient Nepal: Journal of the Department of Archaeology* (ed. K. M. Shrestha), no. 136, pp. 51–75. Kathmandu.

Singh, K. 1915. "Narrative of an exploration of the Nam or Tengri Nor Lake by Pandit Kishen Singh," in *Explorations in Tibet and Neighboring Countries: Records of the Surveys of India*, vol. 8, part 1, 1865–1879, pp. 133–49. Compiled by T. G. Montgomerie. Dehra Dun: Office of the Trigonometric Survey.

Snellgrove, D. L. 1987. *Indo-Tibetan Buddhism: Indian Buddhists and Their Tibetan Successors*, 2 vols. Boston: Shambhala.

———. 1967. *The Nine Ways of Bon: Excerpts from the gZi-brjid Edited and Translated*. London Oriental Series 18. London: Oxford University Press.

Snellgrove, D., and Richardson, H. E. 1980. *A Cultural History of Tibet*. Boulder, CO: Prajñā Press.

Snelling, J. 1991. *The Sacred Mountain: The Complete Guide to Tibet's Mount Kailas*. London: East-West Publications.

Sonam Wangdu (Bsod-nams dbang-'dus). 1994. *Art of Tibetan Rock Paintings*. Introduction by Li Yongxian and Huo Wei. Chengdu: Sichuan People's Publishing House.

Sørensen, P. K., and Hazod, G., in cooperation with Tsering Gyalpo. 2005. *Thundering Falcon: An Inquiry into the History and Cult of Khra-'brug Tibet's First Buddhist Temple*. Wien: Verlag der Österreichischen Akademie der Wissenschaften.

Stein, R. A. 2010. *Rolf Stein's Tibetica Antiqua* (trans. and ed. A. P. McKeowen). Brill's Tibetan Studies Library, vol. 24. Leiden: Brill.

———. 2003a. "The indigenous religion and the *Bon-po* in the Dunhuang Manuscripts" (trans. P. Richardus), in *The History of Tibet: The Early Period to c. CE 850; the Yarlung Dynasty* (ed. A. McKay), vol. 1, pp. 584–618. London: Routledge Curzon.

———. 2003b. "On the word *gcug-lag* and the indigenous religion" (trans. P. Richardus), in *The History of Tibet: The Early Period to c. CE 850; the Yarlung Dynasty* (ed. A. McKay), vol. 1, pp. 530–83. London: Routledge Curzon.

———. 1972. *Tibetan Civilization* (trans. J. E. S. Driver). Stanford: Stanford University Press.

———. 1971. "Du récit au rituel dans les manuscrits Tibétaines de Touen-Houang," in *Études Tibétaines dédiées à la mémoire de Marcelle Lalou* (ed. A. Macdonald), pp. 479–547. Paris: Adrien Maisonneuve.

———. 1970. "Un Document Ancien Relatif aux Rites Funéraires des Bon-po Tibétains," in *Journal Asiatique*, pp. 155–85. Paris: Imprimerie Nationale.

———. 1959. *Les Tribus Anciennes des Marches Sino-Tibétaines: Legendes, Classifications et Histoire*. Paris: Imprimerie Nationale.

Stoddard, H. 1994. "Tibetan publications and national identity," in *Resistance and Reform in Tibet* (ed. R. Barnett and S. Akiner), pp. 121–56. London: Hurst.

Takeuchi, T., Nagano, Y., and Ueda, S. 2001. "Preliminary analysis of the Old Zhangzhung language and manuscripts," in *New Research on Zhangzhung and Related Himalayan Languages*. Bon Studies 3 (ed. Y. Nagano and R. J. LaPolla), pp. 45–96. Osaka: National Museum of Ethnology.

Takeuchi, T., and Nishida, A. 2009. "The present state of deciphering Old Zhangzhung," in *Issues in Tibeto-Burman Historical Linguistics*, Senri Ethnological Series 75 (ed. Y. Nagano), pp. 151–65. Osaka: National Museum of Ethnology.

Tang Huisheng. 1993. "Theory and methods in Chinese rock art studies," in *Rock Art Research*, vol. 10, no. 2, November, pp. 83–90. Melbourne: Archaeological Publications.

Tang Huisheng and Zhang Wenhua. 2001. *Qinghai Yanhua*. Beijing: Science Press.

Tenzin Gayden, Cadenas, A. M., Regueiro, M., Singh, N. B., Zhivotovsky, L. A., Underhill, P. A., Cavalli-Sforza, L. L., and Herrera, R. J. 2007. "The Himalayas as a directional barrier to gene flow," in *American Journal of Human Genetics*, vol. 80, no. 5, pp. 884–94. Boston.

Thomas, F. W. 1957. *Ancient Folk-Literature from North-Eastern Tibet*. Berlin: Akademie Verlag.

Thompson, L. G., Yao Tandong, Davis, M. E., Mosley-Thompson, E., Mashiotta, T. A., Lin Ping-Nan, Mikhalenko, V. N., and Zagorodnov, V. S. 2006. "Holocene climate variability archived in the Puruogangri ice cap on the central Tibetan Plateau," in *Annals of Glaciology*, vol. 43, pp. 61–69. International Glaciological Society.

Tong Tao. 2011. "Silks from Han to Jin period found near Kyung-lung dngul-mkhar, the capital of ancient Xiang Xiong kingdom in Ngari, Tibet," in *Chinese Archaeology*, Institute of Chinese Archaeology Chinese Academy of Social Sciences, accessed January 17, 2012: http://www.kaogu.cn/en/detail.asp?ProductID=3120.

Tong Tao and Wertmann, P. 2010. "The coffin paintings of the Tubo period from the northern Tibetan Plateau," in *Bridging Eurasia* (ed. M. Wagner and Wang Wei), pp. 187–213. Mainz: German Archeological Institute.

Topgyal, T., and Tashi Topgyal. 1998. "The lifestyle of nomads," in *The Tibet Journal* (trans. L. Shastri and V. Cayley), vol. 23, no. 3, pp. 34–50. Dharamsala: Library of Tibetan Works and Archives.

Tsybiktarov, A. D. 1998. *Kultura plitochnyh mogil Mongolii i Zabaykalya*. Ulan-Ude: Izdatelstvo Buryatskogo gosuniversiteta.

Tucci, G. 1980. *The Religions of Tibet* (trans. G. Samuel). London: Routledge and Kegan Paul.

———. 1973. *Transhimalaya* (trans. J. Hogarth). Reprint, Delhi: Vikas Edition.

———. 1950. *The Tombs of the Tibetan Kings*. Serie Orientale Roma I. Roma: Is. M. E. O.

Tucci, G., and Ghersi, E. 1934. *Secrets of Tibet: Being the Chronicle of the Tucci Scientific Expedition to Western Tibet (1933)* (trans. M. A. Johnstone). London: Blackie and Son.

Uray, G. 1972a. "Queen Sar-Mar-Kar's songs in the Old Tibetan Chronicle," in *Acta Orientalia Academiae Scientiarum Hungaricae*, vol. 25, pp. 5–38. Budapest.

———. 1972b. "The narrative of legislation and organization of the Mkhas-pa'i Dga'-ston: The origins of the traditions concerning Sroṅ-Brcan Sgam-po as first legislator and organizer of Tibet," in *Acta Orientalia Academiae Scientiarum Hungaricae*, vol. 26, no. 1, pp. 11–68. Budapest.

———. 1968. "Notes on a chronological problem in the Old Tibetan Chronicle," in *Acta Orientalia Academiae Scientiarum Hungaricae*, vol. 21, no. 3, pp. 289–301.

Vernier, M. 2012. "Exploring ancient Ladakh with Martin Vernier," in *Flight of the Khyung*, September 2012, http://www.tibetarchaeology.com/september-2012.

Vitali, R. 2008. "A tentative classification of the *Bya ru can* kings of Zhang zhung," in *Tibetan Studies in Honour of Samten Karmay*, part 2, *Revue d'etudes tibétaines*, no. 15, November, 2008, pp. 379–419. http://himalaya.socanth.cam.ac.uk/collections/journals/ret/pdf/ret_15_10.pdf.

———. 2003. "Tribes which populated the Tibetan Plateau, as treated in the texts collectively called *Khungs chen po bzhi*," in *Cosmogony and the Origins, Lungta*, no. 16, pp. 37–63. Dharamsala: Amnye Machen Institute.

———. 1996. *The Kingdoms of Gu.ge Pu.hrang. According to mNga'.ris rgyal.rabs by Gu ge mkhan.chen Ngag.dbang grags.pa.* Dharamsala: Tho.ling gtsug.lag.khang lo.gcig .stong 'khor.ba'i rjes.dran.mdzad sgo'i go.sgrig tshogs.chung.

Vohra, R. 1989. *The Religion of the Dards of Ladakh: Investigations into Their Archaic 'Brog-pa Traditions.* Ettelbruck: Skydie Brown.

Volkov, V. V. 2002. *Stone Stelae from Mongolia ("Deer Stones").* Moscow: Scientific World.

Waddell, L. A. 1895. *Buddhism and Lamaism of Tibet: With Its Mystic Cults, Symbolism and Mythology, and Its Relation to Indian Buddhism.* Reprint, New Delhi: Heritage Publishers, 1974.

Wangdu, P., and Diemberger, H. 2000. *dBa bzhed: The Royal Narrative Concerning the Bringing of the Buddha's Doctrine to Tibet.* Wien: Verlag der Österreichischen Akademie der Wissenschaften.

Wangdu, S. 2005. "Forty years of archaeology in Tibet," in *China Tibetology*, vol. 71, no. 3, pp. 210–13. Beijing.

Wangyal, T. 1993. *Wonders of the Natural Mind: The Essence of Dzogchen in the Native Bon Tradition of Tibet.* New York: Station Hill Press.

Xuebin, Q., Jianlin, H., Blench, R., Rege, J. E. O., and Hanotte, O. 2008: "Understanding the yak pastoralism in Central Asian Highlands: Mitochondrial DNA evidence for origin, domestication and dispersal of domestic yak," in *Past Human Migrations in East Asia: Matching Archaeology, Linguistics and Genetics* (ed. A. Sanchez-Mazas), pp. 427–42. London: Taylor and Francis.

Yamaguchi, Z. 1977. "The name T'u-fan and the location of the Yang-t'ung: A study of Fu-kuo-chuan and the Greater and Lesser Yang-t'ung," in *Toyo Gakuho*, vol. 58, pp. 313–53.

Index

About the Author

John Vincent Bellezza is an archaeologist and cultural historian focused on the pre-Buddhist heritage of Tibet and the Western Himalaya. He has lived in high Asia for three decades and is a senior research fellow with the Tibetan Center, University of Virginia. Bellezza has published widely on archaic ritual traditions in Bon and Old Tibetan literature. Since 1992, he has comprehensively charted the monuments and rock art of the ancient Zhang Zhung and Sumpa proto-states, revealing the surprising level of cultural sophistication attained on the uppermost reaches of the Tibetan Plateau more than two thousand years ago. Bellezza is the first non-Tibetan to have explored both the geographic and ritual sources of each of the four great rivers that emerge from the Mount Tise region. He has also visited nearly every main island and major headland in the great lakes region of the Changthang.

Bellezza's other books include *Divine Dyads* (1997), *Antiquities of Northern Tibet* (2001), *Antiquities of Upper Tibet* (2002), *Calling Down the Gods* (2005), *Zhang Zhung* (2008), *Death and Beyond in Ancient Tibet* (2013), and *Antiquities of Zhang Zhung*, 2 vols. (2014). For more information about Bellezza's work, see his website: www.tibetarchaeology.com.